# Going Global

## The Professional Practice Series

The Professional Practice Series is sponsored by The Society for Industrial and Organizational Psychology, Inc. (SIOP). The series was launched in 1988 to provide industrial and organizational psychologists, organizational scientists and practitioners, human resources professionals, managers, executives and those interested in organizational behavior and performance with volumes that are insightful, current, informative, and relevant to *organizational practice.* The volumes in the Professional Practice Series are guided by five tenets designed to enhance future organizational practice:

1. Focus on practice, but grounded in science.
2. Translate organizational science into practice by generating guidelines, principles, and lessons learned that can shape and guide practice.
3. Showcase the application of industrial and organizational psychology to solve problems.
4. Document and demonstrate best industrial and organizational-based practices.
5. Stimulate research needed to guide future organizational practice.

The volumes seek to inform those interested in practice with guidance, insights, and advice on how to apply the concepts, findings, methods, and tools derived from industrial and organizational psychology to solve human-related organizational problems.

# Previous Professional Practice Series volumes include:

# Going Global

Practical Applications and Recommendations for HR and OD Professionals in the Global Workplace

Edited by Kyle Lundby

with Jeffrey Jolton

Foreword by Allen I. Kraut

JOSSEY-BASS
A Wiley Imprint
www.josseybass.com

Published by Jossey-Bass
A Wiley Imprint
989 Market Street, San Francisco, CA 94103-1741—www.josseybass.com

Jossey-Bass books and products are available through most bookstores. To contact Jossey-Bass directly call our Customer Care Department within the U.S. at 800-956-7739, outside the U.S. at 317-572-3986, or fax 317-572-4002.

Jossey-Bass also publishes its books in a variety of electronic formats. Some content that appears in print may not be available in electronic books.

**Library of Congress Cataloging-in-Publication Data**

Going global: practical applications and recommendations for HR and OD professionals in the global workplace / edited by Kyle Lundby with Jeffrey Jolton; foreword by Allen I. Kraut. —1st ed.
    p. cm. — (The professional practice series)
  Includes bibliographical references and index.
  ISBN 978-0-470-52533-3 (cloth)
  1.  Personnel management.  2.  International business enterprises.  3.  Globalization.
I.  Lundby, Kyle M. (Kyle Martin)  II.  Jolton, Jeffrey
HF5549.G624 2010
    658.3—dc22

                                                                              2010003736

Printed in the United States of America
FIRST EDITION

*HB Printing* 10  9  8  7  6  5  4
*PB Printing* 10  9  8  7  6  5  4  3  2  1

# The Professional Practice Series

# Table of Contents

# Foreword

This latest volume in the Professional Practice Series deals with the practical impact of globalization on the work done by most industrial-organizational psychologists and their human resource management colleagues in many organizations around the world. The effects of globalization are powerful and growing and are not always well understood. This book will help readers to recognize and deal with many of its important effects in the workplace.

We can easily recognize globalization in our everyday personal and professional lives. The total of the United States' imports and exports from overseas has grown from less than 10% of the gross national product in 1969 to more than 25% today. Our marketplaces in the United States are full of products made abroad, and the same is true in other nations. The overseas membership of the Society for Industrial and Organizational Psychology, which sponsors this book series, has doubled in the last 10 years and now makes up more than one out of every eight members.

The less visible aspects of globalization include the different cultures found in other nations, and how that impacts the way in which we practice our professions. Sometimes, these differences become known only when we start to work overseas or work with people from other countries.

These realities, the need to understand what works elsewhere and what does not, and the need to adjust our mental models and actual behaviors are topics that resonate deeply for me. As a college teacher, I have often told my American students that if you really want to understand what it means to be an American you have to travel and live elsewhere. That is when one begins to understand what is different in other lands. It is sometimes said that "the fish is the last to notice water." Experience in other countries makes it clearer just what assumptions, behaviors, and values are different from your own.

My own interest was piqued by the frequent observations of my European-born parents about how "things are done differently in this country." My awareness of differences in culture was heightened when the U.S. Army gave me the "opportunity" to live in the Far East for a year and a half. It grew when I was later employed as the head of personnel research for the IBM World Trade Corporation for four years, traveling and working all around the globe, with a year off to teach at a Middle Eastern university. During much of this time, my renowned IBM colleague, Professor Geert Hofstede, was developing his landmark theories of cultural differences.

Hofstede's writing about the experience of living in and inter-acting with people from a different culture than one's own includes references to the adventures (and misadventures) of Alice in Lewis Carroll's classic story of *Alice in Wonderland.* The creatures she met and their behaviors were terribly different from any that she knew; her experience illustrates how many people feel when they venture overseas. A less mythical tale is found in *Democracy in America,* the writings of the Frenchman Alexis de Tocqueville based on his first visits to the United States in the 1830s. His trenchant observations of the American character, still studied today, could only have been written by a visitor from another country.

Similarly, the observations and accumulated wisdom of the editors and contributors to this book are based on their work overseas. Both Kyle Lundby and Jeffrey Jolton have had extensive experience working in various countries. Moreover, they have assembled an all-star cast of more than two dozen smart and well-rounded organizational psychologists with experience overseas to bring us up to date on useful ideas and practices out of the United States. Much of their writings are based on global organizations, not merely U.S. firms abroad.

Today's global organizations operate at an extraordinary level of complexity. Many have evolved from international firms with a plant or two overseas, and have gone beyond a multinational stage of having several similar firms in different countries to becoming truly global firms with worldwide operations, interests, and viewpoints. People in these global organizations cope with complexities that go far beyond language and culture. They must also deal with the differences based on national boundaries, organizational size, product and services mix, functional specialization, and customer sets (some of which are themselves global in reach). People working in such firms must deal with a large array of overlapping matrices of purpose and responsibility.

Our contributors' chapters help us to understand how practices must be adapted to take account of such organizational complexities. Their work will also will help us to tackle a question raised by Hofstede forty years ago, when he asked *"Do American theories apply abroad?"* He concluded that they often do not apply, or do so only partly. But the recent experience of this book's contributors suggests that they do, or at least that many of the practices based on those theories do reasonably well, when different cultures are taken into account and adjustments are made.

Lundby and Jolton have done us all a great service by bringing together a set of authors who give us useful input about the entire life cycle of employees, ranging from recruiting to training and development, to expatriate assignments, and much more. The broad coverage in this volume will bring new understanding and skills to a wide range of professionals in applied psychology and human resource management.

This is the first volume under the current editorial board, many of whom advised the book's editors. It is especially fitting to the topics in this book that three of the eleven members of the board are based overseas.

The purpose of the Professional Practice Series is to bring the best available knowledge and leading-edge practices, based on solid theory and concepts, to practitioners and those entering practice. The intent is to share the best of what we know and do in order to guide the field and improve the overall level of practice. I think that readers of this book will find that Lundby and Jolton, along with their associates, have accomplished that mission very well, with energy and great skill.

Allen I. Kraut, Series Editor
Baruch College, CUNY

# Preface

## What Is Global?

What does it really mean to be a "global organization"? When people talk about global organizations, they typically describe parts of the whole, but not necessarily the whole itself. For example, an organization may say "we're global" because they have offices in Europe or Asia as well as the United States, or because their final product uses parts manufactured by affiliates in Brazil or South Korea, or because they sell their products around the globe.

Yet successful global organizations are typically more than just the sum of pieces scattered about the world. Their value comes from interactions, processes, and opportunities that exist in a unique combination that could not happen in a business working in a single location or within the same general geography.

Merriam-Webster defines "global" as "relating to, or involving the entire world" or "relating to, or applying to a whole." Global, then, refers to something that is universal, total, and inclusive. From this whole, organizations can derive something more than if they were operating as either separate or noninteracting entities.

There are at least four important components having to do with structure and strategy that differentiate the nonglobal or "run-of-the-mill" multinationals from those that effectively leverage and capitalize upon their global footprint:

- *Physical Dispersion:* This is the most obvious and common differentiator; a business that operates in multiple locations is very different from a business with only one location. And an organization that operates in multiple countries across the globe is different still.

- *Diversity of Thought, People, Culture*: Global organizations gain value from having the diversity of thought, diversity of people, and diversity of culture that comes from being physically located in different geographies. It is important, however, that there be a strategic objective to leveraging this diversity. A lot of global organizations may have diversity but fail to use it to their advantage. Effective global organizations actively capitalize on their diversity.

- *Physically Dispersed and Diverse but Unified*: A third characteristic of effective global organizations is being unified in spite of being dispersed and diverse. At some level, the organization identifies itself as one business, one entity. However it is segmented or however it defines its global elements, there is some singularity to the organization's identity.

- *Global for a Reason*: A final component of effective global organizations is that they are self-aware of their global reach, and leverage that geographic and cultural diversity to maximize success, however success is defined. In other words, they are not simply big by "dumb luck"—there is an underlying purpose.

In addition to structure and strategy, however, we must consider the role of people and how they define and contribute to effective global organizations. There tend to be two basic approaches to "people management" in global organizations. One approach is to focus on the **commonalities** of people—to manage from what seems universal across all workers. This approach tends to create a more task-oriented leadership style, managing processes and getting people to do the roles assigned to them. Organizations may focus on common elements of engagement, such as people wanting to feel valued as part of a successful organization, with capable leadership and opportunities to develop and grow. In this approach, there is an expectation (or assumption) that organizational culture will trump local (geographic or national) culture. In this sort of an organization, we would expect to see relative consistency in selection criteria, training curricula, and internal branding.

The other "people management" approach does not seek commonality, but rather operates with a sensitivity that people in different locations are going to be most in tune and responsive to their local culture and leadership. **Variability** is assumed, acceptable, and in fact desired. In this case, there is a focus on each location of the business creating an environment that maximizes the potential and performance of the people working there. In this approach, the organization's own culture is considered secondary to the needs and norms of the local culture. Naturally, one would expect to see greater variability in selection criteria, training curricula, and other important factors.

The reality is that neither approach to structure or strategy nor "people" strategy is necessarily better. What works for one organization may not work for another. Neither is it the case that either approach must be applied exclusively. Most global organizations are a blend. We believe there is no absolute answer to the question "*What is global?*" Instead, there are shades of gray. However, at the risk of oversimplifying, we think it can be helpful to think of global organizations as varying along two continua—*identity alignment* and *process alignment* (see the following figure).

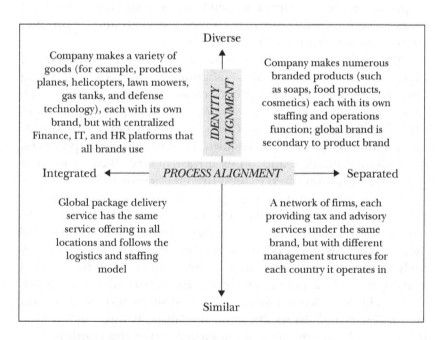

An organization's **identity alignment** has to do with the extent to which diversity is embraced by the organization in the management of its people, product or service offerings, and brand identity. At one end of the spectrum you have *diverse* perspectives. Such an organization will embrace the differences in local cultures, have a more diversified offering of services based on location, and even represent its brand differently to suit the different markets it serves. This allows the organization to tap into the unique strengths and opportunities that exist within each market.

On the other end of the continuum you have *similar* perspectives. These organizations have a greater drive for consistency in people management, the products or services that are offered, and how the brand is represented. The goal is to drive a "joined up" business and maximize on more unified business practices and strategies. There are obviously risks for organizations at either end of this continuum. For example, an extreme emphasis on diversity may result in an organizational structure that is disconnected and difficult to manage in any coherent way. Conversely, an extreme emphasis on cohesiveness may cause an organization to miss out on creative local solutions that could increase brand or product attractiveness to local customer groups.

Although identity alignment looks at the diversity of practice and strategy, **process alignment** concerns underlying operations—how business processes are or are not integrated. At one extreme, you have *separated* business processes. These organizations allow each part or key unit to operate relatively independently, often with its own IT structure, HR practices, performance metrics, and other infrastructure. Businesses built through acquisition often exhibit this characteristic.

On the other end of the spectrum are businesses that are *integrated* in their processes. These companies are more likely to have a single platform for technologies, unified HR systems, and measures of business performance. One can go into any part of such an organization and find a commonality in how information is accessed or how people are hired. Businesses that have grown organically often keep a more integrated set of processes, as they are all "growing" from the same overall platform. Once again, there are risks to organizations at either end of this continuum.

Most global organizations fall at neither one extreme nor the other on these continua, but it helps to think from these perspectives as you consider the various practices that are described in this book. Whether considering selection programs, change models, global mobility programs, leadership strategies, or performance management systems, having a sense of where the organization falls on these two axes can help ascertain what approaches may work best and how best to apply them.

Additionally, the science underlying I/O psychology and HR have not always kept pace with the practical application of their concepts to global organizations. There are many reasons for this, but the net result is that "going global" can be mistakenly and over-simplistically seen as doing the same thing in more places. Fortunately, the tide is turning and our field is now focusing more attention on some obvious questions, such as whether a selection program developed in the west is generalizable to a global organization, if a unified HRIS system can truly meet the needs of different markets, or if national culture trumps a multinational's efforts to create a common internal brand.

Answering these questions and understanding/creating best practices in these areas can serve three important stakeholder groups. First, there are the organizations themselves. Understanding these issues will help them get the greatest value out of being global. Second, understanding these issues and some of the best practice solutions makes HR and OD practitioners better resources for their clients. Finally and most important, it is the millions of workers around the globe who stand to benefit from our robust and valid selection systems. It is the workers who grow and prosper as a result of our on-boarding and leadership development programs, and it is their families and loved ones who benefit from our guidance around work-family balance.

## Audience

The primary audience for this book will be human resources (HR) and organizational development (OD) practitioners and consultants, or industrial/organizational (I/O) psychologists currently working with (or wanting to work with) global organizations. Another audience will be instructors and graduate students interested in such disciplines as industrial/organizational psychology, human resources, organizational behavior, and organizational development.

## Overview of the Book

In this volume, the authors discuss critical aspects of HR and OD practices as they relate to global organizations. Although there are several elements that provide some "how to" guidance, our primary purpose is to help HR and I/O professionals better understand how they can support global organizations, and to help businesses realize the value these practitioners hold.

*Going Global: Practical Applications and Recommendations for HR and OD Professionals in the Global Workplace* is organized into thirteen chapters in three parts. Each chapter represents an area of importance to the intended audience. Part One ("Practical considerations for HR and OD practitioners working across geographic-cultural boundaries") provides a review of some higher-level topics of interest and relevance to HR and OD practitioners and consultants to global organizations. These chapters examine the increasingly global nature of work and such important topics as culture, values, and teamwork. Part Two ("Attracting and selecting employees in the global workplace") looks at the process of organizational entry. Chapters address such critical issues as attracting employees, global selection, and on-boarding practices. Part Three ("Maximizing performance in the global workplace") considers issues relevant to maximizing employee effectiveness, including training for intercultural competence, employee engagement, work-family balance, and the expatriate experience.

Effective global organizations understand why they are global and have a clear strategy for success. It is important to recognize, however, that every global organization is unique and will vary based on the characteristics mentioned. For example, selection and on-boarding may be very different in an organization that promotes variability versus one that promotes commonality. Organizations that seek to create a common leadership style or way of thinking may develop leaders and select expatriates based on a very different set of criteria from one that promotes localization.

In short, readers of this volume will not find a one-size-fits-all solution. The practices that work best will depend upon your type of organization. The chapters will provide current best practices and advice for global organizations, but it is up to HR and OD practitioners in those organizations to choose which practices will work best in their particular situation.

Kyle Lundby
Jeffrey Jolton

# The Contributors

**Allen I. Kraut** is Professor Emeritus of Management at Baruch College, CUNY, where he has taught for the last twenty years. Before then, he was the longtime manager of personnel research for the IBM Corporation. His experience includes four years in IBM's overseas division, the IBM World Trade Corporation, during the time that his colleague Dr. Geert Hofstede was doing the landmark research that described global cultures.

Kraut has been directly involved in international applications of employee selection, management assessment and training, and organizational surveys. He is currently series editor of the SIOP Professional Practices Series, published by Jossey-Bass. He has edited three books in the series, including two on organizational surveys. In 1997, he received SIOP's Distinguished Professional Practices Award.

**Jeffrey A. Jolton**, PhD, is director of consulting at Kenexa, overseeing the development and thought leadership for many of Kenexa's largest global survey and organization research projects. Dr. Jolton has over 15 years of extensive consulting experience, working with a variety of global businesses such as Accenture, Allianz, CVS, DPWN, Ernst & Young, Gap Inc., Hewlett-Packard, HSBC, The Home Depot, PricewaterhouseCoopers, and Xerox. Dr. Jolton works with leaders to help them understand the issues their organizations are facing, and establish actions to help address these issues and meet business objectives and strategic goals.

Dr. Jolton is a regular presenter at numerous professional conferences and has many publications in professional and scientific journals. His research includes a focus on organization dysfunction, engagement, high-performance cultures, and people management strategies. He holds a doctorate and a master of science degree in industrial and organizational psychology from Ohio University.

**Mariangela Battista** is currently responsible for Leadership and Organizational Development at the Interpublic Group of Companies (IPG). Prior to IPG, Mariangela spent eight years at Starwood Hotels & Resorts Worldwide, Inc. as vice president, Organizational Culture and Effectiveness. In her role she was responsible for strategic design and oversight in the areas of Internal Communication, Organizational Measurement, Community Affairs, and People Programs including mentoring, recognition, and ethics and compliance. During her career at Starwood, Mariangela was responsible for the design and implementation of broad talent management and leadership development processes and systems, including competency modeling, performance management, executive and leadership development programs, 360-degree feedback programs, executive coaching, succession planning, engagement surveys, change management, and the Starwood Associate Relief Fund.

In her 21-year career, Mariangela has also been part of the Human Resources function of the Pepsi Bottling Group, American Express, and IBM. She has given numerous presentations at national conferences and is a published author in the areas of competency modeling and engagement.

Mariangela earned a PhD in industrial/organizational psychology from the City University of New York. She is a member of the American Psychological Association, the Society for Industrial/ Organizational Psychology, and the Academy of Management.

**Patricia R. Pedigo, PhD,** is an executive consultant in IBM's Corporate Development HR organization, where she assesses leadership, organization, and culture risks as part of the acquisition of Due Diligence and then works with the leaders and employees in both the acquired and acquiring IBM organizations to make the integration successful. Pat is currently working with several of IBM's complex international integrations in Sweden, the United Kingdom, and Israel. Prior to this assignment, Pat led IBM's Integrated Talent initiative, a global project to integrate and transform IBM's high-potential, technical, and executive talent management practices. Pat also has extensive consulting and project management experience and was an associate partner in the Organization Strategy and Human Capital practices at PwCC and IBM Consulting.

Pat has a PhD in organizational psychology from the University of South Florida and is a licensed psychologist in Connecticut. She is the past publication award winner from the Academy of Management with coauthors Allen Kraut, Marvin Dunnette and Douglas McKenna.

**Erica Desrosiers, PhD,** is the director of Organization and Management Development for PepsiCo, Inc., based in New York at the company's headquarters. Erica works on leadership and management assessment and development initiatives across the company, including the PepsiCo 360-degree feedback process and executive coaching. Prior to joining PepsiCo in 2004, she led the Organization Development function for Applied Systems, a software company. Erica also previously worked for Saville and Holdsworth Ltd. (SHL), where she partnered with clients to design competency models, assessment centers, and other customized solutions. Erica received her PhD in industrial organizational psychology from Purdue University. She lives in Connecticut with her family.

**Dr. Vesselin Blagoev** is director of the University of Portsmouth Program and dean of International University College, Sofia, and chairman of the Bulgarian Marketing Association. He is the former chief secretary of the Council of Ministers of Bulgaria (1994), executive director of the Bulgarian Privatisation Agency (1995–1997), chief executive director of Credit Bank Plc (1997–1998), and Editor-in-chief of *BusinessWeek Bulgaria* (2006–2008). He is also the author of 10 textbooks on marketing and culture, and innovation management, two of them published in the United Kingdom and Russia and author or coauthor of over 40 articles and one novel published in Bulgaria and France (2007). Blagoev has been consultant to over 100 companies.

**C. Shawn Burke, PhD,** is a senior research scientist at the Institute for Simulation and Training at the University of Central Florida. She is currently investigating team adaptability and issues related to multicultural team performance and multiteam systems. This work is conducted with an interest in team leadership and the training of teams operating in complex environments. Dr. Burke has published over sixty articles and chapters related to the above topics. Dr. Burke earned her doctorate in industrial/organizational psychology from George Mason University.

She has coedited a book on adaptability and another on advances in team effectiveness research.

**Marissa L. Shuffler** is a doctoral student and graduate research associate for the Institute for Simulation and Training at the University of Central Florida. Ms. Shuffler has experience in conducting research and analysis for a range of military, private, and nonprofit organizations. Ms. Shuffler's current areas of research include team training, cultural influences on collaborations and negotiations, trust development, critical social thinking, and multinational/multicultural distributed teams. She has presented research at national conferences and published articles in scholarly journals and edited books on these and other topics. Ms. Shuffler holds a master's degree in industrial/organizational psychology from George Mason University.

**Eduardo Salas, PhD,** is trustee chair and professor of psychology at the University of Central Florida, where he also holds an appointment as program director for the Human Systems Integration Research Department at the Institute for Simulation and Training. Previously, he was the director of UCF's Applied Experimental & Human Factors PhD Program. Before joining IST, he was a senior research psychologist and head of the Training Technology Development Branch of NAWC-TSD for 15 years. Dr. Salas has coauthored over 300 journal articles and book chapters and has coedited 19 books. His expertise includes teamwork, team training strategies, training effectiveness, decision making under stress, and performance measurement tools. Dr. Salas is a Fellow of the American Psychological Association, the Human Factors and Ergonomics Society, president-elect of the Society for Industrial and Organizational Psychology, and a recipient of the Meritorious Civil Service Award from the Department of the Navy.

**Michele J. Gelfand, PhD,** is professor of psychology at University of Maryland. She received her PhD in social/organizational psychology at University of Illinois. Her work explores cultural influences on conflict, negotiation, justice, and revenge; workplace diversity and discrimination; and theory and methods in cross-cultural psychology. Michele received the Ernest J. McCormick Award for Early Career Contributions from the Society for Industrial and Organizational Psychology and the LL Cummings Scholar Award from the Organizational Behavior of the Academy of Management. She is currently president of the International Association for Conflict Management.

**Mario Di Loreto** is responsible for Group Human Capital and Human Capital Strategy of Barilla worldwide, providing guidance to HC corporate functions and HC Business Partners. Prior to this, Mario was the human resources director for Mediterranean Region at Starwood Hotels & Resorts for about ten years, where he was part of Divisional HR Board and several innovation project management teams at the corporate level. He started his career in human resources with two airline companies, Alitalia and Air One (where he was part of the start-up of the company). Mario graduated in philosophy and earned a PhD in philosophy of science and history of ideas. He also earned an MBA at Bocconi University in Milan. Mario has been the author of several books and articles in both disciplines, management and philosophy.

**Mukta Kulkarni** is an assistant professor and Young Faculty Research Chair at the Indian Institute of Management Bangalore. She received her PhD in organization and management studies from the University of Texas at San Antonio. Her research articles have appeared in *Leadership Quarterly, Human Resource Management,* and *Academy of Management Journal.* Her coauthored paper on radical change won the Academy of Management Journal best paper award in 2007. She has also worked as a human resource generalist at Lehman Brothers.

**Mathian (Mat) Osicki** currently works for IBM as a Global HR Partner. She received her bachelor's degree from the University of Calgary in Canada and then her PhD degree in industrial/organizational psychology from the University of Tulsa in Oklahoma. She joined IBM as a researcher in the Global Workforce Research area of HR. A few years later she lived in India while conducting a workplace climate study for IBM. Upon her return she worked within the Executive Compensation area of HR before starting her current generalist role. Mat was also an adjunct professor at New York University, teaching graduate-level courses for a couple of years. Mat has presented at SIOP conferences on a variety of corporate topics.

**Tim Carey** is an industrial and organizational psychologist with over 10 years' experience, including extensive corporate expertise in leadership assessment and development. Currently, he is a professional consultant with the Psychology Department at the Chinese University of Hong Kong, where he lectures at the graduate and undergraduate levels in psychology and trains and places undergraduate and graduate students in various companies across Hong Kong and Shanghai for internships. In addition, he is active in delivering assessment and development services around the region for managers and executives. Tim served with a global consulting firm for four years before joining the university. With that organization, his last position was director of consulting services for Greater China. He has delivered consulting services across the Asia Pacific region, as well as in Europe and the Middle East, for clients in many industries, including Shell, the Mandarin Oriental Hotel group, Credit Suisse, EADS, CLP, Walmart, and HP.

A permanent resident of Hong Kong, Tim has lived in the city for eight years. He completed his MA and PhD in industrial/organizational psychology at the University of South Florida, in the United States.

**David Herst** is an instructor at Florida Atlantic University in sunny Boca Raton, Florida. He has published on work and family conflict, the intricacies of online instruction, and cross-cultural test construction. Dr. Herst teaches organizational behavior, human resource management, and cross-cultural communication and negotiation at both the graduate and undergraduate levels. Prior to becoming an academic, he worked for TMP Worldwide (now Monster.com) as a codeveloper of a career management system, which included measures of personality, value systems, and organizational culture preferences. Dr. Herst has also worked as an assessor for a large energy company's executives, consulted with numerous local human resources offices to create everything from resume tracking systems to full bonus systems, and while in graduate school worked on the validation of the Armed Services Vocational Aptitude Battery.

Dr. Herst is currently working on a wide range of research topics including cross-cultural differences in test construction, the validity of manipulation checks, and various collaborative measures with individuals from other departments. He holds a PhD in industrial/organizational psychology from the University of South Florida.

**Wynne Chan** is currently working with Standard Chartered Bank in Hong Kong. She is a graduate of the industrial-organizational psychology master's program of the Chinese University of Hong Kong (CUHK) and earned her bachelor's degree with a double major in economics and psychology from the University of British Columbia, Canada. Having studied and worked in both Canada and Hong Kong, Wynne has gained a cross-cultural perspective of the business world from several regions. During her two years of study at the CUHK, Wynne carried out consultancy projects and training workshops for different organizations in Hong Kong and China, including Hutchison Port (China), the Social Welfare Department of Hong Kong, Eurogroup Far East Limited,, and the Nansha Grand Hotel.

**Mary Mannion Plunkett, PhD,** is the global head of People and Organizational Development for Heineken International, responsible for talent management, leadership development, performance management, and organizational capability. Previously, Mary was the senior vice president for Lehman Brothers, responsible for Talent Management in Europe and the Middle East, and vice president Executive Development, for BP Plc. She has more than 18 years of experience in the field of leadership and organization development, including roles with the Boeing Company, Ernst & Young LLP, and McDonnell Douglas Aircraft Company. Mary also served as an adjunct professor in the Organizational Behavior Department at Seattle Pacific University.

**Dr. Tommy Weir** serves as vice president of leadership solutions at Kenexa. He is a thought leader specializing in strategic leadership for fast-growth and emerging markets, a gifted speaker, and author of *The CEO Shift*—a book that explores the new global business environment and challenges corporate leaders to shift their practices in order to survive in the new economy. Dr. Weir has a rich history of leadership development experience and has held top management and teaching positions throughout his career. He has taught organizational leadership and management courses at the graduate and university level, and consulted with global organizations, including many Fortune 100 companies. His latest position was as the head of learning and development at Nakheel (in Dubai), where he was named the Middle East's HR Professional of the Year. While there, Dr. Weir spearheaded the creation of an innovative learning architecture and leader development program that was as unique as the company's explosive growth. Additionally, he played an instrumental role in the diverse multicultural environment, with more than eighty nationalities working together in one location. Dr. Weir holds a doctorate in strategic leadership from Regent University. His writings on leadership in the fast-growth and emerging markets are featured in numerous publications.

**Jeffrey Saltzman**, CEO OrgVitality and an Associated Fellow at the Center for Leadership Studies at Binghamton University, has been a consultant to some of the world's largest, most successful organizations, a pioneer of new organizational concepts such as Variance Optimization and Employee Confidence. He is experienced with manufacturing, financial services, heath care, retail, media, high technology, service companies, not-for-profits, and government agencies. Based in New York, he has traveled and worked extensively in Europe, Latin America, and Asia-Pacific. He is author of several books and book chapters including, most recently, *My Jeans Are Irregulars* (2009), and is a frequent blogger covering organizational performance topics, management and research.

**Scott Brooks**, PhD, is VP of Consulting Services and Partner at OrgVitality. He has nearly 20 years of external consulting experience working with organizations to help drive performance through listening and responding to the views of employees and customers. Much of his consulting and research work has focused on developing and leveraging human capital metrics to drive customer satisfaction and business results. Along with consulting assignments, Scott has led a regional office, a global consulting function, and firmwide R&D programs. He also worked internally within the organizational development for a division of Target, Inc.

Scott has authored numerous presentations and publications based on strategic human resources, linkage research, surveys, and other job attitude and measurement topics. He frequently speaks at national conferences and company meetings. Scott holds a PhD in industrial and organizational psychology from The Ohio State University and a bachelor of arts from Cornell University.

**Jessica L. Wildman** is a doctoral student in the industrial/ organizational psychology program at the University of Central Florida, where she has been a graduate research associate at the Institute for Simulation and Training since 2007. She has been working on a variety of projects related to culture, teams, and performance. She has published four book chapters and two peer-reviewed journal articles, and has presented over 10 presentations or posters at professional conferences. Her current research interests include multicultural performance, team process and performance, virtual teams, and interpersonal trust.

**Luiz Xavier** is a doctoral student in the industrial/ organizational psychology program at the University of Central Florida. He currently works as a graduate research assistant at the Institute for Simulation and Training. Xavier received a B.S. in psychology and M.S. in industrial/organizational psychology from San Francisco State University. His research interests include teamwork, training, diversity, and conflict.

**Mitchell Tindall** is a doctoral student in the industrial/ organizational psychology program at the University of Central Florida. He is a graduate research assistant at the Institute for Simulation and Training. There he has been involved in several research projects related to culture and teams. He received his M.S. in industrial and organizational psychology from the University of Central Florida. During that time he worked as a contract consultant in the selection of personnel using both cognitive ability and personality tests. His current research interests include the effects of culture on performance of teams, diversity, training, and motivation.

**Paul M. Mastrangelo**, PhD, has over 15 years' experience in organization development, HR research, and adult education. As a senior consultant and director of the Analytic Consulting Team for CLC-Genesee, Paul collaborates with leaders from global companies to evaluate employee perceptions and motivation. His experiences include designing and analyzing employee surveys, advising senior executives, developing small and large change interventions, creating competency-based training, and building selection instruments. He coauthored the 2008 book *Employee Surveys in Management* and has over 25 professional publications. Paul earned his doctorate in industrial and organizational psychology from Ohio University in 1993.

**Paula Caligiuri** is a professor in the Human Resource Management Department in the School of Management and Labor Relations at Rutgers University, where she is the director of the Center for Human Resource Strategy (CHRS). Paula researches, publishes, and consults in three primary areas: strategic human resource management in multinational organizations, global leadership development, and international assignee management. As an academic, Paula Caligiuri has been recognized as one of the most prolific authors in the field of international business for her work in global careers and global leadership development. Her academic publications include articles in the *International Journal of Human Resource Management, Journal of World Business, Journal of Applied Psychology, Personnel Psychology,* and *International Journal of Intercultural Relations.* With a focus on global careers, she has coauthored a book with Steven Poelmans, entitled *Harmonizing Work, Family, and Personal Life* (Cambridge Press, 2008). Her book (with Dave Lepak and Jaime Bonache) *Global Dimensions of HRM: Managing the Global Workforce* (Wiley) is forthcoming. Paula holds a PhD from Penn State University in industrial and organizational psychology.

**Thomas Hippler** is lecturer in Human Resource Management and International Business in the School of Business and Economics at Swansea University (UK). He holds a PhD in international human resource management from the University of Limerick (Ireland). He is a member of the Academy of Management, Academy of International Business and is serving as a member of the Editorial Review Board of the *Journal of Managerial Psychology.* His research interests are in the area of International Human Resource Management, particularly international assignments and expatriate management as well as adjustment to domestic and international job transfers. Dr. Hippler has published in the *International Journal of Human Resource Management* and has book chapters in *New Directions in Expatriate Research* and *International Human Resource Management and Expatriate Transfers: Irish Experiences.* Dr. Hippler understands global experiences firsthand; being a German citizen, he completed his PhD in Ireland

and then moved to the United Kingdom, where he currently resides and works.

**Tammy D. Allen** is professor of psychology at the University of South Florida. Tammy's research centers on individual and organizational factors that relate to employee career development, health, and well-being. Specific interests include mentoring relationships, work-family interactions, career development, organizational citizenship, and occupational health. Tammy is coauthor of *Designing Workplace Mentoring Programs: An Evidence-Based Approach* and coeditor of *The Blackwell Handbook of Mentoring: A Multiple Perspectives Approach*. She is associate editor for the *Journal of Applied Psychology* and the *Journal of Occupational Health Psychology*. She currently serves on the executive board of the Society of Industrial and Organizational Psychology. Tammy is a Fellow of the Society for Industrial and Organizational Psychology and the American Psychological Association.

**Kristen M. Shockley** is a doctoral candidate of industrial/organizational psychology at the University of South Florida. Her research interests are centered on the intersection of work and family, with a focus on organizational responses to work-family conflict, dual-earner couples' work-family management, and the relationship of these issues to health outcomes. She has published her work in the *Journal of Vocational Behavior*.

**Andrew Biga** is a manager in the Employee and Organization Research and Sensing (EORS) HR practice for the Procter & Gamble Company, headquartered in Cincinnati, Ohio. Andrew is the owner of P&G's engagement survey program, delivered annually to more than 138,000 employees worldwide. In addition, Andrew is the global leader for P&G's People Sensing and Analytics program that delivers systemic research-based talent solutions. Responsibilities include influencing strategy and communication for senior leadership. Andrew joined P&G in 2007 and completed his PhD in industrial/organizational psychology from the University of South Florida.

# PART 1

# Practical Considerations for HR and OD Practitioners Working Across Geographic-Cultural Boundaries: The Changing Workplace

# CHAPTER 1

# Navigating the Complexities of a Global Organization

Mariangela Battista, Patricia Pedigo, and Erica Desrosiers

We live and operate in a global world. A flu outbreak in Mexico has an impact on fruit pricing in Asia. A mortgage meltdown in the United States has an impact on world financial markets. Globalization brings with it a web of interconnectedness that did not exist previously, or at least not to the extent that it does now. Organizations today are affected by nearly everything that transpires around the world, not just the local markets or communities in which they operate. Although global supply chains have created huge market efficiencies, they have also brought vulnerabilities. Disruption to a key node in the supply chain can cause dramatic and unpredictable turbulence in the whole system. The financial and economic events of 2008 have demonstrated how tightly intertwined globalization has made the world and its systems.

Globalization has also had significant implications for organizational processes, systems, and operations. Years ago, when most of an organization's employees were generally in the same country and most of their business was conducted in their home country, life was simple. There was no need to worry about cultural differences, language differences, time zones, or local relevance. That luxury has long since disappeared and the reality of organizations today is that operating globally is a more complex undertaking than one might have expected. Becoming a truly global operator entails far more than simply selling the same thing in more places, hiring the same people in more locations, or just pushing out the same processes and procedures around the world. Operating in this mind-set is likely a recipe for failure. Globalization requires a business model that is adaptable and employees who openly welcome new ways of thinking.

Human Resources professionals provide value to their organization by successfully navigating the complexities of a global organization, and in doing so they bring the business strategy to life for their employees. They understand the human dynamics of operating in different cultures and how to facilitate the organization's success. HR professionals are tasked with the strategy and execution of all people-related processes and initiatives in the organization. In global organizations, that role takes on the additional complexity of operating across cultural and language barriers, operational differences, local relevance and appropriateness, time zones, and peak business and holiday schedules, just to name a few. This chapter will highlight examples of situations and contexts often encountered by HR practitioners operating within global organizations that may present challenges and offers specific suggestions for how to navigate in these global waters.

## What Does It Mean to Be Global?

Although we live in a globalized world, there are still challenges in defining a global organization. Think of global organizations as snowflakes—no two look exactly alike. Organizations can operate under four distinct stages of globalization (Hewitt, 2009)—multinational, international, transitioning to global, and global. *Multinational* organizations have cross-border operations that are primarily decentralized and autonomous. *International* organizations have a headquarters that retains some decision-making control but the organization is still largely decentralized. Organizations *transitioning to global* are taking concrete steps to develop worldwide business strategies and policies (note that most organizations identify themselves as transitioning). Some organizations are truly *global* in that they develop strategies and policies on a worldwide basis and share resources across borders. Even for domestically focused organizations, globalization is just as salient, given relationships with suppliers, investors, and even nonnative employees.

What are the implications of those differences in globalization? In more decentralized organizations operating in the earlier stages of globalization, systems and processes are largely independent and disconnected. There are certainly advantages of this, in that these systems and processes can be tailored to the unique needs of the local operation and are often easier to create, execute, and adapt when local conditions warrant. A local operation can often be more nimble when not restricted to the longer and more effortful design and implementation of a global process (Sirkin, Hemerling, & Bhattacharya, 2008). If everyone is working independently and autonomously, however, the organization is not poised to leverage the best practices created and implemented within their very own organization. In addition, there is a significant amount of duplicated and wasted effort, as everyone works to re-create the wheel over and over again.

Understanding and leveraging organizational-level insights is also difficult. For example, assessing and securing enterprise-wide talent pools becomes much more of a challenge when there is little consistency in how things are measured and what information is tracked or shared. In organizations that are further along on the "global" continuum, everything often takes longer because of the required alignment and integration needed to be successful, but the synergies that are created are quite beneficial to the organization in the longer term. Getting to that point, however, requires a significant amount of work.

## The Inherent Complexity of Globalization

The people in and related to organizations—whether employees, shareholders, or customers—bring with them cultural, geographical, geopolitical, and language attributes. How these different and varying attributes are managed and leveraged across constituent groups within the organization has an impact on how well organizations are run and ultimately on the organization's success. Cultures vary, even within countries, and certainly within and across continents. Understanding the complexity both within regions and on a global scale is especially important based on the significant increase in regional and global trade since 1959 (Kim & Shin, 2002). In the geographically structured organization, where divisions are represented by geography or country, as opposed to product or brand, understanding cultural complexities is critical to business success. For example, leaders responsible for an Asia Pacific division must understand the cultural differences that exist between Taiwan and New Zealand, or Japan and China, and modify their products and marketing appropriately. This is similar for a North American division—one cannot assume that what works in the United States will work also in Canada.

### Cultures

These cultural implications apply to customers as well as to employees. In the late 1990s Walmart decided to open stores in Germany as part of their strategic growth initiative. Walmart purchased some small German retail chains and had a successful Walmart executive from Bentonville, Arkansas, run the operations. Nine years and one billion dollars later, Walmart pulled out of Germany. Their planned expansion was a total failure (Solomon & Schell, 2009). Walmart made a then common mistake by assuming that what worked in the United States would work everywhere. They expected that German shoppers would react the same way that American shoppers do to the greeters at the door and the clerks bagging their purchases at checkout. However, the German culture is more hierarchical. Shoppers were not as comfortable receiving the "How are you?" greeting at the door, nor were the German Walmart employees comfortable giving the greeting. German employees also participated in daily morning cheering sessions led by store managers, a practice in all U.S. stores. Corporate culture and national culture clashed. The successful Bentonville executive did not even speak German and required his management team to speak English. Walmart exported its entire U.S. corporate culture without appreciating the differences—and suffered significant consequences.

### Governments and Regulations

Cultures are shaped by geography, language, politics, and leadership. Italy has seen over 60 governments in power since World War II. Changing governments and administrations imply changing laws and regulations. For example, if you are a global organization with operations in Italy, the changing government may affect how your business operates and ultimately your very success. Western organizations did very little business in Asian markets a generation ago. As governments lifted trade barriers, organizations recognized opportunities for new markets. For example, Pepsi was one of the first brands in Vietnam as soon as the trade barrier was lifted. Navigating geopolitical relationships can also be a challenge and can often influence how geographic organization structures are established. Do you put China and Taiwan in the same geography? How do you manage the Middle East? These political relationships spill over into how the organization is structured and even how products are transported and services provided.

In order to conduct business in a particular market, more and more global companies are relocating key operations and production facilities to high-growth countries. In addition to providing a significant local presence, this often enables the company to more effectively compete for local governmental contracts.

### Languages

One cannot underestimate the power of language. In many global organizations, English is the official or de facto language of the business. Yet, if an organization wants to engage the hearts and minds of its employees, then communication in the native tongue is essential to ensure effectiveness.

We know that the way an organization communicates has huge implications for the engagement of the employees and the success of the organization (Welch & Welch, 2008). Literal translations often do not communicate the correct message or with the passion needed to motivate employees. Conducting translations and having in-country employees review the translation often works to ensure that the right message is being communicated. Even that may not be enough, though. Just because a message is translated accurately, the content of the message itself may be perceived as headquarters-centric. This may serve to alienate business units rather than bring them closer together as global units; they may feel that "corporate doesn't 'get us.'"

Other examples can be quite basic in their headquarters-centric style. One of the authors worked with senior HR leadership to create a global communication regarding an upcoming global survey, noted as coming "later this summer." That was fine for employees who would actually be in the summer months but for some regions, it would be winter. Such missteps are confusing at best, and divisive at worst, implying a very headquarters-centric mind-set and attitude. For many HR practitioners, it usually takes at least one or two such missteps before they start to operate in a truly global mind-set, more appropriate for the organization.

### *Organizational Structure*

As described earlier in the various stages of globalization, organizations can have very centralized or decentralized operations. In a centralized organization there are typically centers of excellence which exist in a headquarters-type environment where they are responsible for the design and execution of programs and initiatives implemented in the field business units. Centralized organizations create standards of operation and performance to ensure consistency in global deployment. For example, the Disney experience is expected to be the same whether it is in Orlando or Paris. The organization is dependent upon the highest-quality customer experience for business success. In decentralized organizations, every business unit operates independently with its own set of processes and initiatives. For a business whose success is dependent upon local adaptability and flexibility, this model enables rapid response to changes in local markets. Each approach has its advantages and disadvantages depending upon the business model and market requirements. In at least one large global company we know of, and likely many more, both models are operating, centralizing some functions while decentralizing some operations. HR can and should help organizations match the right design with the business model and strategy.

To add to the complexity, many large, global organizations are matrixed in structure. There are product or brand lines overlaying geographies. If leaders think that managing multiple product lines is a challenge, it becomes exponentially more complex when product lines become matrixed with geographies. Key concern areas of staffing, resources, and customer coverage require ongoing negotiation between the local geography and the brand and products to ensure the right balance. Although global companies go to great lengths to interlock these requirements as part of their annual planning processes, modifications and adjustments are often needed during the year. Helping employees and leaders navigate the matrix structure is an important contribution that HR can make to overall organizational effectiveness, especially when employees join through acquisitions or external hiring.

Successfully managed global organizations have a clear understanding of how they work. As mentioned earlier regarding the continuum of definitions of globalization many companies understand which key business models are the sources of revenue. Even within the same industry, we see different operating or business models that drive how people interact and bring value into the organization. For example, PricewaterhouseCoopers defines itself as a network of partners and limits its top-down influence. Accenture sees itself as is a matrixed organization that is ultimately project-centered with the focus on what is right for the client project. PepsiCo and Starwood Hotels & Resorts are both collectives of clearly defined brands with a common set of core organizational values. Through its structure, each organization has defined for themselves how headquarters (HQ) and field are connected and how they work together to be successful. IBM is also a highly matrixed organization with the integration of products and services to meet customer needs as the core of its business success.

### Headquarters versus the Field

For centralized organizations with centers of excellence, it is critical that input from the divisions or the field be solicited on a regular basis. It is a grand mistake to design a program or make decisions in headquarters without "vetting it" through the global divisions so that issues of culture, language, and operational reality are addressed and a successful implementation can be ensured. Nothing kills an initiative faster than saying it is a mandate from headquarters.

Even more than soliciting input from or vetting plans with the field, the best results come from true partnerships between the headquarters center and business partners in the field. The field partners are the ones with their "finger on the pulse" of the organization and can provide valuable input at all phases. Not only does a partnership result in a better end product or process, but there is a sense of ownership and buy-in that comes from this collaborative effort. This regular dialogue secures critical local ownership and sponsorship of the initiatives and their implementation. For instance, some organizations create global councils or task forces that meet regularly either for the duration of a discrete project or on a more extended basis to ensure true global representation and partnerships. Business and field representatives that participate are able to share not only how things should work, but also how they really are working, and what needs to change and how.

Centers of excellence should be pragmatic in approach. The reality is that programs and initiatives always seem to take much longer to implement than a project plan would suggest. Just because a decision is made and leaders are in agreement that an initiative is the right course of action does not mean that execution is as smooth and flawless as envisioned. Behavior change takes time. New initiatives and processes take time to become inculcated into the organizational culture, and new behaviors and expectations take time and effort to learn. This becomes exponentially more complicated when one considers issues of culture, language, and so on, not to mention the time and effort required for a cascaded rollout, communications strategy and plan, and possibly training for local HR, managers, and employees.

Centers of excellence (headquarters) should not assume that just because an initiative has launched that it is actually operating as it should. Some anecdotal research suggests that it takes three years, or three cycles, for the new initiative to take hold. Ironically, just as processes are taking hold out in the field, leaders in headquarters believe it is time to update and refresh or reengineer the process. Though there may be a business-driven need for the change, sometimes for the good of the organization it is better to keep the process consistent longer to ensure the business value is returned. Any type of change becomes a change-management issue facing even more complexity associated with culture, language, and local support. Some initiatives may need a longer shelf life than organizational development (OD) practitioners are willing to give.

Although eventual change may be inevitable, it is also a "must-do" for HQ to remember that employee consumers of HR processes do not have a singular focus on all things HR. They're busy and often overwhelmed with the content of their own jobs, of which HR process plays but a small part. It is easy to forget in HQ or center-based jobs that employees in the field need additional communication, explanation, and context to keep everything straight. How does everything fit together? Why am I doing this? What do I do with this? Why are we changing things...again? HQ practitioners in global organizations often have significant distance between themselves and the employees that are ultimately the consumers of their goods, so the importance of a communications strategy and a set of well-designed and field-tested tools should not be underestimated.

Having a close connection and working relationship between the headquarters center of excellence and the field is critical for organizational success. There must be constant dialogue and feedback from the field so that the organization is balancing global organizational needs with local field needs. Global programs and initiatives must be designed with the field in mind and, given the variety of countries, cultures, languages, skill levels, and so forth, simplicity and ease of use are nonnegotiable design elements. This can be a challenge when the center of excellence is designing something perhaps ten steps removed from where they actually sit. For example, if the designer sits in the western United States, and the end user sits in Dubai, then there has to be some input from the employee in Dubai to secure effective implementation. If a program cannot be easily implemented then it is often deemed too complicated by the end user and chances of successful implementation are reduced. Practitioners can address this issue by conducting the appropriate focus groups, field testing, or pilot testing. Program execution without adequate field input and testing will likely fail in deployment.

The key for organizations and practitioners is to walk the fine line between designing the framework with instructions to implement and customize locally and trying to create consistent, global standards of excellence. Depending on the business model and sources of value to the company, organizations might be better served by erring on the side of encouraging local tailoring within defined boundaries to ensure that the program makes business sense at the field or local level.

## Organizational Values

Most organizations have vision and values that define their organizational culture. Vision and values provide a common framework across the organization. They communicate what the organization stands for and how employees should conduct business and interact with one another and with customers. They set the tone for behavioral and performance expectations. Reward systems are based upon these values.

Many of these values espouse socially desirable behaviors, such as "treat others with respect and dignity," "the customer is always first," "value teamwork and collaboration." Almost no one would argue against these values.

Yet how organizational values are defined and interpreted may be a source of confusion that can lead to conflict. How do organizational values and national or ethnic values coexist? Although socially desirable, organizational values are not necessarily fully in line with national or ethnic values (Nelson & Gopalan, 2003). There may be some overlap, especially in the area of personal behavior toward other employees, but there are also some differences. Tensions and conflicts can arise between the two if they are too divergent. For example, "treat others with respect and dignity" seems pretty innocuous. However, ethnically, it may be interpreted quite differently. In Asian cultures "treating others with respect" may be interpreted to mean that feedback is kept rather mundane and to a minimum, whereas in Western cultures "treating others with respect" could be interpreted as the opportunity to provide every possible bit of detailed feedback. As reward systems are based on organizational values, organizations then must take steps to ensure that there is consistency in communicating and rewarding expected behaviors.

Recently one of the authors experienced the conflict of organizational versus national culture over including a question on the global engagement survey regarding a willingness to challenge a superior when faced with a values issue. Though intended to address issues of integrity and candor, there were cultural implications to a question like this. In some cultures, employees would never think to challenge a superior; it is just not done. However, in order to create and maintain an ethical organizational culture the company's employees are encouraged to challenge others, especially at a higher level. From a compliance standpoint it is important to ask questions like this, but care is needed in the interpretation of the results, keeping in mind the biases of national culture.

Values tend to be identified and set at the top of the organization. Senior management has a role in defining what the organization stands for. Sometimes these values come from an organization's founder and sometimes they are defined by current management. If the organization is reexamining and redefining their values as a result of a new business strategy or leadership team, this is a great opportunity to get employee perspective and input—especially global input. IBM did this several years ago with their "value jams" initiative. The new CEO, Sam Palmisano, and the senior leadership team held an online, interactive dialogue with all IBM employees to identify and select the appropriate values for the "new" IBM (Hempel, 2006). The "values jam" ensured that the new IBM values would be embraced by all employees worldwide and reflect the global IBM culture. The "value jams" were a success with tens of thousands of global employees providing input and over a million employees and partners viewing the discussion.

### Organizational versus Local Culture

Another interesting intersection revolves around organizational culture and local culture. Organizations tend to have a clear and somewhat dominating culture which may or may not be consistent with local culture. For example, an organizational culture of rapid response, results orientation, and working late nights and on weekends may not sit well in local cultures that place a heavy emphasis on family life, activities, and relaxation. Many have asked the question of which will win out when the two are in conflict—organizational culture or local culture? The easy answer here is probably the correct one—it depends. It depends on the strength and saliency of both cultures, and it depends on the individual and his or her desire for approval, and from whom. Another factor is likely to be the level of the individual employee. As individuals rise in the ranks within an organization, at a certain level they are often considered "corporate assets." There is more interaction with senior leadership, and more impact and influence from the top. At this level, individuals are more likely to be driven by or at least influenced by organizational culture to a greater extent. Lower in the organization, where most if not all interaction and collaboration is with other local employees, local culture is likely to be the dominant one.

## Global Mergers and Acquisitions

Global mergers and acquisitions carry unique challenges for the HR professional. Not only do you need to worry about the integration of two companies, but also the national cultural nuances of the acquisition. Key issues to consider include:

- Being acquired by a U.S.-based company (or one based in another country) and national-istic attitudes associated with the acquisition on both the acquired and acquiring sides
- Managing the inte-gration locally with a nonnative integration team and the potential language barriers
- Recognizing that local laws will govern the rate and pace of some inte-gration activities—for

## U.S.-Centric Not Always the Right Approach

As part of U.S.-based multination-als, we like to think that we are global and inclusive, and that we operate with a global mind-set, but too often it is easy to fall into bad habits. No matter where one sits in the world, that is the perspective that is usually taken. Considera-tion of our global colleagues in planning and decision making will lead to more effective outcomes.

### Time Zones

Conducting conference calls with multiple participants can be quite a challenge. Managing different time zones can also be difficult. Conducting conference calls with an international audience, however, requires the coordi-nation of a space shuttle launch. Conference calls scheduled for early morning New York time are still predawn hours in the western United States, middle of the night for Hawaii, and late evening for most of Asia. It will always be the middle of the night, or non-working hours, for someone in example, when the teams can meet to plan integration, works council involvement, and so on

- Sensitizing the integration team to company and national culture differences between the acquiring and acquired organizations
- Planning for the travel costs associated with securing the productive working relationships needed for acquisition success
- Understanding that reactions to the change will differ widely by local country culture
- Securing local professional change management support to deal with the acquired employees in their language and consistent with their culture
- Recognizing that effective acquisition integration requires trust and dialogue, which are much more complex and challenging in a global environment

When there are global acquisitions, effective integration is always a local activity.

the world. If global representation on a project or initiative is critical for its success, how do you minimize the personal impact of this coordination so that it is not burdensome for employees outside of headquarters? If scheduling makes it difficult for employees to participate then you defeat the purpose of having global representation. Ensuring that everyone shares equally in the work, and the burden, has been a workable solution adopted by many global companies. Rotating conference call times so everyone shares equally in off-hours calls is often the fair approach.

### Work-Life Balance

Work-life balance is also taking on global meaning. Work-life balance has predominately been discussed and studied as a U.S.-based issue. Organizations striving to create great places to work have focused on work-life integration programs such as flextime, job shares, compressed work weeks, and so on. Recent research from the Boston Consulting Group (2008) on global HR challenges has found that work-life balance is now a global issue. In Latin America, Africa, and the emerging Asian markets of China and India, this issue has an impact on retention and development. In addition, European Union policymakers are now looking at work-time regulations of global organizations and creating policies to ensure balance.

### Vacations

The culture of vacations is a related phenomenon. Outside the United States, employees actually use all their allotted vacation time. In European countries, employees receive a minimum of 30 to 40 days paid vacation which they will take seemingly regardless of the business environment. Vacation is viewed as a time to relax and renew, and employees are not in contact with the office. It is not uncommon to postpone important projects or meetings during the July and August months to avoid the European and Latin American holidays. Americans, on the other hand, are notorious for not using all their vacation time and working while on vacation. "Blackberry vacations" are quite common in the United States while unheard of (and not considered healthy) outside the United States. Unfortunately, this can set up different expectations regarding a person's availability.

### Meetings and Conferences

Promoting or espousing a global focus is critical but sometimes there are practical considerations. What constitutes a "global meeting" really? For U.S.-based multinationals there is sometimes push-back from the international managers (or non-U.S. managers) to have to travel to headquarters or a U.S.-based destination. "If we want to think and act like a global organization, we should not have all our meetings in the United States," was a statement often heard by one of the authors. This is a valid point that would often be in conflict with practical reality. It is usually cheaper and much more cost-effective to have meetings in the United States. Most of the meeting attendees (assuming management team) are already in the States, making for cheaper flights and accommodations. There are also perception issues to contend with. Global meetings held in exotic locations (anything outside the United States seems exotic) can be perceived as perks and boondoggles for those attending, creating bad press among employees and, potentially, among shareholders. Locations chosen for such meetings need to be tied to the meeting purpose and justified. If you are building new operations in China, a meeting in Beijing is definitely more appropriate than Chicago. If you're holding a global strategy meeting with representatives from all regions, it may make sense on some level to hold the meeting outside the United States, but when you realize you're flying eight people from the States to an international location to meet with three more people, it does raise a question of practicality.

## Program Implementations

Business initiatives are more difficult to implement in a global organization. One has to maneuver language barriers, cultural issues, and business opportunities. It is a naïve assumption to believe that whatever business strategy or initiative that is created in headquarters will execute flawlessly worldwide. It is critical to work closely with the field. Gaining local program managers to implement the initiative will ensure the right rate and pace of the deployment in order to manage the change effectively. These local resources are also a key link back to the HQ organization on issues and challenges so that appropriate modifications can be made.

### Compromise Is Golden

Another key challenge is to balance different business needs with successful implementation. Launching product initiatives and related training programs during an atypically busy time in the business calendar does not make good business sense, and the program is likely to receive limited attention. It also does not make sense to launch an initiative if the target audience— employees—will not be there to participate. One of the authors experienced just such a scenario with the launch of a worldwide employee survey at a global hospitality company. Although a global task force of OD practitioners representing all the divisions was in agreement that a two-week survey administration window was appropriate, there was much disagreement as to when in the calendar year to administer the survey. Some hotels and resorts were seasonal with increased staffing during these peak periods. However, when resorts hit their peak, business travel or urban hotels were slowing down. The compromise was a month-long window during which each hotel determined the two-week administration period that would best fit their individual occupancy and staffing cycle. Many global organizations today face similar challenges with diverse business models and busy times coexisting within the same organization. As always, the key is a true collaborative effort across boundaries to manage that delicate balance required to be successful.

### Communication Is Key

Communication becomes an extraordinarily complex issue in global organizations. The organization needs to ensure that the intended meaning of the message is understood by the receiver. Unfortunately, one cannot assume that translated messages actually maintain the integrity of the original message. For communication to be clear and accurate, it is important that the meaning is translated—not just the words. There are subtle nuances of language that get lost in the literal translations, not to mention the added complexity with local dialects When addressing a lower-skilled, lesser-educated employee population, it can be challenging to ensure that communications use the appropriate level of language and convey the intended meaning.

Translations can be very expensive and time consuming. Although translation agencies are a great resource with a fairly quick turnaround time, an external agency may not be intimately familiar with the organization, its business, or its culture. All of these elements play into the meaning of the intended message. Literal translations often do not capture the entire meaning of the message, leaving out the important nuances that are critical to the full meaning. For example, one of the authors was involved in the launch of a brand campaign. Translations conducted by an external vendor, though accurately translating the words, missed some subtleties that were reflective of the industry and specific to the customer interaction. This could have been a huge problem for the organization if not identified and corrected. Most organizations have a translation faux pas story to share as a result of failure to fully vet translations *before* significant communications are already being launched.

We recommend that translations, whether conducted in-house or externally, should always be followed by a back-translation. Back-translations will identify issues such as the one mentioned above.

If the language of origin is English, the subsequent translation should be independently retranslated and compared to the original English to ensure that the translation captured the intended message. If original translations are conducted by an external agency, back-translations should be conducted by an in-country employee who understands the business, the company culture, and the local culture. Also, trying to keep translations in-house can keep costs down, and participating in a translation exercise can also be a great developmental opportunity for employees to have exposure to an organizational initiative outside their immediate scope of work.

It is possible to say something multiple ways—all of which may be correct. There may be disagreements between translations and back-translations. How to reconcile and choose the more appropriate version (knowing that technically both are correct)? If the meaning is consistent, it is usually best to accept the employee translation over the translation agency as it assumes a better understanding of the organization and culture, employee buy-in to the process, and the creation of an invested employee stakeholder. Translation and retranslation take a great deal of time. There are usually back-and-forth discussions taking place in order to validate the translation. If employees are doing this, remember that they are doing so in addition to their regular jobs. Translations do take time and should be explicitly planned for in any project plan. Unfortunately, too often they are an afterthought and schedules are tight.

Given the expense of translations, how should a global organization choose which languages to translate? Some organizations provide global communication in English only and expect local management to handle translations locally if necessary. Other organizations, which have the resources, coordinate translations globally from a central location working with in-country employees or translation agencies. In a global organization there can be hundreds of languages spoken. Some organizations may have identified their standard list of languages and all communication is translated in those languages. This creates a standard and a process for communication. In other organizations, which languages are chosen will depend on the nature of the communication For example, in the case of a U.S. multinational where the official language is English, communications geared mostly toward managers will often be communicated in English.

If the communication is meant for all employees then one has to decide whether all possible languages should be covered or if there is a logical list based upon the population. For example, one author was faced with translating the Code of Conduct for the global population. Through various survey data it was determined that 12 languages covered 80% of the organization. These 12 languages became the standards used for major communication. This ignored the other 30 potential languages that were identified. The Code of Conduct was communicated in the 12 major languages and local human resources professionals were encouraged to translate locally, and share globally, if they needed an additional language. Some locations translated the Code of Conduct in their local language (Turkish and Hebrew are two examples). They shared the translated Code of Conduct with the ethics and compliance team and these additional translated documents were posted on the company intranet for other HR professionals to use for any Turkish- or Hebrew-speaking employees.

Depending upon the initiative, there may be a grander purpose than just communicating a company message. Organizational inclusion may be just as important. For employees to feel a sense of belonging and inclusion in the organization, translations become a key mechanism to build this connection. An employee engagement survey is an example of building this connection between the organization and its employees. When an organization implements an employee engagement survey, by its very nature it is requesting employee input and participation. Employees cannot participate in the process if they cannot read or understand the survey's questions because it is not written in their language. In a situation such as this, a more inclusive list of languages for translation is appropriate because the organization needs to create a sense of belonging and inclusion for every employee.

### Privacy Is the Law

Working in a global organization requires an awareness of the different laws and regulations that affect employees. Employment policies are guided by local laws and statutes including unions in the United States and work councils in Europe.

In recent years, organizations now also have to address international data privacy laws including whistleblower guidelines and data transfers (EthicsPoint, 2009). In response to the growing use of technology in database management, and the concern regarding technology intruding on personal privacy, the European Union passed a broad law a decade ago that impacts cross-border transfer of personal data—including HRIS (Human Resources Information Systems) data. Data privacy laws have tremendous implications for HRIS databases and the kinds of information that organizations can collect. Data collected in European countries cannot be transferred to the United States easily. This law frustrates U.S.-based multinational organizations, the headquarters of which need to access HR data about their own European workforce. The EU data laws impose tight restrictions on transferring personal data outside of Europe, especially to the United States and other countries whose local laws do not offer EU-caliber protections. The cross-border transfer restriction is an obstacle for any organization trying to create a global HRIS.

Data privacy laws have also made some HR-specific operations more challenging. France, Belgium, Spain, Canada, Germany, Ireland, and Japan all have data privacy laws which are different from U.S. laws (Wugmeister, Retzer, & Rich, 2007). This creates conflicting parameters by which to conduct business. For example, precoding of demographic information in employee surveys becomes problematic in countries where data privacy laws prohibit capturing, and transferring, this information. In those situations, demographic information must be captured as self-report data, adding more time for the survey participant. Precoded data adds complexity when not consistently deployed. For example, ideally an organization should administer an employee survey in the same manner enterprise-wide to reduce any potential variance, or noise, in the data. However, if organizations are looking to provide some ease of use by precoding demographics, this may work in some countries and not in others. It is often required to create multiple versions of surveys and other instruments to accommodate such differences in practice, or to complicate the single version with assorted caveats regarding "do not complete this information if doing so would be considered illegal in your country.''

EU data privacy laws are being enforced with large fines and criminal penalties such as prison time for the offenders who commit unauthorized data disclosures. Compliance is key to the successful transfer of employee data. Organizations can transmit HR data cross-borders if they implement one of the six EU-approved tools such as collecting consent from employees and the safe harbor model (Dowling, 2007).

## Summary

The global organization presents a set of complex challenges to the HR professional in designing, implementing, and managing global programs. The best practices and recommendations will be presented in subsequent chapters. The global organization is a reality and requires embracing a new set of operating principles to ensure success.

Globalization will be with us forever; there is no going back. Even though we may have seen some trend toward deglobalization or relocalization, the reality is that the world is now more interconnected than in any previous time. How we manage this spells the difference between success and failure.

## References

Boston Consulting Group (2008). *Creating people advantage: How to address HR challenges worldwide through 2015.*

Dowling, D. (2007). Global HR hot topic—Global HRIS and EU data privacy law compliance. *White & Case LLP Newsletters*, May 2007.

EthicsPoint (2009). www.ethicspoint.com.

Hempel, J. (2006). Big blue brainstorm. *BusinessWeek*, August 7, 2006.

Hewitt Associates (2009). *Managing HR on a global scale: Findings from Hewitt's 2009 Global HR Study.*

Kim, S., & Shin, E. H. (2002). A longitudinal analysis of globalization and regionalization in international trade: A social network approach. *Social Forces*, *81*(2), 445–471.

Nelson, R. E., & Gopalan, S. (2003). Do organizational cultures replicate national cultures? Isomorphism, rejection, and reciprocal opposition in the corporate values of three countries. *Organizational Studies*, *24*(7), 1115 –1151.

Sirkin, H. L., Hemerling, J. W., & Bhattacharya, A. K. (2008). Globality: Challenger companies are radically redefining the competitive landscape. *Strategy & Leadership, 36*(6), 36–41.

Solomon, C. M., & Schell, M. S. (2009). *Managing across cultures: The seven keys to doing business with a global mindset.* New York: McGraw-Hill.

Wugmeister, M., Retzer, K., & Rich, C. (2007). Global solution for cross-border data transfers: Making the case for corporate privacy rules. *Georgetown Journal of International Law, 38,* 449–498.

Welch, D. E., & Welch, L. S. (2008). The importance of language in international knowledge transfer. *Management International Review, 48*(3), 339–360.

# CHAPTER 2

# Culture: Values, Beliefs, Perceptions, Norms, and Behaviors

## Vesselin Blagoev

> *Globalization seems pervasive. So, one might think, the world's cultures must be converging into one homogenized global value system. But they are not. We not only do not find evidence of convergence—we actually find that the gap between the value systems of rich and poor countries has been growing, not shrinking.*
> — RONALD INGLEHART, CHAIRMAN OF THE WORLD VALUES SURVEY EXECUTIVE COMMITTEE

During the 2003 annual conference of the Central and East European Management Development Association, a keynote speaker told the audience that there had not been a single example of a successful French-Dutch joint venture. He attributed that to the differences between French and Dutch national cultures. In his words, the Dutch employees of his company, Martinair, were extremely disturbed by the news of the impending merger with Air France, as it could result in authoritarian French management, something that is strongly resented in the Netherlands. As the speaker explained, the clash between the two types of management could have emotional as well as financial consequences. Or consider another case. Heineken NV, one of the largest beer producers in the world, had a similar problem with its French subsidiary. To solve it, that multinational had to buy 100% of its stock ahead of the time specified in the acquisition contract and at a huge premium. "I used this case," the speaker said, "to illustrate the fact that the outcome of some joint ventures can be decided solely by cultural issues." This speaker was not just some industry researcher but Gerard van Schaik, chairman of Martinair, former chairman of the board of Heineken NV, and president of the European Foundation for Management Development. His words reflect an observation that is shared by growing numbers of international managers: If cultural differences are not properly understood and managed, they can be a major obstacle to the success of any cross-national venture, especially if it involves very different cultures. The point of this is not to suggest that cross-national activities cannot work, because there are success stories out there. However, culture is pervasive and often operates at an unconscious level. To successfully manage across cultures, leaders today—whether they are crossing geographic boundaries or not—really need to have an appreciation of what culture is, its ability to influence behavior, and ideally they will have a mind that is open to different ways of interacting with the world.

This chapter will explain what culture is, how cultural differences can be studied and understood, and how that knowledge can be useful to anybody involved in a cross-cultural encounter, including international managers. More specifically, I will briefly examine the scientific approach to the study of the main elements of culture: shared values, beliefs, norms, and behaviors. I will show how the complex picture that emerges from such analyses can be simplified so that it is easily understood by nonacademics. The next section will present some of the main cross-cultural differences that affect management and organizational behavior. Finally, I will address the main implications for international managers.

The reader of this chapter will not find any one-size-fits-all solutions or quick fixes. After all, culture is as complex and varied as the organizations in which leaders lead. Instead, this chapter will provide some serious food for thought, even if this means that some readers may find it somewhat indigestible. As Geert Hofstede, one of the world's most quoted cross-cultural experts, once put it, studying culture is asking for trouble. A discussion of the facts that cross-cultural research has revealed often results in bruised feelings, indignation, and denial.

Thus, the goal of this chapter is not to tell international managers how to do their jobs. Rather, it is conceptualized as a first step of a long psychological process. Somewhere down this road, after a long exposure to cultural differences, some international managers naturally find themselves reevaluating their own values, beliefs, and behaviors vis-à-vis those in the host society. Depending upon their particular situation, some may even need to think about how much of the local culture they can or should assimilate. After all, cultural traits can be very durable and resistant to change; we believe that some degree of acceptance of the host culture is more practical and realistic than trying to convert the local population. In essence, I believe that becoming bicultural, or even polycultural, is key to success in international endeavors. It is not a matter of possessing recipes for specific situations. It is about being able to see the world through at least two different pairs of eyes.

## What Is Culture?

Culture has been defined in innumerable ways. A good short definition has been proposed by U.S. anthropologist Donald Brown: "patterns of doing and thinking that are passed on within and between generations by learning" (Brown, 1991, p. 130). Hofstede's metaphor (2001)—shared mental software—also gives a good idea of how culture can be construed. However, the patterns of doing and thinking, or mental software, represent culture only if they are durable and are shared by at least some of the members of a stable group of people, such as a nation or an ethnicity.

Can a large multinational organization have its own distinct culture and spread it throughout its national branches? Multinationals are interested in promoting a shared culture across their subsidiaries because it is viewed as some kind of glue that should help achieve integration and coordination (Schneider, 1988). Yet, the subsidiaries often have an entrenched national culture that may resist what headquarters would like to impose (Adler, 1997; Hofstede, 2001; Schneider, 1988; Trompenaars & Hampden-Turner, 1999). This means that national values normally supersede those of the corporation. Quoting research evidence, Adler (1997) explicitly dispels the myth that corporate culture can erase national culture. Hofstede (2001), Trompenaars and Hampden-Turner (1999), and other leading experts are of the same opinion.

What about management practices across the globe? Is it fair to say that they are not converging either? Not quite. After reviewing the literature on this issue, Dorfman and House (2004) concluded that there is some convergence of management practices across many countries but there is no gravitation toward a single focal point. In their view, most likely there is some convergence toward U.S. practices, some toward Western European practices, and some toward Japanese practices. Nevertheless, the practical reality is that there are bound to be strong residues of local practices in every country. Ultimately, this means that a typical multinational will exhibit a variety of management styles around the globe, consisting of various mixtures of imported and homemade elements. As a result, it is highly unlikely that a single style will prevail in most countries in the foreseeable future.

And what of beliefs? It is certainly easier to change one's outward behavior (such as management practices) than one's inner self. Thus, when multinationals create commonality across subsidiaries, it mostly consists of shared practices, and not necessarily values and beliefs (French et al., 2008; Hofstede, 2001). So if underlying values and beliefs are resistant to change, how can multinationals promote the shared practices that the leaders of an international company wish to see in all their subsidiaries.

## The Main Measurable Elements of Culture

By now it is largely accepted in mainstream social science that culture can be studied objectively and that the results of the analyses can be used to make verifiable predictions, though not with engineering precision. Culture consists of components that cannot be quantified and compared (such as local customs, ceremonies, and so forth) as well as of measurable elements that can be woven into statistically derived dimensions. The measurable elements of culture form two distinct groups: observable and invisible. The first group consists of behaviors and practices that can either be seen directly or deduced from national statistics, such as suicide rates, murder rates, birth rates, road death tolls, alcohol and tobacco consumption, and the like. The second group comprises what is commonly known as values, beliefs, perceptions, and norms. Because these are studied by means of questionnaires, the easiest way to understand what they are is to look at how the corresponding questionnaire items are worded.

- **Values** are measured by asking the respondents what is important to them in their personal lives. Studies of values have revealed for example that religion, work, and family are far more important to people in some countries than in others (Inglehart & Baker, 2000; Minkov, 2007).
- **Beliefs** are measured by presenting the respondents with statements and asking them if they agree or disagree. For instance respondents in some countries are far more likely than other respondents to believe that men make better leaders than women (World Values Survey, 2006) or that caring for societal affairs only brings trouble (Bond et al., 2004).
- **Perceptions** are measured by asking the respondents how they perceive some abstract aspects of their own lives, such as their happiness, health, and life satisfaction, or the degree of control that they think they have over their own lives. Studies of perceptions (World Values Survey, 2006) have revealed enormous cross-cultural differences.
- **Norms** are measured by asking the respondents what values others should have and what they should do or should not do. Thus, norms can be called values (or desirable behaviors) for others. It is crucially important to understand the difference between people's personal values and the norms that they prescribe to others. because these may coincide or be diametrically opposed. For example, a person who is striving for power may advocate submissiveness as a norm for others (Smith, 2006). The two largest cross-national studies of nationally representative samples, the World Values Survey (2006) and the Pew Research Center (2002; 2007), have revealed significant cross-cultural differences in norms, such as the degree to which respondents agree that poor people should be helped by the government or their fellow citizens.

## Are Some Cultural Ingredients *Better* Than Others?

The bewildering diversity of values, norms, and practices that one can observe in different societies often brings up the question of whether some are better than others. The answer, however, is highly context-specific. For instance, the values that promote national economic growth in a particular historical period may not be the same as at different times or even at the same time in a different society. Thus, unless the context is clearly specified, it is difficult to evaluate values and norms in an absolute sense.

Some authors, however, downplay the importance of context or *cultural relativism,* as it has become known. Dowling and Welch (2004), for example, promote the idea of universal values, such as the biblical "Thou shalt not kill." They ask whether corruption is really acceptable in a country like Indonesia, even though it is a relatively common. Their answer is no, on the grounds that it is "morally wrong." However, some would argue that this answer is culturally specific. In some cases, corruption is viewed quite differently. For example, I know of East Europeans, North Africans, and Middle Easterners who have expressed indignation after Western officials declined their bribe offers. From their own cultural viewpoint, the Western officials had spurned an offer of collaboration and friendship. In short, the same practice is viewed very differently as a function of one's own cultural context.

This is not a call for Western expatriates to engage in corrupt practices while working outside their home countries. Quite on the contrary, as already stated, values are very difficult to change and Westerners cannot be expected to trade theirs for a different currency just because it appears to be "semi-legal tender" in a foreign country. I simply use this example to expose the fallacy of the idea of a universal morality, and to drive home the notion that when some Western values are served up to people who have not grown up with them, they may be as reluctant to adopt them as some Westerners may be unwilling, or just afraid, to engage in corruption.

# Main Cultural Dimensions with Implications for Cross-Cultural Management

The research literature provides many accounts of cultural dimensions that seem to explain various societal differences, some of which have implications for management and organizational behavior. The following is a brief presentation of those that may be most useful to an international manager, while being scientifically sound and reliable.

## Individualism versus Collectivism (Universalism versus Exclusionism)

This is an extremely robust dimension in the sense that it has appeared in a number of large-scale studies, involving more than 45 nations each, the first of which was that by Geert Hofstede around 1970 (Hofstede, 2001), followed by Smith, Dugan, and Trompenaars (1996), Gelfand, Ghawuk, Nishii, and Bechtold (2004), and Minkov (2007).

There are some divergent opinions concerning the right interpretation of this dimension and what exactly is at its core. Many view individualism as being synonymous with selfishness and a preference to *go it alone*. It has also been interpreted as competition-orientation. Collectivism, on the other hand, is often described as a willingness to follow others, to cooperate, and to work in teams. However, these concepts are not meaningfully correlated with the previously mentioned large-scale measures of individualism versus collectivism, as the latter reveal a different picture.

Individualism versus collectivism also reflects some of the important differences between Western and non-Western cultures. Economically poor societies are often thought of as collectivist because they are characterized by strong and cohesive in-groups, consisting mainly of clansmen, close friends, and relatives, although the circle may be extended to include other groups, such as one's loyal customers and employees. People in collectivistic societies usually feel a strong moral obligation toward in-group members, which may sometimes assume the form of self-sacrifice. Out-group members, by contrast, tend to be treated with comparative indifference, which can escalate into outright neglect, negligence, disrespect, derision, and discrimination. In worst-case scenarios, the result can be open hostility and abuse. As Triandis (2000) puts it, "people in collectivist cultures are extremely supportive of their in-group members, but they have a cold, and even hostile, relationship with out-group members" (p. 29).

To avoid misconceptions, and to emphasize the practical implications of these cultural differences, Minkov (2007) proposed a new name for the individualism-versus-collectivism dimension: universalism versus exclusionism. Exclusionism (collectivism) can be viewed as a tendency to treat people on the basis of their group membership, refusing privileges to out-group members by means of nepotism and discrimination. Universalism (individualism) is about the opposite: the degree to which a society is serious about stamping out nepotism and discriminatory attitudes and practices. This dimension is also a very strong predictor of corruption, as measured by Transparency International. Poorer and more exclusionist countries invariably have more corruption. Businesspeople from a state official's in-group deserve a preferential treatment that others are excluded from. If they wish to receive a service or obtain a contract that is not meant for them, the only recourse that they normally have is a bribe.

**Shades of gray**. It must also be noted that there are shades of gray with regard to the distinction between individualism and collectivism. For example, research has shown that the indifferent or cold attitude toward out-group in collectivistic societies may disappear in some collectivist countries when strangers are perceived as being in need of help (Levine, Norenzayan, & Philbrick, 2001). Moreover, it would be incorrect to say that the distinction between in-groups and out-groups is totally unknown in the individualistic West, but it is far less pronounced. For example, while it is clear from the World Values Survey that racism (expressed as an unwillingness to have neighbors of a different race) is much stronger in Asia, Africa, the Middle East, and Eastern Europe, the same survey shows that "tolerance and respect for others," as a value that children should learn, is strongest in the West.

## Implications for Organizations

Individualism and collectivism have many implications for organizations, and we now turn to a few of the more obvious or potentially challenging ones.

**Nepotism**. Whereas Westerners tend to view nepotism as morally wrong, it is viewed as more acceptable in poorer exclusionist (individualistic) societies. In those societies, a person can be dead (literally) without the support of his or her in-group and is therefore obliged to prioritize commitments in their favor.

In a poor society with limited resources, this is only natural. By contrast, refusing preferential treatment to a member of one's in-group can result in severe sanctions.

As a result, organizations in poor collectivist-exclusionist societies may look more like families in that personal and professional relationships are intermixed (Hampden-Turner & Trompenaars, 1996; Trompenaars & Hampden-Turner, 1999). A boss may ask his subordinates to help him paint his house or run personal errands for him. He is a father figure who disburses privileges on the basis of the loyalty and obedience that he receives, not necessarily on the basis of personally achieved professional goals.

Thus, in exclusionist societies, nepotistic practices can be quite strong, as are attempts to cover the misdemeanors of in-group members. "Nothing personal" is a meaningless statement in this type of culture because nearly everything is personal. Any direct criticism of an employee's professional performance may be interpreted as an assault on his character. Hiring, firing, and promotions in a company's hierarchy also reflect the quality of personal relationships. The idea of sacking an employee for failing to achieve targets may sound alien. My own consulting practice shows that when the Western logic of this phenomenon is explained to people with a strongly exclusionist (collectivist) mind-set, they find it abhorrent and unworkable. Of course, layoffs do occur in the poor world during crises, but firing people on the basis of their mediocre performance, with no concern for their personal relationship with their manager and peers, can be viewed as shockingly immoral and incomprehensible.

By contrast, in Western societies, an employee that does not visibly contribute to the success of the organization is viewed as a burden that should be jettisoned as soon as possible. A good illustration of the diametrical opposition in management philosophies that these cultural differences can produce is provided by the narratives of two of the world's most famous managers: Jack Welch, former chief executive of General Electric, and Akio Morita, the late founder and president of Sony. Welch was proud of a human resource management system that required the heads of the company's different businesses to rank all their managers each year and lay off the lowest 10 percent (Welch & Byrne, 2001, quoted in "Jack and the People Factory," 2001, p. 38.). Morita, by contrast, practiced Japanese management, based precisely on the opposite philosophy. Once he complained to some American colleagues about an exasperating employee and admitted he did not know what to do with him. The Americans advised him to fire the person. "I was stunned by the idea," Morita wrote, "I had never fired anybody and even in this case it had never crossed my mind. But to solve the problem by firing a man was the American system" (Morita, Reingold, & Shimomura, 1986, quoted in Hampden-Turner & Trompenaars, 1996, p. 175).

**Contracting**. Universalist (Individualist) societies have a tendency to produce rigid formal contracts that must be respected, whereas exclusionist ones have a much looser attitude toward agreements, especially when they involve out-group members (Minkov, 2007; Trompenaars & Hampden-Turner, 1999). For a contract to be honored in an exclusionist culture, one may need to form a very close relationship with one's business partner, which effectively guarantees the status of an in-group member (Trompenaars & Hampden-Turner, 1999). The universalist cultures of the rich world and their higher concern for others, regardless of their group affiliation, have produced formal legislation that makes it very risky to renege on agreements.

**Punctuality**. The anecdotal evidence in Trompenaars and Hampden-Turner (1999), as well as research by Levine and Norenzayan (1999), shows that Western cultures differ from the rest of the world in terms of their greater respect for punctuality and faster speed of life. This difference has been confusingly interpreted in terms of a "synchronic" or "polychronic" versus "sequential" dimension (Trompenaars & Hampden-Turner, 1999, p. 123). In fact, it simply reflects differences in empathy: lower levels in the poor exclusionist world where people are less likely to show tolerance and respect for others, higher levels in the rich universalist world. As Trompenaars (2003) admitted, an acquaintance of his once made the following statement: "The problem of being late is actually the problem of those who are on time." This means that a lack of punctuality need not be explained as a different perception of time. It reveals a lack of empathy and respect for those who are waiting. Similarly, the so-called polychronic behavior of a clerk in an exclusionist society who is talking to a friend while dealing with a customer simply means that the friend is more important to this person than the business.

**Communication**. One of the potentially exasperating differences between exclusionist and universalist cultures has been defined as high-context versus low-context communication (Hall, 1959). High-context means *beating around the bush:* the message is implicit and parts of it have to be inferred and guessed from the situation in which it was made or from some external information about the speaker. Low-context communication involves explicit statements that leave little room for subjective interpretations. The fact that Western societies prefer long and precise contracts, which are atypical in the developing world, owes a lot to this cultural difference. Western culture is low-context: speaking one's mind clearly and precisely and being direct is considered a virtue as long as one remains polite. But in the high-context exclusionist world, direct communication of bad news is normally viewed as rude and inconsiderate. By way of example, Trompenaars and Hampden-Turner (1999) tell a story about a Western doctor who was killed by a colleague in a developing country for criticized his work. Such extreme behavior is very rare but cases when criticising permanently damages a personal and professional relationship are very frequent.

**Products, services, and safety**. One of the most important implications of universalism versus exclusionism differences for international managers is the different attitude toward product and service quality, as well as safety, in the West and the poorer parts of the world. Alvazzi del Frate and van Kesteren (2004) report a study evidencing far more frequent consumer fraud in exclusionist countries than in universalist ones, whereas Trompenaars and Hampden-Turner (1999) quote an IMD report on international competitiveness that includes a ranking on product safety in 24 developed economies. There is higher concern for safety in the rich universalist countries.

This is an extremely serious issue for management. In principle, it is multinational companies that bring to the developing world the idea of consistent product and service quality for all customers and implement it after some considerable effort. For example, although Bulgaria is considered the homeland of yogurt, it was not until Danone set up shop in that country in the 1990s that

Bulgarian customers could finally buy some yogurt of predictable quality. Even today, the poor and inconsistent quality of many food products in Bulgarian stores and the fraudulent practices of quite a few local producers are hotly debated topics in the country's media.

## Power Distance and Authoritarianism

Power distance, another key component of culture, has been thought of in different ways. Hofstede (2001), for example, conceptualized this dimension as the emotional distance between leaders and their subordinates. GLOBE focuses more on the distribution of power (Carl, Gupta, & Javidan, 2004) and finally, Euwema, Wendt, and van Emmerik (2007) talk about directive leadership as the degree to which managers supervise their subordinates closely and expect precise and immediate execution of their orders. Despite these differences, the three concepts are more similar than different. The basic premise is that leader-follower relationships are more authoritarian in poor countries, which means that this dimension creates a geographic distribution that tracks closely with individualism and collectivism. For example, anecdotal evidence suggests that Asia has greatest authoritarianism, evident in rigid hierarchies and caste systems, autocratic leadership, and submissive subordinates. The Scandinavian countries and the Netherlands, by contrast, are at the opposite extreme where an employee challenging the decision of a manager would not necessarily be viewed as shocking or disrespectful.

For managers crossing these sorts of boundaries, it can be challenging, to say the least. For example, a manager from northwestern Europe or an Anglo-Saxon country who is not used to subservient yea-saying subordinates, but expects initiative and independent action, may find it terribly frustrating to work with those who prefer to sit back and wait for direction. In a high-power distance culture, these sorts of qualities are found primarily in top leaders and entrepreneurs, whereas middle managers and employees at lower levels are simply supposed to execute orders. Even senior staff, such as a company's director of sales or human resources manager, may be reluctant to make any move without the chief executive officer's blessing. Attempts to change this type of culture and introduce notions like participative management, independent decision making, empowerment, devolution, delayering, and flat company structures often fail miserably.

And even when one thinks that changes are executed, the truth could be far different. Examples from Hofstede (2001), Trompenaars and Hampden-Turner (1999), and my own practice demonstrate that even when some change is visible at the surface, the underlying situation may remain unchanged. A Slovak executive from a large German company in Slovakia once told us that the German leaders had spent a year on a delayering project. But the final result showed only on the new company chart. In practice, the old hierarchies remained in people's minds and many employees still expected guidance and orders from those who had been their bosses.

## Uncertainty Avoidance

Hofstede's uncertainty avoidance (2001), in a nutshell, refers to the way that cultures respond to changes and deal with ambiguity. High–uncertainty avoidance cultures are generally thought of as conservative and law-abiding whereas low–uncertainty avoidance cultures are open to change, innovation, and diversity. There has, however, been some confusion around rule orientation and specifically whether or not this is indicative of one's own personal values. For example, if personal values guide behavior, then people in Southern and Latin Europe, where Hofstede's uncertainty avoidance reaches its highest scores, should be the most law-abiding, but many observers have been puzzled by what they have seen in reality—a seeming South European tendency to break rules. What are we to make of this? The answer lies in the difference between personal values and norms for others. In Bulgaria for instance, the typical philosophy seems to be *others should be very rule-oriented but I must be allowed to break the rules if it serves my own interest.* Thus, while Hofstede's uncertainty avoidance may explain how people in some countries react to other people's transgressions it does not necessarily tell us about people's personal rule orientation.

And like anything else, there are shades of gray. For example, regardless of where they fall on the uncertainty avoidance scale, no society on earth is without some unbendable rules that everybody respects. People in southern Europe make more traffic violations than those in northwestern Europe, but they respect various other stringent rules that others may not have heard of. For example, Bulgarians never give a woman an even number of flowers. Another example: Indonesians drive in a way that can make a Westerner's hair stand on end, but they have innumerable indigenous social regulations from which they never deviate.

## Masculinity versus Femininity

Hofstede's "masculinity versus femininity" dimension is also often misinterpreted, at least in two ways. First of all, it has nothing to do with male dominance over women, as many people think. Second, it is not a measure of achievement orientation or competitiveness in an absolute sense. It is about the prioritization of achievement versus personal relationships in the workplace. It reveals which of the two would be more important if employees had to choose only one of them. According to Hosfstede's data (2001) from IBM around 1970, employees in so-called masculine cultures (such as Japan) attached a higher importance to achievement than to relationships, whereas the situation in so-called feminine countries (such as Guatemala) was precisely the opposite. Nevertheless, Japan's achievement orientation score was far lower than the score of Guatemala. In an absolute sense, Guatemala was much more achievement oriented than Japan.

The World Values Survey, which relies on nationally representative data, rather than matched samples from one and the same corporation, shows a somewhat different pattern of work-goal prioritization. In the majority of poor countries, the most important goals are earnings and job security, whereas achievement and relationships are usually lower on people's priority lists. In the United States and Australia, the most important goals are achievement and earnings; relationships are less important. But in Japan, Germany, and the Scandinavian countries, relationships come first.

## Societal Cynicism

Bond and associates (2004) proposed a research-based cultural dimension called "societal cynicism." It is measured by responses to statements such as "To care about societal affairs only brings trouble to yourself," "Kind-hearted people usually suffer losses," "Old people are usually stubborn and biased," "People will stop working after they secure a comfortable life," and so on. It also reflects a view that powerful people are arrogant exploiters. According to the available data, societal cynicism is strongest in Eastern Europe, East Asia (Korea, Taiwan), Pakistan, and Thailand. It is weakest in Norway, the United States, and Canada.

If this relatively new dimension is replicated and confirmed in further studies, it may have serious implications for international management. For example, American managers in Eastern Europe often wonder why they have to go to unusual lengths to gain the trust of their subordinates. Societal cynicism may provide a plausible explanation: in cynical cultures, employees and managers may form oppositional identities that are hard to dismantle. It is also likely that differences in societal cynicism partly account for different attitudes toward corruption.

## Utilitarian Versus Loyal Involvement

Smith, Dugan, and Trompenaars (1996) studied the norms and beliefs of 8,841 managers and employees from 43 countries and identified a dimension they called "utilitarian versus loyal involvement." What it measures is the propensity and willingness to work in a team and share responsibility with others. Their research revealed that individuals in Asia show the highest level and Eastern Europeans score lowest. This dimension captures a phenomenon that any Bulgarian, and probably some other East Europeans, will be aware of. My colleague Michael Minkov and I have asked various groups of Bulgarians—business students, company employees, and even high school students—whether they like to work in teams, and have often heard a resounding "no," often accompanied by a wry grimace. Attempts by managers from English-speaking countries to change this attitude are not likely to result in quick success in any society where people prefer to be given individual tasks and then be left alone.

## Economic Dynamism

Minkov and Blagoev (2009) have proposed a new cultural dimension extracted from World Values Survey data. Starting from the views of leading development economists concerning the determinants of economic growth, and in particular of the East Asian economic miracle, we show a parallel between the factors proposed by the economists and a number of cultural values. We demonstrate that nations that attached a higher importance to thrift and a lower importance to leisure in the 1998–99 wave of the World Values Survey registered considerably faster economic growth in the next decade. We also found that these nations attach a lower importance to personal relationships. The highest scorers on this dimension, which we called "economic dynamism," are East Asian and East European nations. The lowest scorers are the Latin American countries.

This dimension provides serious food for thought not only to national governments but also to international managers. When expatriates from a country that scores high on economic dynamism become managers in one with a low score, they may perceive the local workforce as indolent and unacceptably fun-oriented. Paik and Derick Sohn (1998) quote South Korean managers in Mexico who were upset by the fact that their workers listened to radios and talked a lot, instead of concentrating on their work without getting distracted, which seems to be the normal state of affairs in South Korea.

# Project GLOBE's Leadership Dimensions

During the 1990s, Project GLOBE studied the preferred leadership style in 62 societies (House et al., 2004). The results specific to leadership from this study are presented in Dorfman, Hanges, and Brodbeck (2004). Six preferred leadership dimensions were extracted, describing broad leadership styles. Although these dimensions are still new to academics and practitioners alike, they are interesting. For example, they reveal that charismatic leadership, which captures the attention of many American researchers, is indeed highly valued in the Americas, but far less so in many other countries, where employees rank the importance of effective leadership traits in a different way.

Although the GLOBE study is well known and widely cited, it is not without controversy. One issue of contention has to do with the fact that the authors asked respondents to describe their societies as well as the personalities of their fellow citizens. McCrae, Terracciano, Realo, and Allik, (2007; 2008), however, argued that this approach yields meaningful results only when the issues that the respondents are asked to discuss are very simple and very salient. A simple and salient issue could be the size of the typical family in a given society. Any question at a higher level of abstraction can result in answers that do not contain meaningful information for cross-cultural comparisons. Question v163 in the World Values Survey Association (2008), for example, asks the respondents how much "democraticness" there is in their own countries. According to the nationally representative samples, there is more democraticness in Ghana, Vietnam, and Jordan than in any Western country, such as Switzerland, Germany, the United States, Sweden, and Finland.

There is a very important practical lesson here that international managers and consultants should remember. Asking a country's citizens to provide information about their own culture can be double-edged. It can result in valuable information or meaningless statements, depending on what you ask about.

## Cultural Diversity: A Nuisance or a Competitive Advantage?

In this chapter, we have presented just a fraction of the bewilderingly rich cross-cultural variation in the world. The full extent and depth of cultural differences are hard to fathom and probably impossible to ever catalogue completely. And as we ponder those differences, it is worth revisiting the notion of cultural diversity and whether it is an aid or a hindrance to organizations. The answer is complicated and depends on how you look at this topic.

### Managers Managing Cultural Diversity

As international managers attempt to navigate these challenging waters, there are probably two obvious ways that they can quickly run into problems with respect to culture. Understanding these problems can help turn culture from a nuisance to an advantage. The first is when managers are simply unaware of the many nuances around cultural differences. The good news is that, to some extent, lack of awareness can be remedied through cross-cultural training, coaching, time on the ground, and so forth. And while this may not guarantee cultural "fluency," it can go a long way toward giving the manager a good working knowledge of the relevant norms, values, and expected behavior.

The second way that managers can get into trouble is perhaps more problematic, and that has to do with individuals who may or may not be aware of the cultural nuances but regardless seek to impose their own norms and values and discount those of others. A statement by two consultants with substantial cross-cultural knowledge and experience perhaps exemplifies the challenge of trying to change others: "Perfect integration between Western expatriates and local executives appears to be impossible" (Browaeys & Price, 2008, p. 294). And this is not a subjective opinion without basis in evidence. It summarizes the findings of a study of Afro-Occidental teams by African and Western scholars. And it is a sobering call for realism. Instead of expecting easy and complete solutions to all cross-cultural problems, managers may sometimes have to accept that some serious and possibly unpalatable differences will remain. There may be no further solution but to accept the situation by simply grinning and bearing it.

International managers also need to keep in mind that there is often a logic behind the differences that they may come across. Specifically, different geographic, historical, and social environments will have created different cultures, all of which are quite logical in their particular settings, even if a foreign national fails to see this right away. Understanding this can be a major first step toward a reduction of the discomfort that people often experience in an unfamiliar society, where things can seem to be upside down. Then, managers can work out ways to deal with the challenges of the local culture by accommodating its own logic. A study of Korean management in Mexico provides a good illustration of culture-sensitive conflict resolution. The Korean managers realized the great importance of the family in Mexican society and helped their workers deal with various family-related problems. As a result, the Mexican workers responded with greater commitment and work motivation. Trompenaars and Hampden-Turner (1999) provide an account of how forming a strong personal relationship in a collectivist culture can improve professional relationships between business partners.

It is also important to remember the adage that each half-empty glass is also half-full. Although cultural differences may be assumed by some to be an impediment to the development of a company, the opposite may actually be true. Instead of an impediment, those unique cultural aspects could actually be an advantage that does not exist at home. For example, Western managers may chafe at the tendency in some cultures for subordinates to be passive, unwilling to assume personal responsibility, and lacking initiative, but the other side of the coin is that managers' decisions could actually be implemented more swiftly. At the end of the day, it would seem that what's really key is that international managers (and their organizations) understand the cultural nuances as much as is reasonably possible, and adjust their practices to make the best of the situation for their employees, the organizations, and other relevant stakeholders. After all, there is enough research to prove that different branches of one and the same multinational may use different management styles—authoritarian versus participative—and obtain the same financial results. The ability to see different paths to one and the same goal and assess the utility of one and the same cultural trait from different angles should be a major goal of cross-cultural training.

## It's All Relative

Let us also once again address the issue of cultural relativism. This relativism itself is also relative and not at all absolute. But the reasons for this are practical and have nothing to do with a universal morality. For example, it is true that company growth and profit can be achieved in different ways and by making use of different cultural values, beliefs, norms, and behaviors. But it is not true that just any cultural values, beliefs, and behaviors can be conducive to growth and profit. For instance, a strong distinction between in-groups and out-groups in an exclusionist society is often maintained in business relationships as well: in-group members are entitled to goods of better quality and better service. However, this practice generally hinders company growth because it creates a dividing line between a limited number of in-group members and the unlimited number of out-group members. Evidently, this particular aspect of a strongly exclusionist mind-set needs to be treated as a cause of concern by any manager who believes in company growth.

Another example has to do with the entrenched belief in the West that men and women are equal and must be treated accordingly. Even if a company in a developing country can discriminate against women and still achieve strong profit, this practice will never be accepted by the representatives of mainstream Western culture. Trompenaars (2003) explains how a Western female manager was rejected in a country where men do not believe in gender equality, only to be fully accepted after the local people were informed that she was an extraordinary person at home, commanding very high social prestige. However, this may not work equally well for local women. How to resolve gender inequality problems in societies where women have been kept away from leadership for millennia is not a question that has an easy answer for multinationals operating in those societies.

## Not Comfortable, Just Wait . . . a While

For those who find some cultural practices to be in the marginal zone of what they consider ethically acceptable (that is, a nuisance), they may find solace in the knowledge that economic development generally brings about profound cultural change, generally toward Western universalist values. Before it became wealthy, the Western world had a strongly exclusionist culture. And though it took centuries of economic development for it to become as universalist as it is today, it also seems to be the case that many of the developing countries around the globe are changing at a faster pace than ever before. In China, for example, thinking around thrift that developed over centuries seems to be changing overnight. And though the deep underlying values may not turn on their head quite so quickly, there is no question that technology and the easy access to information that comes with it are having a dramatic impact on these developing societies. Thus, elements of culture which may be a nuisance now in terms of creating competitive advantage, in time, may abate over time.

## Organizations as a Nuisance Variable

Finally, some seemingly cultural problems are simply generated by poor management. At the 2008 annual conference of CEEMAN (Central and East European Management Development Association) in Tirana, the owner of various large businesses in the Republic of Macedonia—who is a national of that country—complained that the typical employee in the Balkans is not sufficiently motivated to work hard because he does not have the Protestant values of the Anglo-Saxon world. Complaints that other East Europeans also have a poor work ethic and are almost unmanageable are often heard from prominent local entrepreneurs. A better understanding of these apparent nuisance factors, however, can be gained by looking at recent history. After the breakup of the socialist-communist system, some businesses ended up in the hands of self-made people who thought that effective management could be practiced without any understanding of human psychology and motivation. As a result, some of their practices were downright awful, consisting mainly of military methods. The natural result was disgruntled employees with cynical attitudes toward their companies, something that had nothing to do with the local culture. So the final lesson for international managers is that what may at first blush seem like "culture" could, upon further examination, be revealed as the result of something quite different.

# References

Adler, N. J. (1997). *International dimensions of organizational behavior.* Cincinnati, OH: South-Western.

Alvazzi del Frate, A., & van Kesteren, J. (2004). *Criminal victimization in urban Europe; Key findings of the 2000 international crime victim surveys.* United Nations Interregional Crime and Justice Research Institute. Internet publication. Retrieved Jan. 8, 2007, from www.unicri.it/wwd/analysis/icvs/pdf_files/CriminalVictimisationUrbanEurope.pdf.

Bond, M. H., et al. (2004). Culture-level dimensions of social axioms and their correlates across 41 cultures. *Journal of Cross-Cultural Psychology, 35,* 548–570.

Brown, D. (1991). *Human universals.* New York: McGraw Hill.

Browaeys, M. J., & Price, R. (2008). *Understanding cross-cultural management.* Harlow, UK: Prentice Hall.

Carl, D., Gupta. V., & Javidan, M. (2004). Power distance. In R. J. House, P. J., Hanges, J. Mansour, P. W. Dorfman, & V. Gupta, V. (Eds.). *Culture, leadership, and organizations. The GLOBE study of 62 societies.* Thousand Oaks, CA: Sage.

Dorfman, P. W., Hanges, P. J., & Brodbeck, F. C. (2004). Leadership and cultural variation. In R. J. House, P. J., Hanges, J. Mansour, P. W. Dorfman, & V. Gupta, V. (Eds.). *Culture, leadership, and organizations. The GLOBE study of 62 societies.* Thousand Oaks, CA: Sage.

Dorfman, P. W., & House, R. J. (2004). Cultural influences on organizational leadership. In R. J. House, P. J., Hanges, J. Mansour, P. W. Dorfman, & V. Gupta, V. (Eds.). *Culture, leadership, and organizations. The GLOBE study of 62 societies.* Thousand Oaks, CA: Sage.

Dowling, P. J., & Welch, D. E. (2004). *International human resource management.* London: Thompson Learning.

Euwema, M. C., Wendt, H., & van Emmerik, H. (2007). Leadership styles and group organizational citizenship behavior across cultures. *Journal of Organizational behavior, 28*(8), 1035–1057.

French, R., et al. (2008). *Organizational behaviour.* Chichester, UK: Wiley.

Gelfand, M. J., Ghawuk, D. P. S., Nishii, L. H., & Bechtold, D. J. (2004). Individualism and collectivism. In R. J. House, P. J., Hanges, J. Mansour, P. W. Dorfman, & V. Gupta, V. (Eds.). *Culture, leadership, and organizations. The GLOBE study of 62 societies.* Thousand Oaks, CA: Sage.

Hall, E. T. (1959). *The silent language.* New York: Anchor Books.

Hampden-Turner, C., & Trompenaars, F. (1996). *The seven cultures of capitalism; Value systems for creating wealth in the United States, Japan, Germany, France, Britain, Sweden, and the Netherlands.* London: Piatkus.

Hofstede, G. (2001). *Culture's consequences. Comparing values, behaviors, institutions, and organizations across nations.* Thousand Oaks, CA: Sage.

House, R. J., Hanges, P. J., Mansour, J., Dorfman, P. W., & Gupta, V. (Eds.) (2004). *Culture, leadership, and organizations. The GLOBE study of 62 societies.* Thousand Oaks, CA: Sage.

Inglehart, R., & Baker, W. E. (2000). Modernization, cultural change, and the persistence of traditional values. *American Sociological Review, 65,* 1, 19–51.

Jack and the people factory. (Sept. 17, 2001). *Fortune*, 38 .

Levine, R. V., & Norenzayan, A. (1999). The pace of life in 31 countries. *Journal of Cross-Cultural Psychology*, *30*(2), 178–205.

Levine, V. R., Norenzayan, A., & Philbrick, K. (2001). Cross-cultural differences in helping strangers. *Journal of Cross-Cultural Psychology*, *32*, 543–560.

McCrae, R. R., Terracciano, A., Realo, A., & Allik, A. (2007). Climatic warmth and national wealth: Some culture-level determinants of national character stereotypes. *European Journal of Personality*, *21*, 953–976.

McCrae, R. R., Terracciano, A., Realo, A., & Allik, J. (2008). Interpreting GLOBE Societal Practices Scales. *Journal of Cross-Cultural Psychology*, *39*, 805–810.

Minkov, M., & Blagoev, V. (2009). Cultural values predict subsequent economic growth. *International Journal of Cross-Cultural Management*, *9*(1), 5–24.

Minkov, M. (2007). *What makes us different and similar: A new interpretation of the World Values Survey and other cross-cultural data*. Sofia, Bulgaria: Klasika i Stil.

Morita, A., Reingold, E. M., & Shimomura, E. (1986). *Made in Japan: Akio Morita and the Sony Corporation*. New York: Dutton.

Paik, Y. S., & Derick Sohn, J. H. (1998). Confucius in Mexico: Korean MNCs and the maquiladoras. *Business Horizons*, *41*(6), 25–33.

Pew Research Center. (2007). *Global opinion trends 2002–2007*. Internet publication. Retrieved Feb. 20, 2008, from http://pewglobal.org/reports/pdf/257.pdf and http://pewglobal.org/reports/pdf/257topline-trend.pdf.

Pew Research Center. (2002). *What the world thinks in 2002. How global publics view their lives, their countries, the world, America*. Internet publication. Retrieved Nov. 8, 2005, from http://people-press.org/reports. (Survey results in http://people-press.org/reports/pdf/165topline.pdf).

Schneider, S. C. (1988). National vs. corporate culture: Implications for human resource management. *Human Resource Management*, *2*(2), 231–246.

Smith, P. B. (2006). When elephants fight, the grass gets trampled: The GLOBE and Hofstede projects. *Journal of International Business Studies*, *37*, 915–921.

Smith, P. B., Dugan, S., & Trompenaars, F. (1996). National culture and the values of organizational employees: A dimensional analysis across 43 nations. *Journal of Cross-Cultural Psychology*, *27*, 231–264.

Triandis, H. C. (2000). Cultural syndromes and subjective well-being. In E. Diener, & M. E. Suh. (Eds.). *Culture and subjective well-being.* Cambridge, MA: MIT Press.

Trompenaars, F. (2003). Presentation at the *Presidents' Forum,* October 2003, International Executive Development Center, Bled, Slovenia.

Trompenaars, F., & Hampden-Turner, C. (1999). *Riding the waves of culture.* London: Nicholas Brealy.

Welch, J. F., & Byrne, J. A. (2001). *Jack: Straight from the gut.* New York: Warner Books.

World Values Survey (2006). *On-line data analysis.* Retrieved in June–November, 2006, from www.worldvaluessurvey.com.

World Values Survey Association (2008). World Values Survey 2005 official data file, v.20081015. Madrid: ASEP/JDS. Retrieved Nov. 12, 2008, from www.worldvaluessurvey.com.

# CHAPTER 3

# Multicultural Teams: Critical Team Processes and Guidelines

C. Shawn Burke, Marissa L. Shuffler,
Eduardo Salas, and Michele Gelfand

In the twenty-first century, global organizations are no longer the exception, but the norm. Global organizations and the resulting multicultural workforce can have tremendous benefits as talent and resources are no longer limited by geography. Having a global workforce has been argued to be a way to drive innovation and competitiveness by facilitating access to a wider pool of approaches, resources, and networks. Therefore, it is often the case that even organizations that are solely located within a single country have a culturally diverse workforce when members are recruited based on talent and not location.

In addition to organizations becoming increasingly global, another trend that has emerged is the move toward team-based organizations where a predominant amount of the work is facilitated through the use of work teams. Such teams have been characterized as being composed of two or more individuals who interact adaptively and interdependently toward a common goal (Salas, Dickinson, Converse, & Tannenbaum, 1992). Recently there has been increasing interest in what happens when these two trends intersect, thus resulting in the use of multicultural work teams. Multicultural teams are defined as a team (see Salas et al., 1992) whose members have diverse values and beliefs based on their cultural orientation. The interaction within these teams primarily reflect intercultural interaction versus intracultural interaction.

In seeking to provide guidance to organizations, there has been a fair amount of work conducted that examines intracultural differences in group- or team-based work. For example, research has shown that cultural differences have implications for cooperation (for example, Kirkman & Shapiro, 2001; Cox et al., 1991), communication (Conyne et al., 1999), feedback (Earley et al., 1999), conflict type (Elron, 1997; Mortensen & Hinds, 2001), cohesion (Man & Lam, 2003; Elron, 1997), team efficacy (Gibson, 1999), adaptation (Harrison, McKinnon, Wu, & Chow, 2000), decision making (Kirchmeyer & Cohen, 1992), and team performance (Elron, 1997; Gibson, 1999; Kirkman & Shapiro, 2001; Man & Lam, 2003; Matveev & Nelson, 2004; Gelfand, Erez, & Aycan, 2007). However, as organizations increasingly rely on multicultural work teams, often overlooked are the challenges inherent in leading and working within teams in which individuals have vastly different backgrounds, traditions, motivations, and concerns (Dinwoodie, 2005).

If there are cultural differences in teamwork when looking intraculturally across cultures, the challenges they pose are compounded when multiple cultures are placed within a single team; however, it has been argued that these teams can be effective to the degree to which they are able to manage the need for consensus versus the need for diversity (Argote & McGrath, 1993). Although diversity in skills and perspectives may benefit multicultural teams, the team also needs a degree of common ground in order to facilitate coordinated action and the understanding that leads to that coordination (Argote & McGrath, 1993). Within organizational teams diversity is often a feature that cannot be escaped, but is a function of the operating environment. The question becomes "What does within team diversity in multicultural teams mean for team interaction and correspondingly teamwork?"

The purpose of the current chapter is to first highlight some of the challenges inherent in working within multicultural teams. In doing so, key processes and emergent states will be briefly described, resulting in a framework within which to think about multicultural teams. Next we identify several guidelines that may be used by practitioners. These guidelines are grouped based on their temporal nature (that is, whether they occur before interaction, during interaction, or post interaction).

## What Are the Implications of Intracultural Differences for Teamwork?

National culture has been defined in many ways: as (1) "...a coalescence of discrete behavioral norms and cognitions shared by individuals within some definable population that are distinct from those shared with other populations" (Lehman, Chiu, & Schaller, 2004, p. 690), and (2) "shared motives, values, beliefs, identities, and interpretations of meanings of significant events that result from common experiences of members of collectives and are transmitted across age generations" (House & Javidan, 2004, p. 15). Although there is no universally accepted definition of culture, after reviewing the multitude of definitions within the social sciences, Triandis (1996) argues that there is wide agreement across definitions that culture consists of "shared elements that provide standards for perceiving, believing, evaluating, communicating, and acting among those who share a language, a historic period, and a geographic location" (Shweder & LeVine, 1984, p. 408).

The challenge within multicultural teams lies within the fact that individuals who often have extremely disparate conceptualizations of how teams should function are required to engage in interdependent interaction (Ilgen, LePine, & Hollenbeck, 1997). Moreover, these culturally based differences are often implicitly held and are only recognized once the team is heading down a path to derailment. Gibson and Zellmer-Bruhn (2001) empirically examined the idea that individuals from different cultures may have different teamwork prototypes (i.e., metaphors), which in turn, reflect underlying assumptions about a team's functionality and structure. Specifically, interviews were conducted in which individuals from a variety of cultures were asked general questions about teamwork. The transcripts from these interviews were then content coded and sorted based on thematic similarities.

Results indicated the emergence of five differential metaphors for teams (for example, sports, military, family, associates, and community). Within individualistic cultures there was a tendency for teams to be described in terms of sports and associate metaphors. Sports metaphors reflected a conceptualization of teams whereby roles are explicitly defined, there is little hierarchy, membership tends to be voluntary, scope of activity is fairly narrow, and objectives tend to be well defined (Gibson & Zellmer-Bruhn, 2002). Associate metaphors were used to conceptualize a view of teams in which there was little role definition, a narrow scope of activity related to professional work, and objectives were explicit, yet evolving and not focused solely on task-related outcomes (Gibson & Zellmer-Bruhn, 2002).

Conversely, metaphors reflecting family and community tended to be used most often with collectivists. Herein, teams were conceptualized using a family metaphor in which there was a paternalistic hierarchy, activity scope was broad, and objectives were more social in nature (Gibson & Zellmer-Bruhn, 2002). In contrast, community metaphors indicated a conceptualization whereby roles were informal and shared, activities and objectives were broad in scope and somewhat ambiguous. Perhaps used less often was the military metaphor, being primarily used by those valuing power distance (Gibson & Zellmer-Bruhn, 2001). This metaphor reflected a strict hierarchical structure, limited scope, and task-focused salient outcomes. These differences in metaphor use point to the potential difficulty in building shared cognitive structures (for example, shared mental models, transactive memory systems) within multicultural teams.

Similar in nature is work that has shown that culture has an impact on what is considered success in work groups. For example, Sanchez-Burks, Nisbett, and Ybarra (2000) reported that cultures that were more collectivistic (for example, Mexico) valued socioemotional outcomes over task-based outcomes. The reverse was true for a sample of Anglos. The work by Sanchez-Burks et al. (2000) as well as that by Gibson and Zellmer-Bruhn (2001; 2002) offer important insights into challenges that may arise for individuals working within multicultural teams, as well as for the leaders responsible for directing and shaping those teams. For example, Gibson's work suggests that within a multicultural team it is likely that the members may come to the team with disparate ideas pertaining to role structure, activity scope, and team functioning. In turn, these expectations will drive different behavioral responses and attributions. These disparate expectations are often latent and, in turn, foster misattributions. Similarly, the work by Sanchez-Burks et al. (2000) suggests different motivational bases for members from different cultures. In turn, these differences may result in frustration and a lack of psychological safety within multicultural teams. Leaders must take into account and balance these disparate motivations so that the team as a whole remains motivated.

Given this complexity, we next discuss several processes and states which must be enacted and sometimes culturally negotiated in order for multicultural teams to be effective and overcome the inherent challenges often caused by diversity. Multicultural teams who are able to implement these processes in a culturally appropriate manner have the potential for positive team outcomes. The following list provides a summary of these critical components.

*Critical Components Driving Effectiveness in Multicultural Teams*

- *Process Components*
    1. Engaging in leadership—creating and maintaining coherence
    2. Ensuring clear and meaningful communication
    3. Engaging in supportive behaviors to maximize team synergy
    4. Engaging in perspective taking to develop a cultural foundation
    5. Engaging in negotiation to find common ground

- *Emergent States*
    6. Creating a sense of psychological safety to facilitate interaction
    7. Forming compatible cognitive structures to aid coordination

## Components Driving Effectiveness in Multicultural Teams

There has recently been a notable distinction in the teams literature; researchers are beginning to better delineate the nature of team process. Marks, Mathieu, and Zaccaro (2001) argue that researchers have not been conceptually disciplined when it comes to the constructs which are identified as process, often confounding process with emergent states. Accordingly, team process refers to "members' interdependent acts that convert inputs to outcomes through cognitive, verbal, and behavioral activities directed toward organizing taskwork to achieve collective goals" (Marks, Mathieu, & Zaccaro, 2001, p. 357). Conversely, emergent states are viewed as a bit more static than process and have been defined as "constructs that characterize the properties of the team that are typically dynamic in nature and vary as a function of team context, inputs, processes, and outcomes" (Marks et al., 2001, p. 357). These constructs often represent cognitive, affective, and motivational components and can be viewed as inputs to and outcomes of team process. Due to the diversity present within multicultural teams, it is often difficult to promote these emergent states. In turn, this has important implications for the manner in which processes (such as leadership, communication, supportive behaviors) are enacted within the team.

In delineating a framework (see Figure 3.1) within which to examine the components which facilitate effectiveness in multicultural teams we rely on the current state-of-the science and employ the distinction between process and emergent states. In addition, while there are a multitude of process and state variables which could be argued to be challenging and essential for multicultural teams space constraints limit discussion to those we believe are most essential.

## Delineation of Process Components

In the United States teams have been defined as two or more individuals interacting together in an adaptive interdependent manner towards a shared or common goal (Salas et al., 1992). While we expect this definition will hold across cultures the operationalization of the behaviors contained within might be expected to differ. However, at a bare minimum we argue that in any type of multicultural team the following three process variables are going to form the foundation of effective teamwork: negotiation, communication, and supporting behavior. In addition, especially important within multicultural teams are the additional processes

**Figure 3.1.  Framework for Thinking About Multicultural Team Performance.**

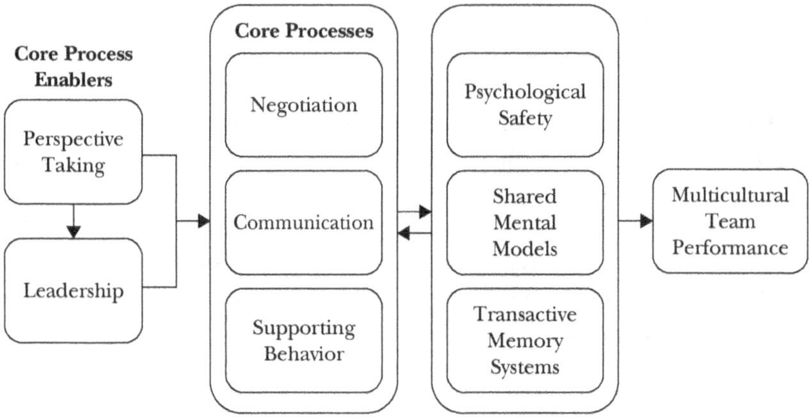

of perspective taking and leadership as these two processes assist in providing a way forward amongst the challenges that may be posed in enacting the other process variables. See Figure 3.1 for a visual illustration.

### Critical Process #1: Engaging in Leadership—Creating and Maintaining Coherence

Leadership has been argued to play a pivotal role in determining team effectiveness (see Burke, Stagl, Klein, Goodwin, Salas, & Halpin, 2006). Specifically, leadership is the mechanism through which the shared cognition, affect, and behavior within teams is promoted so that coordinated action can occur. Leaders ensure that the team has clear, compelling direction, an enabling structure, supportive organizational context, and expert coaching available (Hackman, 2002). It is within this vein that leaders can facilitate a team's ability to adapt by choosing the timing and mechanisms through which to intervene in team process to allow reflection upon methods and procedures to take place (Gersick & Hackman, 1990; Hackman & Wageman, 2005).

Within multicultural teams, leadership actions become even more important given the likelihood of the team's exhibiting degradations in its coherence (shared understandings, behavior, and affect), which in turn, promotes the coordinated action indicative of effective teams. Leadership interventions can help teams adapt to difficulties in execution and process loss. For example, it has been argued that within multicultural teams leaders should promote a hybrid culture (Earley & Mosakowski, 2000) in order to mitigate process challenges. This hybrid culture is not reflective of any one culture that currently exists within the team, but reflects a new superordinate culture. Yet the picture is complicated, as research has indicated that there are differences across cultures concerning what is deemed "effective" leadership (House, Hanges, Javidan, Dorfman, & Gupta, 2004; Bantz, 1993). Moreover, even when leadership prototypes are similar across cultures (for example, charismatic leadership), often the manifestations of these prototypes are culturally contingent (see Mehra & Krishnan, 2005; Pillai & Meindl, 1998; Den Hartog & Verburg, 1997). As such it is not enough to simply train leaders to act in a charismatic fashion, because what is charismatic may differ across cultures.

Also important to note for leaders of multicultural teams is that theoretical work has suggested that when there are large variations in values pertaining to uncertainty avoidance within multicultural teams it may be more difficult for stable norms to emerge (Bantz, 1993). This is important, for it is often a leadership function to set the norms for the team. It has also been argued that key leadership functions such as boundary spanning are encouraged more within collectivistic as compared with individualistic settings (Golden & Veiga, 2005). This can have a tremendous impact on the team as boundary spanning is the manner by which teams adapt to the environment and the way in which new information comes into the team. Thus, although there are several challenges to providing leadership within multicultural teams, leaders can assist in preventing communication breakdowns (Ayoko et al., 2002) and facilitate the sharing of unique information among the team (Baba, Gluesing, Ratner, & Wagner, 2004). Moreover, within multicultural teams there is likely to be more attention paid to interpersonally related leadership behaviors as compared to task leadership behaviors (Watson et al., 2002). Leaders should be cognizant of this and set cooperative goals and, when conflict occurs, employ cooperative conflict management strategies (Chen et al., 2006).

### Critical Process #2: Ensuring Clear and Meaningful Communication

Communication is essential to teams in that it helps members develop and update the shared knowledge structures that serve to guide adaptive action, and it provides the foundation for mutual monitoring and backup behavior. The importance of this process is seen in that cross-cultural communication competence has been shown to be related to performance in multicultural teams (Matveev & Nelson, 2004). Despite the importance of clear communication, difficulties in communication lie at the heart of many of the challenges to interacting within a multicultural team.

Within multicultural teams there are often communication challenges in terms of differences in language and dialect, communication norms, rate, duration, and expressivity of communication (including urgency and affect). In addition, it is often the case that much information—or "the intended meaning" of communication—is lost within multicultural teams. Differences in the rate of communication as well as the structure of communication across cultures can lead to challenges within multicultural teams. For example, cultures differ on the extent to which they expect the meaning to be explicitly stated within the actual communicated message (and thereby communication tends to be more dense) or whether it is implicitly implied based on outside contextual information (see high-low context, Hall & Hall, 1990). Also related to the nature of communication, Earley et al. (1999) found that individual and group-based feedback fostered collective efficacy in members with a collectivist orientation, yet members with an individualistic orientation were more likely to have a sense of collective efficacy when feedback was geared more individually. Finally, within multicultural teams it is not only the structure of communication that may pose challenges. But the actual source of the communication message (that is, the sender) may affect not only the weight or importance assigned to the message, but also the degree to which the information contained within the message is likely to be questioned. For team members with an orientation toward power distance, messages delivered from high-status members will be given more weight and will be less likely to be challenged. In all, communication difficulties present challenges that need to be managed in multicultural teams.

### Critical Process #3: Engaging in Supportive Behaviors to Maximize Team Synergy

One of the defining features that distinguish teams from individuals is the fact that there are supporting mechanisms built into the team structure which, when used appropriately, can facilitate the team's capitalizing on its potential synergy, thereby making its performance greater than the sum of the individual parts. Specifically, team members can engage in mutual performance monitoring, whereby team members jointly observe the actions of members to watch for mistakes, lapses, and overload in an effort to catch and correct potential degradations in a timely manner (McIntyre & Salas, 1995). This process enables recognition of when team members need assistance (Marks & Panzer, 2004). When performance monitoring suggests that a team member is in need of assistance, that assistance may be offered through feedback in the form of verbal suggestions or actual physical aid.

Although mutual performance monitoring and backup behavior have been argued to be essential components of effective teams, they are most often effective when enacted in a team climate of psychological safety (Edmondson, 1999). When a team is multicultural in nature it may become more difficult to create and maintain this climate (we will discuss this in more detail later in the chapter). Psychological safety is but one prerequisite for these supporting functions to be seen as valued. Research has also shown that if backup behavior is provided when it is not needed it can actually lead to decrements in performance due to redundancy of effort (Porter et al., 2003).

Thus, within multicultural teams, despite the fact that these behaviors are argued to be essential due to the complexity present within these teams and the resulting likelihood of errors (task based or social), it may be more difficult to enact these behaviors successfully. Culture may affect not only perception of when backup behavior is needed and when monitoring is seen as important (Gelfand, Nishii, & Raver, 2006), but also the acceptance of any assistance that is offered as well as the likelihood that members will ask for assistance. In addition, if team members misinterpret the cues offered within heterogeneous teams, they may provide backup when it's not needed, neglect the cue that signals help is needed, or provide backup in a manner that is culturally inappropriate. Given this example, it becomes easy to see how heterogeneous teams may have more difficulty in backup behavior because of misinterpretations and miscommunications. Variations in power distance among members may also have an impact on the success of any supporting behavior offered. In multicultural teams with large variations in power-distance orientations among team members, it will become more difficult to successfully engage in supporting behaviors, because team members will vary in their acceptance of these behaviors based on the status differentials between recipients and senders. Further, given some cultural orientations, the explicit manner in which backup behavior is conducted may be seen as threatening, rude, or embarrassing.

### Critical Process #4: Engaging in Perspective Taking to Develop a Cultural Foundation

One of the challenges to interaction within multicultural teams is that cultural differences in values and beliefs lead individual members to expect different things, ranging from how a team should function to the interpretation of members' actions. Yet oftentimes these cognitive assumptions lie hidden. In the absence of explicit recognition of such underlying assumptions members are often likely to use stereotypes to explain behavior or will engage in faulty attributions as they assume that fellow team members are operating under the same set of rules, expectations, and preferences as their own. Perspective taking may be one of the most important transition processes (see Marks et al., 2001) that occur within multicultural teams. It involves "understanding how and why another person thinks and feels about the situation and why they are behaving as they are" (Sessa, 1996, p. 105). Perspective taking is not empathy, but reflects a more cognitive process.

Perspective taking has been shown to have a number of benefits such as: (1) reducing stereotypic responses and increasing the overlap "between representations of the self and representation of the outgroup" (Galinsky & Moskowitz, 2000,

p. 708), (2) encouraging social coordination and helping behavior (Galinsky, Ku, & Wang, 2005), and (3) facilitating better communication. Specifically, Sessa (1996) found that perspective taking caused people to disclose more information and frame their conversations in such a way that they were easily understood. This, in turn, leads to overall greater success in multicultural communications. In essence, perspective taking is a key aspect of effective intercultural team interaction; it provides the foundational knowledge pertaining to a recognition of the need to adapt behavior in some manner and offers a mechanism through which likely member actions can be projected in the future. However, perspective taking is not a natural tendency. This is especially true when it involves taking the perspective of members of another culture. Though it has been argued that individuals who are high in self-monitoring (Densten & Gray, 2003) are better at perspective taking than those who are low self-monitors, there may also be interventions that can be designed and implemented to facilitate this process (we will discuss this more later in the chapter).

***Critical Process #5: Engaging in Negotiation to Find Common Ground***
Negotiation is a process that is often ignored or minimized when it comes to the delineation of important team processes. However, within a multicultural setting negotiation becomes key to effective interaction. Negotiation has been defined as "the ways in which individuals manage their interdependence" (Walton & McKersie, 1965 as cited in Gelfand, Fulmer, & Severance, in press). In addition, whereas negotiation may differ across cultures, Gelfand et al. (in press) argue that there are several core characteristics that should apply across cultures: there is a perception of conflicting interests, communication is involved, a joint outcome exists, and although there are mixed motives, compromise is possible.

Within multicultural teams negotiation is critical because members often come to the team with disparate cognitive structures that are based in their cultural orientations. These knowledge structures, in turn, serve to affect the way each individual member views the world, team interaction, and the attributions that are made. Though there are situations in which the knowledge structures are different but still compatible, it is often the case that the differences are not initially compatible.

It is the team leader's job to facilitate a negotiated reality for the team such that coordinated, adaptive action is enabled. Researchers have argued that the emergence of a third culture within multicultural teams is one of the mechanisms that facilitates effective interaction (see Earley & Mosakowski, 2000). However, negotiation is a complex process even when conducted within a single culture; it becomes even more complex when conducted within the context of a multicultural team. For example, culture has been shown to affect the types of negotiation strategies, the nature of the influence used in negotiation, as well as the valued outcomes (Gelfand et al., 2002; Morris et al., 2004; Gelfand & Brett, 2004). Although viewing negotiation as the process by which differences in cultural values within a single team are resolved is not the normal way this behavior is examined in the literature, taking this approach within teams is essential in order to achieve the common ground that allows coordinated action. In engaging in this process Gelfand and Dyer (2000) report that emotional appeals are thought to be more impactful within collectivistic cultures, and rational appeals more effective within individualistic cultures. Leaders need to be cognizant of this difference when seeking to facilitate a negotiated reality. For more detailed treatment of the role of negotiation, the reader is referred to a recent review by Gelfand, Fulmer, and Severance (in press).

## Delineation of Emergent States

Although processes explain the manner in which interaction occurs within multicultural teams, it is also essential to recognize the effect that emergent states may have on multicultural teams. Specifically, these cognitive and motivational states can arise as the result of multicultural team interaction and, in turn, serve as inputs to future interaction. As with the process variables, there are many emergent states that have been identified within the teams literature that may be argued to be important for the successful interaction of multicultural teams, but due to space constraints we limit our focus here to a few which we feel form the foundation for success: psychological safety, shared mental models, and transactive memory systems. See Figure 3.1 for a visual representation.

## Critical State #6: Creating a Sense of Psychological Safety to Facilitate Interaction

Psychological safety has been defined as a shared belief regarding the degree to which the team is perceived to be a safe environment to engage in interpersonal risk taking (Edmondson, 1999). As such, psychological safety reflects a team climate characterized by mutual respect and trust. Edmondson (2003) found that psychological safety was important in culturally diverse teams (such as medical teams) because it facilitated team interaction. For example, as the degree of psychological safety within multicultural teams increases, members will be more willing to take interpersonal risks, such as speaking up and offering contributions during plan development or engaging in supporting behaviors. One of the potential benefits of multicultural teams is the diversity of vantage points that exist within these teams; psychological safety helps the team to take advantage of this diversity by promoting a climate in which members feel free to question suggestions and decisions, in essence allowing members to play a type of "devil's advocate." Furthermore, though cultures vary in the degree to which they may engage in these actions, based on power differentials and concerns about saving face, psychological safety might play a role in mitigating some of these tendencies by promoting a collective, holistic view of the team setting in which out-groups are diminished.

Edmondson (2003) found that team leaders could promote psychological safety within culturally diverse teams by engaging in motivational, interpersonal activities and fostering a climate of inclusion so that power differences were minimized and the input of all members was recognized. As psychological safety reflects a climate of trust and mutual respect, activities that promote trust would be expected to facilitate a sense of safety. Within multicultural teams, research has shown that not only does trust have different relational bases, but also that cultures vary in their motivational bases. Specifically, Yuki et al. (2005) found that in more collectivist cultures (such as Japan) an important basis on which team members based their decisions to trust each other was the indirect interpersonal ties that existed between them. Conversely, within more individualistic cultures (such as the United States) decisions to trust were related to how well team members identified with each other, based on a shared category of membership.

### Critical State #7: Forming Compatible Cognitive Structures to Aid Coordination

The possession of compatible knowledge structures have been shown to facilitate performance and adaptation within teams (Mathieu, Heffner, Goodwin, Salas, & Cannon-Bowers, 2000; Entin & Serfaty, 1999). However, achieving these emergent states is often very challenging within multicultural teams, because most often members come to the team with very different knowledge structures. These knowledge structures, as partially witnessed through the metaphors used (see Gibson & Zellmer-Bruhn, 2002), guide member expectations, attributions, and interactions. Shared mental models and transactive memory systems are two categories of knowledge structures which, though difficult to construct in multicultural teams, are essential for coordinated action.

Both shared mental models and transactive memory are aspects of shared understanding. Transactive memory system (TMS) is defined as the collective knowledge within a group that is coupled with the coordinated awareness of the knowledge distribution among group members (Wegner, 1987). When TMSs are effective, team members can easily assess who should be responsible for which task based on a mutual understanding of expertise, thereby reducing the cognitive load through more efficient social information searches. Thus, using TMS within multicultural teams may affect communication patterns in that the perceptions of where expertise lies within the team will differentially guide interaction based on perceived expertise-based power differences. In addition, when TMSs are accurate and knowledge within them made explicit this may counter the tendency of individuals within multicultural teams to rely on false stereotypes and inaccurate attributions.

TMS involves three primary components: specialization, or the differentiation of information among team members; credibility, or the beliefs of members regarding the accuracy and reliability of others' knowledge; and coordination, or the organized knowledge processing of information (Akgun, Byrne, Keskin,

Lynn, & Imamgolu, 2005). Essentially, the root of this theory lies upon distributed complementarity and compilational emergence, where team members work as social information searchers to determine who possesses which knowledge and expertise, and then coordinate to ensure that the correct individuals are called upon to utilize such knowledge.

Shared mental models (SMMs) are analogous to but unique from TMS. Though SMMs are also a type of shared cognition that works through distinct aspects of efficiency, there is not really anything in the theory that mentions specialization of information. This may be because SMMs were developed in teams, in which a level of specialization is understood, as team members have an inherent level of interdependency. Instead, SMM theory relies more upon implicit coordination instead of social information searchers (Edwards et al., 2006). SMMs are defined as organized knowledge structures held in common among team members in order to allow them to act in coordinated ways (Mathieu, et al., 2000).

SMMs are characterized by four main types of models: *technology/equipment,* which hold information such as equipment functioning, operating procedures, and system limitations; *job/task,* which hold information such as task procedures, likely scenarios, and task strategies; *team interaction,* which hold information such as roles, responsibilities, and information sharing; and *team,* which hold information such as teammates' knowledge, skills, and attitudes (Cannon-Bowers, Salas, & Converse, 1993). In order to be successful, it is expected that team members need to not only possess accurate and similar information regarding tasks, but also must be able to work together well as a team (Edwards, Day, Arthur, & Bell, 2006). Whereas compatible task-related mental models may be fairly straightforward within multicultural teams, it is the knowledge structures governing team interaction that are typically more divergent. It is these more complex knowledge structures which need to be negotiated, or at a minimum made salient, so team members are cognizant of member preferences and can predict and adapt to member action as needed. In all, compatible knowledge structures are especially critical to develop because of the inherent diversity of cognition within multicultural teams and the misattributions these can cause.

## Guidelines for Improving Multicultural Teamwork

Certainly, the aforementioned processes, states, and associated challenges of multicultural teamwork can be difficult to overcome. Indeed, developing methods for reducing problems and maximizing the benefits of multicultural collaboration has been a struggle for researchers (van Knippenberg & Schippers, 2007). However, drawing from what is currently known regarding how to prepare diverse teams to work together, and about general team training principles, it is possible to provide guidelines that can aid practitioners in reducing some of the challenges to successful performance in such collaborations. These guidelines can be divided according to the temporal frame in which their implementation is most effective: pre-interaction, during interaction, and post-interaction.

Guidelines targeted at the pre-interaction phase on setting a common ground for members of multicultural teams before team processes are initiated. This will facilitate shared cognition and skill-based processes that will encourage team members to utilize a sense of cultural awareness in their multicultural environment, while also reducing the negative impact of ethnocentric tendencies. Guidelines that can be implemented during interaction are primarily targeted at enhancing coordination across team members, as this is a particularly challenging issue for multicultural teams. Finally, guidelines can also facilitate post-interaction as a means to improve future multicultural team interactions, either within the same team or as team members move on to new teams. These guidelines are centered on facilitating feedback to team members regarding what went well during interaction, what could be improved, and how to approach future interactions successfully. The next section provides a more in-depth look at the processes occurring within each phase and corresponding guidelines to enhance multicultural teamwork that can be implemented to enhance multicultural teamwork. The following list provides a summary of guidelines.

*Guidelines for Improving Multicultural Teams*

1. Utilize training that incorporates cultural self-awareness as well as mitigation of ethnocentric tendencies.

2. Implement training that emphasizes perspective taking.
3. Incorporate advanced organizers into training.
4. Utilize textual & video vignette-based situational judgment tests to promote cross-cultural skill development.
5. Establish a set of team norms, behaviors, and beliefs to create a hybrid culture that emphasizes a combination of team member cultural characteristics.
6. Encourage team members to discuss their similarities, especially at the socio-contextual level.
7. Enhance coordination through the use of regulatory communication and realignment.
8. Facilitate cognitive emergent states and behavioral-based processes through the execution of AARs following team interaction.

## Pre-Interaction Phase

Before members of multicultural teams even begin to interact, there are several phases that can be leveraged to ensure that effective team processes occur. First, a primary issue in multicultural teams is the proclivity for a lower degree of shared understanding among team members due to cultural differences (Cramton & Hinds, 2005). Shared understanding among team members can be captured through shared mental models; the shared mental representations held by team members; the team's transactive memory system; or the collective knowledge within the group (Wegner, 1987). Therefore, addressing this prior to team performance can aid in reducing some of the misunderstandings and communication failures that arise from differences in logic and information storage (Kayworth & Leidner, 2002; Baba, Gluesing, Ratner, & Wagner, 2004).

In addition to forming accurate shared understanding among team members, a strong foundational set of skills that are necessary to interact in multicultural environments can be cultivated prior to multicultural interaction. Doing so will enhance cultural awareness and ensure that team members have the appropriate skills in their repertoire when faced with new or challenging cultural situations (Salas, Wilson, & Lyons, 2009). Encouraging team members to practice their skills in a safe environment, such as through the use of situational judgment tests, should aid in facilitating the transfer of these skills during real inter-actions (Bhawuk & Brislin, 2000). The following discussion pro-vides a more detailed explanation regarding how both shared knowledge and skill-based processes can be developed during pre-interaction.

## Facilitating Shared Mental Models & TMS

Developing at least some degree of a shared understanding among multicultural team members is a critical pre-interaction step. As previously discussed, shared mental models and transactive memory systems can enable team performance by reducing con-fusion regarding who can provide a particular expertise. Shared understanding will also streamline communication, coordina-tion, and comprehension of new knowledge (Cramton, 2001). However, it is often the case in multicultural environments that the development of shared mental models and transac-tive memory is much more complicated than in homogenous environments. Individuals in homogeneous teams tend to report stronger feelings of affinity and ease of interaction than those in multicultural environments (Ibarra, 1992). Individuals from different cultures bring their own methods for storing, retriev-ing, and exchanging information, which while at times can be advantageous (for example, in preventing groupthink and promoting creativity), can also be detrimental to the forma-tion of a shared knowledge system (Adler, 1991; Williams & O'Reilly, 1998).

However, this does not mean that developing a shared understanding among multicultural team members is impossible. Indeed, multicultural teams should strive to develop a shared meaning system in order to overcome the negative impacts of cultural diversity and promote effective interactions (Gibson & Earley, 2002). Furthermore, establishing shared mental models and a transactive memory system early on in multicultural team development can aid in reducing or preventing later conflicts and setting the tone for information sharing within the team. To accomplish this, several strategies can be enacted during the early stages of team development in order to promote a lasting and beneficial shared knowledge system.

### Guideline #1: Utilize Training That Incorporates Cultural Self-Awareness as Well as Mitigation of Ethnocentric Tendencies

The first strategy that can help establish a shared understanding in multicultural teams is the use of cultural self-awareness training to mitigate ethnocentric tendencies. Cultural awareness training is based upon the idea that individuals who have a better understanding of their own culture will be more effective and aware of the cultural norms, beliefs, and behaviors of other cultures (Bennett, 1986). Therefore, this type of training is designed to first educate an individual about his or her own culture so that when interacting with individuals from different cultures the trainee will appreciate differences instead of ignoring them or reacting negatively (Littrell & Salas, 2005). Furthermore, as individuals are driven by their cultural beliefs and norms, it is often the case that a tendency to view one's own culture as superior will cloud interactions with others from different cultures (Bussema & Nemec, 2006; Salas et al., 2009). Therefore, before cultural interactions begin, bringing team members "back to the basics" by encouraging an awareness of their own cultural beliefs, biases, feelings, and responses to culture can aid team members in developing a common understanding of cultural similarities, differences, and biases. This can in turn reduce ethnocentric behaviors and lead to greater tolerance and flexibility in cultural perspectives, leading team members to be more effective in creating shared knowledge structures as they begin to perceive commonalities and acknowledge beneficial differences with their team members.

### Guideline #2: Implement Training That Emphasizes Perspective Taking

In relation to enhancing team member cultural self-awareness as a means of improving the development of shared knowledge, multicultural teams can also benefit from training in perspective taking, which is a social cognitive process of perceiving something from the viewpoint of another person (Fiske & Taylor, 1984). Perspective taking is particularly beneficial in cross-cultural environments, as it allows an individual to assume the perspective of another person during interactions, therefore enhancing understanding and the likely success of the interaction. Perspective taking has been found to be a valuable skill in cross-cultural interactions, as Imai and Gelfand (under review) noted in their study of cross-cultural negotiations. Their study demonstrated that individuals adept at perspective taking were more effective in maintaining cooperative sequences of behavior and ultimately achieving higher outcomes with individuals from a different culture.

For the development of a shared knowledge system in multicultural teams, perspective taking is pivotal. Being able to take another's perspective can facilitate a better understanding as to why one team member may view a construct differently from another, and can aid in reaching a consensus regarding that construct (or agreeing to disagree in the case of equally viable quality mental models). Furthermore, perspective taking can aid team members in being able to better predict each other's actions, regardless of their cultural origins.

In order to train perspective taking, providing safe opportunities to practice may be most beneficial. Practice-based training methods offer a mode of active learning that is necessary for team members to more completely develop their repertoire of skills; this is particularly beneficial for a more complex skill such as perspective taking (Salas & Cannon-Bowers, 2000). There are a number of practice strategies that can be utilized, ranging from low-fidelity role playing with actors or team members to high-fidelity computer-based simulations of a real person (Fowler, 1994). No matter which type of practice is selected, it is necessary to ensure that these practices occur in a "safe" environment in which team members can make errors without the same consequences that they would experience in the real world. Scenario-based training may also be useful for perspective taking, as it provides team members with examples of critical incidents, leading to both positive and negative outcomes, to which they can apply their knowledge of perspective taking and reflect upon how they would have responded in the given situation (Bhawuk & Brislin, 2000). Regardless of the approach utilized, ensuring that team members have the opportunity to practice taking perspectives prior to their interactions as a team can enable more open and effective communication that will lead to better shared knowledge systems.

### Guideline #3: Incorporate Advanced Organizers into Training

A final way to enhance a shared understanding across members of a multicultural team during training is to provide team members with advanced organizers, which are commonly utilized in the beginning of a training program to provide a guiding theoretical framework to trainees (Kraiger, Salas, & Cannon-Bowers, 1995). As novel content is more likely to be understood and recalled when linked to existing knowledge, providing an advanced organizer as a conceptual framework aids in the facilitation of training organization and retention of the new information gained (Mayer 1979; 1989). Advanced organizers may be as simple as a brief outline of the training modules and objectives or as complex as a complete reference guide that can be consulted throughout the training program.

Advanced organizers have been found to enhance training effectiveness, particularly for programs such as cultural training where content is complex. Bhawuk (1998; 2001) proposed that cultural assimilators are more successful when linked to a cultural theory that gives trainees a means by which to make sense of cultural differences. Furthermore, by providing the entire team with an advanced organizer, a shared understanding can be facilitated through a common understanding of the training and its goals, thus enhancing not only the training itself, but also serving as an initial foundation upon which team members can begin to develop a shared knowledge system.

## Facilitating Skill-Based Processes

An effective shared knowledge system is not the only area in which to target multicultural team enhancement prior to actual team process and performance. Team members can also work to refine their cross-cultural skills before performing as a team, in order to ensure that they will be able to operate effectively in a multicultural environment. As many different types of cross-cultural skills, including flexibility, social intelligence, and adaptability, have been recognized as being important for success in multicultural teams; instead of focusing on particular skills, we will address the training techniques that can best foster development of these skills in a pre-interaction environment—namely, through the use of situational judgment tests (SJTs).

### Guideline #4: Utilize Written and Video Vignette–Based Situational Judgment Tests to Promote Cross-Cultural Skill Development

SJTs are a form of practice that can be implemented quickly and easily, either through the use of written tests or through video vignettes, in order to ensure that team members possess necessary cross-cultural abilities prior to interacting (Fritzsche, Stagl, Salas, & Burke, 2006). This ease of implementation provides a fast way to provide feedback to team members and address any major gaps in skills prior to actual interaction, potentially preventing conflicts and misunderstandings. Furthermore, the ability to incorporate both written and visual information into SJTs by using different media can provide a richer and more interactive learning environment that enables active learning and promotes better skill development.

Situational judgment tests typically consist of a set of incidents and the alternative actions that could be taken to deal with each incident (Chan & Schmitt, 1997). SJTs have most commonly been used as a selection tool or a method to assess performance (Motowidlo, Hason, & Crafts, 1997). However, for the purpose of preparing team members to interact in multicultural environments, they can be used to create an immediately active experience on the part of learners and provide useful information about their present understanding of and attitudes toward the importance of cross-cultural skills. The ease with which these SJTs can be adapted to a team situation is also beneficial, as critical incidents can be designed for a range of cross-cultural skills and implemented as needed by multicultural teams. This allows a team to receive feedback on the skills most pertinent to its given situation and context, as opposed to a mix of relevant and irrelevant skills.

Although SJTs typically are conducted using text-based critical incidents, video SJTs are increasing in popularity, particularly as a training tool (Fritzsche et al., 2006). Video SJTs show trainees a sketch or situation that they are then asked to respond to, just as in a paper-based SJT. In learning environments, video vignettes are used to demonstrate or allow individuals to practice a single skill or set of skills. Because they can lend context and richness to a learning environment, video vignettes have been proven useful in numerous domains. For example, there are results suggesting improvements in the reflective thinking of teachers (Calandra, Gurvitch, & Lund, 2008) as well as potential for teaching business ethics (Meisel & Fearon, 2006). Developing cultural skills appears to be a prime use for video-based SJTs, as they can highlight slight cultural nuances, such as nonverbal cues or cultural artifacts, which a paper-based SJT cannot communicate as richly. In culturally sensitive situations video vignettes have been used to evaluate inappropriate behaviors and promote the use of culturally appropriate behaviors (Molinksy & Perunovic, 2008). Exposing multicultural teams to such safe practice environments in which they can further develop their skills prior to real interaction is therefore a critical advantage to the use of both text- and video-based SJTs.

## During Interaction Phase

As discussed, there are many critical components to consider when interacting in multicultural teams. Though multiple processes occur during the interaction phase of multicultural collaborations, for the purposes of identifying guidelines, the majority can be grouped into one of the following categories: communication, coordination, and cooperation. As noted, team communication involves the management of information flow, development of plans and strategy, and the solicitation of feedback (Sims & Salas, 2007). Team cooperation involves the desire of team members to work together and perform as a team. Team coordination is vital to team performance, as it is a composition of the behavioral and cognitive mechanisms required for task performance (Marks et al., 2001). Combined, these three larger facets represent the factors that comprise, contribute to, facilitate, and detract from effective team performance during the interaction phase. Breakdowns in any of these processes can lead to lasting damages to multicultural team performance.

Unfortunately, as multicultural teams begin to interact through these three processes, it is very possible that despite the best efforts prior to interaction, negative effects of multiculturalism will reemerge to some degree. These effects can include the highlighting of differences, the development of fault lines, and the emergence of conflict (Jarvenpaa & Leidner, 1999; Lau & Murningham, 1998). Therefore, it is important to recognize what strategies can be utilized during interaction to maximize performance during this action phase and minimize any negative effects of multiculturalism. The following discussion provides three suggested guidelines that can be utilized to facilitate coordination, cooperation, and communication during interactions, namely through the development of a hybrid culture, emphasizing similarities among team members, and establishing a systematic means for coordination.

### Guideline #5: Establish a Set of Team Norms, Behaviors, and Beliefs to Create a Hybrid Culture That Emphasizes a Combination of Team Member Cultural Characteristics

It is undeniable that multicultural team members bring their own cultural influences, norms, and beliefs into their team interaction. However, this does not have to be a detriment to team performance if members are able to meld their cultural values into a new, hybrid team culture (Earley & Mosakowski, 2000). A hybrid team culture is a new set of norms, rules, expectations, and behaviors that individuals within a team create themselves after some period of interaction. The degree to which these values are shared determines the strength of the culture, but the establishment of any degree of team culture that can unify members would be a benefit during team interaction. Indeed, Earley and Mosakowski (2000) found in their qualitative field study of transnational teams that highly heterogeneous teams who created their own team identity were more successful than moderately heterogeneous groups lacking a team identity. Recognizing that they had a high degree of diversity and differences among their team members, the highly heterogeneous groups decided to minimize the negative impacts of these effects by creating of a team culture that could bridge their cultural differences. The moderately heterogeneous teams who did not recognize the benefit of such a shared identity were less successful. Therefore, multicultural teams, regardless of how diverse they are, may benefit from the development of a team hybrid culture.

### Guideline #6: Emphasize Similarities Among Team Members

Even if cross-cultural skills are fine-tuned and shared knowledge systems are established before interaction, it is still likely that as team members begin to work with one another their cultural differences may impede on successful performance. Therefore, a continued emphasis on similarities and a "superordinate team identity" among team members can further aid in the maintenance of a healthy team environment. Individuals tend to have a preference for working with others similar to themselves and often find this type of interaction much easier than interacting with those who are perceived as different (Williams & O'Reilly, 1998). Furthermore, team member similarity is positively associated with team effectiveness (Tsui, Egan, & O'Reilly, 1992).

Although it may be difficult for team members in very heterogeneous teams to find similarities, it is important that teams move beyond surface-level similarities. Similarities do not need to be merely obvious, such as gender, race, or age, to be effective at drawing team members together. In fact, in terms of establishing long-term ties, homophily based on such surface-level factors is less important than homophily stemming from deeper sociocontextual characteristics (Yuan & Gay, 2006). Therefore, it may be beneficial to provide opportunities for team members to recognize their similarities. This could be achieved through a simple question-and-answer session with team members or through periodic reminders of similarities from the team leader. Regardless of the strategy, encouraging team members to find similarities among themselves should aid in enhancing team interaction.

### Guideline #7: Enhance Coordination Through the Use of Regulatory Communication and Realignment

A final means by which to successfully maintain multicultural team processes of coordination, communication, and cooperation during the interaction phase is to introduce a systematic means of coordinating and communicating. This may tie in with the development of a hybrid culture, as it involves creating a systematic method by which team members can expect regular communications regarding their performance, and a way for teams to determine if they need to realign their efforts based on their current performance status. Essentially, this idea builds upon the premise of team self-correction, in that team members develop an approach for communication and coordination that enables them to work together in order to identify breakdowns as early as possible and to provide a systematic means by which to correct these breakdowns (Sims, Salas, & Burke, 2005). Self-guided correction in teams is a successful strategy for enhancing team performance, as has been found in both laboratory and field settings (Smith-Jentsch, Zeisig, Acton, & McPherson, 1998).

Though beneficial for homogenous teams, for multicultural teams this strategy can be particularly invaluable, as it sets up formal procedures—based on or as a part of the team's own hybrid culture—that regulate how communication should be conducted and how members can address problems or malfunctions in team performance. As cultural differences can often restrict individuals' comfort level about reporting errors, this provides a structured, acceptable method by which such feedback can be provided, maintaining a balance between individual cultural needs and the needs of the team as a performing entity.

## Post-Interaction Phase

The completion of interaction in a multicultural collaboration is not simply the end of performance; instead, lessons learned from the interaction itself can provide a rich basis for success in future multicultural collaborations. These lessons are best facilitated through the use of an after-action review (AAR).

### Guideline #8: Facilitate Cognitive Emergent States and Behavioral Based Processes through the Execution of AARs Following Team Interaction

AARs are guided debriefings which usually occur after a period of performance and are designed to review behavior in order to determine what went well, what could be improved, and how future scenarios will be approached. These guided debriefings provide team members with a means by which to "discern the rules of behavior which transcend the specifics of a given scenario" (Smith-Jentsch, Cannon-Bowers, Tannenbaum, & Salas, 2008, pg. 311), thus enhancing adaptive transfer to novel situations. AARs have been heavily leveraged as a training mechanism within military settings (such as team dimensional training or guided team self-correction) and have demonstrated significant, positive impact on shared mental models, team processes, and both individual and team performance (see Ellis & Davidi, 2005; Smith-Jentsch et al., 2008; Smith-Jentsch et al., 1998). For example, Ellis and Davidi (2005) compared the impact of traditional failure-focused AARs (FAAR) to the impact of AARs which focused on both failures and successes (FSAAR) during hands-on navigation training in a sample of elite military defense forces. Results demonstrated that both groups significantly increased performance over the course of three hands-on navigation training exercises, however, individuals who partook in the FSAARs demonstrated significantly greater performance gains. Additionally, trainees who participated in FSAARs demonstrated richer mental models of their performance, suggesting more systematic, critical thinking.

These types of AARs can be very beneficial for multicultural teams, as they provide a means by which team members can analyze both their cultural skill and their performance as a team. Providing multicultural teams with both performance and process feedback is critical, as these teams should be aware not only of their capabilities to work with others from different cultures, but also of how they worked as members of a team. If team members are only provided with overall team results and no feedback regarding the specific processes that led to their success or failure, performance may be falsely attributed to cultural differences or similarities, or to team abilities. Therefore, developing a formal feedback process such as an AAR by which team members can analyze their performance and gain insight will only enable them to perform more effectively in future multicultural teams.

## Concluding Comments

Multicultural teams are by no means a new phenomena, for global organizations have been in existence for decades. However, most of the work that has been conducted on cultural differences within teams has taken an intracultural perspective. Recently, there has been an emerging shift within this literature to also examine intercultural differences. It is only through this focus that researchers and practitioners can better understand the challenges and guidelines for teams in which members have disparate cultural orientations.

Much of what is currently known about multicultural inter-action is leveraged from our knowledge of teams, diversity, and culture—but few efforts have focused on the actual intercul-tural differences. Within this chapter we have highlighted a few of the processes and emergent states which, based on the sci-entific literature, may be argued to be critical for the effective functioning of multicultural teams. Specifically, negotiation, com-munication, and supporting behavior provide the foundation and the processes of perspective taking and leadership can facilitate the mitigation of faultlines and process decrements which often exist early in the team's lifespan. These processes will, in turn, have an impact on the resulting cognitive structures (such as shared mental models, transactive memory systems) and attitudes (such as psychological safety). Although these processes and states are important to multicultural team effectiveness, there are many challenges in implementing them; therefore, we have begun to identify an initial set of guidelines that can be targeted along a continuum of pre-action intervention, real-time intervention, and post-action intervention. It is our hope that this will serve to stimulate further research and discussion.

## Acknowledgment

This work was partially supported by funding from the Army Research Laboratory's Advanced Decision Architecture Collab-orative Technology Alliance Cooperative Agreement (AAD19-01-2-0009) and the Office of Naval Research MURI Grant to Dr. Michele Gelfand, Principal Investigator, UMD (W911NF-08-1-014), subcontract to UCF (Z885903). The views expressed in this work are those of the authors and do not necessarily reflect the organizations with which they are affiliated or their sponsoring institutions or agencies.

## References

Adler, N. J. (1991). *International dimensions of organizational behavior.* Belmont, CA: Wadsworth.

Akgun, A. E., Byrne, J., Keskin, H., Lynn, G. S., & Imamgolu, S. Z. (2005). Knowledge networks in new product development projects:

A transactive memory perspective. *Information & Management*, *42*(8), 1105–1120.

Argote, L. & McGrath, J. D. (1993). Group processes in organisations: Continuity and change. In C. L. Cooper & I. T. Robertson (Eds.), *International review of industrial and organisational psychology*, Vol. 8. New York: Wiley.

Ayoko, O. B., Hartel, C. E. J., & Callan, V. J. (2002). Resolving the puzzle of productivity and destructive conflict in culturally hetero-geneous workgroups: A communication accommodation theory approach. *The International Journal of Conflict Management*, *13*(2), 165–195.

Baba, M. L., Gluesing, J., Ratner, H., & Wagner, K. H. (2004). The contexts of knowing: Natural history of a globally distributed team. *Journal of Organizational Behavior*, *25*, 547–587.

Bantz, C. R. (1993). Cultural diversity and group cross-culture team research. *Journal of Applied Communication*, *21*(1), 1–20.

Bennett, M. (1986). Towards ethnorelativism: A developmental model of intercultural sensitivity. In R. M. Paige (Ed.), *Education for the intercultural experience* (pp. 21–71). Yarmouth, ME: Intercultural Press.

Bhawuk, D. P. S., & Brislin, R. W. (2000). *Cross*-cultural training: A review. *Applied Psychology: An International Review*, *49*(1), 162–91.

Bhawuk, D. P. S. (1998). The role of culture theory in cross-cultural train-ing: A multimethod study of culture-specific, culture-general, and culture theory-based assimilators. *Journal of Cross-Cultural Psychology*, *29*(5), 630.

Bhawuk, D. P. S. (2001). Evolution of culture assimilators: Toward theory-based assimilators. *International Journal of Intercultural Relations*, *25*(2), 141–163.

Burke, C. S., Stagl, K. C., Klein, C., Goodwin, G., Salas, E., & Halpin, S. M. (2006). What types of leadership behaviors are functional in teams? A meta-analysis. *Leadership Quarterly*, *17*, 288–307.

Bussema, E., & Nemec, P. (2006). Training to increase *cultural* compe-tence. *Psychiatric Rehabilitation Journal*, 30(1), 71–73.

Calandra, B., Gurvitch, R., & Lund, J. (2008). An exploratory study of digital video editing as a tool for teacher preparation. *Journal of Technology & Teacher Education, 16*(2), 137–153.

Cannon-Bowers, J. A., Salas, E., & Converse, S. A. (1993). Shared mental models in expert team decision making. In N. J. Castellan, Jr. (Ed.), *Individual and group decision making: Current issues* (pp. 221–246). Hillsdale, NJ: LEA.

Chan, D., & Schmitt, N. (1997). Video-based versus paper-and-pencil method of assessment in Situational Judgment Tests: Subgroup differences in test performance and face validity perceptions. *Journal of Applied Psychology, 82,* 143–159.

Chen, G., Tjosvold, D., & Liu, C. (2006). Cooperative goals, leader people and productivity values: Their contribution to top management teams in China. *Journal of Management Studies, 43*(5), 1177–1200.

Conyne, R., Wilson, F., Tang, M., & Shi, K. (1999). Cultural similarities and differences in group work: Pilot study of a U.S.-Chinese group comparison. *Group Dynamics: Theory, Research, and Practice, 3*(1), 40–50.

Cox, T. H., Lobel, S. A., & McLeod, P. L. (1991). Effects of ethnic group cultural differences on cooperative and competitive behavior on a group task. *Academy of Management Journal, 34*(4), 827–847.

Cramton, C. D., & Hinds, P. J. (2005). Subgroup dynamics in internationally distributed teams: Ethnocentrism or cross-national learning? *Organizational Behavior, 26,* 231–263.

Cramton, C. D. (2001). The mutual knowledge problem and its consequences for dispersed collaboration. *Organization Science, 12,* 346–371.

Den Hartog, D. N., & Verburg, R. M. (1997). Charisma and rhetoric: Communicative techniques of international business leaders. *Leadership Quarterly, 8*(4), 355–391.

Densten, I. L., & Gray, J. H. (2003). Leadership applications: Organizational effectiveness. (CFLI Contract Research Report #CR02–0620). Kingston, ON: Canadian Forces Leadership Institute

Dinwoodie, D. L. (2005). Solving the dilemma: A leader's guide to managing diversity. *Leadership in Action,* 25(2): 3–6.

Earley, P. C., Gibson, C. B., & Chen, C. C. (1999). How did I do? Versus how do we do? Cultural contrasts of performance feedback use and self-efficacy. *Journal of Cross-Cultural Psychology, 30*(5) 594–619.

Earley, P. C., & Mosakowski, E. (2000). Creating hybrid team cultures: An empirical test of transnational team functioning. *Academy of Management Journal, 43,* 26–49.

Edmondson. A. (2003). Speaking up in the operating room: How team leaders can promote learning in interdisciplinary action teams. *Journal of Management Studies, 40*(6), 1419–1452.

Edmondson, A. (1999). Psychological safety and learning behavior in work teams. *Administrative Science Quarterly, 44,* 350–383.

Edwards, B. D., Day, E. A., Arthur, W., & Bell, S. T. (2006). Relationships among team ability composition, team mental models, and team performance. *Journal of Applied Psychology, Vol. 91*(3), 727–736.

Ellis, S., & Davidi, I. (2005). After-event reviews: drawing lessons from successful and failed experience. *Journal of Applied Psychology, 90*(5), 857–871.

Elron, E. (1997). Top management teams within multinational corporations: Effects of cultural heterogeneity. *Leadership Quarterly, 8,* 393–412.

Entin, E. E., & Serfaty, D. (1999). Adaptive team coordination. *Human Factors, 41,* 312–325.

Fiske, S. T., & Taylor, S. E. (1984). *Social cognition.* New York: Random House.

Fowler, S. M. (1994). Two decades of using simulation games for cross-cultural training. *Simulation & Gaming, 25,* 464–476.

Fritzsche, B. A., Stagl, K. C., Salas, E., & Burke, C. S. (2006) Enhancing the design, delivery and evaluation of scenario-based training: Can situational judgment tests contribute? In J. A. Weekley, and R. E. Ployhart, (Eds.), *Situational judgment tests: Theory, measurement and application* (pp. 301–318). Mahwah, NJ: Erlbaum.

Galinsky, A. D., Ku, G., & Wang, C. S. (2005). Perspective-taking and self-other overlap: Fostering social bonds and facilitating social coordination. *Group Processes & Intergroup Relations, 8*(2), 109–124.

Galinsky, A. D., & Moskowitz, G. B. (2000). Perspective-taking: Decreasing stereotype expression, stereotype accessibility, and in-group favoritism. *Journal of Personality and Social Psychology, 78*(4), 708–724.

Gelfand, M. J., & Brett, J. M. (Eds.) (2004). *The handbook of negotiation and culture.* Stanford, CA: Stanford University Press.

Gelfand, M. J., & Dyer, N. (2000). A cultural perspective on negotiation: Process, pitfalls, and prospects. *Applied Psychology, 49,* 62–99.

Gelfand, M. J., Erez, M., Aycan, Z. (2007). Cross-cultural organizational behavior. *Annual Review of Psychology, 58,* 479–514.

Gelfand, M. J., Fulmer, C. A., & Severance, L. (in press). The psychology of negotiation and mediation. In S. Zedeck (Ed.), *Handbook of industrial and organizational psychology.*

Gelfand, M. J., Higgins, M. Nishii, L. H., Raver, J. L., & Dominguez A., et al. (2002). Culture and ego-centric biases of fairness in conflict and negotiation. *Journal of Applied Psychology, 87,* 833–845.

Gelfand, M. J., Nishii, L., & Raver, J. (2006). On the nature and importance of cultural tightness-looseness. *Journal of Applied Psychology,* 91, 1225–1244.

Gersick, C. J. G., & Hackman, J. R. (1990). Habitual routines in task performing groups. *Organizational Behavior and Human Decision Processes, 47,* 65–97.

Gibson, C. B. (1999). Do they do what they believe they can? Group efficacy beliefs and group performance across tasks and cultures. *Academy of Management Journal, 42,* 138–152.

Gibson, C. B., & Earley, P. C. (2002). *Multinational teams: A new perspective.* Mahwah, NJ: Erlbaum.

Gibson, C. B., & Zellmer-Bruhn, M. E. (2001). Metaphors and meaning: An intercultural analysis of the concept of teamwork. *Administrative Science Quarterly, 46,* 274–303.

Gibson, C. B., & Zellmer-Bruhn, M. E. (2002). Minding your metaphors: Applying the concept of teamwork metaphors to the management of teams in multicultural contexts. *Organizational Dynamics, 31*(2), 101–116.

Golden, T. D., & Veiga, J. F. (2005). Spanning boundaries and borders: Toward understanding the cultural dimensions of team boundary spanning. *Journal of Managerial Issues, 17*(2), 178–197.

Hackman, J. R. (2002). *Leading teams: Setting the stage for great performances.* Boston: HBS Press.

Hackman, J. R., & Wageman R. (2005). A theory of team coaching. *The Academy of Management Review, 30*(2), 269–287.

Hall, E. T., & Hall, M. R. (1990). *Understanding cultural differences: Germans, French, and Americans.* Boston: Intercultural Press.

Harrison, G. L., McKinnon, J. L., Wu, A., & Chow, C. W. (2000). Cultural influences on adaptation to fluid workgroups and teams. *Journal of International Business Studies, 31,* 489–505.

House, R. J., Hanges, P. W., Javidan, M., Dorfman, P., & Gupta, V. (2004) (Eds.). *Culture, leadership, and organizations: The GLOBE study of 62 societies.* Thousand Oaks, CA: Sage.

House, R. J., & Javidan, M. (2004). Overview of GLOBE. In R. J. House, P. J. Hanges, M. Javidan, P. W. Dorfman, & V. Gupta (Eds.), *Culture, leadership, and organizations: The GLOBE study of 62 societies* (pp. 9–28). Thousand Oaks, CA: Sage.

Ibarra, H. (1992). Homophily and differential returns: Sex differences in network structure and access in and advertising firm. *Administrative Science Quarterly, 37,* 422–477.

Ilgen, D. R., LePine, J. A., & Hollenbeck, J. R. (1997). Effective decision making in multinational teams. In P. C. Earley & M. Erez (Eds.), *New perspectives on international industrial/ organizational psychology.* San Francisco: Pfeiffer.

Imai, L., & Gelfand, M. J. (under review). The culturally intelligent negotiator: The impact of cultural intelligence (CQ) on negotiation sequences and outcomes.

Jarvenpaa, S. L., & Leidner, D. E. (1999). Communication and trust in global virtual teams. *Organization Science, 10,* 791–815.

Kayworth, T. R., & Leidner, D. E. (2001–2002). Leadership effectiveness in global virtual teams. *Journal of Management Information Systems, 18,* 7–40.

Kirchmeyer, C., & Cohen, A. (1992). Multicultural groups: Their performance and reactions with constructive conflict. *Groups & Organization Studies, 17*(2), 153–170.

Kirkman, B. L., & Shapiro, D. L. (2001). The impact of cultural values on job satisfaction and organizational commitment in self-managing work teams: The mediating role of employee resistance. *Academy of Management Journal, 44,* 557–569.

Kraiger, K., Salas, E., & Cannon-Bowers J. A. (1995). Measuring knowledge organization as a method for assessing learning during training. *Human Performance, 37,* 804–816.

Lau, J., & Murningham, J. K. (1998). Demographic diversity and faultlines: The compositional dynamics of organizational groups. *Academy of Management Review, 23,* 325–340.

Littrell, L. N., & Salas, E. (2005). A review of cross-cultural training: Best practices, guidelines, and research needs. *Human Resource Development Review, 4,* 305–335.

Lehman, D. R., Chiu, C., & Schaller, M. (2004). Psychology and culture. *Annual Review of Psychology, 55,* 689–714.

Man, D. C., & Lam, S. S. K. (2003). The effects of job complexity and autonomy on cohesiveness in collectivistic and individualistic work groups: A cross-cultural analysis. *Journal of Organizational Behavior, 24,* 979–1001.

Marks, M. A., Mathieu, J. E., & Zaccaro, S. J. (2001). A temporally based framework and taxonomy of team processes. *Academy of Management Review, 26*(3), 356–376.

Marks, M. A., & Panzer, F. J. (2004). The influence of team monitoring on team processes and performance. *Human Performance, 17,* 25–42.

Mathieu, J. E., Heffner, T. S., Goodwin, G. F., Salas, E., & Cannon-Bowers, J. A. (2000). The influence of shared mental models on team process and performance. *Journal of Applied Psychology, 85,* 273–283.

Matveev, A. V., & Nelson, P. E. (2004). Cross-cultural communication competence and multicultural team performance: Perceptions of American and Russian managers. *International Journal of Cross Cultural Management, 4*(2), 253–270.

Mayer, R. E. (1979). Can advance organizers influence meaningful learning? *Review of Educational Research, 49*(2), 371–383.

Mayer, R. E. (1989). Models for understanding. *Review of Educational Research, 59*, 43–64.

McIntyre, R. M., & Salas, E. (1995). Measuring and managing for team performance: Emerging principles from complex environments. In R. Guzzo & E. Salas (Eds.), *Team effectiveness and decision making in organizations* (pp. 149–203). San Francisco: Jossey-Bass.

Mehra, P., & Krishnan, V. R. (2005). Impact of Svadharma-orientation on transformational leadership and followers' trust in leader. *Journal of Indian Psychology, 23*(1), 1–11.

Meisel, S. I., & Fearon, D. S. (2006). Choose the future wisely: Supporting better ethics through critical thinking. *Journal of Management Education, 30*(1), 149–177.

Molinksy, A., & Perunovic, W. Q. E. (2008). Training wheels for cultural learning: Poor language fluency and its shielding effect on the evaluation of culturally inappropriate behavior. *Journal of Language and Social Psychology, 27*(3), 284–289.

Morris, M. W., Leung, K., & Iyengar, S. S. (2004). Person perception in the heat of conflict: Negative trait attributions affect procedural preferences and account for situational and cultural differences. *Asian Journal of Social Psychology, 9*, 127–147.

Mortensen, M., & Hinds, P. (2001). Conflict and shared identity in geographically distributed teams. *International Journal of Conflict Management*, 212–238.

Motowidlo, S. J., Hanson, M. A., & Crafts, J. L. (1997). Low-fidelity simulations. In D. L. Whetzel & G. R. Wheaton (Eds.), *Applied measurement methods in industrial psychology.* Palo Alto, CA: Consulting Psychologists Press.

Pillai, R., & Meindl, J. R. (1998). Context and charisma: A "Meso" level examination of the relationship of organic structure, collectivism, and crisis to charismatic leadership. *Journal of Management, 24*(5), 643–671.

Porter, C., Hollenbeck, J. R., Ilgen, D. R., Ellis, P. J., West, B., & Moon, H. (2003). Backing up behaviors in teams: The role of personality and legitimacy of need. *Journal of Applied Psychology, 3*, 391–403.

Salas, E., Dickinson, T. L., Converse, S. A., & Tannenbaum, S. I. (1992). Toward an understanding of team performance and training. In R. J. Swezey & E. Salas (Eds.), *Teams: Their training and performance* (pp. 3–29). Norwood, NJ: Ablex.

Salas, E., & Cannon-Bowers, J. A. (2000). The anatomy of team training. In S. Tobias and J. D. Fletcher (Eds.), *Training and retraining:*

*A handbook for business, industry, government, and the military* (pp. 312–335). New York: Macmillan Reference.

Salas, E., Wilson, K. A., & Lyons, R. (2009). Designing and delivering training for multi-cultural interactions in organizations. In D. Stone & E. F. Stone-Romero (Eds.), *The influence of culture on human resource management processes and practices* (pp. 115–134). Mahwah, NJ: LEA.

Sanchez-Burks, J., Nisbett, R. E., & Ybarra O. (2000). Cultural styles, relational schemas, and prejudice against out-groups. *Journal of Personality and Social Psychology, 79*(2), 174–189.

Sessa, V. I. (1996). Using perspective taking to manage conflict and affect in teams. *Journal of Applied Behavioral Science, 32*(1), 101–115.

Sims, D. E., & Salas, E. (2007). When teams fail in organizations: What creates teamwork breakdowns? In J. Langan-Fox, C. L. Cooper, & R. J. Klimoski (Eds.), *Research companion to the dysfunctional workplace: Management challenges and symptoms* (pp. 302–318). Cheltenham, UK: Edward Elgar.

Sims, D. E., Salas, E., & Burke, C. S. (2005). Promoting effective team performance through training. In S. A. Wheelan (Ed.), *The handbook of group research and practice* (pp. 407–425). Newbury Park, CA: Sage.

Smith-Jentsch, K. A., Cannon-Bowers, J. A., Tannenbaum, S. I., & Salas, E. (2008). Guided team self correction: Impacts on mental models, processes, and effectiveness. *Small Group Research, 39*, 303–327.

Smith-Jentsch, K. A., Zeisig, R. L., Acton, B., & McPherson, J. A. (1998). Team Dimensional Training: A strategy for guided team self correction. In J. A. Cannon-Bowers, & E. Salas (Eds.), *Making decisions under stress: Implications for individual and team training* (pp. 271–298). Washington, DC: APA.

Triandis, H. C. (1996). The psychological measurement of cultural syndromes. *American Psychologist, 51*, 407–415.

Tsui, A. S., Egan, T. D., & O'Reilly, C. A. (1992). Being different: Relational demography and organizational commitment. *Administrative Science Quarterly, 37*, 549–579.

Van Knippenberg, D., & Schippers, M. (2007), Work group diversity. *Annual Review of Psychology, 58*, 515–541.

Watson, W. E., Johnson, L., & Agourides, G. D. (2002). The influence of ethnic diversity on leadership, group process, and performance: an examination of learning teams. *International Journal of Intercultural Relations 26*, 1–16.

Wegner, D. M. (1987). Transactive memory: A contemporary analysis of the group mind. In B. Mullen & G. R. Goethals (Eds.), *Theories of group behavior* (pp. 185–208). New York: Springer-Verlag.

Williams, K. Y., & O'Reilly, C. A. (1998). Demography and diversity in organizations: A review of 40 years of research. *Research in Organizational Behavior, 20,* 77–140.

Yuan, Y. C., & Gay, G. (2006). Homophily of network ties and bonding and bridging social capital in computer-mediated distributed teams. *Journal of Computer-Mediated Communication, 11*(4). Retrieved April 5, 2007, from http://jcmc.indiana.edu/vol11/issue4/yuan .html.

Yuki, M., Maddux, W. W., Brewer, M. B., & Takemura, K. (2005). Cross-cultural differences in relationship- and group-based trust. *Personality and Social Psychology Bulletin, 31*(1), 48–62.

# CHAPTER 4

# HR in the Global Workplace

## Mariangela Battista and Mario DiLoreto

Globalization has had an impact on how we manufacture and deliver products to consumers but it has also affected how organizations select, develop, and retain their talent to ensure organizational success. As the world is moving more and more toward operating as a single integrated marketplace, a large part of that change is due to the growth of multinational organizations.

As a business function, human resources is the best positioned to help an organization succeed and bring its business strategy to life globally. By harnessing the strengths and talents of their employees, organizations can create competitive advantage. The evolving field of Human Capital is strategically designed to align an organization's talent with its business strategy. HR tools and processes are primarily designed to ensure the alignment between business strategy and human or organizational capability. HR provides value in its ability to attract, develop, and retain the best talent for an organization so that there is optimal competitive advantage. Research from the Corporate Leadership Council (2009) has demonstrated that effective HR functions deliver real business results as measured not just by employee performance and retention but also in revenue and profits.

This chapter will explore the impact of globalization on organizations and the shifting role of human resources. It will also describe how global organizations can fully utilize the human resources function to their advantage by strategically designing their HR practices to focus on both tactical and strategic solutions in local and global settings. This chapter will also outline a "freedom within a framework" approach to managing talent, including a phased approach to global program implementation. Finally, we will look to the future of global human resources and the evolving field of human capital.

## Impact of Globalization

The increase in globalization over the last two decades has changed how we do business and how businesses operate. Growth for many organizations has meant going overseas, whether that means a U.S.-based organization opening operations in Asia or a European-based organization opening an office in New York. Joint ventures abound. Even for domestically based organizations, globalization is just as salient given relationships with suppliers, investors, and even non-native employees. For HR professionals, even if the focus is solely domestic, their work will often be affected by global issues, whether dealing with suppliers or securing visas in order to hire and retain talent.

HR strategies need to support and bring business strategies to life. To do this, HR professionals must be fully conversant and understand the business environment, value chains, core business processes, and key talent. In a global environment all of this becomes much more complex. Not only do HR professionals need to be aware of global economic, market, and labor issues, to be effective, but they must also be intimate with local economic, market, and labor issues. One of the main HR challenges that companies face in trying to manage globalization is ensuring that the right people are in the right roles and that there is an effective and distinctive cross-cultural fertilization of talent. To become a "learning organization" is a competitive advantage for global companies. In a world driven by radical innovation and continuous change, companies need to prepare and coach their people to cope with the complexity and accelerated speed of an increasingly global economy. To play and to win in such an environment also implies the need to create the right links between companies and national education programs, in order to give potential future employees the skills to become competitive within the global labor market.

HR professionals often find themselves in conflicted positions. Globalization creates organizational pressures such as increased growth and innovation but also cost-containment pressures (Corporate Leadership Council, 2009). There is enormous pressure to save money and provide standard HR programs and processes with shared technology platforms. However, standard approaches may not work in a local region. How do organizations reconcile standard policies with local HR direction and strategy? Further, how do HR professionals make employees a source of long-term competitive advantage under these pressures?

HR professionals must create a balance between the needs of the entire organization and the needs of the local country. Standardization of HR programs and policies helps to keep costs down, but they must meet local needs if they are to be effective. Oftentimes "standard" policies need to be customized locally in order for them to have any impact or meaning to employees and to the local business.

HR organizations are evolving to meet the needs of global business and workforces. Recent research has found that HR functions are leading their respective businesses in developing and building global HR strategies and structures (Hewitt Associates, 2009a).

## What Is Globalization?

Hewitt's Global HR Study (2009a) defines the four distinct stages of globalization: multinational, international, transitioning to global, and global. Six percent of study participants stated they worked for a "multinational" organization—an organization with cross-border operations that are primarily decentralized and autonomous. Thirty-five percent identified themselves as working for an "international" organization—one with headquarters that retains some decision-making control but is still largely decentralized. The vast majority—40%—are "transitioning to global" in that they are taking concrete steps to develop worldwide business strategies and policies. Only 15% stated that they worked for a "global" organization—one that develops strategies and policies on a worldwide basis and shares resources across borders. In the next few years one can anticipate a continued shift toward "global" as evidenced by the high percentage claiming to be in transition. This follows as we see continued mergers and acquisitions and consolidations especially in the financial, oil, and pharmaceutical industries.

Most empirical and anecdotal research seems to indicate that the majority of HR organizations are taking a portfolio approach to globalization. Work is done at global, regional, and local levels depending on the needs of the organization. This is the right approach as business needs are different throughout the world. Cultural influences are also different and must be addressed as well. Cultural differences exist even within a geographical area and must be accommodated. For example, China is comprised of multiple diverse regions, yet they are all managed the same. Taking a portfolio approach to globalization demonstrates the value of a strategic HR function—one that understands that there cannot be a "one size fits all" answer to their human resources needs.

There is not a final answer for the "vexata quaestio" (disputed question) that asks what is appropriate at a global level and what is required to be delegated at a local level. Certainly the majority of research assumes that in a global environment, talent attraction and retention, employer branding, compensation and benefits, performance management and reward systems, leadership development, organizational design, managing diversity, and corporate social responsibility should all be managed centrally, whereas employment conditions, including managing demographics, union relations, employee networks, and labor productivity are typically managed at a more local level.

## Shifting Role of Human Resources

Traditionally, HR professionals have been in very administrative functions or roles. Their key deliverables focused on ensuring that employees were paid and that staff came to work on time. The role and expectations of an HR professional have changed greatly in the last decade or so.

In his pioneering work on defining human resources, Ulrich (1997) stated that in order to be successful HR professionals needed to be true strategic, business partners with their line managers. This is a huge shift in thinking and behavior. HR professionals must act as strategic business partners in order to provide value to the organization. This means they must contribute to the development and accomplishments of the organization-wide business plan and objectives. They need to understand where the business is going and the people implications for getting there. It is no longer enough to just be tactical, which is still required; HR professionals today need to be proactive and think ahead to the changing needs of the business.

From the most recent survey conducted by the World Federation of Personnel Management Associations (2005), we begin to see a distinct shift happening in the HR role. Following Dave Ulrich's work, the survey asked HR professionals to allocate their time on the job according to five distinct roles as defined by Ulrich. The answers for the first time demonstrated some significant change. According to HR professionals who participated in the study, 24% of total hours worked were devoted to being a strategic business partner, one who partners with senior and line managers to execute business strategy and helps to move the organization from planning to employee execution. Twenty-three percent of their time was spent in the role of administrative expert. As mentioned, this is a role traditionally held by HR professionals. This role focuses on being an expert on how the work is organized and executed, ensuring operational efficiency and that costs are reduced while maintaining quality. Sixteen percent of hours worked were spent as an employee champion, representing the concerns and needs of employees to senior and line management while simultaneously increasing employees' commitment to the organization and delivering results. Nineteen percent of their time was devoted to being a change agent, creating a culture where the organization is primed and ready for change. Eighteen percent of an HR professional's time was spent as a "player," doing things that make a difference to the organization by acting as a coach, leader, facilitator, keeper of the brand, and so forth.

The human resources function needs to provide value and not be administrative in task and focus. Although we are seeing a shift in strategic focus as documented by Ulrich's research, unfortunately this is not the case everywhere. We still see a predominantly administrative focus in many developing countries

(Yeung, 2005). The HR function needs to demonstrate that it is a true strategic partner and shift away from the administrative label it has carried for so long. Whereas this is still a challenge in many developing parts of the world, strong HR functions from progressive multinational organizations will provide tools and resources and set powerful examples of what is expected in a strategic HR professional. This is necessary to drive the business strategy throughout the organization and the world. HR professionals can be successful by focusing not on the HR activity but on its intended business outcome.

## Human Resources Design Framework

HR professionals need to demonstrate that they understand the business and its needs at multiple levels. Successful HR professionals need to understand that there is no "one size fits all" approach for their human resources strategy. A successful management trainee program in Europe may not work as well in Latin America without some local customization. How organizations implement their human resource strategy—locally versus globally—has implications for organizational success.

Sometimes HR effectiveness lies in the details and not the big picture. There are times when HR professionals must be tactical in approach because it is up to them to manage such administrative issues as monitoring compliance, ensuring managers are providing performance reviews, and ensuring that new employees are registered on the payroll system. If these basics are not addressed it becomes more difficult to resolve the larger strategic issues. Being strategic versus tactical does not imply that one is more important than the other; they are both important. Therefore, understanding when to be strategic versus when to be tactical is critical for an HR professional to demonstrate value.

Being successful tactically means having all the basics of human resources in order. This includes a compensation and benefits program, accurate employee records, policy development and enforcement, hiring, and day-to-day employee relations work. Though these basics are not necessarily what give an organization its competitive advantage, without them it would be difficult to build a strategic platform (Christensen, 2006). The

**Figure 4.1. Human Resources Design Framework.**

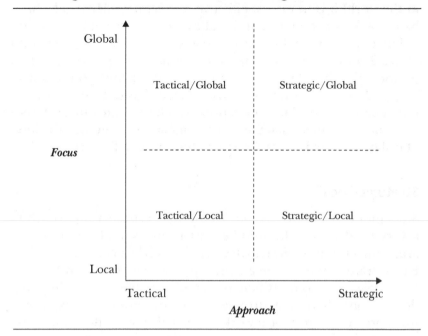

strategic aspects of human resources are what can differentiate an organization and provide its competitive advantage.

Figure 4.1 describes this two-by-two framework of focus and approach or, more specifically, of global versus local and strategic versus tactical. In the section that follows, we highlight examples of business issues and how they can be addressed within this human resources design framework. Each is important, and each cell of the matrix provides value to the organization if it is addressing a business need.

## Strategic/Global

Global organizations with multiple locations are often faced with business challenges that are global in scope and have a strategic impact on the entire enterprise. A case in point is consolidating operations for cost-saving purposes. For example, organizations with large call center operations have to strategically identify where in the world it is most cost effective to operate a 24/7 call center based on salary, benefits, and real estate, but also balance it with a skilled, multilingual workforce ready to provide customers with global 24/7 coverage. It is up to the human resources function to perform the due diligence and identify the talent pool that can staff such an operation on a cost-efficient basis. There are huge implications for business operations which translate into customer expectations and satisfaction. Customer satisfaction with the level of call center service ties directly to bottom-line financial results.

## Strategic/Local

Sometimes an HR professional must take a strategic approach to a very local issue. The Middle East is an example of a growth area with a traditionally expatriate-heavy workforce. As the Middle East is transforming from a largely petro-based economy to more of a service economy (financial services, tourism, and shopping destination) there is a stronger need to convert the expatriate workforce to a more local work force. This is a challenge because the Middle East does not have the structures in place to feed sufficient local talent into the talent pool (Hewitt Associates, 2009b). It becomes an even greater challenge when a country like the United Arab Emirates (UAE) decides to limit visas and make renewal of residence permits more difficult, thus inhibiting expatriate recruitment. HR professionals need to take a very tactical approach to a local problem.

In the UAE, almost 90% of the population is expatriate. Many are low-wage workers from less-developed Asian or Middle Eastern countries. They tend to be employed in construction and domestic services such as hotels and restaurants. Expatriates from India and Pakistan tend to be mid-level managers or technical staff. Senior management personnel tend to come from Europe (notably United Kingdom and Germany) and the United States (Hewitt Associates, 2009b).

Retention is a huge issue in the Middle East as many expatriates view their stay as a temporary, often developmental, career-building assignment. They are waiting for their transition out. If the organization does not ensure that the skill set stays then the local HR professional is scrambling to backfill, probably with another expatriate. There is a huge need to build the talent locally so as to reduce dependence on foreign workers. There may be a need to retain some key expatriates until the skill set can be provided locally. This has obvious implications for pay and rewards.

## Tactical/Global

Sometimes HR must take a tactical approach to a global issue. For example, many organizations conduct employee engagement surveys. Survey data help managers, and their respective organizations, understand what drives employee engagement. Linkage research has shown employee engagement to be related to customer satisfaction and to financial results (Rucci, Kirn, & Quinn, 1998). Employee survey results have huge implications for how managers run their operations.

Collecting employee data can be very tactical but crucial to getting an accurate picture of employee issues. HR professionals must work with line managers to ensure that every employee has an opportunity during their workday to complete a survey whether paper or Web-based. The employee must be able to read and understand the survey in order to participate; therefore, surveys must often be translated. For unskilled labor, language can be a challenge. Even literacy in a native language can be a challenge. The HR professional must ensure that the employee can participate with a level of comfort. They must be able to participate in a nonthreatening, confidential environment. Obviously, there are many administrative details involved in running a successful employee survey program. Tactical administration is important because the data results not only have local impact but global as well. Locally the data will be reviewed by management and employees and a local action plan will be built. Globally the results are important because they may influence global strategy. Linkage research happens at the global level. Without a tactical approach to data collection, there can be no global research.

## Tactical/Local

There may be organizational issues which are local in focus and require a very tactical approach to find a solution. Ensuring that there is adequate office or work space is such an example. As organizations grow and hire additional staff, the original work space may not be sufficient for the growing population. The HR professional is often tasked with projecting staff growth and then identifying and recommending alternative solutions. This can include physically moving all staff to a new facility and location, or moving some staff to a new location. This can also include identifying and implementing innovative solutions such as telecommuting programs, office hoteling programs, and office-sharing programs. Identifying the appropriate solution is a very tactical approach to address such a local issue of ensuring that every employee has his or her own work space.

One can see how identifying the appropriate approach for the specific focus can optimize organizational results. The HR professional, in order to be successful, must be able to balance all these views.

## Managing Talent: Freedom within a Framework

As described earlier, organizations can reflect different stages of globalization. By providing common frameworks in particular HR areas, the organization is creating a common language and set of expectations. One size does not fit all, however, when culture issues are brought into play. In order for these HR programs and processes to work, sometimes local customization is in order. Organizations that can provide a common framework while understanding and accepting that local customization may actually enhance the HR offering have optimized "freedom within a framework" for their local HR professionals. Creating the right balance between global business and local market needs is the ultimate contribution an HR leader can make (Hofmeister, 2005). In the examples that follow we will describe some areas where a common platform coupled with a flexible framework for local implementation has proven successful.

### Competency Models

Competency models, or success profiles, provide a common language and framework for selection, development, and retention within an organization. Competency models are a set of job-related competencies with identified behaviors that are related to successful performance. Having a globally consistent, or common, framework of competencies sets the performance expectations throughout the organization. By identifying competencies for a specific functional area—for example, sales—the organization is stating that to perform successfully in sales these identified competencies are critical. Validation studies provide supporting empirical evidence. This common framework allows for consistency in recruiting talent anywhere in the world. From a talent management perspective, the common language and framework allows for consistent development of employees and career pathing and mobility. A successful pharmaceutical sales manager in Florida should be just as successful in Lisbon when you look at core capabilities. Of course other issues come into play when one is discussing career mobility across countries. The successful sales manager in Florida will not be successful in Lisbon unless she is fluent in Portuguese and also sensitive to and in tune with the Portuguese culture (as well as local regulatory policies).

HR also needs to be attuned to subtle differences in meaning and semantics. The American definition of a competency may not make sense in another country even though the construct may be the same. For example, ''Communicating Effectively'' may be defined in the United States as including the ability to speak up and challenge one's superiors. This is not a behavior that would be demonstrated in Asian countries where the norm is to defer to one's superiors and not to challenge them.

## Talent Management

Competency models act as the foundation for talent management systems. Talent management systems include, but are not limited to, performance appraisal systems, succession planning processes, and 360-degree feedback systems. Global consistency in talent management systems is desirable because it creates a consistent framework and set of performance expectations. ''Strategic thinking'' in India should look like ''strategic thinking'' in Brazil; however, subtle differences in meaning and interpretations can and do exist. To the degree that performance behaviors can be made explicit, therefore, organizations can achieve common understanding. Further, ratings on tools like performance reviews and 360-degree feedback can be culturally biased as well. Some cultures are more direct and blunt in approach (European cultures) and scores from these raters tend to be lower than their Asian or Latin American counterparts who are more genteel or less direct in their feedback.

## Rewards and Recognition Systems

Rewards and recognition systems can be culturally bound. Though organizations may have a global philosophy regarding reward systems, the reality is that reward systems will be most effective if they satisfy the employees' needs. In the United States, health care benefits are an important part of a total rewards system. Employees may actually be attracted to and get recruited by an organization because of its generous benefits package. In other countries where health care is not provided by employers but by the government, other benefits are considered important. One needs to be aware of potential differences in contextual meaning. There is often confusion to the typical survey question ''my company provides me with the benefits my family and I need.'' In the United States, ''benefits'' is generally understood to be health care benefits. In many countries, there is socialized medicine so the organization is not providing health care coverage. Employees in these countries interpret benefits to mean other benefits such as discounts with business partners or suppliers. Sometimes ''benefits'' is not understood at all. Therefore the organization would not be able to use a global rollup of data to make any organizational decisions. In this situation local data, interpretations, and customs are much more meaningful.

When designing global reward programs it is important to remember that what is valued is also different across the world and culturally driven. Cash may be king in certain countries over material goods or awards. When a large global organization, at which one author was employed, tried to design and implement a global recognition program, it was obvious that one design program would not work. HR professionals from the United States wanted to create a program that would be special and pamper the employee so that it would be a memorable award. If the employee was chosen "employee of the month" he or she would win a beautiful award with his or her name engraved on it, and would also be able to choose from a catalog of merchandise. The thought was that employees would be able to have something that they would not normally purchase for themselves, such as a beautiful Tiffany necklace. To give cash as an award was seen as tacky. The HR professionals from outside the United States, though, had a totally different perspective. For many employees in the Middle East or Asia, cash is king. Though the award would be appreciated, many front-line employees had left their family in their home country to live elsewhere and earn a living to support their families back home. A statuette with their name on it and a Tiffany necklace might be beautiful, but their immediate need and concern was to earn money to help their family. A catalog of merchandise would not be well received. In fact, it would be seen as frivolous and actually might reduce the perceived value of the recognition.

## Technology

Technology plays a huge role in uniting an organization and its common mission. IBM leverages the same intranet and database of resources whether the employee works in New York, Germany, or Japan. Technology can enable global conversations and the sharing of important work or client information almost instantly.

A common technology platform provides consistent input and output of data. It allows for rollup of information at a local, regional, country, and global level. The common technology unites the organization in its mission and development goals for its employees. Although most technology platforms operate in the organization's official language (often English), customizing the technology so that local languages can be used may allow for greater participant utility. For example, creating common intranet pages that can be translated locally allows for greater information sharing.

A successful global HR function leverages technology. Technology becomes the enabler that allows HR to streamline talent management, workforce management planning, and workforce analytics. It can address many of the administrative tasks for HR in order to allow HR professionals to focus their energies on the more strategic aspects of their work.

## Employment Law

As seen with compensation and reward, not all aspects of human resources programs and policies can be applied globally, because employment laws are specific to each country. Laws, work councils, and unions can govern who is hired, how work is performed, and how employees terminate. The differences between the specific social welfare programs should be interpreted as an opportunity to share best practices, identifying which kind of employment conditions could be culturally adopted across geographical boundaries. Particularly within the European labor market, the number of legal dispositions that are commonly used within the European Union (EU) are progressively increasing and allow the opportunity to adopt general programs such as health care, integrative pension plans, job-on-call, job sharing, work from home, and part-time work for experienced employees who are not ready for permanent retirement. Across European companies, the interdependent role of the European Works Council, which is focused on sharing information and best practices, rather than on negotiating with local trade unions, provides a common framework to link local economics, business objectives, employment conditions, and training programs.

## HR Metrics

As mentioned throughout this chapter, creating commonalities across the organization produces common and consistent language and business goals. HR metrics can play an important role in creating this common language. Both authors were involved in the development of a global engagement survey. The dimensions and items reflected common issues across the organization that needed attention and monitoring. The survey dimensions communicated to managers globally that these were issues in which the organization was interested and intended to hold managers accountable for. Regression analysis indicated common themes across the different geographical divisions. Feedback and action planning had the most impact at the local level. Here is a situation where local is more powerful than global. Although the organization identified some consistent themes and global issues, data analysis, feedback, and action planning are much more effective at the local manager level.

Other key HR metrics that organizations may capture and analyze at a national level can be action planned at a local level. One could argue they have more effect at a local level. Application rates, turnover rates, and so on reflect the local employment conditions and local organization more than they do the entire enterprise. If the data trends are consistent across the organization, then there are truly enterprise-wide issues to look at.

## Staffing: The Off-Shoring Experience

Off-shoring is a challenge to the HR function because off-shoring presents a shift in how HR professionals have traditionally operated. Instead of moving the talent to where the work is, off-shoring is moving the work to where the talent is.

The trend toward off-shoring of work started in the early part of this century as organizations identified rich talent and cheaper operating expenses in India. Organizations with large call center operations, such as airlines and information technology (IT) service companies, have tended to gravitate toward this trend. IBM and Accenture have led the way with major operations in India. Some organizations have more staff off-shore than they do in their domestic locations. There has been such angst and backlash around off-shoring, however, that most organizations will not even publicize employee populations by country because they do not want to be accused of off-shoring.

### Shifting to Right-Shoring

By the end of this decade we will have seen the shift from off-shoring to right-shoring. As off-shoring has leveled out, companies are now searching for the right answer, rather than the least expensive solution. Right-shoring is the restructuring of an organization's workforce to find the perfect mix of jobs that can be moved to foreign countries or be performed locally. In right-shoring, a company outsources its simpler and not-so-important processes to other countries, while retaining the complex processes in-house. Organizations feel that by handling the complex and important requirements of their business they can benefit from improved customer relationships and have a better control over their business. Right-shoring is all about maintaining a balance about the work that can be sent overseas and the work that can best be done within the organization.

The HR professional plays a huge role in whether or not right-shoring is a success for the organization. The HR professional must understand the work that needs to be done, the skills necessary to be successful, and then identify where those skills exist in abundance. Once the region, or location, is identified, then the critical task of selection begins.

## Human Resources Program Implementation

In a global organization it is naïve to believe that whatever is created in headquarters, a center of excellence, or one of the divisions will be flawlessly implemented throughout the organization. With globalization comes complexity in program design and implementation. We cannot assume that the common platforms described in the previous section will result in local success without some specific attention. For flawless implementation, we outline some recommended steps in this section.

### Role of Human Resources Professionals

The human resources function and its professionals play a critical role in ensuring that the organization's business strategy is executed and successful. As mentioned earlier in this chapter, human resources is the best positioned to help an organization succeed and bring its business strategy to life globally. By harnessing the strengths and talents of its employees, organizations can create competitive advantage.

HR professionals must be able to understand the tools and processes developed to operate the business. Only by their knowledge can they communicate and educate constituents on the value and use of the tools. Performance management is an obvious example. The value of a performance management process is not in completing the forms but in setting the goals and having the performance discussion. Is the employee on track to achieve the goals? This is important because goal achievement should be directly tied to organizational performance and success. Too often HR professionals are in the policing role, checking for compliance if the goal and appraisal forms are complete rather than taking the time to educate their managers and employees on the value of the tool to operate the business. They also tend to focus on the quantity of reviews completed versus the quality of the reviews and discussions. This occurs because the HR professionals themselves do not truly understand the value. In order for HR to be advocates and to champion the tools and processes, they themselves need to be educated. Too often organizations implement HR systems without ensuring that the users or advocates actually understand them. Again the focus is on the HR activity instead of the intended business outcome. Further, human resources specialists, such as compensation and benefits professionals, talent management, learning and development, and selection and staffing professionals, must work closely with their generalist partners and line management to support the business strategy and goals. Once the business needs and related human capital needs are identified, the specialist and generalist partnership often produces a very effective solution.

## Global Task Force

Creating a global task force of HR professionals representing different geographies (for example, North America, Latin America, Europe, Africa/Middle East, and Asia Pacific) will allow for diversity of thought and input into the program design. Even within geographical areas there will be differences in culture that need to be accommodated for (for example, China is not like Australia even though they might be managed the same way, by the same management team, in Asia Pacific). Having global representation will make the program design and implementation run more smoothly because the representatives will have had a voice from the beginning. Task force members will be able to provide invaluable insight to the design. They can field test the idea in local markets to ensure clarity of message and intent to minimize any confusion before launch. They will be able to identify the nuances that might impact the program locally. They will also be able to identify issues or barriers and be able to offer solutions for flawless implementation. Task force members are now key stakeholders who have a vested interest in the success of the program or initiative. They will be able to galvanize their local management team's support to ensure program success.

## Pilot and Phased Approach to Implementation

It is recommended to start small with any initiative and create a pilot and then a phased approach to implementation. Choose a subpopulation of the larger population but pilot it globally. For example, one of the authors was responsible for the design and global rollout of a 360-degree feedback program. The first year was considered a pilot and only general managers were invited to participate (around 900 employees globally). The following cycle was expanded to include general managers and their direct reports. It also included headquarters managers. By the third cycle, department heads were invited to participate. In a three-year period the 360-feedback participant population went from 900 to 8,000. In every cycle issues were identified and resolved before the next implementation.

## Ensure Functional Buy-In

Human Resources professionals must believe in the value of the tools and processes. They are often participants as well as implementers. If they do not understand the value then it becomes a compliance task for them and for their employees. In order for HR processes to have true business impact, they must be optimized and considered part of business operations and not "another HR program." The task force approach, as mentioned earlier, can play a role in creating functional buy-in. The task force representatives, as part of their role, need to communicate to their local HR teams not only what the program or initiative is about but also the business outcome it addresses and the value of the approach.

Ensuring functional buy-in is critical because HR professionals are tasked with ensuring that employees and managers understand the intended outcome of the initiative.

### Create Local Champions

In order for HR professionals to be the "arms and legs" of implementation, they need to be champions of the process. Creating local champions provides the organization and its employees with local knowledge experts who can ensure program optimization and success.

Local champions can include task force representatives but they should include others not on the task force as well. Champions can be HR or line professionals; this is a great development opportunity for both. They can develop depth of expertise whether it is in selection, talent management, organization development, or another HR area. Depending upon the initiative, the local HR leadership may determine that it makes better sense for local line management or employees to be the champions. In the case of an employee engagement survey, where anonymity and confidentiality are always questioned, a better solution would be to have local employees, and not HR, as champions.

Local champions will be able to identify the best way to implement and utilize the intended initiative. For example, a local champion in Turkey may determine that supervisors in their location should not participate in their local 360-feedback initiative because, although they have a "supervisor" title, locally their responsibilities do not include actual performance management or direct supervising responsibilities. A headquarters mandate that all supervisors participate in 360-feedback should be addressed by the local champion with an explanation of why it would not make practical sense to participate.

## Challenges to Implementation

The recommendations listed above are meant to provide guidance around implementation. However, there are a number of issues to consider when implementing a new HR initiative or even making changes to an existing program or process. Customizing or tailoring these to fit local needs will enhance success.

## Changing Demographics

The complexity of managing demographics (for example in Germany, where hiring skilled immigrants is more complicated and the age range is more skewed than in countries such as the United Kingdom), combined with the pressure on productivity results and profitability margins, are forcing an increasing number of European companies to launch innovative solutions to increase their intellectual capital.

Managing demographics is fast becoming one of the most pressing issues for HR professionals. They must manage skill and productivity loss resulting from turnover of young talent and the retirement of an aging workforce. This is especially true in the United States, Canada, Australia, and much of Europe. Both challenges pose several threats, among them: the increase in absenteeism, health care, and pension plan costs; the potential loss of knowledge as experienced employees leave the company; and the difficulty of motivating older workers. With the war for talent there is concern that there will be fewer qualified employees entering the labor market. Organizations need to identify new staffing solutions based on modeling labor demand by job family in addition to the traditional venues of succession planning, restructuring work, and early retirement.

Though in the United States we have long heard of the war for talent and concern for talent shortages when baby boomers retire, global demographics tell us that the baby boom has not yet occurred in many developing countries. Whereas the United States is concerned that baby-boomer retirement will result in a skill gap, the working age population in developing countries is still relatively young. Populations may be decreasing in Europe but they are increasing in India. That is good news, especially in our emerging economies.

## Languages

In a global organization, translations become a standard operating practice. This is not just for HR initiatives but for any business initiative that must be communicated.

For communication to be clear and accurate, it is important that the meaning is translated—not just the words. There are subtle nuances of language that get lost in the literal translation.

The challenge is that often you are not just dealing with the local language but the local dialect. For a lower-skilled, less-educated employee population, ensuring that the level and meaning are captured is a challenge.

One way to address this issue is to have in-country employees as reviewers to translate and retranslate, or validate, the message content. The original translation can be completed by a translation service (these services tend to employ local country nationals). The translation should be followed with a back-translation by an in-country employee to ensure that it matches to the original meaning. The original translation can also be completed by an in-country employee, however the back translation is key and should be performed by a different in-country employee. Nuances in languages are usually seen here. It is possible to say something multiple ways—all of which may be correct. The decision then is which translation to accept. Sometimes it is best to accept the employee translation over the translation service as it assumes employee buy-in to the process and the creation of an invested employee stakeholder. Translation and retranslation take a great deal of time. Expect some back and forth as translations are validated. This does take time and should be explicitly planned for in any project plan.

It is critical that messages are not "lost in translation" and that the intended message or purpose of the initiative is what is communicated in the end. One of the authors was involved in a situation where a translated performance evaluation form implied that the goals and objectives were optional and not necessarily formal or enforceable (oh, the subtleties of language). In this European country it was actually easier to operate this way because if goals were optional you did not need to get buy-in or approval from the unions or work councils. However, it was critical to the performance and success of the organization that employees understood their job and its required goals and associated objectives.

## Legal Issues

As programs are designed, it is always easy to assume that they will work everywhere. Even with thoughtful due diligence and global representation, sometimes country-specific regulations or legal issues may stand in the way. Assumptions tend to get challenged in a global environment. A case in point—one of the authors was responsible for creating a global employee relief fund. The fund would be used for employees in economic need after a disaster (natural or otherwise) resulting in a loss or hardship. In a global organization, a tsunami in Asia not only affects local employees but it also provokes compassion from fellow employees all around the world. The goal of the program was to raise funds through donations from employees, with a match from the organization. It would seem easy enough in concept, however, not so easy in implementation. It was discovered during the implementation phase that some countries do not allow money to actually leave their country, thereby making donations impossible to collect. China could solicit donations and raise money from employees, but the money could not leave the country and be part of the "global" account. The money had to stay in China and could be used only for Chinese employees in need. Technically this was in conflict with the mission of the program where the goal was a global fund to which all employees could contribute and also apply for a relief fund grant. In addition, though donations to charities are considered tax deductible in most countries, this is not universally the case. Local tax laws had to be identified and communicated with the rollout of the program. which created an added level of complexity.

## Ethics and Compliance Issues

The economic turbulence of 2008 and 2009 has shed new light on ethics and compliance issues. Whereas almost all multinational organizations have ethics and compliance programs (as mandated by their local country's laws), cultural issues affect how they actually operate. In order to develop and implement global ethics programs and hotlines, organizations need to address some challenges, including how to communicate a consistent business ethics policy in many languages. If organizations are implementing a global hotline, the hotline services must be localized to conform to local language and cultural norms. Another development in recent years is that organizations now have to address international data privacy laws, including whistleblower guidelines and data transfers (EthicsPoint, 2009). Data privacy laws have made general business as well as HR-specific operations more challenging. Outside the United States, multinational organizations must tend to the often conflicting requirements of local governments. France, Belgium, Spain, Canada, Germany, Ireland, and Japan are just some of the countries with differing data privacy laws that must be addressed. Global organizations must be aware that many cultures are extremely wary and some are averse to the practice of whistleblowing. In addition, what is considered unethical or illegal behavior can vary widely, further complicating attempts to adopt a uniform ethics program. The data protection requirement and language barrier in many multinationals can make it very difficult to capture information about, and investigate, possible misconduct.

# Future of Global HR Management

With the economic events of 2008 and 2009 behind us, we wonder about the future and the implications for global HR management.

## Shifting Role of Human Resources

The human resources business partner model, as described earlier, has to adapt to meet the changing business challenges which will continue to evolve, for the immediate time being, with uncertainty.

However, all this uncertainty can be to an HR professional's advantage. HR can define the future based on predictable trends (such as demographics or business growth) but it can also step up to the challenge of defining its own future. HR has evolved over the last several decades as businesses have evolved. The administrative and transactional roles of the past have given way to a strategic business partner model. Some are advocating that the next evolution of the role will take us to an internal consultant model (Vosburgh, 2007) where HR is not pushing an HR agenda but instead helping clients in their respective businesses to solve difficult business problems.

Globally, the HR function is in different places in its evolution. In many of the Asian countries we still see remnants of a transaction-based HR function as they are still technically in the first generation of a free enterprise system. Multinational organizations need to ensure that their global HR professionals have the skill sets to support their organizational clients for the future. Creating world-class HR talent globally should be a top priority of every chief human resources officer.

## Emerging Economies

As global markets expand, what are the implications for human resources? Will there be special focus on the BRIC economies—Brazil, Russia, India, and China? For the last several years these countries have been identified as emerging economic powerhouses and, for many multinational organizations, these countries have been a focus for economic growth. It is predicted that by 2035, the combined gross domestic product (GDP) of these four countries will become bigger than the G7 (Kowitt, 2009). This has huge human resource implications as HR professionals will have to select, develop, and retain employees in these emerging economies for years to come. They will have to balance expatriate staffing, which will be necessary for the exploding growth, with cultivating and nurturing local talent development.

Our growing global service economy continues to put the spotlight on talent. Talent acquisition, retention, and development are even more critical in a service economy than in a traditional manufacturing economy.

## Identified Needs

A survey of over 4,700 executives by the Boston Consulting Group (2008) found that managing talent and improving leadership development were consistently top concerns globally. In North America, survey participants perceived the critical challenges to be managing talent and demographics, improving leadership development, managing work-life balance, and transforming HR into a strategic business partner. In Latin America, the top two future HR challenges identified were managing work-life balance and managing talent. In Europe, managing talent and demographics emerged as key challenges. In Africa, executives identified managing talent, work-life balance, globalization, and diversity as major future challenges. The key HR challenges in Emerging Asia (China and India) were identified as managing talent, improving leadership development, becoming a learning organization, and managing work-life balance. Executives in Established Asia (Singapore, Japan, South Korea) were primarily concerned with managing globalization, talent, and improving leadership development. In the Pacific Region, executives named managing talent, improving leadership development, managing demographics, managing change, and cultural transformation as critical HR challenges. We are beginning to see some shift in priorities as now managing the work-life balance of employees seems to be gaining importance, especially in countries where work councils, or unions, play a huge role in the labor market.

## Deglobalization

Given recent world events one might even argue that we are seeing a shift to a deglobalization or relocalization. Sustainability is not only a media topic and popular cause, but it has also become embedded in most organizational strategies. Individuals and organizations are noting and using local resources versus a global supply chain, as evidenced by trends such as the slow food movement. This has implications for talent resources as well. Though it is still too early to conclude whether the pendulum has swung in the other direction, if we do begin to see an increased emphasis on localization, then we will probably also begin to see a decrease in talent mobility with increased emphasis on identifying and growing local talent.

## Human Resources as a Decision Science

For human resources to continue to evolve, we need to maintain focus on human capital as the differentiator of organizational success. A key correlate is the ability to measure success. The successful HR function of the future will have the ability to measure key metrics and become more of a "decision science" (Boudreau & Ramstad, 2007) thereby measuring its impact on business outcomes rather than HR activities. The focus needs to shift from the services that HR provides to the business decisions that HR informs and supports.

Human Resources professionals will also become more aware of capital markets and the role that intangible assets such as human capital play in sustaining those markets. The investor community is now interested in such HR practices as succession planning, leadership development, corporate culture, and executive compensation as data points in buy-or-sell decisions (Ulrich & Brockbank, 2009).

In conclusion, if HR is successful in harnessing the strengths and talents of its employees, it stands to reason that the enterprise will be successful. Understanding our global complexity, the value of human capital, and the value that the human resources function can provide to meet the business challenges can create an exciting future. Organizations are not productive or profitable if they do not have the right talent in the right roles aligned with the business strategy. Human resources professionals are the best positioned to create this alignment and help an organization succeed by bringing its business strategy to life globally.

## References

Boston Consulting Group (2008). *Creating people advantage: How to address HR challenges worldwide through 2015.*

Boudreau, J., & Ramstad, P. (2007). *Beyond HR: The new science of human capital.* Boston: Harvard Business School Publishing.

Christensen, R. (2006). *Roadmap to strategic HR.* New York: American Management Association.

Corporate Leadership Council (2009). Building HR business partner capabilities in continental Europe.

EthicsPoint (2009). www.ethicspoint.com.

Hewitt Associates (2009a). Managing HR on a global scale: Findings from Hewitt's 2009 Global HR Study.

Hewitt Associates (2009b). Foot on the gas: Managing human resources in the Middle East.

Hofmeister, J. (2005). Global and local balance in human resources leadership. In Losey, M., Meisinger, S., & Ulrich D. (eds.), *The future of human resource management.* Hoboken, NJ: Wiley.

Kowitt, B. (2009). For Mr. BRIC, nations meeting a milestone. CNN-Money.com, June 17, 2009.

Rucci, A. J., Kirn, S. P., & Quinn, R. T. (1998). The Employee-customer-profit chain at Sears. *Harvard Business Review, 76*, 1, 95–112.

Ulrich, D. (1997). *Human resources champions*. Boston: Harvard Business School Press.

Ulrich, D., & Brockbank, W. (2009). The HR business partner model: Past learnings and future challenges. *People and Strategy, 32*, 2, 5–7.

Vosburgh, R. M. (2007). The evolution of HR: Developing HR as an internal consulting organization. *Human Resource Planning, 30*, 3, 11–23.

World Federation of Personnel Management Associations. (2005). *Survey of global HR challenges: Yesterday, today and tomorrow.*

Yeung, A. (2005). Becoming business partners in Chinese firms: Challenges and opportunities. In M. Losey, S. Meisinger & D. Ulrich (Eds.), *The future of human resource management*. Hoboken, NJ: Wiley.

# PART 2

# Attracting and Selecting Employees in the Global Workplace

# CHAPTER 5

# Recruitment in a Global Workplace

## Mukta Kulkarni and Mathian Osicki

*The only thing worth more than a bright new idea is a bright new hire.*
— NAKACHE, 1997

Attracting human resources to an organization not only determines the future composition of the organization's workforce, but also the long-term ability of the organization to meet its strategic goals. A good recruitment procedure can function as a sieve, to filter people from the available talent pool. Attracting the right candidate is important not only in booming markets where organizations compete intensely for scarce talent, but also in recessionary markets where organizations have to sift through a large number of applicants who are vying for relatively fewer jobs.

An Employment Management Association report indicates that, on average, organizations spend $1,000 recruiting a nonexempt employee, about $7,000 for an exempt employee, and over $23,000 for executive-level employees in the external labor market. Recruiting efforts therefore have to be targeted toward attracting the right candidate, not only given financial implications, but also because they feed into consequent selection processes. If recruiting strategies don't help identify a sizable and suitable pool of talent, even the most accurate selection process will be of little or no use (Fisher, Schoenfeldt, & Shaw, 2006).

Despite the importance of the recruiting function, a recent survey of 50 CEOs of global organizations paints a grim picture. This survey indicates that even for top management-level recruitment, strategies are ad hoc, vague, and heavily reliant on subjective evaluations. The consequence is that about a third of new hires leave after three years of being with the organization. What is more surprising is the fact that most CEOs do not see the situation as it is (Fernández-Araoz, Groysberg, & Nohria, 2009). Suboptimal recruitment, and the consequent unavoidable suboptimal hiring, especially at strategic levels and for key positions, can cause serious financial setbacks for an organization or, worse, ruin it. Sometimes organizations search too narrowly and try to find candidates from within their own network, only to realize too late that their decision was flawed (Fernández-Araoz, 2007). Indeed, a study by the Center for Creative Leadership shows that one out of four executives selected is the only one considered (Fernández-Araoz, Groysberg, & Nohria, 2009). This may well have been the case with appointing Jill Barad at the helm of Mattel, or Douglas Ivestor at the helm of Coca-Cola. Both were asked to leave after about two and a half years (Charan & Colvin, 2000; Morris, et al., 2004). Could the organizational stories have been different had they cast a wider net and attracted and sifted through other candidates?

## Importance of Casting a Wide Recruiting Net

Traditionally, organizations could scan their local environments for a relevant supply of talent and be reasonably satisfied with the results. Today though, given uneven employment growth (International Labour Organization, 2009), globalization, and competition, organizations have to broaden their scan to include international environments (Schuler & Tarique, 2007). For example, given increased technological sophistication and opening up of markets, companies like Dell, Sony, Apple, Zara, Nike, to name a few, have had to develop a global talent pool and conduct recruiting globally to service expanding markets (Dessler, 2008). To make matters more complicated for organizations, much of the global talent pool now lies outside of the United States and Europe. Thirty-three million young professionals now live in 28 low-wage countries (Despeignes, 2005), and this talent is not uniform in availability. India and China, for example, were predicted to face serious skilled labor shortages by the end of 2009 (Farrell & Grant, 2005; NASSCOM, 2006). Further, available skill sets and numbers do not match organizational requirements in certain parts of the developing or growth economies (Guthridge, Komm, & Lawson, 2008; International Labour Organization, 2009), especially for managerial positions (Ready, Hill, & Conger, 2008).

Given the global nature of business today, organizations have to create very specific and effective recruitment efforts to build a deep reservoir of global as well as local talent to staff all their organizational levels (Guthridge, Komm, & Lawson, 2008). To address these challenges, global organizations such as Procter & Gamble have mapped a global supply-chain process to obtain talent. At the country leader level at Procter & Gamble, for example, there are about 300 executives who come from 36 countries, and 50% are from outside the United States. The top 40 executives of Procter & Gamble come from 12 different nations, and 45% are from outside the United States (Ready & Conger, 2007).

Consider also the example of Renault-Nissan. In 1999, the top brass of Nissan, then in financial trouble, decided to partner with Renault and chose a non-Japanese COO from Renault to transform the organization. The COO was Carlos Ghosn, a Brazil-born French-Lebanese businessman. It was a bold decision for the Japanese company, which usually recruited only Japanese executives, and one that transformed the ailing company into a successful one (Millikin & Fu, 2005).

It is not only large or multinational for-profit organizations that have to cast a large recruiting net to leverage the globally dispersed talent and overcome regional skill scarcity. Consider the involved and successful recruiting strategy followed by Sinai hospital in Baltimore, Maryland. This not-for-profit health care organization reaches out to nurses in the Philippines, spends time explaining their mission and work, and, after determining a fit, invites them to join their campus. This strategy has helped them tremendously in meeting talent demands. These examples demonstrate how casting a wide recruiting net can effectively fill a void that a narrower one may not address.

## Scope and Outline of the Chapter

In this chapter, we draw upon recruitment research and organizational examples to outline various contingencies that managers should consider when undertaking recruitment initiatives, and offer specific recommendations for recruiting effectively in the global workplace. We define recruiting as a process of finding and attracting the right candidates and encouraging them to apply for certain positions (Bohlander & Snell, 2004; Dessler, 2008). Given our scope, we do not detail internal versus external sources of recruitment, content and delivery of recruitment messages, effects of recruiter characteristics, or timing of recruitment initiatives. Comprehensive summaries and reviews on these topics can be found elsewhere (for example, see Barber, 1998; Bohlander & Snell, 2004; Breaugh, 2008; Dessler, 2008).

The chapter is structured as follows. First we discuss the notion that various contingencies have the potential to influence recruiting strategies, and how organizations have to be aware of these contingencies. In the next section we specifically elaborate on external as well as internal contingencies that have an impact on recruiting. In each section we draw upon research and organizational examples to identify key lessons and recommendations for managers. The chapter is broadly summarized in Table 5.1.

## Contingencies to Consider When Recruiting

Organizations function within an external societal and global context as well as an internal organizational context. Both these exogenous and endogenous contexts serve as contingencies that influence human resources practices in general and recruitment in particular. Key exogenous or external contingency factors include the legal, societal or cultural, political, and labor market contexts. Key endogenous or internal contingency factors include the size, age, technology, and structure of an organization (Jackson & Schuler, 1995). To deal with both kinds of contingencies, global organizations typically follow one of three approaches in terms of their human resource practices: They adjust practices to reflect local institutional conditions; they follow common practices regardless of which country they are operating in; or they create some form of a blend to reflect a combinational of local

**Table 5.1. Chapter Summary.**

| Contingencies | Recruiting Guidelines |
|---|---|
| **I. Exogenous** | |
| 1. Social-Cultural Context | • Train/sensitize managers to different values and expectations across the globe<br>• Create clear job descriptions that are understood across locations<br>• Decide if recruiting will be a centralized or decentralized activity<br>• Signal different incentives and perquisites to cater to different expectations across locations |
| 2. External Labor Market | |
| a. Scarcity | • Create a strong campus presence<br>• Differentiate by creating an organizational brand<br>• Actively tap passive job seekers |
| b. Abundance | • Create multiple recruiting rounds to zero in on the right candidate<br>• Leverage an external skills database if available<br>• Leverage employees as ambassadors to spot and attract talent<br>• Target boomerang employees |
| **II. Endogenous** | |
| 1. Size | • Formalize recruiting processes<br>• Leverage the internal labor market |
| 2. Technological Sophistication | • Leverage social networking sites<br>• Deploy creative internet technologies<br>• Create attractive organizational Web sites |

and headquarter practices (Brewster, Wood, & Brookes, 2008; Rosenzweig & Nohria, 1994). Unilever, for example, has allowed for complete decentralization in recruiting across the globe, and each country they operate in has created its own unique locally designed recruitment strategy. General Electric (GE), on the other hand, recruits across the globe with a specific set of criteria, and looks for individuals who fit the GE value system. For instance, in 2007, of the 1,053 students hired into GE's leadership programs, 224 were from Asia; 148 were from Europe, the Middle East, and Africa; and 681 were from the Americas (Hill, 2008).

There is no one best practice or gold standard for recruiting, but there are certainly some practices that organizations have followed which have helped them identify and attract good candidates (Fernández-Araoz, Groysberg, & Nohria, 2009). Typically, when human resource practices fit exogenous contingency factors such as national culture and laws, as well as endogenous organizational factors such as size or technological sophistication of the organization, they most effectively help enhance organizational performance (Immelt, Govindarajan, & Trimble, 2009; Lengnick-Hall & Lengnick-Hall, 1988; McGaughey & De Cieri, 1999; Schuler & Tarique, 2007). In the next two sections we outline key external and internal contingency factors that may influence organizations' recruiting efforts, and call for managerial attention to these when chalking their recruitment strategies.

## Exogenous Contingency Factors in Recruitment

Exogenous contingency factors are those that are outside of the immediate control of the organization, but are those which may significantly influence organizational functioning. In this section we focus two factors that can impact recruiting strategies and outcomes—the macro societal or cultural context and the external labor market in which the organization is situated. We especially focus on these two factors because of their direct impact on recruiting strategies and activities. Given the various cross-country and sometimes within-country differences in legal elements such as employment standards, worker compensation, unionization, human rights, and the availability of niche literature regarding the legal context of human resource practices (Berkowitz & Muller-Bonanni, 2007; Shilling, 2008), we do not delve into the legal context in terms of recruiting in this chapter. We also do not outline cross-country political factors in recruiting for similar reasons.

## Societal or Cultural Context

Managerial assumptions and work values are shaped by the societal and national cultures in which they operate (Laurent, 1986) and human resource practices may not always trump sociocultural boundaries of different countries (Mendonca & Kanungo, 1996; Sparrow & Budhwar, 1997). Thus, although the "what" question in human resource philosophy may be universal (for example, effective employee recruitment), the "how" question may be culture-specific (for example, criteria and sources of recruitment) (Tayeb, 1995; 1998). This is especially the case because historical legacies, social stratification, educational system, and pressure groups all have their origins in national culture, and exert their own influences on work values, attitudes, behaviors, and thus on organizational human resource policies and practices (McGaughey & De Cieri; 1999; Tayeb, 1995; 1997). Overall, criteria as well as methods and sources of recruitment may be culture bound.

Managers in individual-oriented or self-oriented countries may recruit differently as compared with managers in collective or socially oriented countries (Kulkarni, Lengnick-Hall, & Valk, 2010). In individually oriented countries, recruitment may be based more on hard criteria such as competences and skills. In socially oriented countries, recruitment may be based more on soft criteria such as social and interpersonal skills, or socially ascribed status. For example, whereas education and past work experience may be specific recruitment criteria in the United States, in Asia or the Middle East a criterion may be whether or not the candidate belongs to the manager's "in-group." Specifically, managers from mature economies such as the United States may be individualistic in that their in-group may not include the workplace (Tayeb, 1995), whereas managers from growth or developing countries are generally more family- and community-oriented in that members from the workplace may be viewed as the in-group (Mendonca & Kanungo, 1996). Although the personnel function in Asia and the Middle East is becoming more strategic and objective, networks based on social contacts, caste, and other social connections still influence human resource policies and practices. Indians, for example, are relatively more collectivist, clan oriented, and caste conscious (Tayeb, 1987), and Taiwanese and Malaysians are rooted in traditional Chinese values of group or collective orientation. People in Thailand, China, and Vietnam are also known to administer preferential treatment toward network or in-group members (Zhu, Warner, & Rowley, 2007).

Networks or the collective in-group may also be determined by religion. A large body of research shows that religion is important in Islamic countries, particularly in the Middle East. Numerous studies across countries such as Egypt (Leat & El-Kot, 2007), Oman (Aycan, Al-Hamadi, Davis, & Budhwar, 2007), Iran (Namazie & Frame, 2007), United Arab Emirates (Rees, Mamman, & Braik, 2007), and Saudi Arabia (Alsahlawi & Gardener, 2004), to name a few, indicate that managers may target familiar others based on religion. The tendency to recruit from the known social network, some argue, reflects uncertainty avoidance (Leat & El-Kot, 2007), and a social or collective orientation (Aycan, Al-Hamadi, Davis, & Budhwar, 2007). This tendency may be reflective of developing countries in general (Kanungo & Jaegar, 1990), given that there is generally more uncertainty in developing countries as compared with mature ones.

Overall, societies that value interpersonal relationships will gear recruitment efforts to identify candidates that fit the social network in the organization (Aycan, 2005). This has a direct and substantive influence on where and who managers recruit. Recruitment may be especially driven by ascribed status driven by familial and social connections—that is, personal relationships—a situation that may not be overt or explicit in European organizations (Budhwar & Khatri, 2001; Sharma, 1984; Sparrow & Budhwar, 1997). In sum, collective or high–uncertainty avoidance cultures may prefer internal recruitment channels, and informal and network-based recruitment (Aycan, 2005). Considering the fact that people who live and work in countries described as "developing" or "growth" comprise almost 80% of the world's population (Aycan, Al-Hamadi, Davis, & Budhwar, 2007), and this region is where job growth is currently highest (International Labour Organization, 2009), the impact of social factors cannot be overlooked by multinational organizations.

What have organizations done given this situation? Recognizing such regional differences, some organizations, such as Unisys, leverage a hybrid model to tap into global talent. In a hybrid model, each business unit has a recruiting specialist to fulfill functional roles within that designated unit, but targeted recruiting strategies are centralized. Thus the process of implementing the recruiting policy is delegated to the local units which are clearly tuned into local realities (Corporate Leadership Council, 2006b).

Macro societal aspects also influence what the available labor pool values, and consequently what organizations should signal when attracting candidates. For example, whereas candidates in individually oriented countries such as the United States strongly value health benefits, this benefit is among the least valued in Asia and Australia. Recruitment efforts thus have to be targeted. Cendant Mobility, a provider of workforce development solutions, provides an example from India. Indian employees have familial obligations and responsibilities that are complex and often more demanding than a Western notion of family responsibilities. Indians may be expected to care more for their extended families (Budhwar, 2001; 2003; Kulkarni, Lengnick-Hall, & Valk, 2010). This suggests that work-life benefits such as flexible time-off may be more compelling for attracting candidates in India as compared with elsewhere (Corporate Leadership Council, 2006b).

So what should global managers do in regard to the macro social context when recruiting globally? One, global managers should be trained and sensitized to be aware of the significant roles that institutions such as family, religion, education, trade unions, and the state play in shaping employee attitudes and actions across the world. This awareness will help the managers to devise appropriate means to handle diversity at the micro level. Two, managers should clearly describe the jobs for which they are recruiting so that even if certain regions tap into their social networks and leverage informal methods, recruitment and hiring is particular to the job in question. Three, managers must decide if they want to delegate recruiting to local units, and for which levels of hiring this delegation is appropriate. Four, managers should build flexibility into their recruitment strategies to include and actively signal different incentives and perquisites to cater to different expectations across the world.

## Labor Market Conditions

The second macro level contingency which directly and significantly affects recruiting efforts is the condition of the labor market. The labor market is defined as the general area from which applicants have to be recruited. Various factors such as national and regional economies, skill and education level of the workforce, and demographic composition of the labor pool all affect the labor market. This story gets complicated further when we consider the global labor market. Two types of labor markets influence recruitment—scarce and abundant labor markets. Scarcity in the labor market implies that the labor market is tight, and there is low unemployment. Consequently, organizations have to try harder to recruit good candidates. Abundance in the labor market, on the other hand, implies the labor market is loose, and there is high unemployment (Bohlander & Snell, 2004). It is important to note, however, that the labor market is different for different levels within an organization. For example, it is quite possible that even though there is an abundant supply of available labor for lower-level positions, recruiting people for strategic positions may be tough, as that market may be scarce. We first discuss how a scarce labor market influences recruitment efforts, and then focus on how an abundant labor market influences recruitment efforts.

**Scarcity in the labor market.** Consider these examples. The Cheesecake Factory in the United States attracts and hires over 20,000 people per year, operates more than 110 restaurants, and is expanding nationally (Dessler, 2008). Infosys attracts and hires over 24,000 people annually, and is expanding globally. Further, a depleting talent pool is forcing organizations to incur higher costs to source the right talent. How can organizations such as these find good candidates? The solution that most organizations have adopted is innovation in their recruitment efforts and strategies (Dessler, 2008; Kossek, 1987).

Organizations can employ one or all of three strategies to attract candidates in a scarce market—attract candidates through innovative campus recruiting efforts, create a strong organizational brand, actively tap "passive" job seekers—and, if possible, leverage technology for all of the above. The three strategies are *not mutually exclusive* (campus activities can help build an organizational brand) but are discussed separately for tractability.

In the following, we discuss ways in which various organizations have successfully implemented the previous strategies. Use of innovative technologies depends on the technological sophistication of an organization, and we therefore discuss it in greater detail in a later section which elaborates on internal contingency factors.

**Creating a strong campus presence.** A wide variety of organizations with a presence across the world utilize campus recruiting heavily to attract bright candidates. We will consider examples from Ernst and Young (Sullivan, 2008b), Tata Consultancy Services Ltd. (Fernández-Araoz, 2007), Procter & Gamble (Ready & Conger, 2007), Valero (Sullivan, 2006c), and Infosys (Birkinshaw, 2008). What do these organizations do in common? All four organizations have created a strong campus presence and have established robust ties with national or international universities, or both, for campus recruiting.

Campus recruiting is taken very seriously at Ernst and Young, and they have created a campus-centric team approach that includes a coordinating partner, campus recruiter, campus champion (senior manager), a diversity champion, and they have added campus recruiting goals into managers' personal development plans and performance scorecards. They have strong internship program ties with over 300 business schools in North America, and they leverage former interns as campus ambassadors to attract newer candidates. These practices ensure that 90% of their interns join them as full-time hires (Sullivan, 2008b). Similar practices are followed by Infosys (Birkinshaw, 2008).

University recruiting is also a line-led activity at Procter & Gamble, and many senior managers personally lead campus teams at top universities around the world. To strengthen and solidify ties with top universities, which are a key source of talent, the campus team leaders not only lead recruitment efforts, but they also fund research, make technology gifts, and participate in various activities such as conducting talks at the campus, or judging competitions (Ready & Conger, 2007). Valero goes a step further in terms of innovative practices in campus recruiting. They leverage teaching assistants as talent scouts on targeted campuses, allowing Valero to secure interns and full-time employees prior to going for formal on-campus recruiting events (Sullivan, 2006c).

Accenture taps into specific student clubs at elite universities such as Yale to recruit the brightest from campus (McConnon & Silver-Greenberg, 2008). Tata Consultancy Services (TCS) has also implemented a unique recruitment strategy to build strong campus ties. They have partnered with certain schools to design specific classes that fit TCS manpower and skill requirements (Fernández-Araoz, 2007).

Overall, campus recruiting not only helps directly in securing candidates; it also helps indirectly by creating a future pipeline of candidates based on the recruiting organization's past actions and the reputation it builds on campuses from where it routinely recruits. For example, when recruiting on campus, Motorola China offers a variety of services to students including career planning, resume writing, and team-building exercises. As a result, the organization hires about 250 to 400 interns annually from partner colleges, of which 60–80% eventually become full-time employees (Corporate Leadership Council, 2006b). Some organizations target students even before they get to any university. Organizations such as Lockheed Martin, Boeing, IBM, and General Electric undertake various activities to teach U.S. high school students science, technology, engineering, and math skills. Boeing volunteers, for example, teach science with the aid of flight simulators and a mock space shuttle with wireless computers, and Northrop Grumman, a leading global security organization, provides 7,000 high school seniors across North America with 17 weeks of elementary job training. About 6,000 students have found jobs at Northrop since the program started in 1971 (Reveron, 2009).

**Differentiating by creating an organizational brand.** Another strategy that organizations follow to attract candidates is to create a clear employer brand image. Organizations such as Google, for example, have been very successful at branding, and consequently attracting candidates (Sullivan, 2006a) who are attracted to what is implied by the brand. Organizations follow various methods to create a brand image by signaling certain positive attributes and differentiating themselves in a labor market. Branding influences familiarity and recall ability which in turn positively influence candidate attention and job application behaviors (Collins, 2007). The key idea in branding is to make the organization salient in the mind of the labor pool, so that when the opportunity arises, candidates will apply to the organization.

So which recruiting strategies based on branding have organizations followed to ensure that people sit up and take notice of them?

Hiring managers at Intel offer podcasts and host Webinars to explain jobs and opportunities, and answer questions from potential candidates. This is a low-cost method for building relationships and it also focuses on a very specific audience that the organization is trying to target (Institute of Management and Administration, Inc., 2008). Another low-cost but relatively nontraditional method to attract skilled workers is what is referred to as" proximity recruiting." Toxbox, a next-generation provider of a free service that lets you talk with your friends over live video, engaged in innovative proximity recruiting when Yahoo! was laying off its employees. Toxbox set up a taco truck outside Yahoo's campus and offered affected and other employees hot lunch while also advertising employment opportunities at Toxbox. They could thus tap into valuable talent from Yahoo! and garner enormous publicity for their relatively unknown organization (Sullivan, 2008a).

Certis CISCO, the largest auxiliary police force operator in Singapore, traveled a little farther away from their campus to develop their brand and recruit candidates. They wanted to attract relatively large numbers of auxiliary police officers and management personnel to join their growing organization. This was accomplished by sending out a "recruitment bus" to travel to the heartlands. They also organized road shows where they offered iPods to the first 100 applicants, and set up library talks to reach out to people who may not necessarily have been familiar with the force (Lee, 2007).

Organizations across the world have also used visual media to promote their brand and gain attention of applicants by making the organization salient in the minds of people exposed to the media. Donald Trump's "The Apprentice" and ESPN's "Dream Job" are well known. Organizations such as Aviva Life Insurance, Flextronics Software Systems, LG Electronics, Impetus Technologies, DNA, Yes Bank, and Denstu have also participated in a televised recruitment drive. This televised event was hosted in

India by Naukri.com, in association with CNBC TV 18, a leading business news and information channel ("The Job Show," 2006). Deloitte Consulting also leveraged visual media, and in 2007 invited its employees to create a three-minute amateur film answering the question, "What's your Deloitte?" Not only did this initiative spark widespread interest within the internal community, it eventually became a great recruiting tool for the organization (Fugure, 2009).

Finally, to stand apart in a crowded organizational world, some organizations include the applicant's family in the recruitment drive. For example, some organizations pay the expenses for an applicant's spouse to accompany him or her on a site visit. This organizational act suggests to the applicant that the organizational culture is supportive of work-family issues (Boswell, Roehling, LePine, & Moynihan, 2003). Overall, these strategies are designed to make the organization salient in the minds of potential job seekers.

**Actively targeting passive job seekers.** A survey of global CEOs shows that most organizations start their recruitment process reactively when a position opens, but it is clearly more useful to start the search process much in advance for all levels of the organization. Intuit, a software organization, known for such products as QuickBooks and TurboTax, carefully starts their search process in advance of headcount needs. They have created supply-demand maps for all organizational levels and manage to accurately anticipate more than 90% of their talent needs (Fernández-Araoz, Groysberg, & Nohria, 2009).

However, anticipating need and then targeting the correct candidate is tougher than it may seem, especially for strategic positions. In such cases, organizations may actively seek passive job seekers—people currently employed by other organizations, who are happy at their current workplace, and aren't looking actively for jobs (Chatman, O'Reilly, & Chang, 2005). Consider the case of Amazon. Amazon's business model requires the organization to manage a constant flow of new products, suppliers, and customers, as well as deliver orders by promised dates. When Amazon needed a new head for its global supply chain, it recruited Gang Yu, a professor of management science and a software entrepreneur who is one of the world's leading authorities on optimization analytics. Of course, this combination of analytical, business, and relationship skills was difficult to find, and Amazon looked at nontraditional sources to tap someone who can be seen as a "passive job seeker." SAS, a software organization, also needs candidates for niche and state-of-the-art business applications such as predictive modeling or recursive partitioning (a type of decision tree analysis). To fill these niche positions, they begin recruiting up to 18 months before they need to fill such positions (Davenport, 2006).

Consider yet another example. Chiron, a pharmaceutical organization, operates in a very tight labor market where only a few potential candidates exist around the world for certain scientific positions. Chiron recruiters learn the business specifics from various business units and try to build relationships with passive job seeker scientists who are in turn open to talking with someone who understands their work and business (Corporate Leadership Council Recruiting Roundtable, 2006).

Passive job seekers can be sought from various places and in various ways. Cisco recruiters follow innovative recruiting tactics such as attending garden shows or microbrewery festivals—any potential places that their target candidates frequent. At one point Cisco had also rigged its Web site to spot candidates from rival organization 3Com and greeted these people with a page that asked them if they wanted a job at Cisco (Kiger, 2003). Though this may sound like an outrageous strategy, recruiters also frequent bars where unsuspecting target candidates may congregate (Sullivan, 2006b).

The other strategy that organizations are following to tap into key candidates in a tight labor market is to look at the temporary or part-time labor pool. To target such candidates, organizations are leveraging niche job boards. Stay-at-home mothers who are looking for jobs can be recruited through channels such as *Working Mother* Magazine, or bluesuitmom.com; temporary workers can be targeted via channels such as temps.com; retired employees can be tapped through retiredbrains.com; and finally, diverse demographic groups can be tapped into through latina.com or blackcareerwoman.com. Organizations such as United Parcel Service (UPS) that leverage a large temporary workforce customize part of their Web site to target the part-time candidates. For example, their Web site showcases employee testimonials in terms of what the organization has done for the specific demographic groups, and why it is therefore a good fit for other such candidates (Corporate Leadership Council, 2006a). L'Oreal follows a similar strategy and highlights women scientists on their Web site to attract other such employees (Institute of Management and Administration, Inc., 2008). Finally, the U.S. Army uses simulation video games directed at recruits who are technologically sophisticated and avid gamers (Sullivan, 2006a).

In sum, scarcity in the labor market can be dealt with by creating a campus presence, making the organizational brand salient in the minds of potential candidates, and actively tapping passive job seekers. In the next section we discuss how organizations adapt their recruitment strategies when there is abundance in the labor market.

**Abundance in the labor market.** At first glance, it may seem like an ideal situation—organizations have a large pool of candidates to choose from, but surveys and studies show that finding good candidates is tough even in times of high unemployment where the supply from the external labor market is not tight (Dessler, 2008). To make matters worse, many job applicants who are in the labor market looking for jobs have an incomplete or inaccurate understanding of what a job opening involves, are not sure what they want from a position, and do not have insight with regard to their knowledge, skills, and abilities (Breaugh, 2008). Thus, abundance in the labor market implies that organizations have to sift through a deluge of non-matched candidates. What do organizations do in such conditions? There are various strategies—they can create multiple rounds to zero in on the right candidate, leverage an external skills database if available, leverage employees as ambassadors to spot and attract talent, and target boomerang employees.

**Creating multiple rounds to zero in on the right candidate**. Consider the sheer number of applicants at Infosys. Every year, 1.3 million candidates apply for a job at Infosys, and about 17,000 are selected. How does Infosys deal with this large number? Recruiters have created various rounds to zero in on the right candidates. Online applications are screened carefully, and only 10% of the applicants are invited to take an online test designed to measure applicant technical and written skills. This test is conducted by an external vendor and less than 1% of people who do well on this test are considered further (Birkinshaw, 2008). Thus, capitalizing on technology allows Infosys to narrow an immense number of possible candidates down to a more select and manageable amount.

**Leveraging an external skills database**. To sift through the vast number of applications, industry bodies are also helping organizations. For example, The National Association of Software and Services Companies (NASSCOM), the chief industry body for the Indian information technology (IT) and technology services companies, has created a National Skills Registry (NSR), a centralized database of all employees of the technology services and business process outsourcing (BPO) organizations in India. Launched in 2006, the NSR contains third-party–verified personal, qualification, and career information of IT professionals. Organizations in the IT and BPO industry leverage this skills database to inform their recruitment practices.

**Leveraging current employees as ambassadors to spot and attract talent**. Cisco is another organization that gets many applicants. To ensure they hire the correct candidate from many applicants, Cisco follows an innovative strategy by carefully targeting "active job seekers." Cisco noticed that people would click on their Web site for information about the organization, and wanted to know more in terms of the work opportunities available. Cisco created a "make friends @ Cisco" button on their Web site, and when people clicked on this button, they got a call from current Cisco employees who talked about their work. A few years ago, Cisco received 100 to 150 requests per week from applicants wishing to be introduced to a "friend@Cisco," and 60% of the people who joined Cisco did so because they had a friend working there already (Chatman, O'Reilly, & Chang, 2005). Cisco also relies heavily on employee referrals, and about 55–60% of its hires in the sales organization are from referrals ("Perfecting your employee referrals program," *Human Capital*, 2006).

The Cisco example brings up an important point. Employees are a good resource in terms of sifting through candidates as well as attracting candidates ("Perfecting your employee referrals program," 2006). Employees understand how an organization functions and who may be a good fit. Recognizing this, some organizations have very successfully used employee referral programs. At Sasken, 30% of the top management level recruiting is done through referrals, whereas 32% of all hiring is through referrals. Other organizations leverage their social networks to spot the right candidates. At Eli Lilly, for example, key new hires are asked to identify good performers that the organization can eventually target. Eli Lilly also hosts "bring your own rolodex" meetings where senior staff are encouraged to network with passive but high-value potential candidates. Organizations can thus develop a large talent pool proactively and much in advance of actual staffing needs by tapping into networks of employees (insiders) as well as trusted suppliers, customers, and former employees (outside-insiders) (Fernández-Araoz, Groysberg, & Nohria, 2009).

**Targeting boomerang employees**. The final strategy we discuss in this section is called boomerang recruiting. Boomerang employees, also commonly referred to as rehires, are former employees who return to an organization. Oftentimes, employees leave the organization only to realize that their ex-employer wasn't as bad as they'd thought. At the same time, the ex-employer may want the same employee back, given her skill set that was developed within the organization and thus well suited to it. Boomerang recruiting is cost efficient because of lower costs of retraining such employees and building their organizational commitment (naukrihub.com, 2009). Organizations such as McKinsey, Microsoft, Deloitte, Ernst and Young, Booz Allen, and Bain, to name a few, are pioneering corporate alumni programs to track good employees who have left the organization and may want to come back (Puri, 2009). Booz Allen Hamilton has gone further, and has created a dedicated team called the "comeback kids" that has proven very successful in encouraging former employees to return (Sullivan, 2006a).

In sum, abundance in the labor market can be dealt with by creating multiple rounds of recruiting, leveraging an external skills database if available, leveraging employees as ambassadors, and targeting boomerang employees. In the next section we direct our attention to endogenous or internal organizational factors that influence recruitment strategies.

# Endogenous Contingency Factors in Recruitment

Various organizational level or internal factors influence an organization's recruiting strategies. In this section we elaborate on two factors that can have an impact on recruiting strategies and outcomes: the size of the organization, and its technological sophistication. Although various indicators of size such as sales volume or other performance measures are used, the most common indicator of size is the number of employees, as this indicates both current capacity for work and current performance level (Scott, 2003). In this section we also use the word *size* to denote number of employees, as this has a direct relationship with human resource strategies. Technological sophistication of the organization implies organizational comfort with leveraging technology, and this also has a direct relationship with human resource strategies, especially attracting and tracking candidates. It is quite possible that large global organizations are also technologically more sophisticated than small local setups.

## Organizational Size

Organizational size influences the structure of departments, their functioning, and strategies of an organization. As organizations grow, a simple informal model of control through mutual adjustment and social interactions gives way to more standardized control (Mintzberg, 1979). Human resource strategies and recruitment practices in particular also become more formal, bureaucratic, and resource intensive than practices of smaller organizations (Fisher, Schoenfeldt, & Shaw, 2006). Large organizations can follow two broad strategies when recruiting: formalize recruiting processes across the organization, and leverage the internal labor market. This is an especially important point for large global organizations that can systematically comb their own ranks to spot and deploy talent where required.

**Formalizing recruitment procedures**. Formalizing external recruitment procedures is important because large organizations are involved in recurring transactions (such as recruiting many people) and can economize costs per recruit (Bhattacharya, 2008). Recruiting costs of large organizations such as Infosys can be amortized over many hiring decisions. Further, large organizations are more likely to have dedicated recruiters who are formally trained. Larger organizations are also more likely to use more screening procedures than smaller organizations because large organizations have the resources available to design or acquire (and validate) multiple screening devices such as psychological tests, physical abilities tests, and so forth (Birkinshaw, 2008). Finally, formalization is important as large organizations face institutional pressures and public scrutiny and are answerable to multiple stakeholders (Barber, Wesson, Roberson, & Taylor, 1999; Kossek, 1987).

**Leveraging the internal labor market**. Considering that formal procedures in recruiting can be seen through previous sections and examples, this section will focus on recruiting in the large internal labor market that exists in large organizations. A 2004 poll conducted by Development Dimensions International showed that internal recruiting for management positions was at 53% within the 350 organizations polled. This was an increase from 44% in 1999 (Little, 2007).

Why do (or should) organizations recruit from their internal labor pool? Recruiting from within has many advantages. It may be relatively cheaper to attract and hire candidates from within the organization than outside, it is a great retention tool, and, finally, a great way to develop and nurture talent (Plemmons, 2009). In fact, a recent report shows that Skanska, one of the world's leading construction groups, which has a presence across 19 countries and employs over 60,000 employees worldwide, saved several million dollars last year by recruiting internally (Resourcing, 2009). Recognizing the importance of recruiting from within, organizations such as General Electric and United Parcel Service put great emphasis on developing talent that can be leveraged in multiple units of the organization when needs arise (Fisher, Schoenfeldt, & Shaw, 2006).

How do organizations tap into the available labor pool to fill positions as they open up? Consider the cases of Cisco and Houston's M. D. Anderson Cancer Center. Cisco created and launched a software application called the Pathfinder. This software, used by about 20% of the organization's engineers to change jobs, allows employees to load their résumés into the system, sift through openings by location, career level, and other criteria, and then contact the hiring managers in other business units directly (Kiger, 2003). When employees self-attract and apply in some organizations, internal recruiters at M. D. Anderson actively look at the availability of internal talent and projected hiring needs, and target key people (Plemmons, 2009). Managers at ANZ Financial Services (Australia and New Zealand Banking Group Limited) actively mentor junior colleagues, and between half to one-third of the financial planners are recruited from different units of the organization (Egan, 2007). Other organizations such as Merck and the U.S. military have leveraged technology to spot and recruit internal candidates. These organizations use human resources information systems such as SAP and PeopleSoft to tap into the internal labor pool (Bohlander & Snell, 2004).

Organizations endowed with large internal labor markets can also use a process called job posting and bidding to leverage internal talent. This process can be as simple as posting an opening in the cafeteria to putting it up on the internal Web server. Texas Instruments, Xerox, and Cisco, to name a few of many organizations, do this quite effectively (Bohlander & Snell, 2004). Overall, size affords recruiters and hiring managers a large internal pool of talent, and possibly a formalized predetermined recruitment process that can be used across locations.

## Technological Sophistication

The final contingency we discuss in this chapter is the level of organizations' ever-expanding technological sophistication. Whether the organization is recruiting internally or externally, within social networks or outside, or in tight or loose labor markets, organizations can effectively use technology to attract candidates. After all, the world is getting smaller and recruits are sometimes just a click away (Friedman, 2006). In the sections below we describe how various organizations have leveraged technology to recruit candidates. We identify three broad recruiting trends in this section: leveraging social networking sites, deploying creative Internet technologies, and creating attractive organizational Web sites.

**Leveraging social networking sites**. Social networking sites continue to gain enormous popularity and momentum. To target specific types of candidates, and to broaden their recruitment efforts, organizations are increasingly trying to tap into the large number of people active on social networking sites such as LinkedIn. Web sites like Orkut, Facebook, and other social media sites are the new haunting places for human resource professionals these days to scout for talent that can deliver results (Shah, 2007). Technology organizations like Wipro, and Tata Consultancy Services have started recruiting heavily through social media networks. Ernst and Young also heavily leverages Facebook to target students (Sullivan, 2008b). It's not just the traditional civilian large organizations that are leveraging social networking sites to recruit people. The U.S. Central Intelligence Agency, the U.S. Navy, and the Army are also using Facebook and Twitter to recruit talent (Bruce, 2007; MSNBC report, 2009). In fact, a recent survey by Development Dimensions International showed that 25% of recruiters used social networking sites for information about candidates, and 52% of them have used online information to make selection decisions (Recruiter, 2009), a trend that is likely to continue considering the growing millions of active and passive job seekers that throng such Web sites.

Along with organizations, professional head hunters across the world are also making social networking sites a part of their recruitment strategy, and are setting up dedicated resources to sift through these sites for global recruiting (CyberMedia, 2007; Sachitanand & Bhattacharya, 2008). LinkedIn is becoming such a popular recruiting source the world over that professional recruiters are demanding the same full access that organizations have in order to have access to more candidates (Goodfellow, 2008).

**Deploying creative Internet technologies.** Organizations are also increasingly using creative technologies to spot and attract candidates. Some organizations are using the Web site X-raying technique to access the passive talent pool. This technique allows recruiters to see all pages on an organizational Web site that are not protected by a firewall. X-rays can be done using the advanced search feature on Web sites such as Google or Hotbot. Another technique used by organizations is called Web site flipping. Flipping allows recruiters to find all Web pages linked to a given Web site. For example, recruiters can access individual home pages that are linked to organizational Web sites. Such cross-linked sites can yield valuable passive candidate information. One has to keep in mind though, that such techniques are not legal throughout the world.

Yet another technique to get access to job seekers is using name-generating software. This software can be purchased and allows recruiters to sift through the Internet to generate names, profiles, and resumes of individuals meeting the search parameters specified by the recruiter. Intel, in 2004, worked with a vendor to create such customized software. This software "crawled" through a list of pre-programmed sites to access very specific types of candidates (Corporate Leadership Council and Recruiting Roundtable, 2006). Valero also automated part of their recruiting efforts and programmed "Web spiders" to crawl, retrieve, and upload candidates into their internal applicant tracking system based on both current and projected needs (Sullivan, 2006c). Wachovia, on the other hand, paid for this service instead of developing one in-house. Various vendors such as ZoomInfo, LinkedIn, and SearchExpo provide this service for a fee. Other technology-savvy organizations such as Microsoft encourage and actively leverage recruiter and employee blogs. Such blogs can be used to target passive job seekers who are surfing the net. They can be used to build a relationship with the potential employee as well as create an organizational brand.

**Creating attractive organizational Web sites**. The final trend we discuss is how organizations can leverage their own Web site to attract candidates. Skoda Minotti, for example, uses a rather innovative way to attract applicants. Their Web site hosts a game similar to "photo audit," where players spot differences in photos within a given time and have their scores displayed in a competitive fashion against other players. Potential applicants from various campuses, who are playing the online game, get ranked against each other and can see scores of others from their schools. High scorers are given rewards. This increases Web traffic to Skoda's site and gives Skoda a database of potential hires (Ebenstein, 2008). Skoda Minotti and The Cheesecake Factory both use a promotional recruitment video on their Web sites that explains how the organization runs, how people are such a key asset, and how the potential recruit will enjoy working for this great organization. For organizations that cannot host videos on their own Web sites, there are other cyber places such as VlogYourJob.com. VlogYourJob.com is the United Kingdom's first online video recruitment Web site, created by Indigo Red, a U.K.-based recruitment consultancy. This Web site encourages organizations to post vlogs—online short videos—as job advertisements. It also allows recruiters to give potential candidates a taste of what it's like at the organizations by posting a video about their working environment (Marketing Week, 2007). Thus, organizations that have technological sophistication can leverage both in-house and externally developed technologies to recruit.

## Conclusion

We defined recruiting as a process of finding and attracting the right candidates and encouraging them to apply for certain positions. We drew upon recruitment research and organizational examples to outline various contingencies that managers should consider when undertaking recruitment initiatives. So what does all this mean for your own recruiting efforts? How can you create an effective recruiting strategy in your organization? As outlined in Table 5.1, we especially argued for the importance of the macro sociocultural context and the external labor market as the two key exogenous factors that have an impact on recruitment. We also pointed to the importance of organizational size and evolving technological sophistication as the two key endogenous factors that affect recruitment. For each of these contingencies, we have distilled lessons based on organizational theory and examples. For instance, when discussing the social context, we have argued for the importance of sensitizing and training global managers about different values and expectations across the globe, and of creating clear job descriptions that can be implemented irrespective of where the managers recruit from. Further, on the topic of the external labor context, we have highlighted the importance of creating salience in the minds of potential applicants and tapping passive candidates in a scarce labor market. In terms of an abundant labor market, we have pointed out the importance of creating multiple rounds of recruiting, leveraging external databases, internal employees, and targeting ex-employees. We have argued that large organizations can formalize procedures and tap the internal labor pool. Finally, technology can be leveraged to attract candidates. Specifically, organizations can leverage social networking sites, deploy creative Internet technologies, and create effective and attractive organizational Web sites.

Overall, we recognize that no two organizations are the same, and contingencies and recruitment strategies differ per organization. Although there is no magic formula for recruiting, and some of these techniques may force you to think outside the box, the benefits of charting a well-defined recruiting strategy are clear.

## References

Alsahlawi, K. A., & Gardener, E. P. (2004). Human resource and economic development: The case of Saudi Arabia. *Journal of Third World Studies, 21*, 175–190.

Aycan, Z. (2005). The interplay between cultural and institutional/structural contingencies in human resource management practices. *International Journal of Human Resource Management, 16*, 1083–1119.

Aycan, Z., Al-Hamadi, A. B., Davis, A., & Budhwar, P. S. (2007). Cultural orientations and preferences for HRM policies and practices: The case of Oman. *International Journal of Human Resource Management, 18*, 11–32.

Barber, A. E. (1998). *Recruiting employees.* Thousand Oaks, CA: Sage.

Barber, A. E., Wesson, M. J., Roberson, Q. M., & Taylor, M. S. (1999). A tale of two job markets: Organizational size and its effects on hiring practices and job search behavior. *Personnel Psychology, 52*, 841–867.

Berkowitz, P., & Muller-Bonanni, T. (2007). *International labor and employment law: A practical guide (International Practitioner's Deskbook Series).* Chicago: American Bar Association.

Bhattacharya, S. (2008). From talent crunch to cash crunch. *Business Today, 17*, 126–129.

Birkinshaw, J. (2008). Infosys: Computing the power of people. *Business Strategy Review,* 18–23.

Bohlander, G., & Snell, S. (2004). *Managing human resources.* Mason, OH: Thomson/South-Western.

Boswell, W. R., Roehling, M. V., LePine, M. A., & Moynihan, L. M. (2003). Individual job-choice decisions and the impact of job attributes and recruitment practices: A longitudinal field study. *Human Resource Management, 42*, 23–37.

Breaugh, J. A. (2008). Employee recruitment: Current knowledge and important areas for future research. *Human Resource Management Review, 18*, 103–118.

Brewster, C., Wood, J., & Brookes, M. (2008). Similarity, isomorphism or duality? Recent survey evidence on the human resource management policies of multinational corporations. *British Journal of Management, 19*, 320–343.

Bruce, C. (2007). CIA gets in your Face(book). Retrieved on May 9, 2009, from www.wired.com/techbiz/it/news/2007/01/72545.

Budhwar, P. S. (2001) Doing business in India. *Thunderbird International Business Review, 43*, 549–568.

Budhwar, P. S. (2003). Employment relations in India. *Employee Relations, 25*, 132–148.

Budhwar, P. S., & Khatri, N. (2001). A comparative study of HR practices in Britain and India. *International Journal of Human Resource Management, 12*, 800–826.

Charan, R., & Colvin, G (2000). The right fit. *Fortune, 141*, 226–238.

Chatman, J., O'Reilly, C., & Chang, V. (2005). Cisco Systems: Developing a human capital strategy. *California Management Review, 47*, 137–167.

Collins, C. J. (2007). The Interactive effects of recruitment practices and product awareness on job seekers' employer knowledge and application behaviors. *Journal of Applied Psychology, 92*, 180–190.

Corporate Leadership Council Report (2006a). Part-time employee recruiting strategies.

Corporate Leadership Council Report (2006b). Recruiting from a global talent pool.

Corporate Leadership Council and Recruiting Roundtable Report (2006). Creating a passive candidate recruiting strategy.

CyberMedia India Online Ltd. (2007). Network sites become networking platforms. Retrieved on February 17, 2009, from www.ciol.com/News/News-Reports/Networking-sites-become-recruitment-platform/131008111373/0/.

Davenport, T. (2006). Competing on analytics. *Harvard Business Review, 84*, 99–107.

Despeignes, P. (2005). Offshoring: A reality check. *Fortune*, 89 .

Dessler, G. (2008). *Human resource management*. New Delhi: Prentice-Hall of India.

Ebenstein, J. (2008). Hunting for CPAs: Recruiting and retention tactics. *CPA Practice Management Forum, 4*, 5–7.

Egan, L. (2007). Digging deeper for productivity gains. *Money Management, 21*, 40–41.

Farrell, D. & Grant, A. J. (2005). China's looming talent shortage. *McKinsey Quarterly, 4*, 70–79.

Fernández-Araoz, C. (2007). Making people decisions in the new global environment. *MIT Sloan Management Review, 49*, 16–20.

Fernández-Araoz, C., Groysberg, B., & Nohria, N. (2009). The definitive guide to recruiting in good times and bad. *Harvard Business Review. 87*, 74–84.

Fisher, C. D., Schoenfeldt, L. F., & Shaw, J. B. (2006). *Human resource management.* New Delhi: Houghton Mifflin.

Friedman, T. L. (2006). *The world is flat: A brief history of the twenty-first century.* New York: Farrar, Straus & Giroux.

Fugure, B. (2009). Movies with a message: Deloitte employees unleash their inner director and make the company's first-ever film festival a success. *Communication World*, 40–41.

Goodfellow, C. (2008). Anger over limited access to LinkedIn. *Recruiter News*, 6 .

Guthridge, M., Komm, A. B., & Lawson, E. (2008). Making talent a strategic priority. *McKinsey Quarterly, 1*, 48–59.

Hill, C. W. L. (2008). *Global business today.* New York: McGraw-Hill/Irwin.

Immelt, J. R., Govindarajan, V., & Trimble, C. (2009). How GE is disrupting itself. *Harvard Business Review*, forthcoming.

Institute of Management and Administration, Inc (2008). Best practices: How top employers are using web-based recruitment technologies now.

International Labour Organization Report. (2009). Global employment trends.

Jackson, S., & Schuler, R. (1995). Understanding human resource management in the context of organizations and their environments. *Annual Review of Psychology, 46*, 237–264.

The job show—India's first televised job hunt by Naukri.com and CNBC TV. (2006). *Human Capital, 9*, 8 .

Kanungo, R. N., & Jaeger, A. M. (1990). Introduction: The need for indigenous management in developing countries. In A. M. Jaeger and R. N. Kanungo (Eds.), *Management in Developing Countries.* London: Routledge.

Kiger, P. J. (2003). Cisco's Homegrown Gamble. *Workforce, 82*, 28–32.

Kossek, E. (1987). Human resources management innovation. *Human Resource Management, 26*, 71–92.

Kulkarni, M., Lengnick-Hall, M. L., & Valk, R. (2010). Employee perceptions of repatriation in an emerging economy: The Indian experience. *Human Resource Management*, forthcoming.

Laurent, A. (1986). The cross-cultural puzzle of international human resource management. *Human Resource Management, 25*, 91–102.

Leat, M., & El-Kot, G. (2007). HRM practices in Egypt: The influence of national context? *International Journal of Human Resource Management, 18*, 147–158.

Lee, J. (2007). Transforming the HR function from reactive to proactive: A CISCO case study. *Human Capital, 11*, 28–31.

Lengnick-Hall, C A., & Lengnick-Hall, M. L. (1988). Strategic human resources management: A review of the literature and a proposed typology. *Academy of Management Review, 13*, 454–470.

Little, D. (2007). Promotional material. *Journal of Property Management, 72*, 38–41.

Marketing Week (August 16, 2007). Indigo Red unveils UK's 'first' video jobs website. Retrieved on April 8, 2009, from www.mad .co.uk/Main/News/Disciplines/Media/Digital/Articles/ e5d92fac9b704bd4b5695455450f911b/Indigo-Red-unveils-UK's- 'first'-video-jobs-website.html.

McConnon, A., & Silver-Greenberg, J. (2008). Meet your new recruits: They want to eat your lunch. Retrieved on May 11, 2009. from www .businessweek.com/magazine/content/08_21/b4085042677127 .htm.

McGaughey, S. L., & De Cieri, H. (1999). Reassessment of convergence and divergence dynamics: Implications for international HRM. *International Journal of Human Resource Management, 10*, 235–250.

Mendonca, M., & Kanungo, R. N. (1996). Impact of culture on performance management in developing countries. *International Journal of Manpower, 17*, 65–75.

Millikin, J. P., & Fu, D. (2005). The global leadership of Carlos Ghosn at Nissan. *Thunderbird International Review, 47*, 121–137.

Mintzberg, H. (1979). *The structuring of organizations: A synthesis of the research.* Englewood Cliffs, NJ: Prentice-Hall.

Morris, B., Sellers, P., Schlosser, J., Florian, E., Helyar, J., & Neering, P. (2004). The real story. *Fortune, 149*, 84–98.

MSNBC Associated Press, May 1, 2009. Pentagon targets recruits on Facebook, Twitter. Retrieved on May 9, 2009, from www.msnbc.msn .com/id/30513702/.

Nakache, P. (1997). Cisco's recruiting edge. *Fortune, 136*, 275–276.

Namazie, P., & Frame, P. (2007). Developments in human resource management in Iran. *International Journal of Human Resource Management, 18*, 159–171.

National Association of Software and Service Companies. (2006). 2006 IT industry Communiqué for the Academia. Retrieved on February 10,

2009, from www.nasscom.in/Nasscom/templates/NasscomSearch .aspx?cx=018416552530915382824%3Ahxwavbrtgx8&cof= FORID%3A11&q=IT+industry+Communiqu%C3%A9+for+the +Academia&sa=Search#858.

Naukrihub.com. (2009). Boomerang employees. Retrieved on April 2, 2009, from www.naukrihub.com/hr-today/boomeranging-employees.html.

Perfecting your employee referrals program. (April 2006). *Human Capital, 9*, 16–19.

Plemmons, P. (2009). Conducting an internal search. *Trustee, 62*, 26–27.

Puri, S. (2009). Corporate alumni and boomerang recruiting programs. Retrieved on April 2, 2009, from http://toostep.com/insight/corporate-alumni-and-boomerang-recruiting-programs.

Ready, D. A., & Conger, J. A. (2007). Make your company a talent factory. *Harvard Business Review. 85*, 68–77.

Ready, D. A., Hill, L. A., & Conger, J. A. (2008). Winning the race for talent in emerging markets. *Harvard Business Review, 86*, 62–70.

Recruiter Report (April 2009). Retrieved on August 21, 2009, from www.recruiter.co.uk/searchResults.aspx?cmd=GoToPage&val=1.

Rees, C. J., Mamman, A., & Braik, A. B. (2007). Emiratization as a strategic HRM change initiative: Case study evidence from a UAE petroleum company. *International Journal of Human Resource Management, 18*, 33–53.

Resourcing (2009). Skanska's career growth prospects cuts recruitment. *Resourcing, 11*, 7 .

Reveron, D. (2009). Recruiting trends. *US Black Engineer & Information Technology, 33*, 65–65.

Rosenzweig, P. M., & Nohria, N. (1994). Influences on human resource management in multinational corporations. *Journal of International Business Studies, 20*, 229–51.

Sachitanand, R., & Bhattacharya, S. (2008). Working the web. *Business Today, 17*, 170–172.

Schuler, R., & Tarique, I. (2007). International human resource management: A North American perspective, a thematic update and suggestions for future research. *International Journal of Human Resource Management, 18*, 717–744.

Scott, R. (2003). *Organizations: Rational, natural and open systems* (5th ed.). Englewood Cliffs, NJ: Prentice Hall.

Shah, R. (2007). Companies start recruiting through social media websites! Retrieved on February 17, 2009, from www.watblog .com/2007/11/30/companies-start-recruiting-through-social-media-websites/.

Sharma, I. J. (1984). The culture context of Indian managers. *Management and Labour Studies, 9,* 72–80.

Shilling, D. (2008). *Complete guide to human resources and the law.* Gaithersburg, MD: Aspen.

Sparrow, P. R., & Budhwar, P. S. (1997). Competition and change: Mapping the Indian HRM recipe against world-wide patterns. *Journal of World Business, 32,* 224–242.

Sullivan, J. (2006a). 12 best recruiting practices to copy. Retrieved on February 12, 2009, from www.ere.net/2006/09/25/12-best-recruiting-practices-to-copy/.

Sullivan, J. (2006b). Recruiting at bars and other places prospects gather. Retrieved on May 1, 2009, from www.drjohnsullivan.com/content/view/16/27/.

Sullivan, J. (2006c). Six best practices in recruiting. Retrieved on May 1, 2009, from www.drjohnsullivan.com/content/view/27/27/.

Sullivan, J. (2008a). Recruiting strategies—Proximity recruiting using a taco truck. Retrieved on February 12, 2009, from www.ere.net/2008/12/15/recruiting-strategies-%E2%80%93-proximity-recruiting-using-a-taco-truck/.

Sullivan, J. (2008b). Best practices in recruiting: 2008 ERE award winners. Retrieved on February 12, 2009, from www.ere.net/2008/04/07/best-practices-in-recruiting-2008-ere-award-winners/.

Tayeb, M. (1987). Contingency theory and culture: A study of matched English and Indian manufacturing firms. *Organization Studies, 8,* 241–261.

Tayeb, M. (1995). The competitive advantage of nations: The role of HRM and its socio-cultural context. *The International Review of Human Resource Management, 6,* 588–605.

Tayeb, M. (1997). Islamic revival in Asia and human resource management. *Employee Relations, 19,* 352–364.

Tayeb, M. (1998). Transfer of HRM practices across cultures: An American company in Scotland. *The International Journal of Human Resource Management, 9,* 332–358.

Zhu, Y., Warner, M., & Rowley, C. (2007). Human resource management with "Asian" characteristics: A hybrid people-management system in East Asia. *International Journal of Human Resource Management, 18,* 745–768.

# CHAPTER 6

# Global Selection
## Selection in International Contexts

Tim Carey, David Herst, and Wynne Chan

## What Is Global Selection, Anyway?

It is now a cliché to note that the world is changing rapidly and that the notion of work is feeling the effects of that change. But the rapidly changing world's impact on work is being felt more acutely as the pace of that change speeds up. Nowhere is this more important than in selection. Where selection used to be simply finding the person who would fit best in a well-defined and stable job, now it is much more complex. All of the five "W's" of work are changing—who, what, when, where, and why. Different types of people are doing new types of work in different locations and even for different reasons. It is not uncommon anymore for a 20-year-old to create a new industry, such as Adam Zuckerman's Facebook, and a 50-year-old to be considered unfit for many jobs despite his experience, because the technology he learned is so outdated. Moreover, a career may begin in one country but then progress through five other countries before it ends. Finally, as industries disappear and others are born, one person may have several different careers in her lifetime.

Given these aspects of the work world, it is not a stretch to say that selection rules have changed. Moreover, when we add the necessity for dealing with different ethnic groups, nationalities, or cultures, the problem is further compounded—yet moving between different cultures is becoming more important for companies, especially multinational companies (MNCs). A representative of Shell, Inc. notes that: "If you're truly global then you're hiring in here [the United States] people who are immediately going to go and work in The Hague and vice versa. So in essence you wind up in a global job market and the standardization [of staffing systems] ensures that you are applying the same standards and using the same tools to [obtain] the best candidates who are going to be part of a global community" (Ryan, Wiechmann, & Hemingway, 2003, p. 86). Clearly, being able to move effectively from one culture to another is becoming a requirement for at least some employees.

One example of this is the changing nature of companies in the human resource consulting arena in the Greater China region. Where even ten years ago one would have hired a few expatriate (expat) consultants and brought them into the region to deliver services to MNCs that were also just moving in, now one must search for well-educated locals (many of whom were educated out of the region) who speak three languages (Mandarin, Cantonese, and English) and have experience in MNCs. Having an expat who speaks only English or a local who speaks only Mandarin limits the capabilities of that person to deliver a number of services in the region.

The goal of this chapter, then, is to highlight some areas that might have been missed when considering selection in a global context. Specifically, we will discuss some of the major issues when selecting across cultures, including how to effectively develop tests, manage cultural issues in assessment centers, and differentiate among the types of employees who are assessed. We will focus more on practical solutions than theoretical considerations and at times we will be less empirically based than anecdotally relevant, although we do reference some recent research. Finally, Asia, with a particular focus on China, and the Middle East will figure largely in our analysis because two of the authors have significant experience working as consultants in those regions.

One way in which local selection and global selection are similar has to do with the need to distinguish between the selection of more senior-level managers and those at a junior, possibly nonmanagement level. Though most would probably say that the hiring of the more senior-level managers is more important and thus requires more resources, the selection of more junior-level managers has a major impact on not only how the company does in the present, but also how well the company will do in the future, as the junior-level managers are expected to take on the senior roles later (assuming the company can retain them). In any case, each level requires a different approach. One would use mass-selection tools for lower-level selection and more precise, targeted tools for higher-level selection. However, there are significant differences across countries when selecting among lower-level applicants. For example, it is not uncommon to get a request in China to devise a selection system that will sift the applications of 10,000 recent graduates down to 20 candidates who will be offered positions. Similarly, Friedman (2005) mentions a case where a company receives 700 applications per day for entry-level positions. It is probably rare to get that many applications in most markets, and it requires the use of significant resources to ensure that such a process is handled correctly. Thus, this is an issue that should be considered by those selecting lower-level candidates in some international markets—expending significant resources just to get these candidates in the door.

However, selection is further complicated when recruiting across cultures. This is simply because there are cultural differences between the candidates. For example, as Ryan and Tippins (2009) point out, one important difference between cultures is on the assertiveness and emotional expression dimensions. Whether a person is to be hired for a low-level or a managing director position, it is likely that the same selection tools will not work the same way across different countries because of differences in this characteristic. A Thai person may act in a very unassertive manner in a group discussion, whereas an American may be quite assertive in comparison. When both are put into the same group, one risks that the more assertive candidates are rated higher when Western instruments are used, because assertive people are more likely to speak up and be rewarded. If this were a deciding factor for selection, then the company would hire more assertive (Western) candidates and thus end up with a staff that may not relate well to the various local cultures into which they are placed.

At the same time, there are cases in which the use of a Western assessment process in a different culture would be warranted, despite its clashing with some of the incumbents' own cultural mores. First, if that person is tasked with interacting with both her own culture and that of the "parent" country, she will need to be conversant in the parent country's culture. For example, speaking with headquarters is typically an important part of the jobs of many in a foreign office of an MNC, from the country managing director to lower-ranking managers, as the latter are often matrixed with a "dotted line" to the global headquarters function. This will necessitate the candidate being able to successfully negotiate with other, sometimes very different, cultures. If she cannot do so effectively, she should be considered someone who can possibly be effective in her own country (which the assessment process might not be able to indicate) but not in a context where there are other nationalities. So the Western assessment process would effectively weed out these candidates.

Second, in a Western assessment process a number of competencies are typically measured. If the measurement process effectively assesses the other competencies, then even where it is less valid on one or more (in this case, over- or underscoring on assertiveness) the overall results may be positive. Thus, the candidate may not be strong at assertiveness, but if she is able to do other things well (such as demonstrate technical competence, openness, and judgment) she may be a good fit for the position with some assertiveness training.

By the same rationale, when selecting more junior managers, one should probably not expect a strong showing on competencies related to intercultural competence. At this level, expertise in the local context is both necessary and sufficient. One cannot expect a 27-year-old manager who has never been out of his own country to be able to rise above his own culture and deal effectively with those from a second or third culture. Moreover, at this level, he probably will not have to, other than possibly dealing with the senior executives who may be from the host country. Given that, he will have time to learn such skills if put in the right situations and mentored and coached successfully. For this group, then, the Western (or imported) approach probably would not work. Instead, the local culture must be examined by the creator of the assessment procedure and the idiosyncratic aspects of that culture must be built into the process. This includes the necessity to take the local culture into account when creating tests, as will be discussed below.

To summarize, then, the following questions must be asked before assessing a local candidate for a position in a foreign office of an MNC. First, how much will that person deal with the head office? If the answer is "a lot" then cultural competence should be assessed. If that person will be expected to stay in the host country and only much later achieve a position where she would interact with the head office, then a locally based assessment process should be used. Second, of the competencies considered, which are "must haves" and which are "nice to have"? It may be that given strength on some competencies, the overall result may indicate a good candidate who can be trained where necessary.

## Why Bother?

When we are talking about selecting senior managers or high potential employees (HIPOs), these are relatively few within an organization (if there were many HIPOs, they would not be called that—not everyone can be—or wants to be—a HIPO). Consequently, it might seem that organizations should spend more resources and effort trying to accurately and efficiently select entry-level employees, as these are greater in number. A case could certainly be made for this. However, HIPOs and senior executives are expected to have the greatest impact on the company; if the company does not get this right, poor decisions may compromise the growth of the company (Hewitt Associates, 2004) or, in the worst case, seriously damage the company, as happened at Enron ("Enron Scandal at-a-Glance," 2002) and Barings Bank (Chua-Eoan, 2007).Thus, at the end of the day, attention to both very senior managers and HIPOs is prudent.

Another issue to consider when creating a selection system is that there are strong social networks in many collectivist cultures (Goodwin, 1999). Put another way, people talk. If they discuss the poor selection methods used by a given company, that company may be relegated to last choice for the best applicants. Or perhaps even worse, candidates may join the company, get experience quickly, and then move on, thereby decreasing long-term retention rates and organizational stability, requiring more resources to be put toward recruitment, selection, and ultimately decreasing profits. To this point, Harter, Schmidt, and Hayes (2002) demonstrated in a meta-analysis that employee engagement and business outcomes are related. Sparrow, Brewster, and Harris (2004) speak of employees as ambassadors for the company as part of "employer branding." This means that essentially each employee who interacts with external stakeholders can have a profound influence on how the brand offering of the organization is perceived by others. This research points to the critical need to ensure a good fit and keep high-performers happy at the company. Thus, the organization must send candidates clear, consistent messages about what the company needs and wants through the recruitment process.

## Need for Cross-Cultural Skills

Workplaces are becoming increasingly diverse and, in general, cultural diversity has increased significantly across the workforce in the United States (Toosi, 2002) and other countries (Moorhead, 2010). Workplace interactions also take place more frequently with those of different cultures; Friedman (2005) cites examples of large call centers in India representing many U.S. companies, where entry-level employees even practice different accents to make their customers in the United States and Europe more comfortable. As the world becomes even flatter, people of different nationalities will join companies at increasing rates, forcing the host country nationals to deal with those from different cultures, whether in the cubicles next to them, on the teleconference calls with customers, or when reporting to their dotted-line superior, who may reside in another country, as noted above.

This process of increasing cultural diversity is already occurring at the senior levels in companies, at times so much so that it is becoming less clear where the company is actually based. For example, when Lenovo bought IBM's Personal Computer division, Friedman (2005) noted: "This new Chinese-owned computer company headquartered in New York with factories in Raleigh and Beijing will have a Chinese chairman, an American

CEO, an American CPO, and a Chinese CFO, and it will be listed on the Hong Kong Stock Exchange" (p. 210).

Another reason to think hard about global selection processes is that there are employees in MNCs who may be based locally but act globally—that is, interact extensively (beyond just on the phone) with other cultures in terms of both internal and external clients. This may be, for example, the French national who is responsible for the Southern Hemisphere of an energy company and spends much of her time on the road. She will deal extensively with Asians, South Americans, and Africans, including many of the different cultures in those regions. Regardless of where she is based, she will need to have experience with, and work well with, many different nationalities.

Clearly, this will require significant travel. Indeed, Welch and Worm (2006) indicate that the issue of IBTs (International Business Travelers) has been under researched. They quote an Australian executive as saying: "On average, I would go to Asia for two weeks and come back, go to the U.S. for two weeks and come back, go to Europe for two weeks and come back. And the next time I went to Asia [I would] probably go to a different part of it. I guess I was away—if you accumulated it—for 8 to 9 months of the year" (p. 283). Such a lifestyle will certainly involve dealing with other nationalities and cultures on a regular, if short-term, basis. One of the authors worked with a director who manages a country in Asia by flying from the United States every two weeks to spend two weeks "in country." This went on for years.

Aside from the IBTs, however, there are people in many, if not most, MNCs, who travel routinely and are thus required to deal with many different cultures. In regions like Asia where countries are relatively close to each other, traveling from one country to another for a meeting is relatively common for a growing subset of employees. For those who do not travel, moreover, the use of videoconferencing is growing, which enables nearly anyone in the company to interface with counterparts in different offices. Many of these are expatriates who have been living in the region for a relatively short time but are required to routinely interact with many different cultures.

Employees will certainly need intercultural skills as the world grows "flatter" and labor pools begin to flow into each other, creating what might be termed the labor "ocean." At present, it is not unheard of to search globally for a key position, though this is probably more likely for quite senior-level positions. This trend will likely continue and intensify in the future as more positions are opened to international competition. As Lowe, Milliman, de Cieri, and Dowling (2002) put it: "The traditional factors of production (capital, technology, raw materials and information) are increasingly fungible, with employee quality the only sustainable source of competitive advantage to developed country multinationals" (p. 46). MNCs are seeing this as well. A representative of Procter & Gamble said in 2003: "PnG feels that changes in candidate demographics and skills as well as their mobility are creating more intra-regional staffing issues that they must address. Companies that do not address these changes will lose out on the global talent pool being created. In some ways, PnG feels that they have little choice in becoming more global" (Wiechmann et al., 2003, p. 80).

Some dispute the notion of a growing number of transnationals (TNs). Forster (2000) holds that even the traditional expatriate will become a rarity in the future, given better technology and the high costs of those types of postings. Moreover, he notes that they are realizing that they don't necessarily get better jobs when they come home and often have trouble readjusting. In fact, he says, the requirements for globe-trotting international managers are so harsh that very few even have the psychological vigor to deal with "the personal and professional disruption that regular international relocations would entail" (p. 138). The result of all this, he claims, will be shorter postings, more videoconferencing, and less need for the "old type of continual 'hands-on' assignments" (p. 138). Although the expats of the future will be endangered, he holds, TNs are already so rare that they may not even exist.

However, nine years after this study was published, the numbers of expats are higher than ever and there is indeed evidence that their presence is still required (Brookfield Global Relocation Services, 2008). In Hong Kong, though the numbers of expats dropped from a high of 9.6% of the total population to 6.7% in 2001, they are again rising, reaching 7.1% in 2007

(Kingsbury, 2009). The dips in the early 2000s may reflect both the economy at the time and the fact that "hardship postings" have decreased—companies are less willing to pay large amounts for expats to move to countries that are no longer considered difficult to live in, such as China (Brookfield, 2008). It is clear, however, that the trend is toward more, rather than fewer expats.

In addition, indirect evidence for the growth in numbers of TNs can be found in the observation that many people do not do well when they return home (see Forster, 1994). This suggests that staying abroad might be the antidote to the reverse culture shock experienced by some expats. If they lack the challenge and excitement they had when abroad, why go home?

It is clear, then, that expats will be a continuing (and likely increasing) part of the global economy. So for these reasons—the importance of getting it right with the HIPOs, strong social networks, the increasing diversity of employees, the need for those willing to travel and work among different cultures, and the increasing fungibility of labor, it will be ever more important to do effective global selection as time goes on. And this usually means selecting for those who are able to deal with more than one culture, among other competencies.

## Types of Global Selection

Perkins and Shortland (2006) break international careers into three different types. The first is the "Parent" (as in Parent Country), or the typical expat role, where the employee is deployed for a time in a different country but eventually returns to the country from which she left. The "Domestic" is someone who may leave the home country for a quick project or two but largely stays in the home country. "Transnational" staff, however, are those who join the MNC from any given country and "whose professional skills may be used in a variety of markets; who accept that their next posting location cannot be predicted, take this as a condition of employment, and have no preconceptions about where they might conclude their career" (Perkins & Shortland, p. 88). Perhaps the most valuable of these transnationals are the "gold collar" workers—those who are "highly skilled and highly sought-after employees with advanced degrees from other countries who've done research in technical fields'' (Briscoe & Shuler, 1995, p. 233). These are the "new, global manager—one who can do more than one job, in more than one language in more than one country or culture'' (Briscoe & Shuler, p. 232). It should be clear that TNs are also expatriates in the traditional sense, as they live outside their home country. However, only a subset of expatriates are TNs, as most expats go home after one overseas assignment, whereas TNs go on to further overseas assignments, possibly throughout their careers. Suutari (2003) notes that their careers often involve short stays at home in between international assignments and that these managers often were interested in international careers from the early stages of their working lives.

Given these differences, global selection may be different from the more straightforward expat selection. In the latter, a person is selected from the home country to spend a limited time period in the (single) host country (Caliguri, 2000) after which she is expected to return to the home country. An employee is sent abroad for a variety of reasons. Caliguri and Paul (2010) note that this can be for: (1) filling a technical skill gap in the host country, (2) development of high potentials where the goal is to develop not only technical, but also intercultural and professional competencies, and (3) strategic or executive assignments where senior leaders are sent to the host country to either fill a functional gap, such as running a joint venture, or to further develop them as global leaders.

With these goals in mind, narrowing the field of candidates for expat roles becomes relatively easy. For the first issue, all technical experts in the parent company should be considered. For the second and third reasons, the pool of candidates to choose from should be fairly circumscribed—companies generally have relatively few HIPOs and senior executives, as noted. For each group, those who have no interest in going abroad can quickly be weeded out. Once the pool is narrowed to a few candidates, targeted selection measures can be implemented.

The selection for TNs, however, may be more difficult. although there is some overlap between expatriate and transnational employees (for example, both go overseas and both are required to deal with other cultures) there are real differences between the two. Cerdin and Bird (2008) point out that expatriate experiences are usually a one-off period in a given career. Transnationals, by contrast, "have pursued a large portion of their careers in an international arena" (Cerdin & Bird, p. 208); Expatriates have been studied extensively, but TNs are relatively less well studied, though they have grown in numbers recently (Cerdin & Bird, 2008). Adler and Bartholomew (1992) summarize some of the differences between the TN and expat manager in Table. 6.1.

Caliguri and Tarique (2006) point out that the literature on expatriate selection suggests that there are three ways this is usually done—realistic previews, self-selection, and candidate assessment. Vance and Paik (2006), on the other hand, suggest a psychometric approach, an experiential approach, and a clinical risk assessment approach.

But for those who are needed as TNs, the selection process would seemingly be more difficult. Beyond what would be required

**Table 6.1. Differences Between Expat Managers and Transnational Managers.**

| Competency | Expat Manager | Transnational Manager |
| --- | --- | --- |
| Global perspectives | Focuses on a single country and manage relationships between HQ and other country | Understands worldwide business environment from a global perspective |
| Local responsiveness | Expert on one culture | Expert on various aspects of many cultures |
| Transition and adaptation | Works with people from given foreign cultures sequentially | Works with people from many cultures simultaneously |
| Cross-cultural interaction | Adapts to living in a foreign culture | Adapts to living in many foreign cultures |
| Collaboration | Uses cross-cultural interaction skills when on assignment | Uses cross-cultural skills on a daily basis throughout his career |
| Foreign experience | Becomes an expat to get the job done | Transpatriation for career and skill development |

Source: Adapted from Adler and Bartholomew, 1992.

for an expatriate, TNs are expected to stay abroad for long periods of time—some for their whole career. It is rare that a young manager would say, "Yes, I not only want to move abroad for one year, but I'd love to go abroad for many years and perhaps only return home permanently when I retire." How would he know that he wants to go abroad for so long when really, he barely knows his job at home! One way that companies get around this obstacle is to send young managers and technical specialists abroad early in their careers, for shorter periods. Perkins and Shortland (2006) note that this has long been done among oil companies. This helps acclimate the managers to traveling and gets them acquainted with the challenges of managing across cultures. For some, this will prove harrowing and they will want to stay home after one trip or, worse, cut their assignment short. For others, the experience will be exhilarating and they may spend longer and longer periods abroad until they do not come home at all between postings or perhaps until they retire.

This de facto self-selection is similar to Caliguri and Tarique's definition of self-selection (2006), but they note that a more formal technique may involve a self-assessment method where the candidates assess their own fit for an international assignment based on aspects such as personality, career and family preferences, as well as their own characteristics. Many people know whether they want to go abroad and whether they would be willing to brave the challenges they would face; a more formal self-selection helps those who do not have their minds made up.

Candidates for transnational positions would certainly have to think about all the issues considered by an expat, such as the impact of constant travel on their careers, their families, and their post-work life. In addition, beyond what expats will have to face, TNs will have to deal with a multitude of nationalities as they move from country to country as noted above and must fit into each country well enough to manage the locals (that is, host country nationals) and expats (who may be from the same or different countries from that of the TN). This would put additional strain on the family as well as the person himself. For example, moving between countries every few years makes it difficult for the children to fit into schools (particularly when there is a language gap and international schools are unavailable) and for the trailing spouse who has to adjust the household to new cultural mores, possibly while finding a job himself. In addition, if the TN has to travel often from the host country, the comings and goings can upset the rhythm of the family life.

When selecting TNs, instead of approaching it from the traditional HRM way of seeing who will "make it" over there without failing and coming back early, it might be worthwhile to consider who will bring the most value back. Cerdin and Bird (2008) outline three types of knowledge generated through international careers: knowing how, whom, and why. *Knowing why* refers to understanding the reasons the organization has made key moves in the past (such as locating a factory in one country versus another). *Knowing how* and *knowing whom* are both aspects of the employee's experience that the organization can take advantage of as a return on the investment of sending them abroad. *Knowing how* refers to gaining capabilities, such as learning how the organization works globally. *Knowing whom* refers to gains in social capital as the expatriate manager (or TN) makes many new contacts both in the home country and the host country. This gives him more access to information among other benefits, which, if used effectively, can significantly help the organization.

With this in mind, it is clear that the organization will require employees who are sent abroad to have competencies in learning in general and in socializing in particular. As Atul Vashistha, the CEO of a consulting firm that helps U.S. organizations outsource, says, "You have to be skillfully adaptable and socially adaptable" (Friedman, 2005, p. 239). Both expats and TNs will need these skills, but TNs will need them at higher levels. They will have to adapt to more cultures successfully enough to be able to socialize effectively with people from those cultures *and* bring that knowledge to bear on making the organization run more smoothly. In fact, if the TN candidate is not interested in sharing her knowledge with others upon returning (or when questioned by others) then she should not be selected. This adds another competency to the mix—a coaching orientation. These criteria for selection suggest that there are other aspects that must be considered for TNs, beyond what some have suggested are key performance indicators (KPIs) for expats. Expat KPIs include, for example, completion of the assignment, cross-cultural adjustment, and job performance (Caligiuri, 2000). For TNs, we should add: higher levels of a learning and coaching focus, a strong interest in socializing, extraordinary adaptability, a very clear self-knowledge, and strong language skills.

Mesmer-Magnus and Viswesvaran (2008) review a number of characteristics that have been researched regarding success of expats. These include the Big Five factors of personality, views of the host country managers, and general mental ability (GMA). The latter is expected to be more important as job complexity increases—as an expat position is likely to be much more complex in terms of the variables to consider for success than a similar domestic position. For a TN, the complexity should be greater, given the higher number of cultures to navigate, so it is likely that TNs will need a higher level of GMA as well.

## Selecting Transnationals

In terms of the processes needed to select TNs, several considerations must be noted. First, when considering selection for a particular role, considerations of what special skills that role might entail should be investigated. This can be done through a job analysis or competency modeling process. Job analysis is defined by Gatewood and Feild (2001) as "a purposeful, systematic process for collecting information on the important work-related aspects of a job" (p. 269). It should be noted that one of the authors' experience in Asia is that very few companies do job analyses in the region. The process is either not understood, not valued, or seen as taking far too long for jobs that may change at any moment. Currently even in countries where the utility of job analysis as it is now practiced is being questioned, the issues are around the changing nature of jobs and the increasing need for aspects such as teamwork or personality variables (Gatewood & Feild, 2001). It is recognized that for lower-level jobs such as manufacturing line positions, job analysis may be relevant. But as one goes up the managerial ladder, jobs are harder to quantify in job analysis terms (Gatewood & Feild, 2001). In fact, for international jobs, this may be even more true. It is hard to capture every KSAO (Knowledge, Skills, Abilities, and Other) characteristic necessary to be a salesperson in another context. Should one include KSAOs for tasks such as "drinking with customers" or "dealing with bribes that are offered"? In some cultures, these are realistic situations that employees must deal with effectively.

A more acceptable (to companies) approach in Asia, at least, is the concept of the competency model. The use of competency models is becoming more accepted in the region and is easier to understand from a manager's perspective. Moreover, they are more flexible. By identifying general constructs that all managers need (leaving aside technical competence) it is a more efficient way to measure and select candidates. Lievens and Thornton (2005) point out three advantages of competency modeling, including aligning job performance with clear organizational goals, broadening the definitions to include job sets rather than individual positions, and gaining acceptance from senior managers and executives. Though some may say that this is closer to Puerile Science than Pragmatic Science in Anderson, Lievens, van Dam, and Ryan's typology (2004), it is certainly better than nothing, which is what some organizations (generally local or SME ones) present with when asked on what they base their selection process.

The second consideration when selecting TNs is that the assessors must be aware of cultural differences. The same Shell manager quoted previously states that the company ensures that they have a diverse set of assessors who can understand behaviors they see from different cultures. Some organizations request outside contractors from different regions to assist with global assessment processes as a way to show their employees that there is at least an awareness of the need to represent different cultural groups (J. Stempfle, personal communication, August 6, 2009). In any case, the assessors must be able to interpret behaviors based on cultural context and ensure that those selected will be able to successfully deal with people in a number of different cultures.

Third, the tools must be cross-culturally relevant and fair (Sparrow et al., 2004). The following section will focus on developing and using tools that fairly assess competencies across cultures.

## Designing Fair Tools—Testing

Although there are a variety of activities that can be used to assess and select TN candidates, from sending them to the host country to doing a clinical assessment, to talking with their families (see Vance and Paik, 2006; Briscoe and Schuler, 2004; Perkins and Shortland, 2006), we will focus here on two methods of selection, standardized testing and assessment centers. The reasons for this are twofold: both are used extensively as part of international human resource consulting firm selection systems, and each has been shown to be valid in domestic contexts through voluminous research over the years.

Testing, first of all, is used widely as a selection method. As Oakland (2004) puts it: "Test use is universal. Tests are used in virtually every country, with newborns through the elderly...." (p. 157). Oakland estimates there are some 5,000 standardized tests in use today.

There have long been guidelines for creating and using tests, with the bar being set by the standards for educational and psychological testing, created by the American Educational Research Association, American Psychological Association, and the National Council on Measurement in Education (Oakland, 2004). Some of the more interesting issues around test usage are highlighted by Bartram (2001) in a case study below. This is just one example; there are probably many cases like this all over the world.

> An Italian applicant is assessed at a test center in France using an English Language test. The test was developed in Australia by an international test developer and publisher.... The testing is being carried out for a Dutch-based subsidiary of a U.S. Multinational. The position the person is applying for is as a manager in the Dutch company's Tokyo office. The report on the test results, which are held in the multinational's Intranet server in the United States, is sent to the applicant's potential line manager in Japan, having been first interpreted by the company's outsourced HR consultancy in Belgium. [p. 43]

Along with being an argument for the increasing "flatness" of the world, these issues include cultural concerns around test development and administration, data ownership, and interpretation of test results, among others.

Further guidelines for test usage were published by the International Test Commission (2000). These guidelines cover ethics and good practice when administering tests, but do not cover how to create the tests. With so many tests already developed and being used, often with the wrong clients, in the wrong way, and in inappropriate settings, it is worth assessing the current state of the art in developing tests.

In a personal conversation with one of the authors in March 2009, a seasoned test development expert for an MNC testing firm described the steps he takes to develop a test, along with some of the pitfalls he faces. The following passage is based on this discussion (S. Keely, personal communication, March 22, 2009).

> Typically the first step in developing a new test is to determine the goal. Often that will be to develop a test for an MNC that wants to select 20 entry-level managers in 14 different countries. These managers should be able to eventually advance in the company, possibly even out of the country, so they should be relatively equivalent to each other when selected. Making the test equivalent across cultures is the challenge, so the following steps should be considered:
>
> 1. Write the test in English (the MNC is based in an English-speaking country, but as English is spoken by more managers across the world than any other language, this is the norm anyway).
> 2. Translate the test into the local languages for each country, verbatim.
> 3. Revise the test to fit the local culture with the aid of an HR professional and a psychologist from that culture. Since there are many differences between languages and cultures, there are always problems here. First, some terms do not exist in some languages. Even figuring out the Mandarin characters for words like "executive coaching" was difficult a few years ago when the term was not common. Also in China, mentioning a personal checking account in a numerical test will confuse people, so this terminology must be avoided. Second, some concepts are simply understood differently across cultures. For example, there is no such thing as a "good loser" in Italian—a loser is a loser. Thus, a scale measuring competitiveness may need revision to reflect that.
> 4. Back-translate the test. Using a bilingual (and ideally bicultural) translator, translate the test back into English. This is best done with a local psychologist, but one different from the one used in the previous step to ensure there is no bias. As there are fluent English speakers available in most countries, including those who have been educated in English-speaking countries, this is not a

problem. Usually the search for the appropriate person begins at a local university's psychology department.

5. Obtain norms for each country. This can also be done in conjunction with the local university psychology department. Standardizing the test and producing means and standard deviations is done in this step. Note that just because an ethnic group in two countries has the same language (and dialect) does not mean that they will get the same norms. For example, Chinese people in Mainland China tend to do better on analytical reasoning tests than do Chinese outside Mainland China. Norming is thus done for each country separately. Cheung (2004) echoes the necessity for doing this step, noting that "If interpreted directly according to the original norms, test scores of Asian respondents [on personality tests] may be misjudged to be deviant" (p. 180).

6. Validate the test for that population. This step is not always done. Most local governments do not require it and it is costly and time consuming. One way to get around this is to do concurrent validity studies. These are easier and less resource intensive for the organization and can provide acceptable approximations for predictive validity.

7. Do equivalence studies. It is nearly impossible to have the same cut-off scores for two different countries on the same test. However, doing this for validity generalization to establish a worldwide norm sometimes works. The goal is to get the group to a reasonable number for selection purposes.

These steps are summarized in Table 6.2.

Some of the problems faced when going through this process include:

1. Technical problems—the script requires special programming on the computer (for example, it is read up and down versus side to side, or right to left, or it is created in characters or script different from those of English).

2. Equivalence in dialects—is the MNC interested in Central American Spanish or Spanish spoken in Spain? Kuwaiti or Saudi Arabian Arabic? Traditional or Simplified Chinese characters? Each dialect requires a different norm to be created as it cannot be said that the speakers of that language are equivalent across countries.

**Table 6.2. Steps for Developing Culturally Valid, Standardized Selection Tests.**

| # | Step | Notes |
|---|------|-------|
| 1 | Write the test in English | This is the global language of business |
| 2 | Translate the test into the local language verbatim | Usually with the help of a local HR professional or translation vendor |
| 3 | Revise the test to fit the local culture | Usually with the help of a local HR professional or psychology professor |
| 4 | Back translate the test | Using a (different) local HR professional or psychology professor |
| 5 | Obtain local norms for the country | Often with the Psychology Department of a local university or an assessment vendor with experience in that country |
| 6 | Validate the test for the local population | Generally not required by local governments |
| 7 | Do equivalence studies for different countries | Almost impossible to get the same cutoff scores, but it is possible to develop a global norm |

3. With senior managers and executives, testing is not always used, except for personality questionnaires.
4. Verbal reasoning tests do not work when translated into different languages; thus, this is not done.

Since in this company's experience it cannot be said that any test is equivalent to the same test translated into another language, testing is considered to be done locally only. For the MNC mentioned above, the company would try to establish cutoffs that were meaningful but this would have to be done on a country-by-country basis. Thus, the MNC might not get complete equivalence if it was trying to get the top 20 scorers among all test takers. They may end up with five people each from three countries, two from another country, and one each from three others. Thus, among the 14 countries from which they were selecting, the top 20 candidates may come from only 7. But with the difficulties of getting equivalence across borders, the

7 countries that were not represented may contain some of the best candidates—they just did not do as well on the tests. Though there is no easy answer on how to address this problem, another tool that may help is assessment centers.

## Designing Fair Tools—Assessment Centers, Context and Culture

As testing is generally used for lower-level managers or entry-level candidates, other tools are generally used for more senior candidates. Or, when testing is used, it is part of a larger process—often an assessment center. An assessment center comprises a number of different activities, usually including testing, an interview, and various simulations. The simulations may include a meeting with a direct report, a work group, a customer, or a boss, along with an "inbox" or series of e-mails and memos to deal with as part of a case study (Fisher, Schoenfeldt, & Shaw, 2003; Gatewood & Feild, 2005).

The issues with transporting an assessment center across cultural lines, largely involve the cueing for behaviors that either do not exist in the second culture or behaviors that do exist, but are evinced differently, as alluded to in the section above. For instance, expecting negative feedback in a direct report meeting in a Western, individualistic society is not out of the ordinary. An effective manager in that scenario will give the negative feedback, even if it is the first time she has met her "subordinate." If she shies away from doing that, it likely indicates a lack of managerial skills. But to expect the same behavior in an Asian context, such as in China, is to look for behavior that does not often appear in real life. One of the authors has gotten consistent feedback while assessing hundreds of managers in Greater China that the first few times one meets a direct report (or just about anyone else for that matter) the focus is on getting to know that person and establishing a relationship, not changing their behavior. In fact, in such a setting, it would be impolite and unnatural to address shortcomings in behavior. Thus, an assessment center that is developed around Western ideals may not work as intended in an Asian context and may actually select for those who would not be effective in the local culture.

Similarly, in a leaderless group discussion (LGD) mixing ethnic groups does not always work. Having a few Thais among a group of Americans and Germans will likely result in the Westerners running the meeting and the Thais, from a more reserved and less masculine culture (Hofstede, 2001), being nearly invisible. This gives little data regarding the abilities of the Thais and would not work when selecting for local positions in Thailand. Moreover, even if the LGD were conducted with all Thai candidates, other problems would appear, such as deference to the highest-ranking person in the room. If the goal is to select for local leaders, the LGD would provide some useful information but might still mask the capabilities of the lower-ranking people in the room. At the same time, it would not provide information on how the selected local leaders would interact with those from headquarters in a Western company.

With an inbox (IB) simulation, the same problems may appear. With a reserved culture, few confrontations will occur and serious problems may not be addressed. However, the most common problem is generally one of language. Because the IB requires the candidate to sort through a few dozen e-mails of varying lengths and deal with the problems therein, all within one to one-and-a-half hours, if the IB is not in his local language, the candidate will have problems even finishing it. Again, this results in less data available for assessment and generally a lower score on the exercise. And even if he does finish, the recommended actions which may work in an Asian culture may not make sense (and therefore receive lower ratings) to Western raters. It should be noted that in some cases, where it is obvious that the candidate had problems with the language, the IB can be judged on the quality of work done, even if it is a small amount. This can somewhat mitigate the issue of the lack of data.

The interview may be problematic as well. Assuming the language ability of the candidate is good enough to answer the questions, an unfamiliarity with the process may hinder him from giving useful answers to behavioral questions. This will likely disappear as the use of behavioral interviews becomes more widespread. However, the problem around appropriate behaviors for the culture may still remain; because the questions are written and scored by Westerners, behaviors that are proper in the local culture may be scored lower than more Western-appropriate ones.

Other cultural issues may also have a negative impact on the assessment center process. One is power distance (Hofstede, 2004) which can be roughly thought of as the amount of hierarchy in a cultural group. In cultures where there is a high power distance, one might find that candidates are especially hard on their direct reports and more subservient to their superiors. This will obviously result in skewed findings in direct report meetings, IBs, and boss meetings when compared to Western standards.

*Context and culture.* When companies enter emerging markets, often local selection systems based on research studies are not readily available. One possible reason for a lack of research-based systems lies in the culture itself, namely an affinity for nepotism and filial or tribal loyalty (Al-Aiban & Pierce, 1993; Brand & Slater, 2003; Common, 2008). A nepotistic system would invalidate selection devices such as interviews, personality tests, and even skill-based tests because the results cannot be compared to meaningful performance when promotions are not based on merit. This is a particular problem in the Middle East and Africa. As an example of the power of this system, consider the U.S. troop surge into Iraq in late 2007. The surge may not have been successful had the army not realized the importance of nepotism in Iraqi tribal culture. Specifically, before and after the surge, U.S. General David Petraeus implemented a policy of offering work contracts to tribal elders (Sheikhs) in exchange for cooperation against Al Qaida in Iraq (Woodward, 2008). What was different about this system was the use of local tribal Sheikhs instead of the centralized, merit-based bidding system used in the West. The army had realized that Sheikhs would only work with the United States if doing so could increase the Sheikhs' own personal power, which they measured by the number of followers they could attract. The work contracts allowed leaders to attract and hire additional followers within their own tribe, solidifying their local status, and increasing the appeal of working with the United States. In contrast, nonmembers of the tribe were provided with little in the way of job offerings, special assignments, promotions, and subcontracts. Use of selection systems in this type of environment may not even be tolerated, much less taken seriously. Trying to force a merit-based selection system into a culture such as this would result in, at best, a total lack of interest in applying for the jobs among candidates.

This type of tribal loyalty extends into major corporations as well, including a well-known Middle Eastern energy company where two of the authors consulted. There, a multiyear attempt to replace tribal and familial nepotism with a meritocracy has been undertaken. Previously workers rose within the organization based on a combination of personal influence and the influence of individuals to whom they were related directly or via tribal affiliation. Replacing such a system with tests and other measures of merit is no small task. Administrators are literally asking individuals to change cultural norms and expectations while they are at work, then return to them when they make their way home for the night. Clearly this effort can impact interpersonal relationships after work, which is a large obstacle to success in the project.

Another aspect of culture which may impact selection is level of context. According to Hall (1976) cultures run on a continuum between high and low context (see Table 6.3). This categorization of cultures helps to determine how people relate to one another on dimensions such as social orientation, commitment, responsibility, confrontation, communication, and dealing with new situations. Social bonds refer to how deeply involved people are with each other. High-context cultures promote social bonds that imply commitment, expectations, good will, conformity to group norms, and greater distinctions between in-groups and out-groups (Hall, 1976, in Kim, Pan, & Park, 1998). Commitment is the degree to which people do as they say in a culture. People in high-context cultures consider their word to be their bond and therefore are very reluctant to give it freely (Kim, Pan, & Park, 1998). However, when they do give their word, it is, for all practical purposes, as good as a written contract in Western culture. Responsibility refers to how hierarchical and centralized decision making is in a culture. High-context cultures see responsibility as being held at the top, where subordinate errors are blamed on those who are in charge. In low-context cultures, by contrast, responsibility and decision making are diffused and therefore so is accountability for errors (Kim, Pan, & Park, 1998).

Confrontation may be the most complex aspect of cultural context. Due to the strength and intimacy of the bonds between people in high-context cultures, confrontation is avoided, as alluded to above. Kim, Pan, & Park (1998, p. 511) indicate that "people . . . are more likely to repress self feelings and interests to maintain harmony, and . . . there is a tendency to allow for considerable bending of the system." Additionally, to show emotions such as anger or disagreement is to lose control; this causes a loss of "face" which is directly related to reputation and honor (Kim, Pan, & Park, 1998). On the other hand, acknowledging that something has happened between yourself and another person in a high-context culture requires that action be taken, and "action is very, very serious" (Kim, Pan, & Park, 1998, p. 511). Similarly, communication relies upon different things in high-context and low-context cultures. In high-context cultures, messages are highly economical and rarely contain all of the information necessary to understand meaning. Instead, meaning is obtained by placing the statements in the context from which they were derived, such as who the communication was for and who it came from (for example, higher- or lower-status individuals). Again, though this is economical in that short messages can communicate a lot, it does require a high level of "programming" to get to such a point (Kim, Pan, & Park, 1998). Finally, people from low-context cultures are used to the complexities of relying on context-free systems and are therefore very creative even when dealing with novel stimuli. Individuals from high-context cultures work well at being creative within their contextual system, yet when confronted with a situation outside of that system they must create a new one before their innovation reaches its fullest potential.

China, Korea, and Japan tend to be high-context cultures; Switzerland and Scandinavian countries such as Norway and Sweden tend to be low-context cultures; and France, Spain, Africa, and the Middle Eastern countries all fall somewhere in the middle (Kim, Pan, & Park, 1998).

*Cultural context and effect on selection.* When it comes to paper-and-pencil job skill assessments there does not seem to be any kind of link between context and score. Whether people are from a high- or low-context culture, they will likely interpret the questions the same way on a given test, all other things being equal. However, in assessment center situations, such as interviews and the assessment of softer skills or aspects such as personality, context may play a key role in how individuals

### Table 6.3. High-Context Versus Low-Context Cultures.

| Issue | High-Context Cultures (HCC) | Low-Context Cultures (LCC) | Result/Problems |
|---|---|---|---|
| Commitment | Word is bond | Written contract necessary | Agreements can be sealed verbally with HCC |
| Responsibility | Responsibility for decisions is held at top; top-down decision-making | Responsibility for decisions is diffused | Subordinate errors blamed on top for HCC; in LCC everyone has accountability |
| Confrontation | Avoided given intimacy of bonds between people | Done routinely to "air grievances" | Bending of system to ensure no one loses face in HCC |
| Communication | Need programming, but can then be economical | Must be detailed and precise; anyone can understand it regardless of culture | Those outside the HCC miss a lot of what is communicated |
| Creativity | Need a system to be creative within; may have to create a new system | Potentially very creative even with novel stimuli | HCC may have to create a new system to be truly innovative |

Source: Compiled from Hall, 1976, in Kim, Pan, & Park, 1998.

answer questions. For example, should an interviewer ask a job candidate to critique a piece of work as part of a skills assessment, the lack of context in such a situation may lead the job candidate to keep quiet for fear of appearing sassy, abrasive, or causing a loss of face for a superior who may have done the work. In simulations, the person from a high-context culture may view the situation from his own cultural context and respond accordingly. Where the simulations are created in a low-context culture, then, they may elicit the wrong cues. For example, in the Middle Eastern energy company mentioned above, one of the simulations used was a meeting with the candidate's peer. While the low-context competencies were cued for in the simulation, typical responses by the candidates were all around developing relationships. In a high-context culture, relationships are very important (Hall, 1976). Moreover, since all of the assessors were Westerners, it is likely that many of the high-context cultural messages were missed. For both reasons, the use of that particular assessment process might be questioned. However, as discussed above, this project was intended to wrench the company into a flat world; hence, different cultural norms were considered more appropriate than the local norms. As noted above, the use of local norms resulted in the promotion of managers on the basis of affiliations rather than merit. This, it was felt, would eventually cripple the company since the senior management was seen as increasingly less capable (and through the nepotistic system, even lacking the incentive to become capable).

The promotion process may be where context and other aspects of culture such as nepotism and familial or tribal loyalty play their most important role in selection systems. Most Western promotion systems assume that performance in the current job predicts performance in the job to which a person is being promoted. However, little research has been conducted on this assumption and what has been done does not seem to support it (see Bernardin, 2009). In fact, in high-context cultures, individuals who hold their own feelings in check communicate in acceptable ways that do not cause others to lose face (Kim, Pan & Park, 1998). This helps to avoid causing problems related to responsibility because that person is able to avoid making errors and conform to group requirements. As a result, these individuals may be more likely to be rewarded for their loyalty than others who do not act in this way. This has little to do with merit but everything to do with what is prized in a good (that is, docile) worker. In fact, it usually results in little challenging of the system, because avoiding errors and not speaking up against bad ideas from others does not allow for it. In addition, in cultures where nepotism and familial or tribal loyalty are high, it is even less important how well a person does in their current job so long as they are properly connected at the next level and do what they need to do to fit in (Brett, 2007).

Thus, the entire concept of merit may be turned on its head. A high-context assessment center may be better off measuring who "gets" the cultural mores most effectively to ensure those candidates are promoted. However, as Friedman (2005) suggests, those cultures may also be left behind in the flattening world: "What is the motto of the tribalist? 'Me and my brother against my cousin; me, my brother and my cousin against the outsider.' And what is the motto of the globalist . . . ? 'Me and my brother and my cousin, three friends from childhood, four people in Australia, two in Beijing . . . all make up a global supply chain'" (p. 326). This is an argument for merit-based assessment, regardless of which local culture is involved. As such, it is a step toward equal measurement of TN capabilities.

## What to Do?

To ensure that cultural factors do not negatively affect assessment results, there are a number of steps that can be taken. First, there must be a competency modeling project completed to clarify what is to be measured, both for the position in the home country and the same position to be filled in the host country. Where there are differences, there should be a conversation by stakeholders about what is important for the host country position and what the expectations are for the person who fills the position. For instance, is that person expected to stay in-country or move out of the country as her career progresses? As noted above, this will have implications for the knowledge and skills needed. Including the requisite competencies to select TNs versus expats versus domestic employees is therefore important. Currently researchers are examining the particular competencies that should be assessed, usually just regarding expats (see Harzing, 2004), but at present there is no agreement on exactly what those competencies should be.

Second, when there is agreement on what the position should require, the assessment should be designed or modified to reflect those needs. If the needs are for a TN to take on the position, then a process that reflects the corporate culture rather than the local culture should be used. If the person is expected to remain in-country for most of her career, then the process should be designed around and reflect the local culture.

Third, once the process is modified to fit the aims of the center, it is necessary to pilot it. Comments should be solicited on everything, including such details as the names for the players in the cases. One way to do this is to select some internal staff from the relevant culture and request input from them on the simulations and interview. One manager from Shell for example, says that in that company, they use focus groups with which to try out a new exercise or process (Sparrow et al., 2004).

Fourth, the assessment process should be validated. This can be done by examining results of the center for individuals against the later progress of those individuals in the company. Of course, this is not an ideal solution because in the vast majority of cases, companies use the data to make selection decisions (as is the goal here). Thus, the data used to validate the center is clearly biased and thus not entirely useful (Gatewood & Feild, 2005). Most companies, moreover, will not put the data aside for a few years to determine the validity of the center; such action would be too costly and would not help the organizations make selection decisions, which again is the point of the exercise. Nonetheless, a validation effort should be attempted.

Fifth, a consistent reevaluation of the assessment process should take place periodically. Even national cultures now are changing as globalization gathers steam, and the needs of companies often change as quickly. It is imperative that the process measure accurately and according to the needs of the organization. To risk assessing the wrong person for the wrong job in the wrong culture may be extremely expensive, not only in cash, but also in negative publicity and the loss of a valuable resource—namely, some of the organization's talent.

Finally, it is possible that as national cultures change, people are even choosing their own culture (Tipton, 2009). This may complicate the development of tests and assessment centers but also may make it easier. If companies can create a culture that draws people in, perhaps like those of some of the dot-coms, then the assessment tools can simply be made to reflect the company culture and a person's fit with that culture, rather than having to determine fit with the local and corporate cultures, along with any other cultures in which a TN might find himself.

# Conclusion

In this increasingly globalized world, it is becoming more and more important to find, hire, and develop people who can move between cultures freely and easily while remaining productive and advancing the organization's goals. Although many researchers have spent significant time exploring the issues surrounding expats, another type of corporate nomad, the transnational (TN) has become a growing part of the global workforce, and increasingly important to MNCs. Thus, TNs must be considered when deciding on which selection tools to develop and how to develop them. The growing numbers of both TNs and expats, moreover, requires the development of tools including testing and assessment centers that are culture appropriate and fair. We have attempted to show in this chapter that these problems are neither gigantic in size nor Lilliputian in scope. Instead, they simply require a logical, if more complex, consideration of the variables involved and a willingness to step out of one's own culture to consider the more long-term goals of the organization and of the individuals within that organization.

# References

Adler, N. J., & Bartholomew, S. (1992). Managing globally competent people. *The Academy of Management Executive, 6*(3), 52–65.

Al-Aiban, K. M., & Pearce, J. L. (1993). The influence of values on management practices. *International Studies of Management and Organization, 23*(3), 35–52.

Anderson, N., Lievens, F., van Dam, K. & Ryan, A. M. (2004). Future perspectives on employee selection: Key directions for future research and practice. *Applied Psychology: An International Review, 53*(4), 487–501.

Bartram, D. (2001). The development of international guidelines on test use: The International Test Commission project. *International Journal of Testing, 1*(1), 33–54.

Bernardin, H. J. (2009). *Human resource management: An experiential approach* (5th ed.). New York: McGraw-Hill/Irwin.

Brand, V., & Slater, A. (2003). Using a qualitative approach to gain insights into the business ethics experiences of Australian mangers in China. *Journal of Business Ethics, 45*(3), 167–182.

Brett, J. M. (2007). *Negotiating globally: How to negotiate deals, resolve disputes, and make decisions across cultural boundaries* (2nd ed.). San Francisco: Wiley.

Briscoe, D. R., & Schuler, R. S. (1995). *International human resource management* (2nd ed.). New York: Routledge.

Brookfield Global Relocation Services, National Foreign Trade Council (2008). *Global relocation trends: 2008 survey report.* Brookfield Global Relocation Services, LLC, Woodridge, IL.

Caligiuri, P. M. (2000). Selecting expatriates for personality characteristics: A moderating effect of personality on the relationship between host national contact and cross-cultural adjustment. *Management International Review, 40*, 61–81.

Caligiuri, P., & Paul, K. B. (2010). Selection in multinational organizations (Chapter 34). Refereed book chapter in James L. Farr and Nancy T. Tippins (Eds.), *Handbook of employee selection.* Hillsdale, NJ: Erlbaum.

Caligiuri, P., & Tarique, I. (2006). International assignee selection and cross-cultural training and development. In Gunter K. Stahl & I. Bjorkman (Eds.), *Handbook of research in international human resource management.* Northampton, MA: Edward Elgar Publishing.

Cerdin, J. L., & Bird, A. (2008). Careers in a global context. In Michael M. Harris (Ed.), *Handbook of research in international human resource management.* Hillsdale, NJ: Erlbaum.

Cheung, F. (2004). Use of western and indigenously developed personality tests in Asia. *Applied Psychology: An International Review, 53*(2), 173–191.

Chua-Eoan, H. (2007). Crimes of the century: The collapse of Barings Bank, 1995. Time.com. Retrieved August 8, 2009 from www.time .com/time/2007/crimes/18.html.

Common, R. (2008). Administrative change in the Gulf: Modernization in Bahrain and Oman. *International Review of Administrative Sciences, 74*(2), 177–193.

Enron scandal at-a-glance. (2002). BBC. Retrieved on August 8, 2009, from http://news.bbc.co.uk/2/hi/business/1780075.stm.

Fisher, C. D., Schoenfeldt, L. F., & Shaw, J. B. (2003). *Human resource management* (5th ed.). Boston: Houghton Mifflin.

Forster, N. (2000). The myth of the "international" manager. *The International Journal of Human Resource Management, 11*(1), 126–142.

Forster, N. (1994). The forgotten employees? The experiences of expatriate staff returning to the UK. *International Journal of Human Resource Management, 5*(4), 405–27.

Friedman, T. L. (2005). *The world is flat: A brief history of the twenty-first century.* New York ; Farrar, Straus & Giroux.

Gatewood, R. D., & Feild, H. S. (2001). *Human resource selection* (5th ed.). Cincinnati, OH: South-Western.

Goodwin, R. (1999). *Personal relationships across cultures.* Routledge: London. Retrieved from: http://books.google.com/books?id= KwMCG0hahEcC&lpg=PT154&ots=lxIGnOi8Te&dq=social%20 networks%20collectivist%20cultures&pg=PT154#v=onepage&q =social%20networks%20collectivist%20cultures&f=false.

Hall, E. T. (1976). *Beyond Culture.* New York: Anchor Books.

Harter, J. K., Schmidt, F. L., & Hayes, T. L. (2002). Business-unit-level relationship between employee satisfaction, employee engagement, and business outcomes: A meta-analysis. *Journal of Applied Psychology, 87*(2), 268–279.

Harzing, A. (2004). Composing an international staff. In A. Harzing & J. Van Ruysseveldt (Eds.), *International human resource management.* New Delhi: Sage.

Hewitt Associates (2004). Research brief: Growing great leaders key to double digit growth. Retrieved from www.hewittassociates.com/ _MetaBasicCMAssetCache_/Assets/Articles/DDGLeadershipfull .pdf.

Hofstede, G. (2004). *Cultures and organizations: Software of the mind* (2nd ed.). New York: McGraw-Hill.

Hofstede, G. (2001). *Culture's consequences: Comparing values, behaviors, institutions and organizations across nations* (2nd ed.). Thousand Oaks, CA: Sage.

International Test Commission (2000). International guideless for test use, version 2000. Retrieved from www.intestcom.org/Downloads/ ITC%20Guidelines%20Download%20Version%204.doc.

Kim, D., Pan, Y., & Park, H. S. (1998). High- versus low-context culture: A comparison of Chinese, Korean, and American cultures. *Psychology & Marketing, 15*(6),507–521.

Kingsbury, K. (2009, August 8). Hong Kong 1997–2007. Time.com. Retrieved from www.time.com/time/specials/2007/article/0, 28804,1630244_1630282_1630193–1,00.html.

Lievens, F., & Thornton, G. C. (2005). Assessment centers: Recent developments in practice and research. In A. Evers, N. Anderson, & O. Voskuijl (Eds.), *The Blackwell Handbook of Personnel Selection.* UK: Wiley-Blackwell.

Lowe, K. B., Milliman, J., de Cieri, H., & Dowling, P. J. (2002). International compensation practices: A ten-country comparative analysis. *Human Resource Management, 41*(1). 45–66.

Mesmer-Magnus, J. R., & Viswesvaran, C. (2008). Expatriate management: a review and directions for research in expatriate selection, training and repatriation. In M.M. Harris (Ed.), *Handbook of International Human Resource Management* (pp. 183–206). Hillsdale, NJ: Erlbaum.

Moorhead, G. I. (2010). Organizational behavior: Managing people and organizations (9th ed.). Mason, OH: South-Western. Retrieved from: http://books.google.com/books?id=RidV6vh08xMC&lpg=PT65&ots=TPmW2eYm9S&dq=global%20workforce%20changes%20diversity%20statistics&pg=PT65#v=onepage&q=global%20workforce%20changes%20diversity%20statistics&f=false.

Oakland, T. (2004). Use of educational and psychological tests internationally. *Applied Psychology: An International Review, 53*(2), 157–172.

Perkins, S. J., & Shortland, S. M. (2006). *Strategic international human resource management* (2nd ed.). London: Kogan Page.

Ryan, A. M., & Tippins, N. (2009). *Designing and implementing global selection systems.* West Sussex, UK: Wiley-Blackwell.

Ryan, A. M., Wiechmann, D., & Hemingway, M. (2003). Designing and implementing global staffing systems: Part II—best practices. *Human Resource Management,* Spring 2003, *42*(1), 85–94.

Sparrow, P., Brewster, C., & Harris, H. (2004). *Globalizing human resource management.* New York: Routledge.

Suutari, V. (2003). Global managers: Career orientation, career tracks, life-style implications. *Journal of Managerial Psychology 18*(3), 185–207.

Tipton, F. B. (2009). Modeling national identities and cultural change. *International Journal of Cross Cultural Management,* 9(2): 145–168.

Toosi, M. (2002). A century of change: The U.S. labor force 1950–2050. *Monthly Labor Review.* Retrieved from www.bls.gov/opub/mlr/2002/05/art2full.pdf.

Vance, C. M., & Paik, Y. (2006). *Managing a global workforce.* London: M.E. Sharpe.

Welch, D. E., & Worm, V. (2006). International business travelers: a challenge for IHRM. In Gunter K. Stahl & I. Bjorkman (Eds.), *Handbook of research in international human resource management.* Northampton, MA: Edward Elgar.

Wiechmann, D., Ryan, A. M., & Hemingway, M. (2003). Designing and implementing global staffing systems: Part I—leaders in global staffing. *Human Resource Management,* Spring 2003, *42*(1), 71–83.

Woodward, B. (2008). *The war within: A secret White House history 2006–2008.* Simon & Schuster: New York.

# CHAPTER 7

# On-Boarding in a Global Workplace

Mary Plunkett

*The author would like to gratefully acknowledge the contributions of Rod Magee.*

## The Challenge

Although research and common sense tell us that it is wise to invest in preparing employees to be successful in their jobs, this challenge is intensified in today's global business reality. The recent worldwide economic crisis is demonstrating just how global the world economy has become. According to the United Nations the number of multinational corporations has more than doubled in the past 10 years. Today there are more than 60,000 firms deriving at least a quarter of their revenue from operations outside their home country (Buckley & Ghauri, 2004). Assuming an average employee turnover rate of 15–20%, there will always be new people entering into organizations. Historically, new employees—especially senior-level hires—received little more than a basic orientation to their new company. Today's business environment, which requires maximum productivity at minimum cost, has forced reconsideration of the once prevailing mind-set that good, smart people know what to do and can find their way around. New employees can be brought into organizations more efficiently and effectively, a process now commonly referred to as on-boarding.

**Table 7.1. On-Boarding Defined.**

| | |
|---|---|
| **Align** | Make sure your organization agrees on the need for a new team member and the delineation of the role you seek to fill. |
| **Acquire** | Identify, recruit, select and get people to join the team. |
| **Accommodate** | Give new team members the tools they need to do work. |
| **Assimilate** | Help them join with others so they can do work together. |
| **Accelerate** | Help them (and their team) deliver better results faster. |

A comprehensive on-boarding process begins with recruitment and extends well beyond entry into the organization. It is critical to design on-boarding practices from the perspective of the new employee, focusing on the individual's efficient, effective, and emotional transition into the organization. As shown in Table 7.1, the most recent and holistic definition of on-boarding describes it as the process of aligning, acquiring, accommodating, assimilating, and accelerating new team members whether they come from inside or outside the organization (Bradt & Vonnegut, 2009).

The unfortunate truth is that most organizations are not adept at on-boarding employees; the good news is that although proper on-boarding requires time and attention, the process itself is not complicated. Further, research by the Aberdeen Group (2006) shows that as many as 75% of the 600 companies surveyed implement or planned to implement a formal on-boarding process by 2010. For every step in the process, there are integrated accountabilities for the newcomer, the newcomer's line manager, and HR professionals. This chapter is written for line managers and those responsible for designing and implementing an effective on-boarding approach for new team members within a global organization.

## The Bottom Line

To enhance competitiveness, organizations are regularly hiring new employees or relocating employees from one function or geography to another. These individuals have a mandate for change, but unfortunately many don't meet expectations and are forced to leave the organization. The Corporate Leadership Council (2006) reported that 30–50% of newly hired executives fail or are "derailed" within three years. Bradt, Check, and Pedraza (2006) suggest that as many as 40% of leaders going into new organizational roles fail during their first eighteen months. Another study reports that up to 64% of new executives hired from outside the company will fail at their jobs, nearly twice the rate of those failing who have been promoted from within (Ciampa & Watkins, 1999). The costs of failure can be staggering. The direct costs of a failed executive-level hire—including recruitment, relocation, compensation, and severance—could be three to four times base salary (Bossert, 2004). But factoring in indirect costs such as lost opportunities, business delays, and damage to customer and staff relationships can push this number to 20 times salary! (Watkins, 2003).

Providing formal on-boarding processes for new employees helps mitigate the risk of failure. Equally important, on-boarding is also a vehicle for enhancing an employee's engagement to the organization and a means of reducing the time necessary to become productive. Statistics regarding productivity gaps for individuals in assignments outside of their home company are sparse. International assignments present a unique combination of challenges related to the individual and his or her family unit, adding to the complexity of effectively assimilating into role. Research that has been conducted on effectively transitioning into roles, not considering the international component, suggests that it takes a mid-level manager 6.2 months to reach the point where contribution to the organization begins to surpass the company's cost of bringing the person onboard (Watkins, 2003). For senior leaders it can take as long as 2.5 years to completely assimilate into a new organizational context (Gabarro, 1987).

## On-Boarding's Foundation: Socialization

The underlying element of an effective on-boarding process is socialization, broadly defined as the process through which an individual acquires the attitudes, behaviors, and knowledge necessary to successfully become an organizational member (Van Maanen & Schein, 1979). Employees enter into a new organization or new function or geography of their existing organization with a lot of uncertainty; for example, how will performance be evaluated, what personal relationships are critical, what behaviors are normative (Miller, 1996)? Effective socialization reduces these uncertainties. An employee who is successfully socialized will dependably perform job tasks and contribute to achieving the goals of the organization. The individual will demonstrate motivation, organizational attachment and commitment, and overall job satisfaction (Allen, 2006).

Socialization is not a single event. Rather, socialization is the iterative process between the new employee and the organization as the individual develops skills, knowledge, role behavior, and adjustment to norms and values in response to needs and expectations of organization (Smith, 1989). New employees develop an understanding of several key areas through socialization as shown in Table 7.2.

## Multicultural Socialization

As more and more organizations expand beyond their home country boundaries, the importance of effectively on-boarding new

### Table 7.2. Key Areas Developed Through Socialization.

| | |
|---|---|
| **Task Knowledge** | Learning and mastering the knowledge, skills and abilities to perform required work tasks |
| **Relationships** | Establishing successful and satisfying work relationships with managers, direct reports, peers, customers, and other key organizational stakeholders |
| **Politics** | Gaining information regarding formal and informal work relationships and power structures |
| **Language** | Understanding industry language as well as acronyms and jargon unique to the organization |
| **Values/Norms** | Understanding the rules and principles that maintain the integrity of the organization |
| **History** | Learning the organization's historical roots, traditions, customs, background of key organizational members |

team members is heightened and becomes more challenging. To be maximally effective, on-boarding programs need to be customized for each individual in the context of the role, the business and industry, the financial state of the business, and its organizational culture. There is little research that specifically addresses on-boarding practices in global organizations, but a recent survey by Korn/Ferry reported that only 30% of global executives were satisfied with their employee's on-boarding process (Pomeroy, 2006). Further, the most commonly cited reason for new employee failure is the inability to adapt to the organization's culture, and multinational organizations by definition represent many diverse cultures (Scullion & Collings, 2006).

Organizational culture has been defined as the ''normative glue'' that holds an organization together (Tichy, 1983). Communicating cultural values and accepted behaviors is an important aspect of achieving organizational outcomes. In a study of 46 global executives who recently changed jobs, one-third needed a year to "adjust," with 75% citing the organizational culture as the biggest barrier to adjustment (Dai & DeMeuse, 2007).

Culture is a critical component to an on-boarding process as new employees entering into multinational corporations need to understand corporate *and* local expectations, norms, and values. (See Chapter 2 for more information on culture.) A clear understanding of cultural elements will allow individuals to evaluate their behavior and make necessary corrections, if needed (McCall & Hollenbeck, 2002).

A useful framework for beginning to understand cultural differences is provided by Stephen Rhinesmith (1996). This broad framework includes analyzing:

1. How people perceive themselves as individuals or as part of collective group.
2. How people perceive their relationships with others in terms of formality, depth, and obligations.
3. How people perceive the world around them, including relationship with nature and attitudes toward time and space.
4. How people think, including problem solving, linear versus holistic, inductive versus deductive reasoning.

**Figure 7.1. Cultural Difference in Communication: Context Versus Content.**

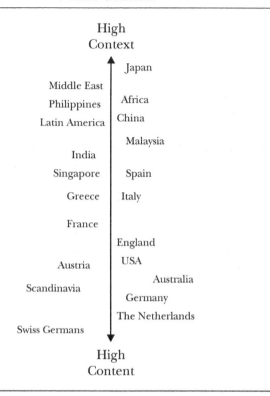

It is important to add communication to this framework, as exchanging information is fundamental to assimilating into a new culture. A useful distinction to consider is high-content versus high-context communication. Different cultures vary on this continuum, as shown in Figure 7.1.

Most of the information is conveyed in words in high-content cultures as compared to high-context cultures where information is carried through nonverbal communication and is more implicit. Unspoken topics and environmental cues are as important as words spoken in high-context cultures where communication is often described as indirect, subtle, warm, and personal. In contrast, high-content cultures are experienced as more direct, impersonal, objective, and logical (Hall, 1976).

A comprehensive on-boarding approach focuses on bringing the new hire up to speed on the internal culture of the organization and the local culture. Table 7.3 shows a list of specific elements that contribute to the culture of an organization.

**Table 7.3. Elements That Contribute to Organizational Culture.**

| | |
|---|---|
| **Awards and Ceremonies** | How are employees recognized for performance? Are there service awards or retirement events? |
| **Social Events** | Are there routine informal events, such as informal gatherings at local pub, or sporting events? |
| **Customer Focus** | To what extent does the organization value customer service (versus production or sales)? |
| **Decision Making** | Does the organization tend toward consensual decision making? Are decisions usually made at the senior level and distributed throughout the organization? |
| **Dress Code** | Is the dress code formal or more casual? |
| **Feedback** | Does feedback occur frequently and informally, or more formally during scheduled sessions? |
| **Information Dissemination** | How much information about the business is shared throughout the organization? How is information disseminated throughout the organization: electronically, in meetings, one on one? |
| **Leadership Style** | What is the style of senior leaders: are they autocratic, participative, heroic, or accessible? |
| **Physical Environment** | What does the typical working environment look like? What is the work space of senior leaders? |
| **Speed** | What is the sense of urgency in the company, to respond to e-mails, telephone messages, work tasks? |
| **Training** | What is the type and frequency of training provided to employees? |
| **Work Hours** | When are employees typically in the office? Are employees expected to work weekends, holidays? |

The new hire's line manager and colleagues play an important role in articulating the internal culture of the organization. This can be effectively accomplished by sharing stories that convey what it is really like to work at your company. Written materials such as policy manuals, internal newsletters, memos from senior leaders, press releases, and so on should be gathered and shared with the new hire as these can also help describe the unique personality of the company and its local operations. Line managers and colleagues and people from the new hire's country of origin are also instrumental in describing the local culture. Additional sources of information such as history books, local art, traditional foods, holiday celebrations, and the like can be very informative about the norms and values of the local culture. Be explicit to include local cultural aspects as well as internal company norms when reviewing the elements shown in Table 7.3.

## Stages of On-Boarding

Because socialization is the foundation of effectively on-boarding new employees, or individuals new to role, we will illustrate on-boarding practices according to the stages of socialization: Anticipatory, Accommodation, and Role Management (Feldman, 1976). Anticipatory socialization occurs before an employee enters the organization. This stage involves practices related to getting into the organization. Accommodation socialization occurs as the individual enters the organization and begins to understand what the organization is really like and attempts to become a participating member. In the role management stage of socialization, the individual masters work tasks, settles into the job role, and becomes a contributing member of the organization.

### Stage 1: Anticipatory or Pre-Entry

Research has shown that the attitudes that newcomers develop toward their new employer form very early and are relatively stable over time (Bauer & Green, 1994). This highlights the importance of paying attention to every detail associated with the candidate selection process as the first stage of on-boarding. New employees begin to develop an impression of the organization based on the professionalism of interactions with recruiters and organizational members. Individuals involved in recruiting and interviewing processes need to provide candidates with a realistic view of the role, the challenges he or she will likely face, and, most important, a glimpse into the culture of the organization. They need to make candidates feel comfortable and welcome while gaining information necessary to make an accurate assessment of the candidates' skills and degree of "fit" within the organization.

Structured interviews are a valuable tool for assessing a candidate's organizational fit; the results from these interviews can be an indicator of the individual's success or failure in role (Lomax, 2001). Structured interviews designed to assess organizational fit should focus on character traits deemed essential by the company. For individuals moving to roles outside their home company, traits such as openness to experience, flexibility, persistence, and empathy have been identified as key predictors of the individual's performance in role (McCall & Hollenbeck, 2002).

GlaxoSmithKline has institutionalized a "Candidate Care" model which is a process and prescribed set of behaviors that applies a customer service model to candidates' recruitment experiences. Treat prospective employees in the same manner as your valued customers, not as traditional job applicants. Ensure that all applicants, those who successfully gain employment and those who do not, have a positive story to share with others. Lou Manzi, vice president of global recruitment, views GSK's candidate care process as a competitive advantage, one that enhances GSK's reputation as a preferred employer while increasing the firm's brand equity.

Practical steps for global hiring managers include the following:

- Provide each applicant with a positive and realistic understanding of the company
- Excite them about your brand by clearly and concisely describing what your firm stands for
- Involve people from diverse perspectives (that is, nationalities, functions, tenure) in the interview process
- Don't overpromise and underdeliver

## Stage 2: Accommodation or Organizational Entry

Effective on-boarding practices implemented during the new-comer's entry into the organization tap into the individual's innate motivation to understand and make sense of his or her new environment. During this phase, three areas require focus: transactional basics, performance expectations, and initial orientation.

### *Transactional Basics*

The transactional basics truly represent a double-edged sword: when executed well they are not sufficient to create an effective on-boarding experience, but any lapses here will destroy even the most comprehensive on-boarding effort.

*Post-Offer Acceptance Communication.* Communicate frequently with the new employee after she has accepted the offer to welcome her into the organization. Carefully craft any formal announcement that will be issued internally or externally to introduce the successful candidate. Include not just the candidate's title and background but introduce the audiences to his mandate: what is he going to bring to the organization? Be sensitive to cultural norms when announcing new employees or employees transitioning to a new role. For example, announcements in Western countries may be more detailed and highlight individuals' accomplishments whereas Asian cultures may downplay past successes.

*The Move.* A sound corporate relocation policy is essential to ensuring a successful relocation. Though this sounds very basic, it is surprising how many multinational corporations have vague policies regarding relocation, whether for a new organizational member or location moves for existing members. The policy needs to be reviewed frequently to ensure relevance and it should adequately address adaptations and exceptions. Service providers, such as move management companies, cultural awareness trainers, language training, and immigration and tax providers, play an important role in most relocations. Ensure that they provide early and frequent predeparture communication with the employee to ensure realistic planning for service delivery. It is the responsibility of the organization, most likely the human resource member of the on-boarding team, to serve as the point of contact for the employee.

A critical component to successful relocation involves the employee's family unit. A now commonly known statistic cites lack of adaptability by the employee's spouse or partner as the number-one reason for assignment failures (see, for example, Frazee, 1998, Lomax, 2001; McCall & Hollenbeck, 2002). A 1999 Global Relocation Trends survey reported data from 177 companies with more than 50,000 U.S. expatriates on active assignments overseas; more than 50% of the companies surveyed listed the following family challenges as critical:

- family adjustment
- children's education
- spouse or partner resistance
- spouse or partner career

Despite the preponderance of evidence and common sense suggesting that early identification and adequately addressing family challenges will establish a comfort zone allowing the employee to concentrate on work, very few companies involve the employee's family in screening and/or selection decisions (Global Relocation Trends, 1999). (See Chapter 12 on Expatriation for more information.)

*Day 1 Experience.* Planning for the employee's first day in the new environment is again very basic, but often overlooked. Take advantage of the employee's enthusiasm on Day 1; make the newcomer feel comfortable and trusting that this assignment is the right one for her. Ensure that there is a plan for greeting the employee upon arrival and assistance with building access and security as necessary. Also ensure that someone is accountable for establishing work station basics including computer, e-mail and intranet access, telephone. The "Day 1" checklist shown in Figure 7.2 provides further examples of important items to ensure the employee experiences a positive Day 1.

## Figure 7.2. Day 1 Checklist.

**Welcome**

☐ Inform existing staff of new arrival and their role
☐ Send welcome announcement
☐ Greet new person and introduce staff

**Facilities**

☐ Car parking
☐ Staff room and kitchen facilities
☐ Telephone—external and internal dialing instructions
☐ Fax machine
☐ Fire extinguishers
☐ First aid boxes
☐ Health and safety notices, including accident book
☐ Utilities, such as lighting, heating, water
☐ Access to buildings, security
☐ Incoming and outgoing mail points
☐ Notice boards
☐ Computer system, Internet access, e-mail
☐ Photocopier
☐ Stationery stocks and systems of reordering
☐ Toilets, cloakroom, and so on

**The organization**

☐ What we do
☐ History of the organization
☐ Organizational structure
☐ Market trends
☐ Future plans
☐ Terminology used in organization

**Figure 7.2.** *(continued)*

---

**Systems**

☐ Office systems—computers, telephones, filing

☐ Courtesies—protocol, etiquette

☐ Hours of work, timesheets

☐ Absence from work—annual leave, bank holidays, sickness

☐ Communications

☐ Meetings

☐ Finance—expense claims, financial responsibilities

**Policies and Personal Development**

☐ Training

☐ Company policies (such as Development; Health and Wellness; Corporate Social Responsibility, and so on)

☐ Performance management process

☐ Salary review guidelines

---

### Performance Expectations

Ensure the employee's line manager is available during the employee's initial arrival at the organization to clarify accountabilities and establish priorities. This needs to be an ongoing dialogue, but the line manager sets the stage on Day 1 for a successful relationship with the new employee. Schedule a two-hour block of time for the line manager and new employee to meet on Day 1. As Gallop's research has shown, the employee's line manager plays the most important role in influencing employee engagement and performance (Buckingham & Coffman, 1999).

The line manager's role in effectively establishing performance expectations for the new hire includes the following:

- Provide an overview of the function's role in the business and its relationship to other functions
- Review the role description and agree on priorities and timetables

- Agree on how performance will be judged, who will be involved in evaluating performance, and how performance will be rewarded
- Define development goals
- Set up periodic informal evaluations

Some organizations highlight the critical role of the line manager in effectively on-boarding new hires by including metrics such as the percentage of time dedicated to on-boarding efforts and turnover rates as part of line managers' performance ratings.

### 3.Orientation

According to a survey by the Society for Human Resource Management, 83% of companies report the use of a formal orientation program for new employees. Unfortunately, the usefulness of such programs from the perspective of the new employee varies significantly. Some programs focus solely on communicating factual information about pay and benefits, company rules and policies, and completing paperwork. Most of these activities can be accomplished more efficiently and effectively with supporting technology, allowing the employee to access the information when necessary.

Table 7.4 highlights some of the common problems associated with orientation programs from the perspective of new employees (Werner & DeSimone, 2006).

Best practice companies approach new employees' orientation in very different ways. They design orientation programs that concentrate on emotional takeaways and many identify a peer coach or "buddy" to help orient the newcomer. The peer coach is preferably the same level as the new employee and has tenure of at least six months with the organization. In addition, the peer coach should:

- Prepare a list of what he or she would have wanted to know about the organization when he or she first entered
- Be available for 15 minutes per day during newcomer's first week
- Provide feedback and encouragement to the newcomer
- Provide guidance on expanding networks within the company

**Table 7.4. Common Problems with Orientation Sessions.**

| Problem | Recommendation |
| --- | --- |
| Too much paperwork | Most documents such as Personal Information, Bank Details, Tax Forms, Medical Information, and so on can be completed prior to the orientation. Many organizations offer access to the company intranet and provide clear guidance on information required along with a contact person for questions prior to the employee's Day 1. |
| Information overload | Don't try to cram 20 hours of information into a three-hour session. Newcomers generally lack the ability to prioritize the information provided; focus on critical pieces of information only. |
| Information irrelevance | Consider your audience. Typically a wide variety of employee skills and roles are represented in the audience. Don't spend time on details that are irrelevant to your general audience. |
| Too much selling of the organization | The new employees have already "bought." Build on this fact. |
| Too much one-way communication | Take advantage of opportunity to allow new employees to ask questions and to begin to build networks. Building relationships with people in the room is more important than any information provided. |
| Lack of follow-up | Ensure that information (including contact details of attendees) from orientation is available post-orientation. Provide a simple check-in with new employees 30 days post-orientation. |

- Serve as a sounding board and informal source of information for questions related to policies, processes, work rules, and corporate or local style and norms, for example.

In terms of more formal orientation sessions, best practice companies use the time to describe the company's history and values and help employees feel connected to the company's business strategy and financial goals. As Diana Oreck, vice president of Ritz-Carlton's Global Learning and Leadership Center said, "People don't remember what you said or what you did but they always remember what they felt." Southwest Airlines is an example of another company that focuses its orientation program on creating a positive emotional experience. The emotions and feelings elicited in effective orientation programs include welcome, comfort, security, pride, excitement, confidence. In addition to sharing key information about the company (such as history, values, strategy, organizational structure, and so on), consider inviting respected employees and leaders to share client success stories. These examples can give newcomers a sense of accomplishment knowing they are working for a company that is respected in the marketplace. In addition, stories relayed from current employees and managers can help new employees begin to visualize how they can help contribute to organizational success.

It is customary for orientation programs to be implemented locally. In more advanced global organizations, common content provided from the corporate group is incorporated into local orientation sessions. Examples of this common content might include a welcome message from the CEO, visions for future, and high-level description of market results and strategic drivers. Stories from senior leaders from around the world may be highlighted through videotaped messages. Depending on the level and role and number of new employees, some organizations may follow a local orientation with a global assimilation event (often held at the company headquarters location). This kind of event is designed to catalyze relationships with senior leaders and with other new employees on a global scale and offers a nice transition from the Accommodation stage of on-boarding to the final Role Management stage.

### Stage 3: Role Management

Building and managing relationships is the focus of the role management stage of on-boarding. This stage takes time, although the combination of the right individual and efficient organizational practices can accelerate the process. The value of establishing solid relationships with the employee's new manager, direct reports, peers, and other organizational members is well documented. Research has consistently shown that people rely on other people to get the information they need to get their jobs done (Cross, 2007). Newcomers are instantly at a disadvantage as they are on the periphery of the web of relationships within the organization. Organizational practices can facilitate and support newcomers to build effective relationships with their manager, team, and larger group of stakeholders.

### Line Manager

The relationship with his manager is one of the most significant in an employee's career (Buckingham & Coffman, 1999). An employee's immediate manager is responsible for performance management and career development processes, as well as providing ongoing coaching and feedback. Managers need to be involved in every stage of the on-boarding experience, but some organizations focus specific attention on ensuring that line managers are skilled in working with new employees to establish objectives, review progress, and provide constructive feedback designed to facilitate the employee's transition into the organization. Further, the line manager plays an instrumental role in helping the employee build important work relationships by providing appropriate introductions and, most important, in carefully considering the first assignment for the new employee. Initial work projects should require assistance from colleagues, especially those in different functions and departments. Avoid assigning initial projects that involve working with external partners or suppliers. When line managers review progress with the newcomer they should ask not only "What have you accomplished?" but also "Who have you established relationships with?"

In global organizations, especially at senior levels, it is likely that the newcomer's immediate manager is not located in close physical proximity. Managing virtual relationships has been touched upon in other chapters (see for example, Chapters 1 and 4), but it is important to highlight here as well. New employees who have remote managers need to assume 100% of the responsibility for establishing and maintaining the relationship.

Find a way to spend time together face-to-face, especially in the early days. It's recommended that the new employee's line manager travel to the newcomer's location in the first week to facilitate introductions and establish objectives. Also agree on regular times and means for checking-in with each other; ideally this will be weekly or biweekly during the initial transition period and over the phone (not via e-mail).

### Direct Reports

A process that has been used successfully at GE for years is focused on relationships between the new employee and his or her direct reports. GE refers to this as the *New Manager Assimilation Process* and similar processes are used at many global companies including Citigroup and Honeywell. A New Manager Assimilation Process centers around three areas:

1. *Relationship Management*: setting the foundation by clarifying roles, relationships of team, work climate, trust, and openness
2. *Boundary Management*: identifying critical priorities of the business, understanding challenges and opportunities, and stakeholders
3. *Leadership Action:* strategy structure, support, follow-up actions of manager and team

The NMAP can take anywhere from a half day to one-and-a-half days, and successful programs have a subsequent follow-up session to check in and evaluate how things are going. The follow-up normally takes place four to six months after the NMAP. In its most basic form, data is collected from the new manager's team, summarized, and returned to the new manager who, together with a coach, reviews the questions and prepares for a face-to-face feedback session with the new team. Questions may include, but do not need to be limited to, these examples:

• What do we already know about [New Manager]?
• What don't we know but would like to know about [New Manager]?

- What are our concerns about [New Manager]?
- What do we want most from [New Manager]?
- What does [New Manager] need to know about us?
- What are the major challenges we face as business, function, or team?

During the feedback session, the new manager responds to the input and the questions gathered from the team. He or she engages in dialogue with the team and agrees on actions. A summary of the feedback session is reviewed three to six months later.

The success of any New Manager Assimilation Process is dependent upon an experienced, trained, and skilled facilitator. Prework for these processes varies but may include an assessment of team learning style and communication style, and could also include a leadership style assessment for the new manager.

At Citigroup the NMAP was focused on the following outcomes:

1. Enable a smooth transition for the new manager and the manager's team
2. Create a dedicated space for open dialogue and to share information
3. Build relationships for effective work flow by clarifying information and addressing misconceptions
4. Clarify vision and objectives through dialogue focused on sharing, enhancing, and refining direction
5. Identify significant actions for the next six months

Generally the NMAPs are used for senior-level appointments but an abbreviated version can be useful for employees at all levels. This approach has been tested and used effectively in Western cultures; see the following NMAP Process Example for an explanation of the process at a major international gas company. As indicated previously, it is important to apply techniques that "fit" into local cultures. A modified version of the NMAP where information is provided to the new manager in written form, for example, may be more effective in high-context cultures.

---

**NMAP Process Example**

*On-Boarding: Framework for Individual Support (12–18 Months)*

- Stage I: Initial integration meeting
  Takes place within first 30 days
- Stage 2: integration meeting (NMAP with team)
  Takes place within first 90 days)
- Stage 3 integration meeting (Check-in)
  Takes place within first 6 months
- Stage 4 integration meeting (Final check-in)
  Takes place between 12 and 18 months

This work is coordinated and facilitated by a member of the corporate executive development team working closely with the local human resources manager and the new manger's boss. The work would include developing a formal integration plan, arranging a mentor, liaising with the line manager, providing 360-degree feedback to the individual, and facilitating the integration with the team meeting. This corporate resource helps the new manager navigate the internal landscape, network with key stakeholders, quickly learn the internal "rules of the road" and is especially significant for those new managers that are globally dispersed away from the corporate center. It is essential for someone knowledgeable about the corporate center and the key players to facilitate the on-boarding process. This process greatly speeds up the new manager's time-to-effectiveness.

---

## Stakeholders

As more organizations realize the importance of social networks, many are investing in a process of gathering stakeholder input and mapping an initial network for the new employee. This investment has resulted in reduced turnover and greater employee engagement in diverse industries including financial services, energy, technology, and health care.

Ideally the stakeholder input is gathered prior to the new employee's first day and focuses on four basic areas:

1. What are the expectations associated with role new leader is stepping into?

2. What challenges might the new leader face?
3. Insights and advice concerning our culture?
4. Who are the key people in the organization that this leader must establish good relationships with?

A skilled transition coach, internal (ideally the HR member of the on-boarding team) or external to the organization, facilitates the process by attending to the details outlined in the following Stakeholder Input Process.

---

### Stakeholder Input Process: Transition Coach Responsibilities

- Communicating the objectives of the process throughout the organization, and specifically with hiring managers
- Ensuring support for the process from the hiring manager
- Meeting with hiring manager to document his or her expectations associated with role, insight or advice regarding culture, and gathering names of key stakeholders to participate in process
- Working with line manager to craft invitation to stakeholders to participate in a brief interview as part of assimilation of new hire
- Interviewing key stakeholders
- Summarizing data, ensuring confidentiality of input
- Reviewing summary report with hiring manager and with new employee
- Providing ongoing coaching and follow-up support to hiring manager and new employee

---

## Putting It All Together

We've discussed a number of elements that contribute to an effective on-boarding process. Table 7.5 shows a time line of key on-boarding activities starting from the time the new employee is identified.

## Table 7.5. Putting It All Together.

| When | What | Who |
| --- | --- | --- |
| 2–4 weeks prior to start date | Prepare on-boarding plan | Line manager |
| 2–4 weeks prior to start date | Organize on-boarding team (for example, HR professional, peer coach) | Line manager |
| 2–4 weeks prior to start date | Plan for move with service providers | HR professional, new hire |
| 2–4 weeks prior to start date | Schedule cultural assessment and coaching | HR professional |
| 2–4 weeks prior to start date | Prepare post-offer acceptance communication (including internal or external announcements) | HR professional, line manager |
| 2 weeks prior to start date | Prepare announcement | Line manager |
| 2 weeks prior to start date | Plan Stakeholder Analysis; schedule and conduct interviews | HR professional |
| Day 1 | Complete Day 1 Checklist | HR professional or peer coach |
| Day 1 | New hire and line manager meet | Line manager |
| Weeks 1–2 | Arrange 1–1 meetings with team members | Line manager, new hire |
| Weeks 1–2 | Arrange 1–1 meetings with peers and role model leaders | Line manager, new hire |
| Weeks 1–2 | Review feedback report from Stakeholder Analysis with line manager | HR professional |
| Weeks 1–2 | Review feedback report from Stakeholder Analysis with new employee | HR professional, Line manager |
| Weeks 2–3 | Manager and new hire complete performance objectives, development plan | Line manager |

*(continued overleaf)*

**Table 7.5.** (*continued*)

| When | What | Who |
|------|------|-----|
| Weeks 2–9 | New Hire visits operations, customer outlets, etc. | Line manager |
| Weeks 2–9 | New Hire meets external vendors, suppliers, customers | Line manager |
| Weeks 2–4 | Complete NMAP: data input | HR professional |
| Ongoing | Schedule weekly or biweekly check-in meetings with line manager | New hire |
| Weeks 4–8 | Complete NMAP: Team dialogue | HR professional, new hire |
| Weeks 16–24 | Follow-up NMAP | HR professional, new hire |

## The Future of On-boarding

As indicated previously in this chapter, there is very little information available regarding on-boarding practices in global organizations. As the number of global organizations continues to increase, and consequently the number of employees working outside of their country of origin continues to increase, there is clearly an adequate sample to investigate basic questions. For example, what best practices exist regarding on-boarding employees into global organizations? We've highlighted some in this chapter, but mostly from our own experience base. Compiling a comprehensive set of best practices, and lessons learned, from employees who have been effectively on-boarded into global organizations would be useful. In addition, it would be important to understand the costs (such as financial, resource commitment) associated with on-boarding practices.

It would be valuable for researchers to investigate the following areas related to on-boarding:

1. What is the failure rate for new hires or employees who transfer to a new location within global company; do failure rates differ if newcomers enter in headquarters locations versus remote

locations? What impact does an effective on-boarding process have on this?

2. Can overall performance of global organizations be compared: those that invest in on-boarding and those that do not?
3. What are the more long-term outcomes of on-boarding, such as career progression, promotion?
4. Do employees who go through effective on-boarding processes build more effective virtual teams? Do their teams score higher on engagement indices that those employees who have not gone through on-boarding?

Organizations that implement on-boarding practices such as New Manager Assimilation Processes and Stakeholder Analyses have a wealth of information within these data sets. For example, stakeholder perceptions of the organization's culture could be analyzed and applied more broadly to other HR processes, including organizational reviews, recruiting, and communication.

## References

Aberdeen Group. (2006). *Onboarding benchmark report: Technology drivers help improve the new hire experience*. Boston: Aberdeen Group.

Allen, D. G. (2006). Do organizational socialization tactics influence newcomer embeddedness and turnover? *Journal of Management, 32*(2), 237–256.

Bauer, T. N., & Green, S. G. (1994). Effect of newcomer involvement in work-related activities: A longitudinal study of socialization. *Journal of Applied Psychology, 79*, 211–223.

Bossert, R. (2004). *Transition coaching activities accelerates leadership success.* Chief Learning Officer on CLOmedia.com.

Bradt, G. B., & Vonnegut, M. (2009). *Onboarding: How to get your employees up to speed in half the time.* New York: Wiley.

Bradt, G., Check, J. A., & Pedraza, J. (2006). *The new leader's 100-day action plan.* Hoboken, NJ: Wiley.

Buckley, P. J., & Ghauri, P. N. (2004). Globalisation, economic geography and the strategy of multinational enterprises. *Journal of International Business Studies, 35*(2), 81–98.

Buckingham, M., & Coffman, C. (1999). *First, break all the rules.* New York: Simon & Schuster.

Ciampa, D., & Watkins, M. (1999). *Right from the start: Taking charge in a new leadership role.* Boston: Harvard Business School Press.

Corporate Leadership Council. (2006). *Attracting and retaining critical talent segments* (Volume I), Washington, DC: Corporate Executive Board.

Cross, R., & Prusak, A. (2002). The people who make organizations go—or stop. *Harvard Business Review, 80,* 1–22.

Dai, G., & DeMeuse, K. P. (2007). *A review of on-boarding research.* Korn/Ferry International.

Feldman, D. C. (1976). A contingency theory of socialization. *Administrative Science Quarterly, 21,* 433–452.

Frazee, V. (1998). Keeping your expats healthy. *Workforce, November,* 19–23.

Gabarro, J. J. (1987). *The dynamics of taking charge.* Boston: Harvard Business School Press.

Global Relocation Trends. (1999). Survey Report. Windham International, National Foreign Trade Council and Institute for International Human Resources, p. 24 .

Hall, E. T. (1976). *Beyond culture.* New York: Doubleday

Lomax, S. (2001). *Best practices for managers and expatriates.* New York: Wiley.

McCall, M. W., & Hollenbeck, G. P. (2002). *Developing global executives.* Boston: Harvard Business School Press.

Miller, V. D. (1996). An experimental study of newcomers' information seeking behaviours during organizational entry. *Communication Studies, 47,* 1–24.

Pomeroy, A. (2006). Better executive onboarding processes needed. *HR Magazine, 51*(8), 16.

Rhinesmith, S. H. (1996). *A manager's guide to globalization.* New York: McGraw-Hill.

Scullion, H., and Collings, D. (Eds.) (2006) *Global staffing.* London: Routledge.

Smith, D. M. (1989). Organizational socialization of physical therapists. *Physical Therapy, 69*(4), 282–286.

Tichey, N. (1983). *Managing strategic change: Technical, political and cultural dynamics.* New York: Wiley.

Van Maanen, J., & Schein, E. H. (1979). Toward a theory of organizational socialization. *Organizational Dynamics, Summer,* 19–36.

Watkins, M. (2003). *The first 90 days.* Boston: Harvard Business School Press.

Werner, J. M., & DeSimone, R. L. (2006). *Human resource development* (4th ed.). Mason, OH: South-Western Cengage Learning.

# PART 3

# Maximizing Performance in the Global Workplace

# CHAPTER 8

# Developing Leadership in Global Organizations

Tommy Weir

Gone are the days of preparing for a single-country career and the days of being a one-country company, as employees and organizations now live in the troughs of globalization and are not bound by geographic borders. Yet many companies still practice a single approach to developing leaders, and many operate on the assumption that "leading" is the same all over the world. It is time to move beyond this ideal. This is a simplistic and risky practice because it is does not contribute to maximizing the investment made in leadership development, nor does the single-source approach result in the sought-after outcomes of employee engagement, performance, and organizational success. This chapter will aid organizations with understanding the implications of the contemporary practices of global leadership development and will recommend what should be practiced when developing leaders in global organizations, highlighting the importance of grafting local identity with the global organization's culture.

There is no escaping the fact that there is a global consistency in "what" leadership is, as every company requires leaders to help direct and fulfill its strategic vision. However, the confusion comes in mistaking the "what" and "how" of leadership, as there are vast differences in terms of styles of leadership, focus on task versus consideration, charisma, and transformation in comparison to tactical knowledge and strategy. To illustrate this point, think about your experiences of traveling abroad and drinking a Coca-Cola (or if you have not traveled abroad perhaps, you have tasted different international versions of Coke in the Coca-Cola museum in Atlanta or at Epcot). Prior to such an experience, the immediate assumption is that Coke is the same all over the world. But is it? Consistently, the color of the liquid is dark caramel, it is best when cold, it has similar ingredients, and the container is the same trademark red color, but the taste varies greatly from one region to another. The "what" of Coke is the same all over the world—a soft drink to quench thirst, but "how" it tastes varies by region to match the local needs. The same concept is true for leadership.

The four-component parts of leadership—the leader, the follower(s), the interaction between the two, and the outcome or goal—appear to be similar all over the world. As the parts appear to be consistent, organizations attempt to import and export the practice of developing leaders from one market to the next, yet this actually falls short of the desired outcome. The problem in this approach is that each of the four leadership components varies from country to country.

The flavor of leading and leadership development should be suitably adjusted to local tastes as well. For example, a universal practice of effective leaders is to provide clarity and direction to the followers. This principle (the *what* of leading) is global, but *how* the leader gives direction should vary by region. During a recent visit to one of the world's leading edible oil companies in an emerging market city, I was given the following advice on directions to give my driver: "Tell the driver that we are located across from the vacant field next to where the toy store used to be." This vague landmark-oriented set of directions was very discomforting for me as I come from a developed city where maps and GPS are commonplace. I was a bit nervous about these directions when I got in the car but arrived at my destination safe and sound, as these directions were very clear to the driver. When leaders are giving directions, they need to take into consideration the regional nuances and practices of the local population. Is the region accustomed to using a map or landmarks? Is it detailed with street names and numbers or visual and reliant on landmarks? Do they rely on Google maps for directions and get detailed sets of directions or simply process the journey one step at a time?

Leaders need to understand this level of difference and translate this everyday practice of moving from one location to another into how they communicate expectations in the workplace. The practical application is that leading requires an awareness and understanding of the local nuances.

Using a simplified definition of leadership as "what and how a leader does to and for his or her followers to achieve a common goal," at the highest level, one can say that the ideals of "what leadership is" are universal but "how" one leads is not universal, nor is the process of leader development. By treating leadership development as though it is the same from one region to another, even though it is not, how can organizations expect to fully realize their desired ROI from their leadership development efforts, something that globally accounts for a staggering multibillion-dollar investment?

Thus, organizations are increasingly saying, "Why is so much invested in developing leaders, yet we don't have leaders?" The short answer is that there needs to be a high degree of localization when it comes to the practice of leader development. The long answer, and the subject of this chapter, is that it requires (1) looking at and understanding the history of leadership development activities—this is the starting point for understanding why organizations employ the methods they use to develop their leaders; (2) looking past the perceived similarities to discover the real demographic insights and leveraging the innate societal development levers; and (3) building a universal yet localized leadership development model that maximizes the investment. This chapter will conclude with a case study outlining what global leadership development looks like in a regional market.

## History of Leadership Development Activities

To understand why global leadership development activities are not yielding the desired tangible result of more effective leaders, let us consider this practical example. Recently, an emerging-market multinational company based in Dubai invested $3 million in a globally top-ranked executive education program to develop a mere 150 high-potential leaders. The company's hope was that by selecting one of the leading executive education programs with several Fortune 100 clients, that they too would raise their level of leadership effectiveness. This program imported the "best of the best" business school faculty and covered topics such as strategy, decision making, team building, emotional intelligence, finance, marketing, and people skills. On paper, the program should have been effective for this company.

Unfortunately, it was not—the results were less than stellar and eventually the emerging-market multinational concluded that they lost their investment, and cancelled the program. What would cause a top-rated global executive education program to miss the mark? Although there are many factors that make or break a leadership development initiative and the impact that it may have on an organization's future success, what went wrong in this program (and many others like it) is that it was heavily steeped in Western thinking and approaches. In this instance, the program was conducted with the underlying assumption that there is a single approach to global leadership. In addition, and perhaps what is most important, the faculty had limited market understanding beyond an extensive literature review. What was missing was an understanding of societal norms and local practices that influence development. Would the results have been different had the executive education program invested in better equipping faculty with an understanding (ideally based on real-life experience) of the local environment?

The reason that this program and many others like it are so heavily influenced by the West is easy to understand when you consider that:

- 18 of the top 20 executive education are in the West
- All but 5 of the top 100 MBA programs are in the West
- Nearly every one of the top-selling leadership books is written by a Western author

Why has the West had such an influence on leadership training as a discipline? The apparent perception from the adopted practices is that leadership development should come from the West. This is a mistake, and this section explains why global organizations retain the overly simplistic thinking that "one leadership model fits all" by walking through the modern history of what is practiced and understanding why. This is important to understand in order to step back from the current practices and learn how to improve developing leaders in global organizations.

## Origins of Leadership Thought

The modern discipline of studying organizational leadership is mono-cultural and has its genesis in the West with the leadership trait studies. This was followed by Frederick Taylor's "scientific management" and by the Hawthorne Works of Western Electric until the 1950s when the studies from the Big Ten schools of Michigan and Ohio State from the heartland of America produced their popular studies. When examining the various leadership theories, it is important to keep in mind what was happening in society and in the workforce at that time, as leadership research is usually a response to the current environment. At that time, the world was still reeling from the effects of the Second World War and much of the thought about leadership and management was shaped by a military mind-set. During this era and particularly in a military situation, leaders were most interested in getting subordinates to follow well-defined mandates. When leaders said jump, that is what was expected. As a result, leadership activity was very mechanistic and top-down. In addition, organizations where the studies took place were not at all concerned with global issues. Today, being multinational is commonplace and in fact highly sought after. Back then, however, the world was much less connected.

It is also a practical reality that while researchers may accumulate knowledge over time, the foundation may remain intact. This was the case with leadership where later practice built on preexisting work, so the original insights and conclusions permeated later thinking. In summary, the elements that created a foundation for leadership thinking and practice included a basis in Anglo Saxon model of traits, centralized control, hierarchical, and mechanistic.

Following the Second World War, the United States played a major role in the world economy, and its industries, ideas, and approaches dominated those of other countries—including thinking about leadership. Since early work and modern leadership research was U.S.-centric, Western ideals remain embedded in the core of leadership thinking and practices. Fast-forward to modern day and this largely Western-driven approach is what is being propagated around the world. And though it is effective in many ways, it falls short in terms of preparing global leaders who must operate in an increasingly interconnected world. In essence, the field of play has changed but much of our thinking about leadership has not.

## Organizational Leadership Development Practices

The Industrial Revolution, which mainly transpired in the West, helped usher in the concept of laboratory training as an organizational practice for knowledge sharing where participants learned from their own interactions and the evolving dynamics of the group. From the likes of these basic skill training groups (T-groups), the popularization of corporate training and learning was born and eventually the creation of many forms of modern leadership development, including individualized instruction, development plans, on-the-job and coaching programs, integrated performance support, 360-degree (multi-rater) feedback, as well as online support. Like the rise of leadership theory and research, leadership development activities were also Western based. An example of three of the globally popular development approaches will illustrate this: leadership centers, executive education, and case studies.

### Leadership Centers (Academy)

One of the first aggressive organizational leadership development efforts started in the 1950s at GE's famed Crotonville site. At that time, GE was growing but realized they had a shortage of qualified managers to run the additional divisions. GE first turned to local universities to see if they could offer a solution to GE's shortage of qualified managers. Concluding that they could not help, GE ultimately established their own internal leader maker center, and began the concept of Leadership Centers (Academies). Over time, the curriculum and approaches have been revamped to continue to produce competent leaders but the concept as a whole has remained more or less intact and true to its foundation.

Not surprisingly, companies around the world have hopped on the GE bandwagon, and hoping for similar results, imitated the hugely successful practice for creating leaders, who are "cut from the same cloth." On the surface, this approach to leadership development appears to have been successful.

The practical value of the Leadership Center (Academy) is producing leaders who are modeled after others who have proven to produce stellar results. The belief is that if an organization can reproduce its best leaders, then the organization will have the bench strength to grow in the future and should be able to grow faster and bigger. But is this true in the global marketplace? Moreover, an approach that is focused more on copying an existing leader archetype than evolving to what is organic or unique to each culture would seem to be a suboptimal strategy.

One of the pitfalls of such an approach is that it does not consider the leaders' backgrounds and how this differs from one region to another. The practical recommendations for global organizations section of this chapter outlines what should be considered when developing leaders, and Leadership Center approach will be stronger by integrating these considerations on the leader level rather than just the organization level.

## Executive Education

As other organizations became interested in the GE Leadership Center approach, leading B-schools realized that they were losing market share to internal corporate leadership programs and that they needed to become more responsive to this new competitive marketplace. Armed with top-quality faculty, these B-schools realized that they could provide an important service to not only degree-seeking students, but also nontraditional students through public short courses, in-house programs for corporations, and executive education programs. In essence, they were offering business school education to those who either needed a refresher or simply could not get away to pursue a formal degree program. Their competitive advantage is their brand reputation, history, and having the leading business thinkers as their faculty. The assumption is that by learning from the best, you can become the best. During the past 20 years, these executive education programs have become widely popular all over the globe. The most sought-after programs are from top-tier business schools in North America and Western Europe.

However, on the global scene there is a significant pitfall as witnessed in the Dubai-based organization. These programs do not always travel well globally. Success in global leadership development requires more than giving the program a passport and clothing it in local culture. Increasingly, executive education programs are recognizing the need have a better understanding of local culture, leader characteristics, and business environment in order to develop leaders who will succeed locally and globally.

## Case Studies

The Harvard Business School made a significant contribution to the practice of developing leaders with the introduction of their "Case Study" approach to growing leaders. Business case studies recount real-life business situations in which leaders are faced with a practical dilemma. By reviewing, discussing, and critically analyzing the situation, students gain valuable insight and thereby develop their own leadership capabilities. Harvard adopted this practice out of necessity; there simply were not adequate business textbooks to develop business executives. Over the years, the case study approach has spread into training and leadership development departments as a standard tool to help grow organizational leaders.

The value of the case studies is significant, as they create a simulated environment allowing potential leaders to use real-life situations. The pitfall, once again, is that they tend to use Western examples and focus on Western business concerns. A common request in the global marketplace is for the case studies to be more relevant to their needs and concerns.

Each of these examples (leadership centers, executive education, case studies) enjoys great success, and they have collectively shaped the approaches that are used around the globe today to train and develop our leaders. Although these approaches are successful at home, they do not always resonate globally as their roots are firmly planted in the West, leaving some non-U.S. organizations scratching their heads and wondering, "Why are we investing so much in leadership development but still do not have leaders?" The answer is that developing into an effective leader is more than attaining a degree or attending a program; it is about developing skill, behavior, attitude, motivation, and role—with a local flavor. Successful leadership development incorporates understanding and adapting the practice to match who the future leader is.

## Global Landscape and Changing Demographics

It is easy to be tricked by global similarities and to make false conclusions based upon them. When traveling around the world, the similarities from one city to another can be startling; my parents recently experienced this when they made their first trip to Dubai in 2008. Upon arriving, they quickly noticed many of the same restaurants and stores as their hometown in the United States. This is true on first glance but deeper investigation reveals more than 200 nationalities who now call Dubai home. With the numerous nationalities come different sights, smells, attitudes, driving patterns, religions, parenting approaches, thoughts on business, educational backgrounds, and so forth, but all clothed in similarities. Whether one is in Paris, Shanghai, New York, Delhi, Nairobi, or just about any of the other major cities, many of the same consumer brands (for example, HSBC, McDonald's, BP, Starbucks) are in evidence and there are striking surface similarities. There is no question that globalization is changing the world's culture on the surface and dressed it with similarities but when it comes to growing leaders it is important to look beyond to see the differences as well.

### The "New" Workforce and Leader Environment

Success in developing leaders in global organizations requires understanding that the "new" workforce is where the future leaders are coming from. A few of the high-level elements that reflect the changing shape of the workforce include shifts in the age of the workforce, urbanization, literacy rate, and microeconomic structure. Each of these in turn shapes what one should consider and how to approach leader development.

- According to the 2008 U.S. Census Data on World Population, 40% of the people in emerging-market countries are under the age of 20 and the total youth population in the emerging markets is eight times larger than in the developed markets. This means that there are significantly more young and inexperienced workers and leaders in developing nations. An obvious challenge for leadership development experts in those areas, then, is that the potential pool (that is, the future leaders) will have less practical experience to draw upon. Because they will not have worked their way up through the ranks and mastered leadership challenges along the way, more remedial action may be needed. This creates a challenge for organizations and current leaders as they need to modify their acceptance of what are the qualifications for leadership position. Additionally, this means that mode of leader development will be dependent on mentorship and the localized practices of assuming a corporate patriarchal development model.

- Every second, two people move from the rural countryside into one of the world's 496 cities with a population in excess of one million, and, according to the United Nations, 52% of the world now lives in an urban setting. In practical terms, this translates into a massive influx of uneducated and unskilled (at least for the urban setting) workers. And though leadership development programs may have historically (that is, since immediately following WWII) dealt with effective leadership for this type of population, the Western-centric programs are currently geared toward modern nonagrarian workers. This a challenging environment on the global scene as it requires understanding a new working class who has not had exposure to formal organizational performance dynamics.

- The literacy rates in the West have been stable for generations whereas in the emerging markets they have been growing steadily. This is truly a great step in the right direction, but it is important to remember that literacy cannot be taken for granted. This has practical implications for leaders, as some of the "new" workforce and their families may not be literate and steeped in organizational traditions or rhythms.

- Finally, one out of six people today are living on less than $2 per day, and many live in the shadow of one of the world's cities with a population of one million or more. For leaders, this is a staggering number of potential employees who are focused more on survival than anything else. Such concepts as inspirational leadership, self-actualization, and communication, though important in leadership development curricula, mean little to employees at the bottom of today's food chain. This is a paradigm-shifting process for leaders, as they have to align their level of thinking on needs with the considerations of the urban poor who are eagerly entering the workforce.

## How Do These Differences and Distinctions Relate to Developing Leaders?

On a daily basis, a scan of the news headlines reveals how different regions view the work of leadership. In some, leadership is synonymous with power. Consider the historic or modern-day warlords, dictators, and the concept of "Big Boss." In others, leadership is synonymous with vision, dignity, and courage. Whatever the view, it is clear that one's concept of leadership is heavily reliant upon his or her culture or region of origin. In a similar fashion, many organizations (consciously or not) formulate ideas about leadership at their home office, and it is these homegrown ideas that so often underpin their leader development programs. However, these home office perspectives are not necessarily universal and can have limited impact on the "new" global workforce. For example, many leadership development programs have recently added the topic, "How to lead different generations" and have adopted the popularized terms, Baby Boomers, Gen X, Gen Y, and so forth. These terms resonate in North America but have limited meaning in countries that did not experience a post–WWII boom in births, let alone those that did not exist at the time. China, by contrast, has a very different leadership challenge that also has implications for training. Specifically, there is an absence of highly qualified leaders among the age demographic that would have been in college during the time of the Cultural Revolution, when universities were closed by the Chinese government. Both of these are extreme examples, but the point is that when adopting an approach and structuring content for leader development programs, global organizations need to consider the local demographics and history when designing curricula to develop leaders.

Thus, you might say that leadership development happens at the point where anthropology, sociology, and psychology converge with organizational behavior. Cultural norms and habits are embedded from birth and are built through the formative years and into adulthood. Developing leaders is complex in a single society, let alone globally, and few organizations have fully leveraged the potential impact that can come through their development programs. All over the world, people are very different—they come from different backgrounds with unique experiences—and the local societies are at different stages educationally, economically, and developmentally.

The global landscape can be summarized in the notion of difference—people are different, companies are different, countries are different, and to excel in global leadership development, these differences have to be leveraged in the creation of appropriate methods that replace the reliance on a "one size fits all" global leader development program. Leadership development needs to connect personally with who the leader is; this happens best through examples and approaches from the leaders' heritage and discipline, specifically merging local industry with the home office leadership environment. Organizations should focus their attention on how leadership development should be happening in their environment and maximize the leadership potential in every culture. What inspires and instructs a leader counts in the development process, and it needs to allow for variation in the global programs.

## Practical Recommendations for Global Companies

Developing executives who are equipped to work in a global environment and developing leaders who are on the other side of the world pose a significant challenge for leadership development experts today. As this chapter has pointed out thus far, it is essential to understand not only the universal truths—the "what" of leadership but also the context-specific and variable "hows" of leadership. However, this is easier said than done. The reality is that a lot of money and time are invested in leadership development with limited ROI. Given this track record, what should organizations do? For leadership development efforts to deliver the desired results, a successful comprehensive and truly global approach to organizational leadership development should: (1) foster an understanding of the uniqueness of experience and environment, (2) maintain a focus on cultural heritage and organizational future, and (3) adapt the leadership model and approach.

## Understand the Uniqueness of Experience and Environment

Just as streetwise business operators get to know the customer and sophisticated organizations invest in consumer insights, leadership development specialists need to get to know who the participants are. Because people are different around the world, organizations need to look beyond their current hypotheses and explore the causal factors that shape how leaders develop, with the purpose of constructing an effective approach to leadership development. Four elements that need to be considered when understanding the uniqueness of experience and environment include the leaders' unique backgrounds, their thought processes, their home societal structures, and the dominant religion of their development cultures.

## Leader's Unique Background

Leadership development specialist need to scrutinize and discover why the differences exist and understand their assumptions as they influence how people think and behave and thus grow in their leadership capability. This requires leadership development specialists to set aside existing notions and constructs about their specialties while they probe the local markets to understand who the people are and how they develop. These three fundamental questions need to be contemplated in the exploration process:

1. Why do leaders learn?
2. How do leaders learn?
3. What do leaders need to learn?

When addressing these questions organizations should consider individual leaders or tightly aligned markets rather than contemplating universal answers for leaders on a global level. Two risk factors are involved in this practice: (1) this activity is heavily reliant upon anthropology and sociology, a skill set not traditionally taught or practiced in organizational leadership development departments, and (2) without broad international experience as an expatriate including significant experience in various countries, it is difficult to set aside individual experiences and be able to question why things are as they are in a particular culture—let alone draw conclusions that affect leadership development.

For example, in the midst of a major leadership development effort, a leading telecom company with an operating office in one of the emerging markets realized that the leaders in the program came from numerous backgrounds. In this particular operating company, they had 35 different nationalities and all but 1 nationality was working outside of its home office. Their leadership development specialist, who had extensive expatriate experience, recognized this reality and hit the pause button to explore what this meant for how they lead and what it will mean for how leaders will develop. They explored the three fundamental questions mentioned earlier and concluded that they needed to take a deep look at their leaders' backgrounds and adapt their global program accordingly.

## Thought Process

Human cognition is not the same all around the world, and at the most elementary level people in the East and West have different basic thinking approaches. Psychologists have assumed universally that Westerns and East Asians have maintained very different systems of thought. For example, Westerners have a strong interest in categorization, which helps them to know what rules to apply to the objects in question. And they rely on logic to play a role in problem solving. Conversely, East Asians attend to objects in their broad context and how they relate to one another.

The need to explore locality in relationship to leadership is apparent through this description of the Western and Asian basic thought processes. Leadership development specialists would be wise to consider the system of thought as they explore the leader's background.

This understanding will aid organizations' efforts to maximize the investment and results from leader development activities. For example, if a company that is based in China and has operating offices throughout Europe and North America decides to export its home market leadership development program to all of its global leaders and managers, it needs to allow for the different systems of thought in order to leverage the natural abilities and thinking processes of the leaders in Europe and North America.

## Social Structures

Social structures are also distinct between various cultures and environments, and they do affect how a person develops as a leader. The way in which groups relate to each other is based on relatively enduring patterns of behavior and relationships within social systems. Norms become embedded into social systems in such a way that they shape the behavior of leaders within them. In and of themselves, social structures are very complex. This complexity intensifies when attempting to cross cultures or integrate various social norms and patterns.

## Religion

As a developmental consideration, religion is more than an approach to spirituality. Unlike the Western idea of the world being divided into two comprehensive domains—one sacred and the other profane—on a global landscape religion presents a common quality for societal character. Religion is a communal system of belief focusing on a system of thought from which come moral codes, practices, values, institutions, tradition, and rituals. Leadership specialists need to understand the broader impact of "religion" on people as members of society. Religion shapes personal practices and group rituals stemming from shared conviction; it is a "way of life." Unlike the homogenous impact of religion when operating in a single market or across European and American markets, on the vast global front the breadth of religious impact on how leaders develop needs to be sought out and understood. Additional thoughts to consider when exploring a society include:

- What is the societal (and parental) support for development and why is it as it is?
- What are general beliefs and what stories shape them?
- What are the learning habits and why are they as they are?
- What is the educational model and approach?
- What does an individual's experience actually include?
- Individual's cultural background and what created the culture.
- What is the perceived value of learning to local culture?
- What developmental patterns existed throughout ancient and modern history?
- Where is the culture in its current life cycle?
- How were the potential leaders parented and how does authority act?
- What types of noneducational activities are relied on in the local culture that build leadership habits?

Leadership development specialists need to have the skills of great connoisseurs; they need to become fully acquainted with and appreciate the differences between the various cultures. Over time, they will develop a taste for both views—the home office and their leaders' backgrounds.

## Maintain Focus on Cultural Heritage and Organizational Future

In addition to understanding the uniqueness of experience and environment, it is the role of the leader development specialist to understand the backgrounds, to remove barriers, and to build a bridge between the cultures of the leader and the organization so that they can graft together the local identity with the multinational company's environment. Success resides in knowing both sides and how to connect them. One of the more important elements in grafting the leader's identity with the company's environment is for the development specialists to understand the depth and development of potential leaders' societal backgrounds. This will facilitate bridge building and help leverage the most effective development approaches.

Most global organizations hold the unconscious belief that potential leaders:

- Are educated, most likely through public education, in a classroom that utilized active learning
- Have an understanding of the idea of organizational life as it is constructed via extracurricular activities at the elementary level and supported in most social interactions
- Have a consistent underpinning stemming from the influence of a Judeo-Christian ethic absorbed through educational programs and cultural rhythms
- Will pursue and be supported to develop as leaders
- Have an understanding of operations from their first jobs held
- Operate from tightly aligned commonalities with coworkers in their organization

But when the company explores the global settings, these unconscious beliefs most probably do not align with those of the regional cultures. Theories or hypotheses about environment and background need to be tested through behavior and then modified depending on the outcome of the testing. The uniqueness of individual experiences creates the uniqueness of personality. An individual's hypotheses about his or her environment not only are a basis for describing the environment but also seriously influence the way the individual behaves toward the environment. Success in leadership development comes as organizations are able to graft the environments and backgrounds together. Attention needs to be given to maintaining focus on the cultural heritage of the leader and the organization's future while bringing the two together.

## Adapt the Leadership Model and Approach

Finally, leadership development activities should be largely influenced by society and the dynamics of the current workforce. Thus, the next step after compiling the leader's dossier is to analyze the existing leadership development activities and discover how they can be modified or adapted to maximize the investment and leadership potential in the various markets. This is the point where organizations should understand the universal components and explore the factors that need to be understood in order to "localize" and shape the leadership model.

Operating companies around the world express that their home offices have difficulty in that they have researched and invested heavily in current programs, yet the field offices know that thee programs need to be modified in order to have a greater impact. If a global organization is serious about developing leaders, it will need to recognize the priority of this approach and make the necessary adjustments.

## Middle East Case Study

When it comes to leading in the Middle East, people often ask, "Is it any different than leading in another country or region?" The answer is a resounding "Yes!"

For anyone working in the Middle East this is a question that cannot be ignored, as it is foundational for business success. Looking around the globe it is clear that leadership initiatives are not the same, nor should they be. It is a grave mistake to think that you can import and export ways of leading in the same way that countries import and export oil.

Successful leadership development requires that you first identify the rhythms and nuances that are present in that culture. Next, focus on understanding the leadership need(s), and establish where they originated from and why they are as they are. Only then should you put energy into seeking the solution of how to develop the leaders. This is especially true in the Middle East, where people are mistakenly importing Western approaches to leadership development without giving consideration to the local cultural rhythms.

Consider a recent example from Beirut, Lebanon, where a training course in time management was being conducted to rectify the notorious problem of arriving late for appointments and events. On the surface, it is easy to think that all time management skills around the world are similar. So the western training company reached into their toolbox to fix this perceived problem. In the midst of their training, the solution was, "if you make better use of your time then you will be on time."

Knowing Lebanese culture, I found this to be laughable. Even more hysterical is how the trainer proceeded to teach the Lebanese managers to use their time. The solution was to turn off mobile phones and only answer calls for two hours each afternoon. At that suggestion, one could see the Lebanese managers' eyes glaze over.

Why? This development solution had a lack of understanding of the local culture and it was addressing a problem that was not really there. In Lebanon (and most of the emerging markets), the mobile phone is the dominant method of communication and a central component of life—they never turn off or ignore their mobile phones.

This lighthearted example is meant to emphasize what can happen when there is a lack of understanding that situations and cultural rhythms are different and that leadership development solutions need to be rooted in the local society. Why do people come into the Middle East (or for that matter any part of the world) and propagate their solutions without an understanding of the local market and needs?

At the time of my research, there was a deep sentiment that Western leadership development solutions would not work in the Middle East, yet many people were still reading Western-oriented business books and attending Western-based leadership seminars in search of success even though the content could not be fully implemented. Why would this be? In order to develop leaders successfully in the Middle East, you have to understand the culture, you have to know what influences it, and you should lead accordingly. When addressing the Middle East, it is critical to look into its history and notice the rich culture and massive achievements.

Successful leadership development in the Middle East (ME) requires an understanding of the elements that influence the society. This case study shows an ME-specific model of leadership development called the "Patriarch Model." If applied in the right context, this model will be the framework for successful leadership development in the Arab world. It is important to note that there is no such thing as "one" Middle East or Arab world. This region is made up of more than 15 countries, half a dozen different religions, and countless regional- and tribal-specific ways of doing things. So even in a tightly aligned geographical region, there are differences to be considered. Although there are many differentiators, a quick look across the Middle East will reveal a few commonalities. This case study utilizes the commonalities in identifying the elements of influence.

## Elements of Influence in the Middle Eastern Society

The most important thing to do when leading in the Middle East is to become familiar with what has and does influence the culture. The following influences—the family, Islam, family business, and colonialism—have shaped Arabic business into what it is today. Likewise these elements shape the way people develop as leaders and should be apparent in a global organizations program.

### *Influence of Family: Patriarchal and Loyal*
Unlike in the West, the influence of family in the Middle East is very strong and has a tremendous impact on how people lead and what employees are looking for in their employers. At the very least, organizations need to be aware of this influence.

Why does the family dynamic have such a powerful influence in the corporate settings? Because the Arab world is a patriarchal society and family focused. In this society, the father is the central figure and he wields a great amount of authority. In the traditional Arab family home, there is a healthy respect and reverential fear of the father as the family looks to him for leadership. It is also typical that this leadership will pass on to the eldest son. The patriarch in the family understands he has the responsibility for the family or tribe and does not take it lightly.

The business environment is a facsimile of this family structure. Employees look to their boss for strong leadership and expect to experience what they would at home. At the same time the boss embraces his responsibility for the stewardship of his employees.

In the Arab home it is common to have centralized power; however, in the business world this often causes problems and creates blockages for the work. The bottlenecks in the decision making, the minimal delegation, and the vast amount of task-oriented leadership are by-products of the misused patriarchal patterns. The influence on the patriarchal family structure can be seen in the structure of organizations in which top-down authority is the norm. The natural outcome of centralized power is control, and this controlling mentality will limit a leader's ultimate influence and success. The tight locus of control and power that is experienced in the business context comes from mimicking the home style of leadership. For an organization to develop leaders in the Middle East, it is essential to understand where these patterns come from and why they exist; this understanding is foundational to success.

## Group Orientation and Relationships

There is also a strong group orientation in the Middle East. An Arab family is a very tight-knit group of people and the extended family is the locus for most social interaction. They live life out as a group, so much so that it is quite common to find cousins as best friends.

How does the group orientation work in a patriarchal setting? On the surface these practices seem to be paradoxical but in reality they work well together. Even though legitimate authority rests ultimately on the apparent absolute power of the patriarch, he nonetheless takes account of family opinion when making decisions.

Even with his given authority, the good patriarch creates a consultative environment where the group orientation supports a group approach to making decisions. The business context is both hierarchal and consultative. This consultative structure offers the basis for understanding how decisions are made in the Arab world. It is fundamentally different than in the West, which primarily endorses individual decision making.

The family takes an active role in deciding whom to marry, where to work and live, and even what type of car to drive, and so forth. Stemming from the family nature of decision making comes the consultative approach to decision making in Arab organizations. Westerners working in the Middle East often incorrectly criticize their Arab counterparts for not making a decision; they do not understand that the reason for this behavior is based on historical decision-making rhythms. They are accustomed to being part of a group decision-making process and then looking to the patriarch to make the final decision.

The impact of relationships is also felt in the way that business is carried out. In the Arab world, business is based predominantly upon relationships. In this highly relationship-oriented society each family works toward the long-term accumulation of position, prestige, standing, relationship, and respect.

## Honor and Loyalty

Because of the relational society comes an intense focus on loyalty. It is expected and often guaranteed as leaders surround themselves with subordinates that they can trust.

Another difference in the Arab world is the practice of giving and preserving honor. The influence of the family is central to understanding the Arab manager's use of time during the working day. When a close family member appears at the office of even a very senior manager, it is regarded as improper for the demands of organizational hierarchy to take precedence over the obligations due to family. In other words, he is choosing to give honor to his family before giving priority to his work.

Leadership is a complex phenomenon in Arab organizations and is related to the ideal of honor. This is challenging concept for western-oriented managers because the West is a guilt-or-innocence culture where something is either right or it is wrong. The Arab world has a very different focus: it is an honor-or-shame culture. These two very diverse orientations generally shape the way work is conducted.

## Influence of Islam

When trying to understand the business culture and provide leadership in the Middle East, it is important to take into account the influence of Islam. This is not speaking of the influence of the local mosque, but the cultural underpinning of Islam in society. Similar to the way the West has been shaped by the practice of Christianity over centuries, the Middle East has become what it is from the influence of Islam.

In the Arab world it is believed that Islam is more than a religion that concerns itself merely with the spiritual aspects of life. Islam is literally a way of living that embraces the spiritual, moral, social, educational, and economic aspects of life. Islam does not separate religious and state authority in the way that is usual in the West. It is a religion of practice and is publicly visible rather than being only a private inner belief. Unlike the private western practices of religion, the business environment through-out the Middle East is deeply influenced by Islamic teaching and practice.

## Community

The idea of group orientation and relationships does not merely stem from the influence of the family. Unity is an Islamic practice that is expressed in the concept of the "ummah." This identifies the community of all believers who are joined as they touch the ground during prayer. The ummah is universal and indivisible, representing in a real sense a "body." This idea clearly proposes a different positioning for individuals in relation to other individuals collectively as a group. Value comes from participation in the ummah, rather than from individual practice.

The concept of group is very strong in Islam and throughout the Arab world. This strong cultural element pours into the business environment. And it must be understood in order to successfully understand how leaders develop in the Middle East. The employees' value and identity in large part come from the relationship network of which they are part.

## Time

Western-oriented people struggle with understanding why time is handled as it is in the Middle East. Unique from many other societies, strong cultural influences come from the application of time. There are three primary practices related to how time is used in the Middle East.

The fundamental difference is the age of time. In the West (specifically in the recently developed parts of the West like the United States), time is an "infant," whereas in the Middle East, time is a "seasoned adult." The idea is that time usage and understanding is comparative to the age of a country or region—just as to a child, time holds a different value than it does for an adult. A small child always wants things now and an adult learns a new set of standards related to what is and is not acceptable concerning the consumption of time. If you say something will happen in one month to a 3-year-old child, that will seem like forever. One month equals 1/36th of the child's life. But to a 55-year-old adult, one month equals 1/660th. The result is that the child and the adult have very different perspectives relating to time. The United States is just over 230 years old, whereas the Arab world is thousands of years old, and this influences the cultures' different views of time.

Another shaper of time is the phrase "Insha' Allah"; literally "If God wills." This can be a simple statement or a form of words covering the strong possibility of inaction or even a negative outcome to apparently agreed-on courses of action. There is a strong belief that time is only in God's hands so how can a mere human have assurance of future time. This idea has to be understood, as it is the heartbeat of the rhythm of life. In parts of the Middle East, it affects how planning is carried out. When outsiders hear Insha' Allah they often wonder if the people are making excuses or if they really mean it. Typically, it is stating a belief, but unfortunately it is abused as well.

Another concept that foreigners struggle with is the concept of "bukrah" implying "tomorrow." Time in the West is most often seen as definite, whereas in the Arab world time has indefinite characteristics. If it is Monday and a Westerner says tomorrow, he literally means Tuesday. He is taking time to mean something definite.

In the Arab world, bukrah combined with Insha'Allah would practically mean in the coming future rather than the precise meaning of the next day. Time is handled with respect for Allah and therefore man cannot make time definite. It is important to attach Arab cultural meaning to the phrases instead of exact western interpretations.

These concepts of time have an impact on how business is conducted, but more than that they have real impact on how to manage. A western-oriented organization has the responsibility to understand and adapt to the principles of the region if it wants to maximize the local leadership potential.

## Influence of the Family Business

The Middle East is ripe with family businesses. This concept is so strong that there are even family-run countries. The history of the family business is a critical component of the influence that the family has on how business is conducted. A westerner must be able to answer, "How does the concept of family business and its culture affect leadership in general?"

Even many of the mega-businesses are family owned and operated. From the exterior, they look very much like an international corporation, but the deep architecture and rhythms are that of a family business. The nature of a family business tends to be more patriarchal.

Although one may not be leading in a family business, it is still critical to understand the dynamics of a family business. For centuries it was the predominant business model, even up to recent times. So most Middle Easterners have adopted the family business model, and many even import similar practices into non–family businesses. Because of the prevalence of family businesses in the ME it is easy for national managers to lead by family business practices and drive them in their work, no matter what type of organization.

## Influence of Colonialism

Much of the Arab world has been subject to Western bureaucracy. This legacy includes a strict adherence to the chain of command, and adherence to secular systems. These systems somehow conflict with the local patterns and customs. There is a dichotomy between adopting Western models and the desire to retain culturally aligned approaches. The Western approaches appeal to the perception of prestige, but are they relevant and appropriate?

If an organization wants to succeed in developing leaders in the Middle East, it is imperative to pause and understand that the various influences are interrelated and do not operate separate from each other. One must see what this means first in terms of how business is conducted, what the needs of the workforce are, and then apply it to leadership development.

## The "Patriarch Model" of Leadership Development

Originally a patriarch was a man who exercised autocratic authority over an extended family. The word patriarch is a composition of "father" and "leader." And that idea is exactly what this model is built around—a leader with fatherly responsibility.

In the West the concept of being a father has a tendency toward viewing parenthood primarily in material terms. The belief is that the role of the father is to see to it that his children are well fed, obtain a good education, and have a good start in life.

Even a limited understanding of Islamic principles will convince one of how erroneous and shortsighted such a viewpoint is. This point is encapsulated in the thoughts that the direction of a child is attributed to the role of the parents. The father is in essence the role model of the child and has been given the pedestal of leadership in the home. The man (father and husband) is the keeper and leader of his family.

Leadership does not imply the right to be overbearing, but in actuality carries the meaning of responsibility. The father is the one who will be held responsible for the development and nurturing of his children. A tremendous responsibility has come to bear upon his shoulders. To view this only in materialistic terms is the height of folly, for one has to realize that sustenance and direction are the father's responsibility. The "Patriarch Model" of leadership is based upon the understanding of the modern patriarch and the key focus is on developing abilities for the future release of control and empowerment.

There is an inherent pride among top Arab leaders that they made it to where they are without leadership development. The question is, "did they?" Perhaps a few did, but most likely they did not. Their version of leadership development just looked different from many of the imported programs. Much of their development would have come in the way that a father develops a son rather than from a formal program. In Arab culture, development starts at the knee of the mother, continues into the classroom, and is broadened by their exposure to people and ideas. During the entire time, the father is the guide who sets the direction.

In the "Patriarch Model" it is a leader's responsibility to develop the abilities of his followers. The best way to mirror this is to learn from the father-son relationship. First, the father relies on the mother in the formative years to establish the rooting. Then a father will take his son with him to observe work and the father (leader) in action. After a period of observation, the father will discuss with the son what is happening. The focus is on developing the way the son thinks and what he sees. When the father is comfortable with the son's thinking patterns and behaviors, he will begin to give him responsibility and the opportunity to demonstrate his ability and value.

Simplifying how to develop leaders in the Middle East comes down to one word—patriarch. It is imperative to understand what this means. For some it is a confusing concept as they translate it to mean "father" in the western sense. This is not what a patriarch is—a patriarch is more than just a father who provides financially for his family. He is a leader with a truly deep fatherly responsibility.

Oftentimes organizations think they have the solution for how leadership development should be carried out in the Middle East. Instead of understanding where they are working, they just plow forward and commit serious faux pas. What they need to do is to begin with learning what influences the society. In the case of the Middle East, this means understanding the influence of the family, Islam, family business, and colonialism. Given this basic understanding the ability to develop leaders greatly improves. Following the understanding of culture, organizations should apply a locally relevant approach to leader development similar to the "Patriarch Model" that is present in this case study.

Although this case study relied upon the geography of the Middle East, the principles are applicable for any culture or region. What is necessary for developing leadership in global organizations is to understand the local influences and adapt the leader development model accordingly to maximize on the potential.

## Conclusion

Parenting is a conservative practice, and most rely on the same practice that their parents used, even if they know it may be out of date. Likewise, organizations tend to be conservative when they attempt to develop future leaders and follow the same routines that they and others have relied on over the years. They do this even if the approaches are outdated or, in the case of global organizations, when they do not export well. After all, those approaches have served them well. But what if there is another way to develop leaders, a better way?

A corporation's leadership development strategies should address the complexities of managing an increasingly diverse and global workforce. Global leadership is more than the popularized concepts of thinking globally, appreciating cultural diversity, building partnerships and alliances, and sharing leadership. It is about maximizing the potential that lies in each and every location that a multinational corporation operates from. Even though, in most markets around the world, there is an admiration for Western ways, global organizations will be well advised to leverage the local culture and combine it with their home office practices to create a globally significant program.

In order to maximize the return on investment in leadership development and to capitalize on the latent leadership potential in all markets, organizations need to break from the centrally created model and learn to balance the universal knowledge with local needs. This includes (1) understanding the uniqueness of the leaders' experience and environment, (2) maintaining focus on cultural heritage and organizational future, and (3) adapting the global leadership model and development approach to be harmonious with the cultures of the potential leaders.

Global organizations are not ignorant about these points; rather they recognize how challenging this is. In the private corridors, they report that their global environments are so hard to work in that attention is diverted from maximizing the potential there and is placed on developing efficient programs, thus utilizing the "cookie cutter" approach, which facilitates the fast-profit motive. But the question is, how does this resolve the original dilemma of "Why is so much invested in developing leaders, yet we don't have leaders?"

# CHAPTER 9

# Strategic Surveying in the Global Marketplace and the Role of Vitality Measures

Jeffrey M. Saltzman and Scott M. Brooks

As the global economy descended into recession in 2008, organizations struggled for survival. For many, short-term performance became the only focus. Long-term performance would not matter should an organization perish. Very few industries and very few corners of the planet were spared from financial threat.

As the recession seemed to stabilize, many organizations realized—at least in the abstract—that the economic lull could be used to build the discipline of becoming more effective. Certainly cost cutting forces prioritization of what an organization values. But questions loomed: What kinds of cuts satisfied the needs of *current performance*, and what kinds sacrificed *future potential*? What kinds of opportunity could emerge from this crisis?

Although these questions are brought into sharper focus by the recession, they highlight the general objective of optimizing present-day operations while investing in the innovation required to remain vital into the future. In fact, according to the *Random House Dictionary* (Dictionary.com, 2009), the second definition of *vitality* is the "capacity for survival or for the continuation of a meaningful or purposeful existence: *the vitality of an institution*" (italics in original). Some of the data we have seen suggests that many organizations in this time period are more strongly focusing on getting their internal houses in order, reorganizing, slimming down, cutting their way to prosperity (perhaps in their view), and putting somewhat less emphasis on modifying products and services to meet current customer desires. Other organizations are striking more of a balance between internal efficiencies and retooling products and services to increase their appeal given the current market conditions.

Although there can be many metrics to address the vitality of an organization, this chapter deals with what employees can tell us that helps to predict and manage future success. We will begin with an illustration of global research addressing *employee confidence,* a construct which taps directly into employee evaluations of the future. Results from countries representing the world's dozen largest economies will highlight a fundamental message: While cultural and national differences may challenge our ability to compare employee opinions across countries, there is still very valuable information remaining enabling us to predict performance, to draw conclusions, and correspondingly to manage the global workplace.

We will then draw the lessons of employee confidence into a larger model of *organizational vitality,* built from a cross-pollination of organizational literatures. There are direct implications from this model for monitoring and managing global organizations via employee survey techniques.

## Setting the Global Stage

For multinational organizations, one goal of a strategic employee survey is to collect a uniform metric that can be used as business intelligence, information gathering, or a monitoring measure to determine how the organization is performing and where the organization can most benefit from interventions. There are many challenges to the successful completion of this goal, and among them is the nature of globalization itself—the attempt to apply in a uniform fashion a measure to an environment that is anything but uniform. The word globalization often implies a uniformity that is just not there, rather than diversity and interdependence.

However, if we concluded that the extent of global diversity prevented any kind of systematic comparison across global units, then we would be at an impasse. One fundamental premise of this chapter is that people are more the same than different, and that although multinational organizations spread across a significant array of cultural, economic, functional, and legal differences, an organization by literal definition is attempting to assert a degree of "sameness" or consistent governance across the enterprise.

In general, if one is on a search for cultural differences, they can be found. The larger question is, however, are those differences of enough substance within the workplace that they should affect day-to-day management decision making and the operational characteristics of an organization? More concretely, do they impinge on our ability to predict traditional measures of financial performance? This point is explored in the program of research discussed in the following section.

## Case Study: Employee Confidence

The premise behind employee confidence is that individual employees know how their organization is faring, each from his or her unique perspective. And though no employee, including the CEO, has a comprehensive or total understanding of how the organization is doing, by collecting employee confidence information from the employee population or a significant cross-section of the employee population, in aggregate that information represents a "group intelligence." If asked the right questions, the providers of this group intelligence will shed light on organizational performance–related issues, offering not only a very good predictor of what is actually happening within the organization but also a road map to organizational improvement, suggesting specific interventions to enhance performance. This "employee as observer" framework has been examined for 30 years (for example, Schneider, Parkington, & Buxton, 1980). By this definition, organizations that exhibit a higher level of employee confidence are more vital.

Employee confidence is measured by asking the employees of an organization about their perceptions within four key areas, two related to organizational performance and two that are related to the individual's personal situation within the organization. A high level of employee confidence is achieved when employees perceive their organization as being effectively managed with good business processes, competitively positioned with attractive products or services, and when they believe that they have a promising future within their organization and, if needed, transportable skills that would be attractive to other employers.

## Measuring Employee Confidence

Employee confidence consists of two subdimensions, *organizational confidence* and *personal confidence,* and each of these subdimensions has an internal and external factor. The internal part of organizational confidence focuses on the internal functioning of the organization (that is, the degree to which it is managed well, the effectiveness of business processes, and its financial health or discipline). The external part of organizational confidence focuses on the environment in which the organization operates (such as industry health, competitiveness, attractiveness of products and services).

The internal part of personal confidence focuses on the employee's future with their current employer and is the traditional driver of how employee loyalty was generated from the employee's perspective (for example, job security, promising future, preparation for future). The external part of personal confidence asks about employees' perceptions of what would happen to them if they had to go onto the job market (that is, skills would allow them to find a similar job, with similar pay, and others are hiring people with their skills). External personal confidence represents "career" security, the ability to work within your profession, rather than "job" security, the ability to remain with your current employer, which is represented by internal personal confidence.

As a model the employee confidence concept can be depicted with a 2 × 2 chart as shown in Figure 9.1. For the study described below, each cell of this 2 × 2 was measured using three corresponding survey items (Saltzman & Herman, 2009).

Beginning in June 2008, quarterly Web surveys were administered to a global sample of approximately 15,500 full-time employees in the private sector, at least 18 years old and working in companies with at least 100 employees. The countries

**Figure 9.1. The Employee Confidence Framework.**

|  | Internal | External |
|---|---|---|
| **Organizational** | Effective management and business processes, financial success | Competitively well positioned, demand for products, attractive to customers |
| **Personal** | Job security, bright future at organization, long-term skill development | Transportable, up-to-date skills, equivalent job opportunities available elsewhere |

included in the sample were Brazil, Canada, China, France, Germany, India, Italy, Japan, Russia, Spain, United Kingdom, and the United States, representing approximately 75% of the world's gross domestic product (GDP). Five thousand employees were included from the United States, 1,000 from each other country with the exception of Russia, where 500 were sampled. Respondents were drawn from panels that have agreed to answer surveys in each country (the respondents from administration to administration are not necessarily the same). The samples were checked to ensure that they conformed to the demographics one expects within each of the countries included (for example, 50% male, 50% female). Twelve core employee confidence items and various outcome measures (such as pride, turnover potential) were asked, along with consumer intention items and those related to demographics and organizational characteristics. In addition, respondents were asked to provide the name of their organization, enabling matching to publicly available financial information.

## Employee Confidence Findings

As of this writing, five quarters of data have been examined within the employee confidence framework: the June 2008 baseline and four subsequent quarters. Within the sample, the responses associated with employee confidence follow a normal distribution and have been found to relate to multiple business performance outcomes and financial or economic measures.

## Gross Domestic Product (GDP)

A rank order correlation between change in gross domestic product and employee confidence for each of the 12 countries in the sample revealed a significant rho of .87 (replication six months later yielded .77). The BRIC countries (Brazil, Russia, India, China) in general had the highest employee confidence scores. In other words, countries with higher levels of employee confidence are more likely to be those with rapidly growing economies (see Table 9.1).

The significant relationships demonstrate that whatever the cultural component of employee confidence, there is a substantial amount of useful and meaningful country-by-country variance related to economic factors. In fact, the most meaningful trends in employee confidence from June 2008 to June 2009 can be readily mapped to economic events and business news within each country (see Table 9.2). Note that these qualitative analyses

### Table 9.1. Employee Confidence Aligns with Rank Order Change in Gross Domestic Product.

| Country | Confidence Rank Order | Δ2006 GDP | ΔGDP Rank Order | |
|---|---|---|---|---|
| India | 1 | 9.70 | 2 | Three of four rapidly expanding economies |
| Russia | 2 | 8.10 | 3 | |
| United States | 3 | 1.82 | 6 | |
| China | 4 | 11.40 | 1 | |
| Brazil | 5 | 5.40 | 4 | |
| Canada | 6 | 1.65 | 8 | |
| Germany | 7 | 1.71 | 7 | |
| United Kingdom | 8 | 1.43 | 9 | Three of four slowest growth or shrinking economies |
| Spain | 9 | 1.84 | 5 | |
| France | 10 | 1.14 | 10 | |
| Italy | 11 | −.04 | 12 | |
| Japan | 12 | 1.01 | 11 | |

$rho = .87$

Notes: Employee Confidence measured in June 2008.

Change in Gross Domestic figures were as of 2006, the most recent available for all countries.

# Table 9.2. Employee Confidence Percentage Scores.

| | Δ 2Q09 – 1Q09 | 2Q09 | 1Q09 | 4Q08 | 3Q08 | 2Q08 |
|---|---|---|---|---|---|---|
| U.S. | 5.3 | 98.9 | 93.6 | 101.4 | 103.4 | 100.0 |
| UK | 4.6 | 99.0 | 94.4 | 102.6 | 103.0 | 100.0 |
| Germany | 7.6 | 99.0 | 91.4 | 101.3 | 100.7 | 100.0 |
| France | 8.4 | 101.4 | 93.0 | 101.5 | 99.6 | 100.0 |
| Canada | 1.6 | 98.9 | 97.3 | 99.9 | 105.4 | 100.0 |
| China | 12.5 | 102.3 | 89.8 | 100.7 | 99.9 | 100.0 |
| India | 8.1 | 99.6 | 91.5 | 99.3 | 100.1 | 100.0 |
| Russia | 12 | 100.9 | 88.9 | 98.3 | 101.6 | 100.0 |
| Brazil | 6.8 | 107.2 | 100.4 | 106.4 | 105.7 | 100.0 |
| Japan | –0.7 | 93.8 | 94.5 | 93.6 | 99.5 | 100.0 |
| Spain | 3.9 | 96.0 | 92.1 | 100.5 | 100.1 | 100.0 |
| Italy | 5 | 97.8 | 92.8 | 100.3 | 101.3 | 100.0 |

Brazil has the most positive employees relative to 2Q08. Brazil's "growth cycle outlook" was also the only one to be rated "downturn" rather than "strong slowdown" in December 2008 by the OECD.

Shanghai, July 16 (*New York Times*)—Fueled by an ambitious economic stimulus program and aggressive bank lending, China's economy grew by 7.9 percent in the second quarter of this year, the government said Thursday, a surprisingly strong showing given the world economic crisis

Tokyo, April 30 (Reuters) – Japan's industrial output rose more than expected in March (1.6%), the first gain in six months.

China and Russia strongly bounced back, as did France, India, and Germany in 2Q09. Four of 12 countries equal or exceed initial score of 100.

These ranking also match events as reported in *The Wall Street Journal*; there is exceptionally high unemployment in Spain, and the United Kingdom's economy is posting sleep drops, which are dashing hopes for a quick recovery.

focus on *changes* in employee confidence. Using each country as its own baseline helps to highlight that growth or decline are less influenced by the myriad factors that make global comparisons difficult. Note that each country's score was set to 100 in June 2008, and changes since then are a proportion against that baseline. Table 9.2 shows whether a country's employee confidence has increased when compared to the June 2008 baseline (numbers above 100) or whether it has declined (numbers below 100). This method provides a reasonably culture-free way of assessing change within each country, as each country has the same starting point of 100 regardless of raw score. It could be argued that certain cultures would have different "rates" of change against the baseline over time driven by culture, but the analyses performed so far have shown no evidence to support that notion. This method could also be used with large international organizations or those with diverse product lines as a method to create an apples-to-apples comparison of change (improvement or decline) across the organization.

### Unemployment

The second quarter 2009 administration of the employee confidence survey, with a bolstered sample of more than 10,000 respondents, enabled a state-by-state comparison within the United States. Additionally, since U.S. economic data are more regularly and readily available than that for many countries globally, we were able to compare unemployment before, during, and after the survey. In short, employee confidence correlated significantly with unemployment, fractionally stronger with the survey measure as a leading indicator of subsequent quarter unemployment $(-.42)$ than as a concurrent $(-.36)$ or lagging $(-.38)$ indicator. Figure 9.2 shows the relationship of employee confidence in the second quarter of 2009 as related to unemployment in the third quarter.

### Company Performance

Aggregating employee opinions to a country or state level helps to illustrate that employee opinions have relevance and usefulness across cultural and governmental borders. However, organizations are typically interested in driving their own financial results as

**Figure 9.2. Employee Confidence and U.S. State Unemployment.**

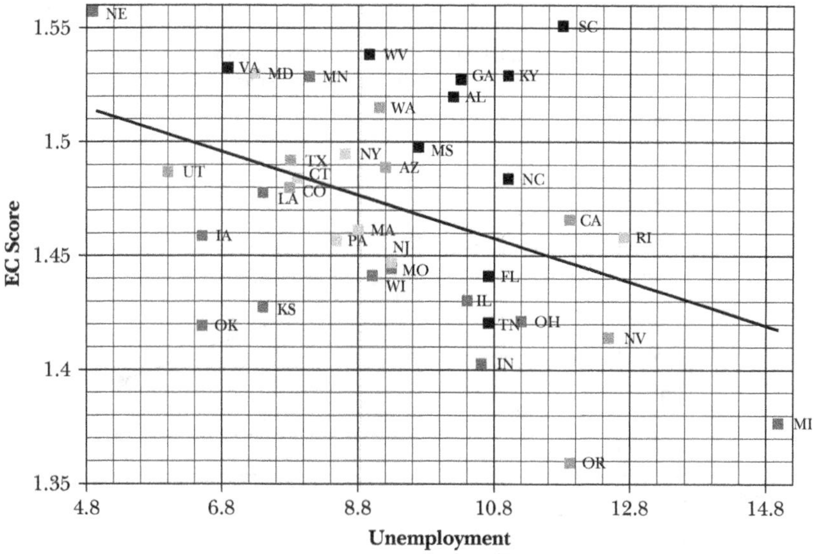

Note: Only states with at least 50 employee survey respondents were included in the analyses.

opposed to macro-economic performance. With a subsample of U.S.-based organizations, public financial records were matched to individuals' survey results. Findings included:

• Companies with top-quartile employee confidence averaged −16.79%, three-year total rate of return (TRR), contrasted with companies having bottom quartile employee confidence at −37.66%. Note that these distressed financial results were due to the study's coinciding with the recession of 2008–2009.
• Diluted Earnings per Share showed a change of +2.33 where individuals had top-quartile employee confidence, versus −5.74 for the corresponding bottom-quartile employee confidence group.

Additionally, employee confidence matched self-report measures of recent organizational performance. Sixty-eight percent of those with high employee confidence reported that their company

## Figure 9.3. Employee Confidence and Organizational Performance.

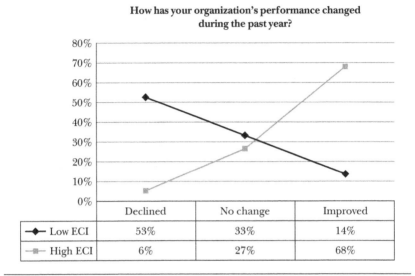

How has your organization's performance changed during the past year?

|  | Declined | No change | Improved |
|---|---|---|---|
| ◆ Low ECI | 53% | 33% | 14% |
| ■ High ECI | 6% | 27% | 68% |

Note: Y-axis scores reflect percent favorable scores on employee confidence.

performance has improved over the last 12 months versus 53% of those with low employee confidence reporting that it has declined (see Figure 9.3). Thus, we can conclude that employee perceptions of performance align with the fiscal reality.

### Consumer Confidence

It could be logically argued that the source of consumer confidence comes from what is happening to the individual employee at work. If workers are concerned about losing their jobs or have other reasons to doubt the health of the organization, they are likely to put off buying that new car, refrigerator, or home. The perception of current financial well-being and people with low versus high levels of employee confidence was examined to see if differences would emerge in their anticipated consumer spending.

It is very clear that those with lower levels of employee confidence express more worry about their personal financial well-being and that this worry carries over to stated intentions

**Figure 9.4.  Employee Confidence and Purchasing Confidence.**

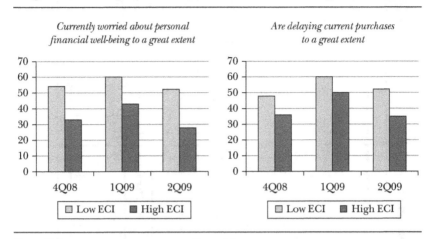

Note: Values represent percentage favorable.

regarding consumer spending (see Figure 9.4). Additionally, Employee Confidence was also found to mirror the pattern seen on the monthly measure of consumer confidence published by the Conference Board (see Figure 9.5).

## Case Study Conclusions

The lessons of this case study are as follows:

- National differences in employee confidence clearly exist.
- Because of the significant relationship with changes in GDP (initial rank order coefficient of .87 and replication of .77), clearly a substantial proportion of country-by-country variance can be explained by economic factors, and not simply cultural factors.
- Employee confidence has worldwide meaning and predictive value.
- Within-country *changes* in employee opinions are more comparable than raw scores. For example, comparing China's raw score to other countries (it has the fourth highest) is much less valuable than comparing China's change from June 2008 to June 2009 (it is the second largest improvement).

# Figure 9.5. Employee Confidence and U.S. Consumer Confidence.

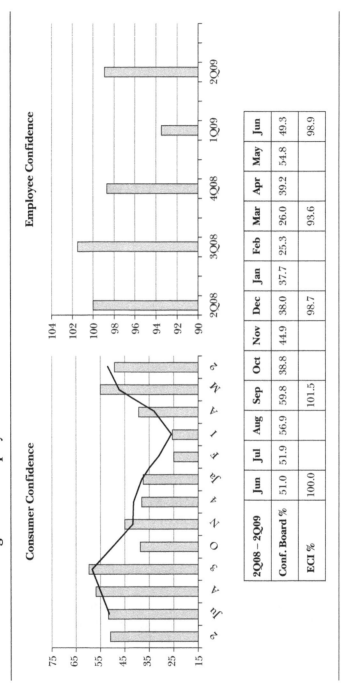

| 2Q08 – 2Q09 | Jun | Jul | Aug | Sep | Oct | Nov | Dec | Jan | Feb | Mar | Apr | May | Jun |
|---|---|---|---|---|---|---|---|---|---|---|---|---|---|
| Conf. Board % | 51.0 | 51.9 | 56.9 | 59.8 | 38.8 | 44.9 | 38.0 | 37.7 | 25.3 | 26.0 | 39.2 | 54.8 | 49.3 |
| ECI % | 100.0 | | | 101.5 | | | 98.7 | | | 93.6 | | | 98.9 |

- Employee opinions about the future (company performance, competitive standing, personal promising future, and so on) reflect organizational vitality, as demonstrated by relationships with a variety of economic health indicators (consumer confidence, unemployment) and company financial metrics (DEPS, TRR).

## Enduring Survey Purposes

What is the real point of organizational surveys? Whatever the specific angle of any given survey effort, survey programs are intended to produce change. Perhaps more progressive systems are designed to promote the *discipline* of change management, of listening and responding to important constituents and feedback about organizational performance. In fact, they share this in common with any measurement system (accounting systems, customer surveys, quality audits, sales forecasts, six-sigma methods, and so on).

Stepping back from surveys in particular, what are the common areas that organizations attempt to change? What are the most common challenges companies face? To address this question, many models of organizational effectiveness exist, from the simple (Five Stages of Organizational Decline, Collins, 2009) to the involved (for example, Burke-Litwin Model, Burke & Litwin, 1992), and the academic (Systems Model, Katz & Kahn, 1978) to the applied (Balanced Scorecard, Kaplan & Norton, 1996; McKinsey 7 S Framework, Peters & Waterman, 1982) to the hybrid (High Performance Model, Wiley & Brooks, 2000). Stepping back from any single model, there appear to be five enduring challenges that virtually any organization faces in its pursuit of growth and financial sustainability or, more generally, vitality:

1. **Customer Loyalty.** Organizations seek to create value by providing customers—particularly paying customers—with valued and competitive products and services.
2. **Progressive Innovation.** This reflects the creation of value through refining and inventing future products and services.
3. **Quality Work Processes.** Products need to be efficiently created and, along with services, effectively delivered.

4. **Engaged Employees**. Organizations need to create an engaging experience to encourage the most from the people who fuel the processes, create the innovation, and deliver for the customers.

5. **Clear and Compelling Leadership**. The overarching mission and direction of the organization needs to be developed and translated through its leaders in order to properly secure and align resources.

We do not present these five as the only challenges that an organization may face. Certainly there can be crises of ethics, weak financial discipline, regulatory issues, progressive sustainability interests, and so forth. But these five reflect core challenges that apply virtually universally to any organization.

The employee confidence case study illustrates one version of slicing across these areas, touching particularly upon engagement, leadership, and customer competitiveness. There is, in fact, a rich history of research linking these topics to organizational climate and performance. Recent reviews for each topic include Brooks et al. (2006) for Customer Loyalty; Bledow, Frese, Erez, Anderson, and Farr, (2009) for Innovation; Miron, Erez, & Naveh (2004) for Quality; Macey and Schneider (2008) for Employee Engagement; and Efron, Greenslade, & Salob (2005) for Leadership.

We argue that the vital organization is the one that can focus on improving these disciplines, becoming a change-ready organization, enabled to meet its challenges.

## Organizational Ambidexterity

Each of the five challenges can be addressed on two levels: maximizing current performance and developing future potential. For example, the Leadership challenge can involve enhancing current leadership behaviors (for example, communication and prioritization), as well as developing a succession plan for the next generation of senior executives. Because no organization has unlimited resources—whether those resources are money, talent, or time—the appropriate balance, one leading to maximum vitality, must be struck between current performance and future potential. Table 9.3 provides examples of how each of the five areas can have a current performance and a future potential component.

**Table 9.3. Enduring Challenges Involve Both Current
Performance and Future Potential.**

|  | Clear, Compelling Leadership | Quality Work Processes | Engaged, Confident Employees | Progressive Innovation | Loyal Customers |
|---|---|---|---|---|---|
| **Current Performance** | Effective Senior Management | Quality, Reduced Waste | Discretionary Effort | Market Competitiveness | Service |
| **Future Potential** | Leadership Development | Continuous Improvement | Employee Retention | Product Pipeline | Customer Retention, Growth |

The pursuit of maximizing current performance generally involves streamlining systems, increasing scale, decreasing costs, and other efforts to control and standardize the organization's efforts. The pursuit of developing future potential generally depends less on control and more on creativity. The latter is an inherently riskier endeavor. Thus, there is a built-in tension between *exploiting* current opportunities and *exploring* future potential. The management of this tension is called *organizational ambidexterity* (see, for example, O'Reilly & Tushman, 2004).

A full elaboration of organizational ambidexterity is bigger than the scope of this chapter, but to summarize, it represents an emerging organizational science of balancing priorities focused on building efficiencies (process within a paradigm) against priorities encouraging creative exploration (into new paradigms; see Bledow et al., 2009). Though it may not impact a traditional survey program, any model of organizational effectiveness needs to incorporate this tension, and perhaps new survey programs need to take it into account.

## Organizational Change and Resilience

Organizations are run by people, and people face challenges in pursuing common goals and in their day-to-day efforts to enhance performance. Striking just the right balance regarding how to invest in organizational improvements—for example, choosing between maximizing current performance and developing future potential—is a chief concern with which organizations—and people—struggle. Being resilient in addressing these challenges is a necessary component to maximizing the vitality of the organization. As described below, resiliency is an organizational characteristic as well as a personal attribute that, in conjunction with balancing the resource allocations associated with maximizing current performance and future potential, would lead to increased levels of organization vitality.

Measuring the organization on a global scale, as can be done with employee confidence, is one effective way of predicting and managing an organization's future—in effect, to manage organizational change. "The pace of change is quickening" is a true statement, not just within an industry, geopolitical entity, or by level of industrialization, but globally. How an organization deals with change and its pace, both at an individual and at an organizational level, will determine its long-term success. The old notion that an organization can achieve long-term stability in its customer base, product line, operating processes, or technology is unrealistic if the organization is to thrive and cope with today's ongoing challenges. Today's environment is more volatile than ever and will remain so for the foreseeable future. Challenges will become more and more "routine," and responding effectively to them will be a "normal" issue that organizations need to be equipped to face. Organizations need to be able to cope with challenges and to do so in a way that is sustainable and does not limit future options. In fact, balancing the need to drive performance in a definitive fashion while keeping future options open are two goals that are somewhat in opposition. Both are required for success (Berkes, Colding, & Folke, 2003). Organizations that perform well in these areas as they deal with their challenges will be by definition more resilient to threats and will be exhibiting higher levels of vitality.

> If a corporation aspires to perform as well as the market indexes over the long term, it will have to change at the pace and scale of the market, but without losing control. Companies, of course, do not have to change at the pace and scale of the market, but if they do not, then the research from McKinsey's Long Term Performance Database shows that they are more than likely to underperform for their investors. [McKinsey & Company, 2009]

Resiliency is a construct that has generated increasing interest since the 1990s and has been studied at the individual and organizational level. Being resilient is the notion of positive adaptation when faced with significant adversity or environmental threats (Rutter, 1993). This definition implies that significant threats or severe adversity are present and that the individual or organization positively copes with those threats. Being more resilient rather than less has been shown to lead to positive outcomes for both individuals and organizations (Cohn, Fredrickson, Brown, & Mikels, 2009; Berkes, Colding, & Folke, 2003).

Vitality is the aggregation of resiliency measures and other critical metrics of organizational performance that, when tracked and improved upon, enhances the organization's ability to deal with the increasing volatility seen in the organization's environment. Under normal conditions, the data suggest, an organization whose vitality measures are appropriately designed, accurately measured, and higher than the competition will not only achieve higher levels of resiliency but will also outperform that competition. It is important to note that the vitality data represented by these concepts have been found to be malleable, that is, changeable over time if the correct measures are teamed up with appropriate change processes. Protection from a loss of vitality and resilience does not only involve the factors impinging at the moment, but rather the way the organization deals with the ongoing and future risks and threats—processes which are potential inflection points in the organization's life.

Being able to maintain the vitality of the organization and its level of functioning when environmentally challenged will be dependent on:

1. The level of the threat or degree of risk that the organization is facing, including the performance of the organization on the five common challenges cited earlier:

    a. Customer loyalty
    b. Progressive innovation
    c. Quality work processes
    d. Engaged employees
    e. Clear and compelling leadership

2. The organization's response to the threat or risk and its ability to turn that risk into opportunity
3. The appropriateness of the vitality measures that the organization is tracking
4. The processes and mechanisms that the organization has in place to maintain those vitality measures at a high level

Three broad areas—the environment within which the organization resides, the investments the organization is making, and the achievements which the organization celebrates—contain six key vitality processes which can be brought to bear to help address the threats that the organization faces, including:

1. **Environment**

   - **Monitoring:** Information collection or environmental monitoring (for example, employee, customer and supplier surveys, the gathering and analysis of other business metrics).
   - **Reducing:** Minimizing the occurrence of negative chain reactions that can occur from one threat, before they spiral out of control (for example, strong internal and external communications networks).

2. **Investment**

   - **Warding:** Investing in a shared vision, a shared operating style, senior leadership, employees, products and services, and quality—the standardization of those products and services as well as organizational procedures.
   - **Transforming:** Turning risks into opportunities by developing a culture of innovative and creating organizational capabilities.
   - **Enhancing:** Increasing organizational effectiveness and efficacy (for example, cost control, state-of-the-art business processes, contingency planning).

3. **Achievement**

   - **Celebrating:** Celebrating and rewarding organizational and personal accomplishments (for example, successful completion of goals; reward and recognition systems).

Overall a well-designed framework builds in a positive fashion off outcomes traditionally cited as the marks of resiliency in a person or organization, including reduced failure probabilities, reduced consequences from failures, and reduced time to recovery (Holling, 1973). Specific vitality factors have been linked to increasing organizational performance (Brooks et al., 2006), and the organization's ability to achieve satisfied customers (Kendall, 2006). Though they should be tailored to each organization, specific factors can include:

1. Having a confident, engaged workforce
2. Not taking success or customers for granted
3. Producing quality products and services that meet customers' current needs
4. Delivering products and services with a customer service orientation
5. Creating products and services with perceived value
6. Operating with a disciplined growth orientation
7. Implementing effective business processes
8. Having effective leadership
9. Ensuring the right people in the right jobs, overall
10. Developing a strong new product and service pipeline
11. Operating in a sustainable fashion
12. Operating with ethics and transparency

## Measuring Vitality and Other Metrics in a Globalizing World

Organizations work hard to maximize performance by increasing their effectiveness. Efficiencies are strived for, the ability to do more with less—and if at the same time the organization can minimize risk to itself, that is just icing on the cake. The complexity of these goals increases exponentially as the size and complexity of the organization increases. Global organizations that need to deal with varied divisions or business units spread across multiple countries—with unique cultures, political situations, infrastructures, and so forth—face particularly challenging situations. Much research has been done to quantify the differences and the similarities that are apparent within the work-force across various countries and cultures. Some of the research seems to focus chiefly on the differences that exist (Hofstede, 1984), whereas others focus more on the similarities (Lundby & Hui, 2008). But in many respects everyone is after the same thing: increasing organizational effectiveness.

We can derive models that highlight our similarities or models that highlight our differences, but the main question is, are we collecting, monitoring, and analyzing information that makes a difference in the performance for the organization under study? That question is often answered by undertaking linkage studies, where employee opinions are aggregated by work group or business unit, and matched to various measures of performance (such as customer satisfaction, financial performance) and then analyzed for impact. Though there are methodological approaches to controlling for cultural or other geographic differences, this kind of research is based on the notion that creating a similar measure of employee opinions across various countries and cultures is in fact legitimate. One challenge that researchers of organizational culture face is to determine whether broad, across-the-globe measures of opinions are appropriate, and, in fact, if they measure anything approaching the same constructs in differing societies. The questions emerge: Are we more similar when it comes to how you measure attitudes or are we more different, requiring perhaps a differing measurement instrument depending on where you happen to be located? Do individual differences outweigh our ability to develop a uniform measure, or can well-worded questions embedded within robust paradigms win out in creating global measures of psychological constructs seen within organizations?

As the case study presented earlier demonstrates, there can be enough commonality across employee opinions aggregated at a country level to result in significant and meaningful relationships with changes in gross domestic product. Accommodating for cultural differences would likely only improve upon this already substantial relationship. For researchers and for organizational leaders of global organizations, this is a fortunate and perhaps necessary foundation. With some measures, like employee confidence, more is better no matter where—or how—you live in the world.

This view is similar to emerging conclusions regarding cultural influences in selection and assessment (J. Weekley, personal communication, 22 September, 2009). First, culture does not change the important constructs to assess. Second, culture can change the benchmarks or average scores to a degree (though more for personality than for general mental ability). Third, the validity of these constructs in predicting important performance criteria appears comparable across cultures.

Though it may sound like an oxymoron, we human beings are all fundamentally the same and yet all of us, each and every one of us, is uniquely different. We are all human and our humanness forces each of us to operate and experience the world within the evolutionarily derived boundaries of Homo sapiens. Yet what we celebrate (or perhaps should celebrate) most about our humanness is our individual differences and the freedom we have to make choices, which together yield an infinite number of ways in which we can express our humanity. We all may have a unique fingerprint, but we all have fingerprints.

Some of us choose to work in health care, others plant crops, some sell goods or services, others teach, drive a taxi, work in construction, practice law, become an accountant, sing on a stage, play sports, operate a business, or a whole host of other activities. Some of us prefer to live in urban environments, whereas for others only rural will do. Some of us prefer to travel and others are homebodies, perhaps even living within a few miles of where they were born. Some of us take comfort in being religious and others are not religious. Some get married, perhaps having children, and others prefer to stay single. The great majority of us will have opinions and ideas throughout our lives that will be strongly shaped by the cultures and societies in which we grew up, the experiences we had—and our choices will be influenced accordingly.

As we make those choices we are creating a unique set of outcomes that helps to define ourselves. For instance, look at the rural construction worker who married his high school sweetheart, has three kids and a dog, and likes to travel to new places each time the family takes a vacation. That is a combination of characteristics that is accumulated over the course of one's life that helps to differentiate each and every one of us from the others. However, as we pick and choose between the enormous numbers of choices that are possible as we experience our lives, we are all in pursuit of the same thing. We have the expectation that should we be able to achieve our goals, whether they are to work in health care, construction, plant crops, travel, or to get married and have kids, that somehow we will be happier. We make these choices and live our lives in the pursuit of happiness, an underlying fundamental of our humanity. When people feel that they have no or few options available to them they tend toward depression, and one intervention to assist those who feel like they have few options is to help them understand the choices that they do in fact have (Wake & Miller 1992).

Defining ourselves, our organizations, or our societies by focusing on the sameness that exists between them is both illusory and real, as it is focusing only on their uniqueness that defines them. It is illusory for we, our organizations, and our various societies are clearly not the same. But it is real in that they all have shared underlying characteristics. The richness that describes the diversity of humanity, or our lack of sameness, yields a more robust humanity, with individuals bringing differing experiences, knowledge, skill sets, characteristics and abilities, and with differing cultures and societies contributing uniquely to the powerful mix. But we would defy you to find a worker anywhere in the world, of any generation or any other demographic you would care to choose, who did not want to be treated respectfully and in a dignified fashion, or want to feel valued, with a sense of accomplishment springing from their efforts, a sense of fairness of treatment with respect to equity, and pride in their organizations and themselves. And one who would not want to have confidence in the future of his or her organization. We could go on describing other shared characteristics of workers, but the point is simply that a large number of commonalities do in fact exist.

As we measure ourselves and our organizations from a characteristics standpoint, do we focus on our similarities, our differences, or do we somehow attempt to measure both? Is it legitimate to use the same measures of employee satisfaction or loyalty, and so on in a highly industrialized country with a high standard of living as it is in a country under the constant threat of famine, disease, war, or terrorism? We have argued that we humans are both similar and different. We further contend that our similarities make it possible to create a measurement with enough robustness to work across the wide spectrum of situations in which organizations are enmeshed.

As great an impact as globalization has had so far, the people of the world today are not homogenous culturally, economically, politically, or demographically. And by extension the organizations that operate in a global fashion are not homogenous, culturally, economically, politically, or demographically either. Organizations that operate globally work to maximize their performance across a wide variety of cultures, economic conditions, political systems, and demographic characteristics of the local populations. It is a challenge. Many of these multinational, multicultural, multipolitical, and multidemographic organizations, in their attempt to assess their organizational cultures, use standardized measures across their internal organizational components—and this raises a question. By doing this are they measuring the simple fact that each of these divergent components has fingerprints, or are the standard measures and the methodologies employed with them sensitive enough to capture the unique characteristics of each fingerprint within the organization? What is lost and what is gained in this approach?

## Conclusion

Global, multinational surveys are difficult. But they are simply a microcosm of all efforts designed to respond to organizational challenges and to improve organizational functioning in some way. With this in mind, the major themes of this chapter can be wrapped up in a handful of key points:

- Organizational surveys, perhaps especially those in large, global organizations, need to drive toward improving effectiveness.
- Accordingly, the purpose of surveys is not to characterize differences in work climate or culture. There is no denying the impact of culture. However, it is more important to focus on the common "something" that the organization pursues.
- Thus, a survey strategy, if truly strategic, is part of a larger organizational change strategy, one that maps into the five enduring

challenges reflected by leadership, quality processes, employee engagement, innovation, and customer loyalty. Employee confidence provides one example of such a measure.

Thinking of surveys in this way parallels the evolution of Human Resources, with the ongoing efforts of HR professionals to become increasingly strategic business partners. HR interests and objectives are more and more defined first by the needs of their line management clients and second by their human resources functional requirements (Vosburgh, 2007). As mentioned in the introduction, *vitality* is the "capacity for survival or for the continuation of a meaningful or purposeful existence," and thereby reflects this notion of starting with the end in mind. Building this capacity is about nurturing the overarching disciplines of resiliency and ambidexterity.

## References

Berkes, F., Colding, J., & Folke, C. (2003). *Navigating social-ecological systems*. Cambridge: Cambridge University Press.

Bledow, R., Frese, M., Erez, M., Anderson, N., & Farr, J. (2009). A dialectic perspective on innovation: Conflicting demands, multiple pathways, and ambidexterity. *Industrial and Organizational Psychology: Perspectives on Science and Practice, 2*, 305–337.

Brooks, S. M., Wiley, J. W., & Hause, E. L. (2006). Using Employee and Customer Perspectives to Improve Organizational Performance. In L. Fogli (Ed.), *Customer service delivery: Research and best practices*. San Francisco: Jossey-Bass.

Burke, W. W., & Litwin, G. H. (1992). A causal model of organizational performance and change. *Journal of Management, 18*, 523–545.

Cohn, M. A., Fredrickson, B. L., Brown, S. L., & Mikels, J. A. (2009). Happiness unpacked: Positive emotions increase life satisfaction by building resilience. *Emotions*, 361–367.

Collins, J. (2009). *How the mighty fall*. New York: Harper Collins.

Dictionary.com. (2009). Definition of "Vitality." Retrieved from http://dictionary.reference.com/browse/vitality.

Efron, M., Greenslade, S., & Salob, M. (2005). Growing great leaders: Does it really matter? *Human Resource Planning, 28*, 18–23.

Hofstede, G. (1984). *Culture's consequences: international differences in work-related values*. Thousand Oaks, CA: Sage.

Holling, C. (1973). Resilience and stability of ecological systems. *Annual Review of Ecology and Systematics*, 1–23.

Kaplan, R. S., & Norton, D. P. (1996). *Translating strategy into action: The balanced scorecard.* Boston: Harvard Business School Press.

Katz, D., & Kahn, R. L. (1978). *The social psychology of organizations* (2nd ed.). New York: Wiley.

Kendall, S. (2006). Customer service from the customer's perspective. In L. Fogli (Ed.), *Customer service delivery: Research and best practices.* San Francisco: Jossey-Bass.

Lundby, K., & Hui, H. (2008). Employee engagement across Asia Pacific: Same or not the same? In M. Battista (Chair), *Associate engagement in Asia—Myth or mystery?* Symposium/forum presented at the Twenty-third Annual Conference of the Society for Industrial and Organizational Psychology, San Francisco, CA.

Macey, W. H., & Schneider, B. (2008). The meaning of employee engagement. *Industrial and Organizational Psychology: Perspectives on Science and Practice, 1,* 3–30.

McKinsey & Company. (2009, June 15). *Managing in turbulent times, the pace of change.* Retrieved June, 2009, from McKinsey & Company: www.mckinsey.com/ideas/MITT/paceofchange/index.asp.

Miron, E., Erez, M., & Naveh, E. (2004). Do personal characteristics and cultural values that promote innovation, quality, and efficiency compete or complement each other? *Journal of Organizational Behavior, 25,* 175–199.

O'Reilly, C. A., III, & Tushman, M. L. (2004). The ambidextrous organization. *Harvard Business Review, 82,* 74–81.

Peters, T. J., & Waterman, R. H. Jr. (1982). *In search of excellence: Lessons from America's best-run companies.* New York: Harper & Row.

Rutter, M. (1993). Psychosocial resilience and protective mechanisms. In J. Rolf, *Risk and protective factors in the development of psychopathoplogy* (pp. 181–212). Cambridge: Cambridge University Press.

Saltzman, J. M., & Herman, A. (2009). *Understanding employee confidence in today's environment: 3Q09 Invited presentation delivered at the Fourth Annual Kenexa World Conference.* Dallas, TX.

Schneider, B., Parkington, J. J., & Buxton, V. M. (1980). Employee and customer perceptions of service in banks. *Administrative Science Quarterly, 25,* 252–267.

Vosburgh, R. M. (2007). The evolution of HR: Developing HR as an internal consulting organization. *Human Resource Planning, 30,* 11–23.

Wake, M. M., & Miller, J. F. (1992). Treating hopelessness. *Clinical Nursing Research,* 347–365.

Wiley, J. W., & Brooks, S. M. (2000). The high-performance organizational climate: How workers describe top-performing units. In N. S. Ashkanasy, C. Wilderom, & M. F. Peterson (Eds.), *The handbook of organizational culture and climate,* (pp. 177–191). Thousand Oaks, CA: Sage.

# CHAPTER 10

# Best Practices for Training Intercultural Competence in Global Organizations

Jessica L. Wildman, Luiz F. Xavier, Mitch Tindall, and Eduardo Salas

Consider the following set of facts regarding global business: research findings indicate that between 16–40% of expatriate managers end their foreign assignments early, often due to poor performance or an inability to adjust to foreign environments (Black & Mendenhall, 1990; Rahim, 1983). Even if expatriates stay the length of their assignment, oftentimes their assignment can be viewed as a failure because of lost opportunities, delayed productivity, or damaged relationships (Bennett, Aston, & Colquhoun, 2000; Littrell, Salas, Hess, Paley, & Riedel, 2006; Selmer, Torbiorn, & Leon, 1998). With the direct cost of sending expatriates to their foreign assignments as high as $220,000 (Birdseye & Hill, 1995), having a substantial proportion of expatriate assignments failing can cost organizations substantially. For example, it has been estimated that each failed expatriate assignment costs organizations between $50,000 and $150,000, with cumulative annual costs of expatriate failures totaling around $2 billion for U.S. organizations (Copeland & Griggs, 1985; Harris & Moran, 1979; Misa & Fabricatore, 1979). Furthermore, even if the expatriate assignment is successfully completed, a large proportion of expatriates leave the organization within a year of returning to their native country because they have difficulty readjusting to U.S. life and culture (Gomez-Mejia & Balkin, 1987).

As workforce globalization increases, intercultural experiences such as expatriate assignments are becoming more commonplace. The grim state of expatriate assignments just described highlights the growing need for effective cultural interventions. Encouragingly, there has been an increased focus in both science and practice on improving the quality of intercultural interactions (Byram, 1997; Deardorff, 2009; Hall, 1992; Landis, Bennett, & Bennett, 2004). Many organizations are now using training programs to make their employees more "culturally competent" before sending them abroad. Intercultural competence training is often touted as a method of increasing the success of expatriate assignments and repatriation. Holtbrügge and Schillo (2008) further argue that intercultural training has the potential to benefit not only expatriates and others in face-to-face intercultural situations, but also virtual delegates interacting with people from other cultures.

Despite an increase in intercultural training use, there is very little consensus in both science and industry regarding what intercultural competence actually entails or the best way to train for it. Moreover, organizations tend to use any training intervention they can get their hands on without a clear understanding of why and how to most effectively implement them. Therefore, this chapter is aimed at providing practical guidance regarding the training of intercultural competence in employees of global organizations. The chapter will take four main thrusts toward this goal. First, we describe intercultural competence and the various constructs that can be considered part of intercultural competence. Second, we delineate several extant intercultural competence training approaches that have grown out of organizational science. Third, we look at the criticality of proper training assessment, and directly apply the science of training assessment to the arena of intercultural competence training. Finally, we integrate the previous sections into several best practices for global organizations that desire to train their employees effectively in intercultural competence.

## What Is Intercultural Competence?

Before we can discuss how to most effectively train toward intercultural competence, it is necessary to clearly define intercultural competence as a construct. Some have defined intercultural competence as skills that allow an individual to be sensitive to interpersonal dynamics, be perceptive to complex interactive situations, and be able to control their emotions (Lonner & Hayes, 2004). Others have described intercultural competence simply as the ability to function effectively in another culture (Gertsen, 1990). This latter broad description of intercultural competence allows for a wide variety of knowledge and skills to be considered that can contribute to an employee's intercultural competence. Accordingly, our chapter adopts this broad approach to the conceptualization of intercultural competence by discussing a variety of skill sets that could potentially contribute to an individual's success in intercultural situations. Restated, we adopt Gertsen's (1990) broad definition of intercultural competence as the ability to function effectively, and consequently include several theoretical constructs considered to be integral to success in an intercultural context. In the following sections, emotional intelligence, social intelligence, adaptability, and perspective taking are introduced as the critical skill sets that make up intercultural competence. Finally, cultural intelligence is introduced as the newest theoretical development in the arena of intercultural training.

## Emotional Intelligence

Emotional intelligence is a set of skills focused on self-awareness, impulse control, and empathy (Goleman, 1998). This includes the ability of individuals to perceive and respond appropriately to the affective states of culturally similar others, as well as to self-regulate their own emotions. Thomas (2006) defines emotional intelligence as "the ability of people to perceive the emotional states of others and to regulate one's own emotional state in the service of improved interactions" (pp. 79–80). As Earley and Peterson (2004) state, this particular competency, as defined by the literature, assumes that individuals are interacting with others that are culturally similar to themselves. Simply stated, an individual who is emotionally intelligent in their own cultural context may or may not be effective at perceiving and responding to the emotional cues of others when placed in a cross-cultural context. However, emotional intelligence is critical to effective interaction in any social context, including intercultural ones, and therefore is an important facet of intercultural competence.

## Social Intelligence

Social intelligence is a set of skills focused on getting along smoothly with others around us (Cantor & Kihlstrom, 1987). Marlowe (1986) developed a model of social intelligence comprising four core components: social interest, social self-efficacy, empathy skills, and social performance skills. Social interest refers to an individual's concern for others. Social self-efficacy refers to an individual's feelings of confidence in social situations. Empathy skills include the ability to both cognitively and affectively understand others, and social performance skills are the observable social behaviors that an individual engages in. Again, though this set of competencies is critical for individuals performing in any social context including intercultural situations, it lacks any direct acknowledgment of culture in those situations. It is possible that a socially intelligent individual may be very effective at responding to social situations in his own culture while being completely confused in a cross-cultural context. However, an individual who is socially intelligent in intercultural contexts will likely be more successful than a socially unintelligent individual, making social intelligence another necessary, but insufficient, component of overall intercultural competence.

## Adaptability

Adaptability is another individual attribute that has been associated with overseas success (Zakaria, 2000). Adaptability in the workplace has been broken down into several basic job-related skills: solving problems creatively, dealing with uncertain work situations, learning new tasks, demonstrating interpersonal adaptability, demonstrating cultural adaptability, demonstrating physical adaptability, handling work stress, and handling emergency situations (Pulakos, Schmitt, Dorsey, Arad, Hedge, & Borman, 2002). In other words, to the extent that workers are able to perform these skills, they will be more effective in intercultural contexts. Adaptability has been discussed in a variety of organizational contexts, including the context of global organizations where employees are required to quickly adapt to new cultures. Adaptability has been shown to be an important attribute for someone interacting in a multicultural setting.

A person who is easily able to adapt to a new situation should have less difficulty adjusting in a multicultural setting, compared with someone who is less flexible.

## Perspective Taking

Perspective taking is a skill that has been defined in several different ways. According to Whaley and Davis (2007), perspective taking consists of cognitive flexibility or problem-solving skills. Galinsky and Moskowitz (2000) define perspective taking as the ability to embrace the perspective of another person. In the field of counseling and clinical psychology, perspective taking is seen as an integral attribute of a culturally competent mental health service provider (Lopez, 1997) and vital to appropriate social functioning (Galinsky & Moskowitz, 2000). McAllister and Irvine (2000) suggest that gaining an understanding of others' perspectives is a critical aspect of cross-cultural learning. Perspective taking has been found to be positively correlated with social competence and self-esteem (Davis, 1983). According to McAllister and Irvine (2000), during the final stage of becoming interculturally sensitive (integration), a person is able to analyze phenomena from a different perspective or within the cultural context. Consequently, someone who is able to actively take the perspective of another will have a better understanding of that person's behavior and, in turn, will be able to relate with that individual to a larger degree. Therefore, one's level of perspective taking can be considered another skill set critical to being successful in an intercultural work setting.

## Cultural Intelligence

Cultural intelligence (CQ) is a concept developed in response to the lack of attention paid to culture in other concepts such as emotional and social intelligence. Earley and Peterson (2004) point out that emotional intelligence and social intelligence, though clearly relevant, are void of a cultural context in terms of explaining how and why people behave as they do. CQ can be described as a "multifaceted competency consisting of cultural knowledge, the practice of mindfulness, and the repertoire of behavioral skills"

(Thomas & Inkson, 2004, pp. 182–183). This set of knowledge and skills allows individuals to interact effectively across a multitude of cultural situations. Some have described CQ as having four basic components: meta-cognition, cognition, motivation, and behavior (Crowne, 2008). Meta-cognition is an individual's knowledge of and control over their different cognitions (Ang, Van Dyne, & Koh, 2004). Cognition is an individual's knowledge of self and social environment, and in terms of CQ, it also includes the knowledge about the structures of a given culture. Motivation refers to an individual's genuine interest and desire to learn and function in cross-cultural situations. Finally, behavior refers to a person's ability to exhibit the appropriate verbal and nonverbal behaviors when placed in a cross-cultural situation. This may also include the ability to refrain from engaging in inappropriate behaviors.

In a more practically oriented interpretation of the concept, Earley and Mosakowski (2004) suggest that there are three basic sources of cultural intelligence: head, body, and heart. In other words, individuals must first devise learning strategies for acquiring new knowledge when in a cross-cultural situation (head). Second, they must learn to mirror the customs and gestures of a particular culture (body). Finally, an individual will never become culturally intelligent unless they are truly motivated to do so and confident in their ability to learn (heart). This approach is a much more practically oriented system aimed at helping professionals to be more behaviorally effective in cross-cultural business situations.

Thomas (2006) adopts the Earley and Ang (2003) definition of cultural intelligence, which is the ability to interact effectively with people from other cultures. However, Thomas goes on to offer a revised three-pronged approach to developing CQ that includes knowledge, mindfulness, and behavior. Knowledge includes an individual's basic understanding of culture and cross-cultural interactions in general. Mindfulness is a process linking knowledge and action. More specifically, mindfulness is a heightened awareness of and attention to current experience or reality. This component of CQ suggests that culturally intelligent individuals are constantly aware of their cultural surroundings, as well as their own assumptions and thoughts regarding those surroundings. Finally, behavior is the ability to choose and enact culturally appropriate behaviors based on the specific cultural context.

The term cultural intelligence has also been used in a more general sense to describe people's overall success when attempting to adjust to another culture (Brislin, Worthley, & Macnab, 2006). This very broad understanding of cultural intelligence is similar to the broad understanding of intercultural competence mentioned previously. It has been suggested that cultural intelligence, regardless of which particular set of competencies is considered, can be increased through experience, practice, and a positive attitude toward learning (Brislin et al., 2006). For the remainder of the chapter, in an effort to be as comprehensive as possible, we do not limit our discussion to any one of these theoretical approaches, but instead describe a variety of training programs and strategies aimed at improving the effectiveness of intercultural work interactions via any of the skills mentioned here.

## Current Intercultural Competence Training Approaches

Intercultural competence training can be described as any formal effort toward "preparing people for more effective interpersonal relations and for job success when they interact extensively with individuals from cultures other than their own" (Brislin, Cushner, & Yoshida, 1994, p. 183). Similarly, Littrell and colleagues (2006) define intercultural competence training as an "educative process used to improve intercultural learning via the development of cognitive, affective, and behavioral competencies needed for successful interactions in diverse cultures" (p. 356). Gudykunst and Hammer (1983) developed a typology for classifying various intercultural training approaches based on two core criteria: the training method and the training content. Training methods can be described as either didactic or experiential, whereas training content can be culture general or culture specific. Didactic training, for the most part, tends to be primarily culture specific, whereas experiential training is often focused on developing culture-general skills. In the following sections, we briefly describe the current approaches for training intercultural competence, including didactic, experiential, and mixed approaches.

## Didactic Training Approaches

Didactic training refers to any training intervention that focuses on information giving. In other words, didactic training is usually what most people imagine when they think of training: classroom-based lectures, readings, assignments, and quizzes. Kealey and Protheroe (1996) identify three types of didactic cross-cultural training: practical information, area studies, and cultural awareness training. Practical information training is one of most common types of cross-culture training used in industry and is focused on providing information regarding the living conditions of a culture such as travel arrangements, shopping, appropriate attire, and the realities of the job (Kealey & Protheroe, 1996). Area studies provide trainees with information regarding the history, values, economy, and political structure of the culture in which they will be living. Information is usually conveyed either through self-directed reading, audio or video files, or in-person lectures. Oftentimes practical information training and area studies are combined and given simultaneously. Cultural awareness training takes a less information-based approach than the others; it attempts to get trainees to see and feel things from the perspective of host nationals. The most common, validated, and well-known cultural awareness training intervention is known as the culture assimilator. Because the culture assimilator is often the benchmark by which other cross-culture interventions are evaluated, it is discussed in further detail.

The culture assimilator is a training intervention that is designed to expose members of one culture to the basic concepts, attitudes, role perceptions, customs, and values of another culture in a time span of two to five hours (Fiedler, Mitchell, & Triandis, 1971). The specific content of culture assimilators can vary but typically include information regarding the other culture's customs and values. Traditionally, culture assimilators are culture specific, with culture assimilators having been developed for Iranian, Thai, Honduran, and Greek culture (Fiedler et al., 1971). More recently, however, culture-general assimilators have been developed that focus on how cultures, across the board, vary.

A culture assimilator is first developed by having host nationals and expatriates with experience in the other culture identify critical incidents that occur on the job. These subject-matter experts are asked to describe a work incident in which an expatriate interacted with a host national but misinterpreted or was confused by the actions or reactions of a host national. Ideally, a critical incident should be easy to interpret once a person has sufficient knowledge of the culture. When a sufficient number of critical incidents have been gathered, the incidents are developed into training scenarios. Trainees typically go through culture assimilators at their own pace. Trainees read each scenario describing a multicultural work incident and select one of four possible responses. Each response is accompanied with feedback that provides the trainee further information regarding the culture. If the trainee selects an incorrect answer, she is asked to select another answer until she gets the correct answer.

Brislin, Cushner, Cherrie, and Young (1986) developed a culture-generic assimilator consisting of critical incidents covering themes such as anxiety, disconfirmed expectations, time and space, roles, language, and in-group or out-group distinctions. Theory-based cultural assimilators have also been recently developed (Bhawuk, 1998; 2001); these assimilators integrate cultural theories into the training material in order to provide trainees with a guiding framework. For instance, the cultural dimension of individualism and collectivism has been used to develop a cultural assimilator. Trainees learn about individualism and collectivism and are taught the importance of understanding these concepts when evaluating the behaviors of individuals from other cultures. Culture assimilators have been used to train American humanitarian aid volunteers, military officers, and civilian advisors for overseas operations in Honduras, Thailand, and Greece. Across these diverse groups and cultures, culture assimilators have been found to be quite effective at improving job performance and interpersonal adjustment overseas (Fiedler et al., 1971; Worchel & Mitchell, 1972).

## Experiential Training Approaches

Experiential training consists of training interventions that involve learning by doing. The focus is on gaining experience in intercultural situations rather than just listening to lectures or reading about other cultures. A common theme linking various experiential intercultural competence training interventions is that trainees participate in activities that they are likely to face in other cultures. The primary goal of experiential training is to develop and practice skills that will enable employees to interact more effectively with host nationals. A secondary goal of experiential training is to help trainees to see things and interpret situations from the host culture's point of view (Littrell & Salas, 2005).

Common experiential cross-cultural training interventions include role playing and simulations (Littrell et al., 2006). Role playing usually requires trainees to act out fictional intercultural business situations. One particular intercultural simulation, the BaFá BaFá simulation created by Simulation Training Systems (Summers, 2004), has trainees divide into fictional cultures and then walks them through interactive scenarios designed to make them more aware of how culture influences behavior in organizations, and how to most appropriately interact with people from other cultures. Royal Dutch Shell utilizes a similar intercultural simulation known as "Cultural Detective" that provides face-to-face as well as online interactive role-playing situations for their employees (Rodriguez, 2009). Overlaps (that is, on-the-job training) can also be considered a form of experiential training. Trainees taking part in overlaps work closely with an experienced expatriate in-country who fills the trainee in on both work practices and adjusting to the culture.

Behavior modification training is yet another form of experiential training. This training is based on social learning theory and has four components: attention, retention, reproduction, and incentive (Bandura, 1977). Trainees first observe examples of effective behaviors and then practice the observed behaviors. Trainers provide positive reinforcement and constructive feedback to ensure that trainees perform culture-appropriate behaviors. Incentives such as rewards and motivation help ensure that trainees attend, retain, and reproduce trained behaviors. Behavior modification training for intercultural competence in particular consists of having trainees learn and practice culture-appropriate behaviors and avoid culture-inappropriate behaviors.

## Mixed Training Approaches

Some intercultural training interventions contain elements of both didactic and experiential training and therefore can be categorized as mixed training approaches. For example, GoldStar Electronics Corporation of South Korea has implemented an integrated cross-cultural training program that is focused on providing trainees with cultural information as well as practical exposure to common intercultural situations (Montagno, 1996). Three such mixed training interventions that will be discussed in greater detail are language training, integrated cultural assimilator and behavior modeling training, and relational ideology training.

Language training is considered separately from other training methods because it often includes both didactic and experiential elements. That is, trainees are provided with rote information and knowledge about the language and culture, but also actively practice speaking the language as well. Language training consists of teaching trainees the language of the host country. In practice, the success of language training varies depending on the complexity of the language being taught, the methods for teaching, and individual differences in the trainees. For example, tonal languages like Japanese or Thai are much harder to learn for speakers who natively speak nontonal languages like English or French. Immersion classes are often more effective than other approaches because they force the students to engage more fully in the use of the language. And finally, some people are just more adept than others at learning new languages. Therefore, language training may be more useful as a supplemental intercultural training approach than as a stand-alone intervention.

Harrison (1992) developed an integrated training program that incorporated both cultural assimilators and behavioral modeling training. On the first day, trainees received an overview of the training program and were given a culture assimilator consisting of 60 critical incidents to complete at their own pace. The next day, trainees were given the behavioral modeling training which consisted of trainees (1) learning key principles, (2) viewing a film of a person utilizing key principles, (3) practicing key principles in role plays, and (4) receiving reinforcement from trainers and other group members. The two approaches complement each other as the culture assimilator allows for the trainees to be exposed to a wide variety of cultural critical incidents, and the behavioral modeling training allows for direct practice of culturally competent skills.

Relational ideology training is a recent cross-cultural training intervention developed by Sanchez-Burks, Lee, Nisbett, and Ybarra (2007) based upon the theory of Protestant relational ideology. The theory of Protestant relational ideology proposes that individuals who are members of cultures heavily influenced by Protestant values, such as the United States, will be less relationally attuned at work and believe that relational and emotional concerns are inappropriate in work settings (Sanchez-Burks, 2005; Sanchez-Burks et al., 2007). A consequence of having a high level of Protestant relational ideology is that individuals from these cultures encode fewer emotional and relational cues, have poorer memory for interpersonal information, and are less aware of others' nonverbal behavioral cues in work settings (Sanchez-Burks et al., 2007). In short, individuals with high Protestant relational ideology will be less adaptive and sensitive to others in intercultural situations.

Relational ideology training has two phases. In the first phase of training, trainees receive area studies. The second phase of training consists of the actual relational ideology training intervention, which is focused on how Protestant relational ideology differs from the other ideologies of other cultures. Trainees first complete three self-assessment exercises that provide information regarding how sensitive trainees are to relational cues in work settings. After completing all the self-assessment measures, the trainer leads a discussion about how the trainees' responses are similar and different from cultures with different levels of Protestant relational ideology. The purpose of the guided discussion is to encourage trainees to be aware of their own ways of thinking and realize how people from different cultures may think differently.

## Summary

The intercultural competence training approaches previously described represent several of the most commonly studied and evaluated forms of intervention in the science of global business. Specifically, we discussed three general types of training interventions: didactic approaches including area studies and culture assimilators; experiential approaches including behavior modeling, role playing, and simulation; and mixed training approaches including language training, integrated behavioral modeling and culture assimilator training, and relational ideology training. Unfortunately, there is a paucity of knowledge regarding which of these theoretically based training interventions is being practically applied in organizations, or the extent to which these programs are effective in real-world settings. However, there is a relatively broad base of literature examining the outcomes of various intercultural training interventions in experimental or quasi-experimental settings. The next section summarizes these findings.

## Intercultural Competence Training Outcomes

The research on intercultural competence is abundant with studies examining the outcomes of various cultural training interventions. Some of these studies suggest that cultural training is integral to successful global interaction (for example, Waxin & Panaccio, 2005), whereas others have suggested that training has no real impact on behavior overseas and that only practice and experience can result in true intercultural competence (for example, Puck, Kittler, & Wright, 2008). In general, however, the outcomes of intercultural competence training investigated in the literature can be organized based on the nature of the outcome in question. More specifically, Kraiger, Ford, and Salas (1993) divide learning outcomes into three basic categories: cognitive, skill-based, and affective outcomes. Cognitive outcomes are concerned with the trainees' gains in knowledge, skill-based outcomes are concerned with the development of behavioral skills, and affective outcomes are concerned with changes in the trainees' attitudes or motivation. The following sections summarize the empirical findings regarding the effectiveness of various intercultural competence training approaches in terms of these three learning outcome categories: cognitive, skill-based, and affective outcomes (see Table 10.1).

### Cognitive Learning Outcomes

The vast majority of empirical research examining the effectiveness of intercultural training has focused on culture assimilators.

**Table 10.1. Summary of Training Approaches and Learning Outcomes.**

| Training Approach | Cognitive Learning Outcomes | Skill-Based Learning Outcomes | Affective Learning Outcomes | Selected References |
|---|---|---|---|---|
| Area Studies | Increased knowledge of culture | Higher supervisor-evaluated performance and self-reported adjustment | No impact on attitude change | Bird et al., 1993; Earley, 1987; Gannon & Poon, 1997 |
| Culture Assimilators | Culture-general assimilator resulted in better learning outcomes than the culture specific or control | Higher self-reported and supervisor-rated performance and adjustment | Theory-based culture assimilator resulted in more intention to change behavior | Bhawuk, 1998; Cushner, 1989; Mitchell & Foa, 1969; O'Brien et al., 1971; Worchel & Mitchell, 1972 |
| Behavioral Modeling Training | Increased learning of customs, conflict avoidance, and group orientation | No impact on behavior in a role-playing exercise | Increased positive attitudes toward target culture | Harrison, 1992; Sorcher & Spence, 1982 |

*(continued overleaf)*

**Table 10.1.** (*continued*)

| Training Approach | Cognitive Learning Outcomes | Skill-Based Learning Outcomes | Affective Learning Outcomes | Selected References |
|---|---|---|---|---|
| Combined Behavioral Modeling/Culture Assimilator | Increased learning of customs, conflict avoidance, and group orientation | Better performance on a role-playing exercise | N/A | Harrison, 1992 |
| Other Experiential Interventions | N/A | Higher supervisor-evaluated performance and self-reported adjustment | N/A | Earley, 1987; Gannon & Poon, 1997 |
| Relational Ideology | N/A | Resulted in higher self-reported performance and adjustment | Trainees experienced less awkward, more comfortable, more enjoyable cross-cultural interactions | Sanchez-Burkes et al., 2007 |

Harrison (1992) performed a comparative study of behavioral modeling, cultural assimilator, and combined training, and found that trainees given an integrated behavioral modeling and culture assimilator training intervention demonstrated better verbal knowledge on an eight-item multiple-choice test than trainees receiving only one of the two interventions, or trainees placed in a control condition. Bhawuk (1998) compared the effectiveness of a culture-general, a cultural-specific, and a theory-based cultural assimilator to a control condition and found that trainees given the culture-general and theory-based cultural assimilator tended to have better learning outcomes as measured by trainees' performance on nine difficult critical incidents and a free recall task than those in the culture-specific and control conditions. Cushner (1989) also found that trainees given a culture-general assimilator had better verbal knowledge outcomes than trainees placed in a control condition. Overall, the literature seems to demonstrate that cultural assimilators do have a positive impact on trainee knowledge.

A smaller subset of research has examined cognitive outcomes in area studies interventions. For example, Bird, Heinbuch, Dunbar, and McNulty (1993) found that trainees given area studies courses had better declarative and conceptual knowledge regarding the course content than trainees placed in a control condition. Gannon and Poon (1997) had trainees self-assess their knowledge gained and found that trainees who received either video training or integrative training, which were both area studies approaches, reported more knowledge gained than trainees who participated in role playing. In general, area studies seems to be an effective intercultural competence training approach if the desired outcome is an increase in knowledge regarding a particular culture or topic. However, intercultural competence training is often aimed at improving much more than knowledge, and the impact of area studies on skill-based and affective outcomes has yet to be determined.

## Skill-Based Learning Outcomes

A few experimental studies of intercultural training have used performance in a role-playing exercise as a measure of behavior.

For example, Harrison (1992) found that trainees who received the integrative training program that combined a cultural assimilator with behavioral modeling training demonstrated superior behavioral responses in role-play exercises as compared with trainees receiving only a cultural assimilator or behavior modeling training alone, and trainees receiving no training. Bhawuk (1998), using the same behavioral role play used in Harrison (1992) as an outcome, conversely found no significant difference in behavior between trainees receiving theory-based, culture-general, and culture-specific cultural assimilators and trainees placed in the control condition. Therefore, the impact of cultural assimilator training on intercultural behavior is not perfectly clear.

Several of the studies examining the outcomes of intercultural training in the field have focused on expatriate adjustment as an outcome. Waxin and Panaccio (2005) examined the impact of four types of cross-cultural training (general conventional training, specific conventional training, general experimental training, and specific experimental training) on the adjustment of expatriates in India and found that all four types of training accelerate expatriate adjustment. However, they found that experimental training interventions, in which the trainees engage in simulated real-life situations, were more effective than conventional training methods, in which trainees just receive information via lectures, text, or other materials.

Puck and colleagues (2008) conducted a survey of 20 German multinational corporations and found that cross-cultural training did not have a significant impact on expatriate adjustment, but that foreign language competence did, suggesting language training is an effective strategy when adjustment is the outcome of interest. It has been suggested that having expatriates learn the host culture's language facilitates interpersonal adjustment by demonstrating that the expatriate is interested and respectful enough to learn the language and improves job performance because expatriates are able to follow along and catch critical pieces of information that are communicated, and have an easier time adjusting (Littrell & Salas, 2005; Littrell et al., 2006; Puck et al., 2008).

Finally, some research has focused on more distal behaviorally related outcomes such as self-reported performance. Specifically, it has been shown that cultural assimilators (both culture general and culture specific) result in better job performance when compared to a control condition (Cushner, 1989; Mitchell & Foa, 1969; O'Brien, Fiedler, & Hewett, 1971; Worchel & Mitchell, 1972). Earley (1987) found that trainees given either area studies or experiential training received higher job performance ratings and reported less interpersonal adjustment difficulties compared with trainees placed in the control condition. Finally, Sanchez-Burkes and colleagues (2007) found that trainees given relational ideology training reported higher perceived performance and intercultural adjustment compared with trainees given cultural assimilators. Though the number of studies examining the transfer of intercultural competence training is small, results to date seem to indicate that training interventions, such as cultural assimilators, area studies, experiential training, and relational ideology training, do have positive impacts on performance and adjustment on the job.

## Affective Learning Outcomes

Compared to studies examining skill-based outcomes, there have been fewer empirical investigations regarding how intercultural competence influences affective outcomes. Three notable studies that have examined affective intercultural learning outcomes are Bhawuk (1998), Bird and colleagues (1993), and Sorcher and Spence (1982). In Bhawuk's (1998) study, trainees who were given the theory-based cultural assimilator showed more intention to change behavior as measured by the intercultural sensitivity inventory than trainees given either the culture-general, cultural-specific, or control training interventions. Bird and colleagues (1993) found that area studies had no effect on trainees' attitudes toward Japanese people, culture, management, products, and art when compared with trainees placed in a control condition. Sorcher and Spence (1982) assessed attitude change via self-report and interviews and found that behavioral modeling training resulted in no changes in attitudes compared with a control condition when assessed by a self-report, but resulted in significant changes in attitudes compared with a control condition when assessed by an interview. This study, in particular, highlights the importance of using a multimethod approach to assessing learning outcomes. Taken together, these results suggest that intercultural competence training can have an influence on trainee attitudes.

## Summary

Cultural assimilators, whether in culture-specific, culture-general, or theory-based form, clearly emerged as the most frequently studied intercultural competence training intervention. Cultural assimilators were found to increase rote knowledge, intercultural adjustment, job performance, and intercultural sensitivity attitudes. Area studies appear to be ideal for increasing trainee knowledge of a culture. Behavioral modeling and relational ideology training have also emerged as promising training interventions that have positive impacts on intercultural performance and adjustment. Unfortunately, the limited body of research on intercultural competence training effectiveness prevents making any absolute statements regarding superiority, especially given the mixed results found in field survey data. The first step toward improving our understanding of intercultural competence training outcomes is to properly assess all training interventions that are implemented in global organizations. In the next section, we discuss the importance of training evaluation, and provide several tools for assessing the outcomes of intercultural competence training.

# Intercultural Competence Assessment Tools

As the importance of intercultural competence training continues to increase, so too will the importance of developing or identifying methods to assess such programs. Sercu (2004) points out that "employers desire a reliable assessment tool that can predict whether a particular employee possesses the necessary knowledge, skills, attitudes and personality traits to be successful in intercultural (business) contacts" (p.73). There is a consensus among researchers that the systematic evaluation of training programs is critical to the success of such programs (Goldstein, 1993), and this consensus extends to intercultural competence training as well. Training evaluation generally comprises the collection and interpretation of data regarding the utility of training programs (Goldstein, 1986). Training evaluation serves two primary purposes: it ensures that trainees meet learning objectives set forth prior to training, and it diagnoses whether or not the training program as a whole was effective in improving performance (Kraiger et al., 1993). Without such data it would be impossible to conclude that a training program is achieving its aim(s) or to diagnose its inefficiencies.

The proper assessment of any training program requires robust assessment tools. Fortunately for the field of intercultural competence, there are a variety of extant tools and approaches that have been developed specifically for assessing levels of intercultural competence in individuals, as well as more general training assessment methods that can be used to evaluate the effectiveness of intercultural competence training interventions. Although many of the existing intercultural competence assessment tools were originally intended to be used as measures of individual differences in intercultural competence, they can very easily be used as training assessment tools as well. In other words, any tool that can assess levels of intercultural competence in an individual can also be used to assess *changes* in intercultural competence brought about by training. In the following sections, we describe a variety of tools, both general and intercultural-competence specific, which can be used to assess the effectiveness of training interventions. We organize these tools around the three types of learning outcomes that they assess: cognitive, skill-based, and affective (see Table 10.2).

## Assessing Cognitive Intercultural Competence

Often in practice the goal of intercultural competence training is to attain a foundation of knowledge of a specific culture. In these situations, multiple-choice questions, essay questions, true-false questions, open-ended questions, listing of facts, assessment of mental models, or any other knowledge-based assessment that requires trainees to display accurate knowledge of specific cultures would be suitable knowledge-based assessments. Measures of declarative knowledge such as these are often used to measure cognitive learning outcomes in training. In fact, in practice, knowledge tests are often the assessment of choice when trying to assess intercultural competence training. For example, the U.S. Army

**Table 10.2. Intercultural Competence Training Assessment Tools.**

| Learning Outcome | Description | Example Assessment Tools |
|---|---|---|
| Cognitive Learning Outcomes | Measures assessing the trainees' gains in intercultural related knowledge. | • Multiple-choice tests of cultural knowledge<br>• Power tests of cultural knowledge<br>• Cultural situation mental model elicitation<br>• Probed protocol analysis technique |
| Skill-Based Learning Outcomes | Measures assessing the trainee's gains in skills necessary for interculturally competent behavior. | • Behavioral Assessment Scale for Intercultural Communication (BASIC)<br>• Observation and rating of simulated performance<br>• Observation and rating of on the job performance |
| Affective Learning Outcomes | Measures assessing the trainees' changes in internal states and feelings regarding intercultural situations such as attitudes and motivation. | • Intercultural Development Inventory (IDI)<br>• Cross-Cultural Adaptability Inventory (CCAI) |

TRADOC Culture Center offers a variety of classes on culture to soldiers. The majority of these classes are self-administered computer-based didactic area studies (for example, Iraq Culture Overview, Iran: History and Religion) courses that usually include knowledge tests as the form of assessment (TRADOC Culture Center, 2009). However, there are other potential ways to assess trainee knowledge such as power tests, mental model assessments, and the probed protocol analysis technique.

Kim, Kirkman, and Chen (2006) define cognitive cultural intelligence as knowledge about economic, legal, and social aspects of different cultures. These areas of knowledge can be used to develop knowledge tests for assessing the effectiveness of intercultural competence training. More specifically, power tests (tests assessing the total number of correct responses to a set of questions) could be used to assess trainee's levels of knowledge regarding economic, legal, and social aspects of a culture after they have received some culture-specific training. This is a highly relevant measure of intercultural competence given that errors made during an intercultural exchange could be the difference between winning and losing a major contract or sale. These types of tests could also be offered at the beginning of training as a feedback tool because variance in the declarative knowledge among trainees is generally greater at the beginning of training (Kraiger et al., 1993).

Another potential measurement tool that could be used to assess changes in intercultural competence in trainees is a mental model measure. Mental models are representations of various functions that a worker possesses on the job. These models help individuals organize information and allow for attainment of new knowledge (Messick, 1984). A U.S. ambassador working with several distinct cultures can be used to illustrate the utility of assessing mental models to gauge intercultural competence. For each culture, the ambassador may have a separate mental model that assists him or her in behaving appropriately from one situation to the next. One way to assess knowledge organization is to compare the mental models of trainees with that of expert mental models regarding a culture or culturally appropriate behaviors (Kraiger & Salas, 1993). An expert model can be created by having a host national, or perhaps a highly experienced expatriate, create a structure that shows the relationships among important cultural concepts relevant to training. The trainee would then organize a structure based on the mental model. Significant overlap between the expert and the trainee is correlated with transfer of training and performance (Kraiger & Salas, 1993).

Trainee metacognition is another cognitive construct that could be assessed to evaluate a training program's effectiveness. The term refers to the regulation and knowledge of one's thoughts (Brown, 1975; Leonesio & Nelson, 1990). These skills include things such as planning and monitoring (Brown, Bransford,

Ferrara, & Campione, 1983; Schoenfeld, 1985). Kim and colleagues (2006) define metacognitive cultural intelligence as a person's thought processes that enable them to recognize and interpret expectations appropriate for various cultural situations. Based on this definition, it is clear that metacognition is an important process during cultural interaction. The probed protocol analysis technique is an excellent method for evaluating metacognition (Means & Gott, 1988). This technique requires trainees to describe a process step-by-step while being asked prompting questions along the way. Another measure used for evaluating metacognition is self-assessments of knowledge gained. It has been demonstrated that trainees often make accurate assessments of such knowledge states (Schendel & Hagman, 1982).

It is important to note that measures of declarative knowledge alone are often insufficient for assessing trainees at higher levels of cognitive development. Although, in practice, it can be enticing to just throw a multiple-choice test at a group of trainees and call it a day, if the intended outcome of an intercultural training intervention is to improve behavior and performance on the job, the proper evaluation of that training program should include behavioral measures as well. In the following section, we describe several tools that can be used to assess behavioral outcomes of intercultural competence training.

## Assessing Skill-Based Intercultural Competence

Skill-based learning outcomes are concerned with the development of technical or motor skills (Kraiger et al., 1993). Sercu (2004) identifies five precise areas of skills or behavior in relation to cultural training: (1) the ability to interpret and relate, (2) the ability to discover or interact, (3) the ability to acquire new knowledge and to operate knowledge, attitudes, and skills, (4) metacognitive strategies to direct one's own learning, (5) and the ability to evaluate cultural perspectives, practices, and products critically. In order to assess skill development in any of these areas, several measurement tools can be used: questionnaires, role-playing exercises, and on-the-job performance measurement.

Because of the behavioral nature of skill-based outcomes, there are not many preexisting questionnaires designed to assess intercultural skills. To the best of our knowledge, the Behavioral Assessment Scale for Intercultural Communication (BASIC) is the only such scale. Developed by Koester and Olebe (1988), BASIC is used to evaluate intercultural communication competence. BASIC is a 27-item paper-and-pencil assessment that measures seven dimensions of intercultural communicative effectiveness: display of respect, interaction posture, orientation to knowledge, empathy, task role behaviors, relational role behaviors, interaction behavior or management, and tolerance of ambiguity (Ruben, 1976). The dimensions contain more specific subcategories. Each subcategory is evaluated using one question. The question is an in-depth description of the subcategory as part of the broader dimension. Following the description are five expressive or behavioral options. These describe in detail how an individual would respond in that particular circumstance. The respondent is asked to choose the option that best fits how he or she would behave. The BASIC provides a unique means for assessing intention to engage in culturally related behavior, but it is important to note that it measures how an individual *perceives* they would respond to a cultural situation rather than how they actually respond. In order to assess actual responses, some form of role play is necessary.

Depending on the specific purpose of the intercultural training, it may be advantageous to develop an assessment simulation or role play that is intended to measure the culturally related behaviors or skills that are the focus of the training program. For example, Harrison (1992) developed a role-playing exercise in which each trainee had to interact with a videotaped Japanese manager. The Japanese manager approached the trainee with a problem, and the trainee then had to react to the videotaped manager. The participants' responses were then rated on eight dimensions regarding the use of appropriate customs and behaviors. Role-playing exercises such as this one can be developed to match with specific training interventions. Ideally, a host-country native or a very experienced expatriate would help to determine the rating dimensions and to design an appropriate simulated scenario for the trainees.

Finally, on-the-job performance can be assessed after training in order to evaluate the extent to which the training is transferring to the job. Much of the research on expatriate adjustment has taken this approach and measured self-reported levels of adjustment in expatriates after they have gone overseas. Both subjective and objective measures of performance can be useful to collect, depending on the desired outcome of the training intervention. For example, if the training intervention is aimed at improving the host nation's perceptions of the expatriates, an appropriate outcome measure might be self-reported perceptions of the expatriate's conduct from the perspective of host nationals.

## Assessing Affective Intercultural Competence

Affective learning outcomes concern the influential nature of people's internal states or feelings about their decisions and actions (Gagne, 1984). Self-report measures are the most appropriate method for examining changes in affective learning outcomes. Two commonly used affective self-report measures are the Intercultural Development Inventory and the Cross-Cultural Adaptability Inventory. The Intercultural Development Inventory (IDI), developed by Hammer, Bennett, and Wiseman (2003), measures people's *orientations* toward cultural differences. For that reason, it can be considered an affective outcome measure of cultural training. The IDI is a 50-item paper-and-pencil measure that assesses five dimensions of cultural difference orientation, which include denial/defense, reversal, minimization, acceptance/ adaptation, and encapsulated marginality. The first three dimensions are considered ethnocentric in that they measure the degree to which individuals desire to avoid intercultural interaction. The last two dimensions are considered ethno-related in that they measure the degree to which individuals seek intercultural interactions. Thirty-two items make up the ethnocentric section of the inventory and 19 items make up the ethno-related section of the inventory. The IDI has a theoretical base rooted in Bennett's (1986) developmental model of intercultural sensitivity (DMIS) and therefore can be deemed a useful tool in assessing affective learning outcomes of a culturally related training program. Honda has been reported to use the IDI as a cultural competence assessment tool (Bzdega, 2008).

The Cross-Cultural Adaptability Inventory (CCAI) measures an individual's readiness to interact with people from a different culture (Kelley & Meyers, 1995). The CCAI measures dispositional traits that have been found to be related to intercultural competence. The Cross-Cultural Adaptability Scale also focuses on aspects of intercultural effectiveness but emphasizes some of the predictors of adaptability, such as openness to new experiences and interest in adaptive situations (Stanhope, Solomon, Pernell-Arnold, Sands, & Bourjolly, 2005). For this reason it can be considered an affective learning measure. The CCAI is a 50-item inventory that consists of four dimensions. The dimensions include flexibility/openness, emotional resilience, perceptual acuity, and personal autonomy. Flexibility/openness measures an individual's level of openness toward others. Emotional resilience measures an individual's ability to remain positive in unfamiliar territory. Perceptual acuity measures an individual's level of comfort when interacting with someone from another culture. Personal autonomy measures a person's ability to maintain a sense of self while appreciating and interacting with people from another culture. This instrument has been used extensively to examine the effectiveness of cultural training programs. However, it has been found to have limited psychometric properties for its scores (Davis & Finney, 2006). If training content matches the dimensions assessed by the CCAI, then it could still be useful in determining the effectiveness of a cultural training program.

## Summary

This section provided an overview of intercultural competence assessment tools that can be used to evaluate training effectiveness. These assessment tools included measures of cognitive intercultural competence such as knowledge tests and mental model measures, measures of skill-based intercultural competence such as role-playing or on-the-job-performance, and self-report measures of affective intercultural competence. In general, it is important to consider the overall goals of the training program and ensure that the intended cognitions, behaviors, and attitudes are assessed to determine if the training is meeting those goals. Often, intercultural competence training is aimed at improving more than one aspect of intercultural competence, and multiple assessment methods will be necessary to truly evaluate the program. Although the proper assessment of a training program can be quite an investment for an organization to make, without it, the organization could be wasting time and resources on a training program that isn't effective and never even know it.

# Best Practices for Intercultural Competence Training and Assessment

Up to this point, this chapter has described several extant intercultural competence training approaches, provided research-based evidence for the effectiveness of intercultural competence training programs, and discussed several measurement tools that can potentially be used to assess levels of intercultural competence in employees. In general, the literature has demonstrated that there is no single answer regarding the best way to train intercultural competence or the best way to assess the effectiveness of a training program. Due to the proprietary nature of the data, very little public information is available, besides the examples found in the scientific literature, regarding the types and effectiveness of training being used in today's organizations. However, based on the science of training and training assessment along with the limited empirical evidence provided in the literature, several recommendations can be made regarding how to best match training content, design, and methodology to specific intercultural competence training needs. Therefore, rather than attempting to make final judgments regarding the superiority of training approaches, the next section will offer several best practices aimed at guiding both researchers and practitioners in making any intercultural competence training intervention as effective as possible in any given situation (see Table 10.3).

## Best Practice 1: Start with a Needs Assessment, and Pay Special Attention to Culturally Unique Aspects of the Job

A needs assessment must be carried out in order to develop any effective training intervention, including training interventions aimed at developing intercultural competence (Bennett et al., 2000; Littrell et al., 2006). A needs assessment consists of collecting

### Table 10.3.  Best Practices for Intercultural Competence Training.

| Best Practice | Suggestions for Implementation |
|---|---|
| 1. Start with a needs assessment, and pay special attention to culturally unique aspects of the job. | • Assess the task, organization, and person needs for intercultural competence training.<br>• Focus specifically on culturally unique aspects of the task, organization, and person.<br>• Consider spousal and family needs for expatriate trainees. |
| 2. Cognitive learning outcomes are necessary, but not sufficient . . . develop skill-based and affective outcomes too. | • Use experiential training to develop the cognitive, affective, and behavioral aspects of intercultural competence simultaneously.<br>• Use role-playing exercises to simulate the emotions and behaviors that accompany intercultural interaction. |
| 3. Use culture-generic training, especially if trainees could potentially be interacting in multiple cultures. | • Focus on developing transferable competencies such as adaptability or social problem-solving.<br>• Provide opportunities for trainees to practice these competencies across a variety of settings. |
| 4. When using culture-specific training, match the design of training and learning outcomes to the work situation. | • Focus on the work-related aspects of a culture such as cultural business customs.<br>• Tailor the training to reflect the cultural toughness of a given culture. |
| 5. Use longer, more complex training for longer, more complex assignments. | • Match the length of the training components to the length of the transfer assignment.<br>• Avoid wasting resources on extensive training for short-term assignments. |

*(continued overleaf)*

**Table 10.3.** (*continued*)

| Best Practice | Suggestions for Implementation |
|---|---|
| 6. Don't waste time ... individualize training to the trainee (if possible). | • Consider the acculturation profile of the trainee when choosing what training components to implement.<br>• Prioritize various components of the training based on the acculturation profile in order to minimize effort. |
| 7. Provide trainees with an advanced organizer ... use a guiding theoretical framework. | • Give the trainees an advanced organizer early in the training to help guide the process.<br>• Use a clear theoretical framework to develop the advanced organizer. |
| 8. Get the best of both worlds ... use an integrated training approach. | • Do not limit intercultural competence training to any one particular training approach.<br>• Choose the intercultural competence training components based on the needs of the trainees and the transfer situation. |
| 9. Make sure learning occurs during training ... provide developmental feedback on intercultural competence throughout. | • Provide clear, descriptive feedback that provides the trainees with explanation regarding the "why" of their performance.<br>• Provide feedback at multiple times throughout the training process. |
| 10. Evaluation of intercultural competence training should go beyond smile sheets ... assess multiple outcomes with multiple methods. | • Assess changes in trainee cognitions, skills, and attitudes, not just reactions.<br>• Use multiple methods to capture as much relevant outcome information as possible. |

information regarding where training is needed, what needs to be trained, and who needs to be trained (Goldstein, 1993). The three essential components of a needs analysis are task, person, and organizational analysis. Task analysis provides information regarding task duties and difficulty in the intercultural assignment. For intercultural competence training in particular, the task analysis portion of the needs assessment should include information regarding culturally unique aspects of the task requirements. For example, does a certain culture begin each work meeting with a particular formal greeting? If so, this formal greeting should be included as part of the task description. Organizational analysis provides information regarding organizational level factors that can affect training effectiveness, such as organizational culture, social support, and strategic objectives. Again, for the purposes of designing or choosing an intercultural competence training program, the organizational analysis should include a particular focus on culturally unique organizational factors.

Finally, person analysis gathers information regarding the personality characteristics, adaptability, tolerance for ambiguity, and strengths and weaknesses of individual employees. This aspect of the needs analysis is critical for developing an appropriate intercultural competence training intervention as it assesses the skills sets (such as adaptability) necessary for intercultural competence. For example, perhaps the employees at an organization all display high levels of adaptability prior to intercultural competence training. In this situation, it would be most beneficial to focus on other skills sets besides adaptability, as this particular trainee population is already adept in that area. In addition, spousal and family needs may also have to be considered during the person analysis if the trainee is going to be sent overseas for an expatriate assignment. Perhaps training should include strategies for minimizing stress on family members, or other interventions aimed at reducing the negative impact of cultural shock on expatriate's family members. A well-conducted needs analysis will enable trainers to select the most appropriate training intervention based on organizational, task, and individual needs. For a more thorough discussion of needs analysis, refer to Goldstein and Ford (2002).

## Best Practice 2: Cognitive Learning Outcomes Are Necessary, but Not Sufficient—Develop Skill-Based and Affective Outcomes Too

It has been suggested that experiential-based training aimed at developing and practicing the skills necessary to interact effectively in intercultural situations is more advantageous than didactic forms of training (Graf, 2003). In particular, if an intercultural competence training program is aimed at improving the effectiveness of employees in a variety of intercultural situations, rather than in one specific culture, the development of knowledge alone is not an ideal approach. Intercultural interaction is difficult not only because individuals are unaware of each other's customs and practices but also because individuals are unaware of how to deal with the stress and uncertainty inherent in the new situation. Experiential-based training is ideal for training employees to handle any intercultural interaction more effectively because it allows for the development of the cognitive, affective, and behavioral aspects of intercultural competence simultaneously. For example, by engaging in role-playing exercises that simulate commonly occurring intercultural situations, the trainees are simultaneously developing their knowledge of other cultures, experiencing and learning to control the emotions that accompany intercultural interactions, and learning how to respond appropriately in terms of behaviors. This is not to say that didactic methods of intercultural training are not useful; they can be very effective as supplemental training to increase the depth of knowledge regarding a particular set of cultural practices and norms. However, didactic approaches alone cannot effectively develop the emotional and behavioral aspects of intercultural competence.

## Best Practice 3: Use Culture-Generic Training, Especially if Trainees Could Potentially be Interacting in Multiple Cultures

Triandis (1994) argued that culture-general training is superior to culture-specific training because there are so many possible relevant intercultural topics that are not specific to any culture.

Graf (2003) conducted a review of intercultural training that found that only 6 of 27 dimensions of intercultural competence (for example, intercultural sensitivity, social problem-solving capacity, self-monitoring) were culture-specific. Graf (2003) also suggested that intercultural training is most effective when culture-generic because training can then be applied across a variety of settings. Culture-generic training is more widely applicable than culture-specific and thus often represents a better investment for organizations. This generic-competence approach has been utilized in the past in teams, with much success (Cannon-Bowers & Salas, 1997). It could be argued that, given the dynamic nature of work, generic, transferable competencies are more critical than ever before. This is essentially the argument we make regarding cultural competencies: Generic cultural competencies will serve to aid individuals who have to interact with multiple cultures on a regular basis, and therefore should be the focus in intercultural training efforts, especially if the intended trainees will be interacting in multiple cultures.

## Best Practice 4: When Using Culture-Specific Training, Match the Design of Training and Learning Outcomes to the Work Situation

In the preceding best practice, we suggested that culture-generic training is superior to culture-specific training. However, sometimes culture-specific training is already being used, or is a more practical choice because trainees will only ever be interacting in one specific culture. In this situation, culture-specific competence training should be focused on the work-related cultural aspects of the intercultural assignment in order to be most efficient and effective. In other words, though it can't hurt to train individuals on the personal life-related customs and norms for a given culture, it is much more important to focus on work-related cultural differences, such as preference for electronic or face-to-face communication, or cultural business customs. By tailoring the intercultural competence training to match the type of intercultural situation at hand, training will give you "more bang for the buck."

One important issue to consider when designing the training and associated learning outcomes for culture-specific interventions is the cultural toughness of the culture (Black, Gregersen, & Mendenhall, 1992). Cultural toughness refers to the extent to which an individual will experience difficulty integrating into different cultures. For example, a typical U.S. citizen would find it more difficult to adapt to a tribal African culture, or a traditional Eastern culture, though it would be much easier to adapt to more Western cultures, such as Australia, New Zealand, France, and Germany. In essence, employees may need more thorough, rigorous, and integrative training if they are going to a culturally tough culture for an extended period of time than if they are going to a less culturally tough culture for a shorter period of time.

## Best Practice 5: Use Longer, More Complex Training for Longer, More Complex Assignments

Mendenhall and Oddou (1986) recommend that more in-depth experiential training interventions be utilized for more long-term expatriate assignments. Specifically, they posit that the length of language training should be based on the length of stay in the host country. For example, employees may only need less than a week's worth of language training focused on the basics of the host country's language and common courtesies if the trainee stays in the host country for less than a month; one to four weeks of language training if the trainee stays in the host country for two months to a year; and one to two months of extensive language training if the trainee stays for one to three years. This same principle—matching the length and complexity of training to the length and complexity of the assignment—applies beyond language training. As an organization, it is beneficial to consider the ratio of resources necessary to develop and implement any intercultural competence training to the benefits of training (and costs of *not* training) for that particular set of employees. That is, whereas intercultural competence training will not hurt the trainee, it would be a waste of resources to implement an elaborate, multiphase, long-term training program just for employees going overseas for a single four-hour meeting. However, expatriates going out on long-term assignments would benefit from such a complex training approach. It is important to keep in mind that the thoroughness of training should depend on the length of stay in the host culture (Kealey & Protheroe, 1996).

## Best Practice 6: Don't Waste Time—Individualize Training to the Trainee (If Possible)

Another issue to consider when designing intercultural competence training is the acculturation profile of the trainee (Mendenhall & Oddou, 1986). Mendenhall and Oddou (1986) created the acculturation profile as a way to individualize training based on the trainee's specific needs. As resources will be wasted if the organization is training skills that are not needed, and trainees are likely to become disengaged attending useless training interventions, individualizing training can save organizations money and improve training effectiveness. Mendenhall and Oddou (1986) identified seven acculturation profiles: the ideal expatriate, the academic observer, the well-intentioned missionary, the type "A" expatriate, the introvert, the ugly American, and the dependent expatriate. For a more thorough discussion of each profile refer to Mendenhall and Oddou (1986). What is important to note is that different acculturation profiles benefit most from different types of training. For example, a person characterized as a well-intentioned missionary may benefit more from an intercultural competence training program consisting of area studies, culture assimilators, and simulations, whereas a dependent expatriate may benefit more from a combination of informal briefings and area studies (Littrell et al., 2006).

Although we realize that it is not practical, or even feasible, for an organization to design entire training programs for each individual employee who will be interacting in intercultural situations, this information can still be used to individualize training to some extent. Specifically, an organization may develop an intercultural competence training program with several different components such as area studies, simulations, and language training. By using acculturation profiles, organizations can prioritize these components of the training for each trainee, allowing for more flexibility if time constraints are tight by requiring the trainees to complete only the components most beneficial to their individual profile type.

## Best Practice 7: Provide Trainees with an Advanced Organizer—Use a Guiding Theoretical Framework

Providing trainees with a guiding theoretical framework, otherwise known as an advance organizer, has been found to increase training effectiveness (Kraiger, Salas, & Cannon-Bowers, 1995). Several extant intercultural competence training interventions highlight the importance of providing trainees with a guiding theoretical framework early in the training process. For instance, Bhawuk (1998, 2001) proposed that cultural assimilators are more effective if they are linked to a cultural theory that provides trainees with a way of making sense of cultural differences. Relational ideology training, as an example, is proposed to be effective because it gives trainees the theory of Protestant relational ideology to make sense of cultural differences (Sanchez-Burks et al., 2007). Thus, when designing an intercultural competence training program it is important to provide trainees with a tool that will enable them to easily make sense of diverse cultural cues.

## Best Practice 8: Get the Best of Both Worlds—Use an Integrated Training Approach

Although this chapter distinguished between various intercultural competence training interventions—such as behavior modification training, culture assimilators, overlaps, language training, and relational ideology training—it does not imply that these training interventions are mutually exclusive or incapable of coexisting. Many training interventions such as relational ideology training integrate aspects of other cross-culture interventions. We propose that the most effective intercultural interventions likely integrate and incorporate features of a variety of training approaches. To illustrate how an integrated design approach can improve training effectiveness, an example of what an integrated cross-culture training intervention might look like is described here in greater detail.

The first phase of an integrated cross-culture training intervention might include providing trainees with didactic training consisting of practical information, area studies, and cultural awareness training regarding country X. Depending on the resources of the organization, the didactic training can be self-paced or classroom or lecture based. Trainees would be given key information regarding the history and values of the people in country X, as well as tips for how to get by day to day in the culture. In the second phase, a culture assimilator could be used to expose trainees to common scenarios they are likely to encounter in country X. To further develop the behavioral skills needed for successful intercultural interactions, other experiential training could be integrated into the program. Trainees could participate in behavioral modeling and learn appropriate behaviors by practicing in role-playing situations with other employees. Concurrent with the didactic and experiential interventions, trainees could take part in basic language training to further develop their skills in viewing events from the perspective of the host culture. Once trainees begin working in the other culture, they could continue to develop their intercultural competence in an overlap which can provide trainees with information that they may have missed in previous training.

## Best Practice 9: Make Sure Learning Occurs During Training—Provide Developmental Feedback on Intercultural Competence Throughout

Feedback, a topic inextricably tied to training, is a fundamental aspect of developing and reinforcing behavior in any learning situation. As intercultural competence training proceeds, the trainees need to be informed of what they are doing right, what they are doing wrong, and in which competencies there is room for improvement (Geister, Konradt, & Hertel, 2006). In order to achieve the ultimate goal of intercultural competence training, the program must provide specific instructions for how students need to change or adapt their performance (in terms of attitudes, behaviors, and cognitions) in order to improve. It is not enough to inform the students of whether they are correct or incorrect without providing any explanation regarding their correctness. In order for learning to occur, the trainees must be guided through the reasoning behind the correct answers until they are eventually able to arrive there on their own. It is also critical that this detailed feedback be provided to the students multiple times throughout the training event, rather than once. By receiving suggestions for how to improve their performance at each step throughout the training, the trainees will start to build a deeper understanding of the principles underlying the training content, whether that content is perspective taking, adaptability, or any other competency related to intercultural interaction.

### Best Practice 10: Evaluation of Intercultural Competence Training Should Go Beyond Smile Sheets—Assess Multiple Outcomes with Multiple Methods

Quite often in practice, training assessment is performed simply by asking the trainees the extent to which they perceived the training to be helpful. This is problematic; although trainee reactions to training are important (trainees need to be motivated and committed in order to benefit most from training), positive reactions to training are not necessarily indicative of training effectiveness. In order to truly assess the effectiveness of an intercultural training program, the expected learning outcomes of the training must also be assessed. That is, the cognitive, skill-based, and affective outcomes that the training program is intended to change must be measured, both before the training and after the training, in order to determine whether the training is having the desired impact on trainee's intercultural competence. It is not enough to simply ask the trainees if they believe they are gaining new knowledge, skills, and attitudes. Multiple methods of measurement should be used to assess actual changes in trainee knowledge (via multiple-choice tests, written assessments), skills (via situational judgment tests, simulation-based assessment, on-the-job assessment), and attitudes (via attitudinal inventories).

## Conclusion

Beyond the recommendations mentioned in this chapter, there are many issues related to culture and training in need of further exploration. First and foremost, there is a dire need for a better assessment of the types of intercultural training being practically applied in the global business world, and the effectiveness of these programs. To the best of our knowledge, there is almost no information available to the public regarding what organizations are using, the interventions discussed in the scientific arena, and which of these interventions have a positive impact in real-world situations. The closest that research has come to this type of information is general surveys regarding the prevalence and perceived utility of cultural training in business (for example, see Bean, 2009; Shen & Lang, 2009). A more in-depth survey of representative organizations across the globe regarding the type, format, and effectiveness of their cultural training practices seems to be in order.

Not only do we need to understand how and when intercultural competence training can influence intercultural interaction in real organizations, we also need to understand how culture influences training itself. For example, how does culture influence the way employees learn? Are there differences in how cultures prefer to train their employees, and do these differences have an impact on how individuals from culturally different organizations approach one another? Though outside of the scope of this chapter, a dialogue regarding the influence of culture on training practice is an area that future researchers could explore to enhance the success of global organizations.

Furthermore, there is a need for intercultural competence training research to expand beyond the training approaches described in this chapter, and look more deeply at the usefulness of other strategies, such as on-the-job learning and simulation-based training. Though briefly mentioned, these alternative methods of training are relatively unexplored in terms of how they contribute to the development of intercultural competence. For example, how does on-the-job learning compare with other training methods in terms of effectiveness? How can on-the-job learning be designed or enhanced to make it more effective as a training method? With regard to simulation-based training, research should explore what aspects of simulation can be leveraged to improve the impact of training on employee's skill development. Does having an immersive environment lead to better transfer of learning? These questions, and more, are still open for investigation.

This chapter has focused on the increasingly critical issue of intercultural competence training. As technology continues to expand, and the world economy to globalize, this issue will become more salient and central to the success of global organizations. Culture is an issue that has been puzzling psychologists since the beginning of the science, and is here to stay. As interaction between individuals from different cultures increases, so too will the complexity of the influences of culture on that interaction. Therefore, it is imperative that organizations take the time to design and implement intercultural competence training programs that are specifically suited for their particular intercultural needs.

## References

Ang, S., Van Dyne, L., & Koh, C. (2006). Personality correlates of the four-factor model of cultural intelligence. *Group & Organization Management, 31*, 100–123.

Bandura, A. (1977). Self-efficacy: Toward a unifying theory of behavioral change. *Psychological review, 84*(2), 191–215.

Bean, R. (2009). *Cross-cultural training and workplace performance* (ERIC Document Reproduction Service No. ED503402). Adelaide, SA, Australia: National Centre for Vocational Education Research. Retrieved from ERIC database.

Bennett, M. (1986). Towards ethnorelativism: A developmental model of intercultural sensitivity. In R. M. Paige (Ed.), *Education for the Intercultural Experience* (pp. 21–71). Yarmouth, ME: Intercultural Press.

Bennett, R., Aston, A., & Colquhoun, T. (2000). Cross-cultural training: A critical step in ensuring the success of international assignments. *Human Resource Management, 39*, 239–250.

Bhawuk, D. P. S. (1998). The role of culture theory in cross-cultural training: A multimethod study of culture-specific, culture-general, and culture theory-based assimilators. *Journal of Cross-Cultural Psychology, 29*(5), 630.

Bhawuk, D. P. S. (2001). Evolution of culture assimilators: Toward theory-based assimilators. *International Journal of Intercultural Relations, 25*(2), 141–163.

Bird, A., Heinbuch, S., Dunbar, R., & McNulty, M. (1993). A conceptual model of the effects of area studies training programs and a preliminary investigation of the model's hypothesized relationships. *International Journal of Intercultural Relations, 17*(4), 415–435.

Birdseye, M. G., & Hill, J. S. (1995). Individual, organizational work and environmental influences on expatriate turnover tendencies: An empirical study. *Journal of International Business Studies, 26*(4).

Black, J. S., Gregersen, H. B., & Mendenhall, M. E. (1992). *Global assignments: Successfully expatriating and repatriating international managers.* San Francisco: Jossey-Bass.

Black, J. S., & Mendenhall, M. E. (1990). Cross-cultural training effectiveness: A review and a theoretical framework for future research. *Academy of Management Review, 15*, 113–136.

Brislin, R. W., Cushner, K., & Yoshida, T. (1994). *Improving intercultural interactions: Modules for cross-cultural training programs. Multicultural aspects of counseling series 3.* Thousand Oaks, CA: Sage.

Brislin, R. W., Cushner, K., Cherrie, C., & Young, M. (1986). *Intercultural interactions: A practical guide.* Beverly Hills, CA: Sage.

Brislin, R. W., Worthley, R., & Macnab, B. (2006). Cultural intelligence: Understanding behaviors that serve people's goals. *Group & Organization Management, 31*(1), 40.

Brown, A. (1975). The development of memory: Knowing, knowing about knowing, and knowing how to know. In H. W. Reese (Ed.), *Advances in child development and behavior* (Vol. 10, pp. 103–152). San Diego, CA: Academic Press.

Brown, A., Bransford, J., Ferrara, R., & Campione, J. (1983). Learning, remembering and understanding. J. H. Flavell & E. M. Markman (Eds.), *Handbook of child psychology* (4th ed., Vol. 3, pp. 77–166). New York: Wiley.

Bzdega, S. (2008, December 13). Companies start to see value in cultural training. *Business Record.* Retrieved from www.businessrecord.com/.

Cannon-Bowers, J., & Salas, E. (1997). A framework for developing team performance measures in training. In M. T. Brannick, E. Salas, & C. Prince (Eds.), *Team performance assessment and measurement: Theory, methods, and applications* (pp. 45–62). Mahwah, NJ: Erlbaum.

Cantor, N., & Kihlstrom, J. F. (1987). *Personality and social intelligence.* Englewood Cliffs, NJ: Prentice Hall.

Copeland, L., & Griggs, L. (1985). *Going international: How to make friends and deal effectively in the global marketplace.* New York: Random House.

Crowne, K. A. (2008). What leads to cultural intelligence? *Business Horizons, 51*(5), 391–399.

Cushner, K. (1989). Assessing the impact of a culture-general assimilator. *International Journal of Intercultural Relations, 13*(2), 125–146.

Davis, M. H. (1983). Measuring individual differences in empathy: Evidence for a multidimensional approach. *Journal of Personality and Social Psychology, 44*(1), 113–126.

Davis, S., & Finney, S. (2006). A factor-analytic study of the cross-cultural adaptability inventory. *Education and Psychological Measurement, 66*(318), 358–377.

Deardorff, D. K., (2009). *The SAGE handbook of intercultural competence.* Thousand Oaks, CA: SAGE publications, Inc.

Earley, P. C., (1987). Intercultural training for managers: A comparison of documentary and interpersonal methods. *The Academy of Management Journal, 30*, 685–698.

Earley, P. C., & Ang, S. (2003). *Cultural intelligence: Individual interactions across cultures.* Stanford, CA: Stanford University Press.

Earley, P. C., & Mosakowski, E. (2004). Cultural intelligence. *Harvard Business Review, 82*(10), 139–146.

Earley, P. C., & Peterson, R. S. (2004). The elusive cultural chameleon: Cultural intelligence as a new approach to intercultural training for the global manager. *Academy of Management Learning and Education, 3*(1), 100–116.

Fiedler, F. E., Mitchell, T., & Triandis, H. C. (1971). The culture assimilator: An approach to cross-cultural training. *Journal of Applied Psychology, 55*, 95–102.

Gagne, R. M. (1984). Learning outcomes and their effects: Useful categories of human performance. *American Psychologist, 39*, 377–385.

Galinsky, A. D., & Moskowitz, G. B. (2000). Perspective-taking: Decreasing stereotype expression, stereotype accessibility, and in-group favoritism. *Journal of Personality and Social Psychology, 78*(4), 708–724.

Gannon, M. J., & Poon, J.M.L. (1997). Effects of alternative instructional approaches on cross-cultural training outcomes. *International Journal of Intercultural Relations, 21*(4), 429–446.

Geister, S., Konradt, U., & Hertel, G. (2006). Effects of process feedback on motivation, satisfaction, and performance in virtual teams. *Small Group Research, 37*(5), 459.

Gertsen, M. C. (1990). Intercultural competence and expatriates. *The International Journal of Human Resource Management, 1*(3), 341–362.

Goldstein, I. L. (1993). *Training in organizations: Needs assessment, development, and evaluation* (3rd ed.). Pacific Grove, CA: Brooks/Cole.

Goldstein, I. L. (1986). *Training in organizations: Needs assessment design and evaluation.* Monterey, CA: Brooks/Cole.

Goldstein, I. L., & Ford, J. K. (2002). *Training in organizations: Needs assessment, development, and evaluation.* Belmont, CA: Wadsworth.

Goleman, D. (1998). *Working with emotional intelligence.* New York: Bantam Books.

Gomez-Mejia, L., & Balkin, D. B. (1987). The determinants of managerial satisfaction with the expatriation and repatriation process. *Journal of Management Development, 6*(1), 7–17.

Graf, A. (2003). Assessing intercultural training designs. *Journal of European Industrial Training, 29,* 199–214.

Gudykunst, W. B., & Hammer, M. R. (1983). Basic training design: Approaches to intercultural training. In D. Landis & R. W. Brislin (Eds.), *Handbook of intercultural training: Issues in theory and design* (pp. 118–154). New York: Pergamon Press.

Hall, E. T. (1976). *Beyond culture.* Garden City, NJ: Anchor Books/Doubleday.

Hammer, M., Bennett, M., & Wiseman, R. (2003). Measuring intercultural sensitivity: The intercultural development inventory. *International Journal of Intercultural Relations, 27,* 421–443.

Harris, P. R., & Moran, R. T. (1979). *Managing cultural differences.* Houston, TX: Gulf.

Harrison, J. K. (1992). Individual and combined effects of behavior modeling and the cultural assimilator in cross-cultural management training. *Journal of Applied Psychology, 77,* 952–952.

Holtbrügge, D., & Schillo, K. (2008). Intercultural training requirements for virtual assignments: Results of an explorative empirical study. *Human Resource Development International, 11*(3), 271–286.

Kealey, D. J., & Protheroe, D. R. (1996). The effectiveness of cross-cultural training for expatriates: An assessment of the literature on the issue. *International Journal of Intercultural Relations, 20,* 141–165.

Kelley, C., & Meyers, J. (1995). *The Cross-Cultural Adaptability Inventory.* Minneapolis: National Computer Systems.

Kim, K., Kirkman, B. L., & Chen, G. (2006). *Cultural intelligence and international assignment effectiveness.* Paper presented at the annual meeting of the Academy of Management, Atlanta, GA.

Koester, J., & Olebe, M. (1988). The behavioural assessment scale for intercultural communication effectiveness. *International Journal of Intercultural Relations, 12,* 233–246.

Kraiger, K., Ford, J. K., & Salas, E. (1993). Application of cognitive, skill-based, and affective theories of learning outcomes to new methods of training evaluation. *Journal of Applied Psychology, 78,* 311–311.

Kraiger, K., & Salas, E. (1993, April). *Measuring mental models to assess learning during training.* Paper presented at the Annual Meeting of the Society for Industrial and Organizational Psychology, San Francisco, CA.

Kraiger, K., Salas, E., & Cannon-Bowers, J. A. (1995). Measuring knowledge organization as a method for assessing learning during training. *Human Performance, 37*, 804–816.

Landis, D., Bennett, J. M. & Bennett, M. J. (Eds.). (2004). *The handbook of intercultural training (3rd ed.).* Thousand Oaks, CA: SAGE publications, Inc.

Leonesio, R., & Nelson, T. (1990). Do different metamemory judgments tap the same underlying aspects of memory? *Journal of Experimental Psychology Learning, Memory and Cognition, 16*, 464–470.

Littrell, L. N., & Salas, E. (2005). A review of cross-cultural training: Best practices, guidelines, and research needs. *Human Resource Development Review, 4*, 305–335.

Littrell, L. N., Salas, E., Hess, K. P., Paley, M., & Riedel, S. (2006). Expatriate preparation: A critical analysis of 25 years of cross-cultural training research. *Human Resource Management, 5*, 355–388.

Lonner, W., & Hayes, S. (2004). Understanding the cognitive and social aspects of intercultural competence. In R. J. Sternberg & E. L. Grigorenko (Eds.), *Culture and competence: Contexts of life success* (pp. 89–110). Washington, DC: American Psychological Association.

Lopez, S. R. (1997). Cultural competence in psychotherapy: A guide for clinicians and their supervisors. In C. E. Watkins (Ed.), *Handbook of psychotherapy supervision* (pp. 570–588). New York: Wiley.

Marlowe, H. A., Jr. (1986). Social intelligence: Evidence for multidimensionality and construct independence. *Journal of Educational Psychology, 78*(1), 52–58.

McAllister, G., & Irvine, J. J. (2000). Cross cultural competency and multicultural teacher education. *Review of Educational Research, 70*(1), 3.

Means, B., & Gott, S. (1988). Cognitive task analysis as a basis for tutor development: Articulating abstract knowledge representations. In J. Psotka, L. D. Massey, & S. A. Mutter (Eds.), *Intelligent tutoring systems: Lessons learned* (pp. 35–57). Hillsdale. NJ: Erlbaum.

Mendenhall, M., & Oddou, G. (1986). Acculturation profiles of expatriate managers: Implications for cross-cultural training programs. *Columbia Journal of World Business, 21*, 73–79.

Messick, S. (1984). Abilities and knowledge in educational achievement testing: The assessment of Dynamic cognitive structures. In B. S. Plake (Ed.), *Social and technical issues in testing: Implications for test construction and usage* (pp.156–172). Hillsdale, NJ: Erlbaum.

Misa, K. F., & Fabricatore, J. M. (1979). Return on investment of overseas personnel. *Financial Executive, 47*(4), 42–46.

Mitchell, T. R., & Foa, U. G. (1969). Diffusion of the effect of cultural training of the leader in the structure of heterocultural task groups. *Australian Journal of Psychology, 21,* 31–43.

Montagno, R. V. (1996). Integrated cross-cultural business training. *Journal of Management, 15*(4), 57–61.

O'Brien, G., Fiedler, F., & Hewett, T. (1971). The effects of programmed culture training upon the performance of volunteer medical teams in Central America. *Human Relations, 24*(3), 209–231.

Puck, J. F., Kittler, M. G., & Wright, C. (2008). Does it really work? Re-assessing the impact of pre-departure cross-cultural training on expatriate adjustment. *The International Journal of Human Resource Management, 19*(12), 2181–2197.

Pulakos, E. D., Schmitt, N., Dorsey, D. W., Arad, S., Hedge, J. W., & Borman, W. C. (2002). Predicting adaptive performance: Further tests of a model of adaptability. *Human Performance, 15*(4), 299–323.

Rahim, M. A. (1983). A measure of styles of handling interpersonal conflict. *Academy of Management Journal, 26,* 368–376.

Rodriguez, R. (2009, July). Incorporating global diversity into learning. *Chief Learning Officer,* 47–49.

Ruben, B. D. (1976). Assessing communication competency for intercultural adaptation. *Group & Organization Studies, 14*(3), 334–354.

Sanchez-Burks, J. (2005). Protestant relational ideology: The cognitive underpinnings and organizational implications of an American anomaly. In R. Kramer & B. Staw (Eds.), *Research in organizational behavior* (Vol. 26, pp. 267–308). New York: Elsevier.

Sanchez-Burks, J., Lee, F., Nisbett, R., & Ybarra, O. (2007). Cultural training based on a theory of relational ideology. *Basic and Applied Social Psychology, 29,* 257–268.

Schendel, J., & Hagman, J. (1982). On sustaining procedural skills over prolonged retention interval. *Journal of Applied Psychology, 67,* 605–610.

Schoenfeld, A. (1985). *Mathematical problem solving.* San Diego, CA: Academic Press.

Selmer, J., Torbiorn, I., & Leon, C. (1998). Sequential cross-cultural training for expatriate business managers: Predeparture and post-arrival. *International Journal of Human Resource Management, 9*(5), 831–840.

Sercu, L. (2004). Assessing intercultural competence: A framework for systematic test development in foreign language education and beyond. *Intercultural Education, 15*(1), 73–88.

Shen, J., & Lang, B. (2009). Cross-cultural training and its impact on expatriate performance in Australian MNEs. *Human Resources Development International, 12*(4), 371–386.

Sorcher, M., & Spence, R. (1982). The interface project: Behavior modeling as social technology in South Africa 1. *Personnel Psychology, 35*(3), 557–581.

Stanhope, V., Solomon, P., Pernell-Arnold, A., Sands, R., & Bourjolly, J. (2005). Evaluating cultural competence among behavioral health professionals. *Psychiatric Rehabilitation Journal, 28*(3), 227–233.

Summers, G. J. (2004). Today's business simulation industry. *Simulation & Gaming, 35*(2), 208.

Thomas, D. C. (2006). Domain and development of cultural intelligence: The importance of mindfulness. *Group & Organization Management, 31*(1), 78.

Thomas, D. C., & Inkson, K. (2004). *Cultural intelligence: People skills for global business.* San Francisco: Berrett-Koehler.

TRADOC Culture Center (2009, March). *Classes on culture.* Pamphlet distributed at the 2009 Culture Education and Training Summit.

Triandis, H. C. (1994). *Culture and social behavior.* New York: McGraw-Hill.

Waxin, M., & Panaccio, A. (2005). Cross-cultural training to facilitate expatriate adjustment: It works! *Personnel Review, 34*(1), 51–67.

Whaley, A. L., & Davis, K. E. (2007). Cultural competence and evidence-based practice in mental health services: A complementary perspective. *American Psychologist, 62*(6), 563–574.

Worchel, S., & Mitchell, T. R. (1972). An evaluation of the effectiveness of the culture assimilator in Thailand and Greece. *Journal of Applied Psychology, 56*, 472–479.

Zakaria, N. (2000). The effects of cross-cultural training on the acculturation process of the global workforce. *International Journal of Manpower, 21*(6), 492–510.

# CHAPTER 11

# Creating Infectious Change in Global Organizations: Applying Psychology to Large-Scale Planned Interventions

Paul M. Mastrangelo

A large-scale intervention for changing employee behaviors is daunting in any organization, but for a multinational organization the challenges are complicated by sheer numbers, geographical distance, and societal cultures. Globalization means more employees working in locations far away from corporate headquarters, where they speak different languages, experience different cultures, and express different customs. Indeed, the organization is a network of *diverse social groups*; yet, each group contains *similar individuals* in terms of purpose, experiences, skills, language, and so on. Therefore, holistic organizational change can be greatly accelerated if interventions are designed according to three principles:

1. Organizational change is the sum of individual employees' behavioral changes.
2. Individuals change their own behavior in predictable ways, and so environments can be designed to promote individual behavioral change.

3. The rate of individual employee change can be exponential if changes are perceived as the norm across relevant social networks within the organization, starting with early adopters and spreading virally because of psychological conditions.

With these underpinnings, this chapter explores (a) why "change" has become increasingly important for organizations, (b) how employee survey data can guide organizational change efforts, (c) what psychological laws of behavioral change can be taken from social, clinical, and health psychology and applied to organizational change efforts, and (d) what practical techniques can interject these components to create infectious organizational change on a global scale.

## Organizational Change in Our Twenty-First Century Global Environment

The pace of change in work environments has accelerated for many reasons. Computer and telecommunication innovations over the past 25 years have increased customer expectations for the immediate satisfaction of their needs. As a result businesses must strive to deliver ever more customized products and services as quickly as possible. To maintain or improve cost efficiencies, business leaders have sought partnerships, mergers, and acquisitions; yet, the pressure to deliver quicker returns on investments for stockholders has also made leaders eager to jettison units that do not meet expectations for profit, growth, or complementary revenue. The resulting employee climate is filled with the call for more efficient processes, accelerated time lines, and customized solutions even in the most stable organizations, which are rare. Large organizations are continuously reorganizing workgroups. Indeed, it is practically essential to prepare a workforce for change. Yet this accelerated pace has indirectly brought about conditions that complicate organizational change: globalization, multishoring, and geographically matrixed organizations complicate OD interventions designed to create company-wide changes in employee behaviors.

To be clear, I use the term "large-scale planned interventions" to refer to changes that are driven from the top level of the organization (but not necessarily executed from the top) and that are meant to affect all employees (but not necessarily in the same manner). Often multinational organizations undertake such interventions after administering a global employee survey (Kraut, 1996; 2006; Falletta & Combs, 2002). Although an employee survey does not elicit the desired change in itself, it does provide helpful antecedents. The process of creating the content of the survey can help top leaders clarify goals and strategy. As a result the survey provides downward communication regarding what topics are important to the organization. Obviously, the survey also creates upward communication, giving top leadership feedback on levels of employee engagement (that is, emotional commitment, intention to stay, discretionary effort), perceptions of critical processes that drive engagement (such as leadership, execution, talent development), and insights into employees' readiness for change. Furthermore, the employee survey provides an organizational metric, which (like other performance indicators) can be compared to external benchmarks and used to establish an internal baseline for future evaluations. Though it is not the intention of this chapter to review methods of conducting and analyzing a global employee survey (see Chapter 9; Mastrangelo, 2008; Scott & Mastrangelo, 2006; Johnson, 1996), there are two aspects of employee survey research pertinent to global organizational change: (1) societal differences in employee perceptions and expectations of their work environment, and (2) topics where employee dissatisfaction should create increased readiness to change.

## Societal Differences in Employees' Work Perceptions and Expectations

There is a body of evidence suggesting that employees' perceptions of their work environment depend upon the society to which they belong (Hofstede, 1980; 2001; House, Hanges, Javidan, Dorfman, & Gupta, 2004). Generally speaking, employees who share the same language, religion, and geography tend to have more similar perceptions and values. The comprehensive GLOBE study conducted by House and associates between 1994 and 1997 found that countries could be grouped into 10 societal clusters according to similar cultural outlooks on the work environment. Predominantly English-speaking nations formed an Anglo cluster, German-speaking nations formed a Germanic cluster, south Asian nations were distinct from Confucian Asian nations, and so on. Each societal cluster was found to have a fairly distinct pattern of employee perceptions (what is) and expectations (what should be) regarding how work gets done. These patterns were based on nine dimensions:

1. *Assertiveness*: Assertive, confrontational, aggressive in social relationships
2. *Future Orientation*: Plan, invest in the future, delay gratifications
3. *Gender Egalitarianism*: Minimize gender role differences, promotion of gender equality
4. *Humane Orientation*: Reward being fair, altruistic, friendly, generous, caring, and so on
5. *In-Group Collectivism*: Express pride, loyalty, and cohesiveness in their organizations or families
6. *Institutional Collectivism*: Encourage or reward collective distribution of resources and collective action
7. *Performance Orientation*: Reward performance improvement or excellence
8. *Power Distance*: Believe power should be stratified and concentrated at higher levels
9. *Uncertainty Avoidance*: Avoid uncertainty, rely on established social norms, rituals, and bureaucratic practices

The GLOBE study suggests that Eastern European and Middle Eastern societies are similar to each other, but nearly opposite from the Germanic and Nordic societies, which tend to be similar to each other. Latin America is similar to Latin Europe, and southern Asia is similar to Confucian Asia. The Anglo society (which includes the United States) tends to have moderate scores on most dimensions, serving as a midpoint between Europe and Asia. Yet, the most intriguing findings in terms of organizational change are the societal differences found among these clusters. Any societal variability in the gaps between perceptions of "what is" and expectations of "what should be" hypothetically should lead to societal variability in inclinations to change behavior. Consider some of the patterns discovered:

- Employees from most societies had perceptions that matched their expectations in terms of in-group collectivism (that is pride and loyalty in organizations and families), with the notable exceptions of Anglo and Nordic societies, both of which perceived less in-group collectivism than what they thought should be.
- Employees from all societies, but especially southern Asia, perceived more power distance (that is, separation between a supervisor and a subordinate) than what they thought should be.
- All societies observed less performance orientation than they thought should exist, but the gap was smallest for Confucian Asia and largest for Latin America.
- The Nordic society was the only one to report more institutional collectivism than what they thought should be.
- The Germanic society was the only one to report more assertiveness than what they thought should be.
- The Nordic and Germanic societies were also the only ones to perceive more uncertainty avoidance (that is, reliance on bureaucracy, ritual) than what they thought should be, contrasting sharply with Middle Eastern and Eastern European societies.
- The Nordic and Germanic societies were most favorable among perceptions of future orientation, whereas Eastern Europe, Latin America, and Middle Eastern societies observed less than what they thought should be.
- Southern Asian countries had more favorable perceptions of humane orientation than did the other societies.
- The Middle East had the lowest expectations for gender egalitarianism, and their perceptions matched that low level, suggesting that their "satisfaction" in this domain is based on setting a lower bar than what other societies would set.

Given these findings, it may seem logical to assume that employees' readiness to change will vary based on these societal differences in perceptions and expectations of work. Societies with larger gaps between perceptions and expectations should be more dissatisfied with the status quo and thus more amenable to change efforts that seek to close those gaps. If true, then multinational organizations executing planned change efforts would experience different levels of success across locations, depending on what specific action area is being addressed and what intervention is being used. This concept produces intriguing, if not counterintuitive, hypotheses. For example, if an organization were to attempt to improve gender equity throughout the world, one would hypothesize, based on these GLOBE findings, that women in the Middle East would have very little interest in the effort. As another example, empowerment efforts in south Asia that transfer power from supervisors to employees should be welcomed by employees, even though it is radically different from current societal norms.

Of course, there are many reasons to doubt that societal culture moderates the efficacy of planned organizational change initiatives—most notably the lack of empirical studies specifically designed to test these ideas. In addition, the conclusions from the GLOBE study are sometimes in conflict with prior findings from Hofstede (for example, the universal finding that employees perceive more power distance than what they think should be contradicts Hofstede's conclusion that Latin and Asian societies prefer more power distance). Such inconsistencies may be due to the various methodological differences between the two studies or to changes in work perceptions across cultural societies in the past 25 years. Finally, one must also be careful not to erroneously apply cultural level results to the individual level (the Ecological Fallacy). A person's immediate psychological environment is far more predictive of that individual's behavior than is the "average" for his or her society. Even when a society's average is lower than the global average, an individual from that society may surpass the global average. Indeed, for developing societies, multinational companies may employ people who differ substantially from their societal norms (for example, better educated, higher socioeconomic status). To that point, my colleagues and I have not been able to conceptually replicate results from the GLOBE study when using specific organizational survey results, leading us to conclude that the organizational culture of a multinational company can trump the societal culture that presides at a given location (Mastrangelo, Johnson, & Jolton, 2005; Mastrangelo & Corace, 2006; Mastrangelo, 2008). HR and OD practitioners engaged in global change efforts are advised to be aware of societal differences, but not to let these broad generalities overrule specific data relevant to the situation.

## Topics Where Employee Dissatisfaction Should Create Increased Readiness to Change

To the extent that employee surveys measure dissatisfaction with facets of an organization's climate, they should also indicate where employees are most ready to change. According to the DVF "Change Equation" ($D \times V \times F > R$) (Holman & Devane, 1999; Torgeson-Anderson, Gantner, & Hanson, 2006), **D**issatisfaction is one of three necessary elements (along with **V**ision and **F**irst Steps) that must interact to overcome **R**esistance and thus create successful organizational change. Yet, experience with employee survey data indicates that dissatisfaction on certain topics is more important than dissatisfaction on other topics. For example, survey questions that ask about compensation and benefits typically yield the most dissatisfaction, but they hardly ever correlate strongly with engagement questions, subsequent retention, or organization performance metrics.

A review of the topics that do correspond with these outcomes suggests that the most important areas of dissatisfaction concern employees' frustration in accomplishing personal and organizational goals. In a Corporate Leadership Council (2004) study of 50,000 employees from 59 companies, the survey topics that most related to employee engagement (logical and emotional commitment, intention to stay, and discretionary effort) included the link between work and organizational strategy, supervisor effectiveness, and communication practices. In my own analysis of a multinational Fortune 100 manufacturing company, the topics most associated with ratings of the organization as a place to work were customer orientation, quality, and successful product launches. A third analysis from a separate multinational Fortune 500 company indicated that the best predictor of top performers who subsequently left the company was perception of the company's culture for improvement, including use of their employee survey to make changes. Across disparate employee survey questions and measures of organizational performance, the most impactful areas are *not* "what's in it for me" topics like compensation, but rather topics that address business execution. Dissatisfaction with execution is what best predicts both employee behavior (such as turnover) and organizational behavior (such as financial performance). Thus, the employees' perceived ability to personally contribute to their organization's success and improvement is the most important source of dissatisfaction for driving change.

Yet, if employees' survey responses pinpoint their dissatisfaction on topics that clearly align with what leaders want to improve, then why is effective organizational change so elusive? There are several possible explanations for this *survey-change paradox*. Sometimes what appears to be dissatisfaction is actually not. As previously mentioned certain survey topics (such as compensation, work-life balance) elicit high dissatisfaction as a norm, but these expressions of dissatisfaction are typically not associated with detrimental behavior. As one of my clients put it, some employee survey questions are like asking your kids if they have enough toys; you know they will ask for more even if they are completely satisfied with what they have. If post-survey efforts only focus on apparent dissatisfaction, but not the real sources of frustration, then the organization loses the opportunity to create broad support for meaningful change.

Likewise, what appears to be satisfaction or dissatisfaction can be confused because of societal differences in employee survey scores. Normative data show relatively high satisfaction across all topics in Latin America and India, but low satisfaction in Japan. Unless scores in these locations are compared to local normative data, the expressions of satisfaction or dissatisfaction will be misconstrued at the organizational level. The same error can take place when comparing survey scores across job types; for example, normative scores for manufacturing jobs are lower than those from sales, potentially masking strengths of one location and the weaknesses of another. In sum, a likely reason for this survey paradox is that employees' survey responses are frequently misunderstood. Yet, poor interpretation of results is not the only culprit.

Another reason why employees' dissatisfaction with the status quo does not translate into effective organizational change is that there is equivalent or greater dissatisfaction with the *alternatives* to the status quo. Employees often prefer to maintain a known source of dissatisfaction rather than venture into a new situation with unknown consequences. This preference for the "evil we know" has been demonstrated particularly among people with low scores on the personality domain Emotional Stability (for example, highly anxious individuals) (Hirsh & Inzlicht, 2008). A similar phenomenon occurs when employees say they want change to occur, but are not willing to commit to their own behavioral change. I have interviewed employees who blame leaders for their current situation, and, therefore, they expect leaders to deliver them. They want *a* change more than they want *to* change. Furthermore, some employees do not believe that the desired outcome is possible given current circumstances and previous attempts at organizational change, leading them to give up trying to make a difference—a phenomenon known in psychology as *learned helplessness.*

To the extent that employee dissatisfaction with the status quo is not being harnessed to improve the organization, there is unrealized potential for successful organizational change. Given the challenges facing a global organization in need of changing employee behavior, this gap between dissatisfaction and change must be bridged. The next section of the chapter reviews evidence-based theories from clinical, health, and social psychology that describe the conditions under which individuals change their behavior. Evidence-based models of individual change will then be applied to organizational change to create large-scale interventions that take advantage of a "crowd mentality" or "contagion" designed to transform dissatisfaction into behavioral change. Simply put, changing people is about changing each individual in that population, but the rate of change need not occur one individual at a time. Global organizational change can be achieved more quickly and effectively if new behaviors are attractive (infectious) to certain individuals who are likely to become role models of that behavior for other individuals (self-replicating).

## Establishing Social Conditions Where Individuals Change Their Own Behavior

Organizational change occurs when a critical mass of individuals' behaviors differs from time 1 to time 2. The definition of the critical mass varies depending on the nature of what is to be changed; success may require 100% of an organization to change behavior, or success may be achieved at a lower percentage of changed behavior. A holistic change requires different employees to make different changes. For instance, the organization seeking to improve its safety record will need adherence to new procedures from nonsupervisory employees, vigilance and support from direct supervisors to maintain safety compliance, cooperation from union leaders to change disciplinary standards for safety infractions, new performance management goals from HR to assert Lost Workday Case as a critical leadership metric, the redesign of all locations by facilities management to reduce accident risks, and so on. Individual employees throughout this organization will need to prepare for and engage in new work behaviors. Successful organizational change can therefore be defined as the aggregate of individual behavioral changes that are appropriate given each individual's organizational role. Fundamentally, organizational change occurs through just two processes: new behavior from new employees, and new behavior from existing employees. The attraction, selection, and attrition of employees in an organization do affect the climate or culture of an organization (Schneider & Reichers, 1983). Likewise, organizational mergers, acquisitions, and reorganizations create new groups, different social interactions, and heightened ambiguity regarding behavioral expectations. However, solely changing the human composition of an organization is not likely to yield the desired combination of specific behavioral changes necessary for success (although drastic staffing changes may make employees more aware of the need to change their own behavior). Furthermore, replacing or adding employees is not always a viable option because of costs, laws, politics, and other constraints. Focusing on how to change the behaviors of existing employees is a more fruitful path to improving organizational change interventions.

Yet, too often individual behavioral change is treated as a "black box" step in organizational change models. Lewin's classic model (1951) of organizational change (Unfreeze, Change, Refreeze) is a good example of a procedural guideline that does not specify *how* behavioral changes are to occur. Even more detailed models, such as Rothwell & Sullivan's Change Process Model (2005), ignore how employee behaviors will be changed. Burke's Action Research Model (2002) provides some guidelines (for example, Establish the need for change, Deal with resistance), but it lacks specific steps for how to achieve these goals. More recent organizational change models approach specifics, but they often oversimplify what it takes to change individuals' behaviors. The previously mentioned DVF Change Equation $(D \times V \times F > R)$ seems to suggest that resistance to change is overcome through improved communication: show employees reasons why they should be dissatisfied with the status quo, show them a vision of a new desirable end, and show them the first steps toward achieving that end. Yet when one examines large-scale public health efforts to reduce smoking, improve dietary habits, or prevent driving under the influence of alcohol, communication along these lines has not been effective. Why should we expect better results in efforts to change employee behavior? My telling you about organizational efforts to improve safety may motivate you to happily follow new procedures, but it also might motivate you to vigorously resist. If those new safety procedures conflict with how you see yourself (helmets are for wimps), how your boss sees you (safety procedures slow down delivery), or how your friends see you (my workgroup burned the new fire prevention policy), then there is a good chance that the communication, no matter how logical, will be disregarded. Communication must be combined with other psychological conditions in order to create large-scale behavioral change.

A more comprehensive approach to organizational change is found in John Kotter's (1995; 1996) Eight-Stage Process for Creating Major Change:

1. Establishing a sense of urgency
2. Creating a guiding coalition
3. Developing a vision and strategy

4. Communicating the change vision
5. Empowering a broad base of people to take action
6. Generating short-term wins
7. Consolidating gains and producing even more change
8. Anchoring (institutionalizing) the new approaches into the culture

Though some aspects of his process mimic the DVF Change Equation (for example, establishing urgency is similar to creating dissatisfaction, both models emphasize communicating vision), Kotter does introduce actions beyond communication that create the right psychological conditions for behavioral change. Note that Kotter speaks about the creation of a guiding coalition and the widespread empowerment of people. Both of these steps reference a *group* of change leaders. "The solution to the change problem is not one larger-than-life individual who charms thousands into being obedient followers.... Many people need to help with the leadership task..."(Kotter, 1996, p. 30). The implication is that organizational change is moderated by social pressures, which can impede or accelerate the various new behaviors necessary for success. Furthermore, Kotter suggests that organizational change occurs in an iterative fashion, where early success is used to bring more people onboard to engage in still more changes.

From this point of view, organizational change can be likened to a chain reaction or domino effect, where the number of employees participating in behavioral changes increases exponentially and the impact stretches out far from the original source of action. Such a campaign is particularly suited to large, global organizations which need behavioral changes to occur quickly despite great geographical distances and cultural differences. To use a marketing analogy, this approach to organizational change is less about broadcasting repetitive commercials to a broad audience and is more about a viral marketing campaign, where a targeted message is attractive to a certain group of individuals (infectious) who then pass the message on to their peers (self-replicating).

Malcom Gladwell's *The Tipping Point* (2000) describes a spontaneous viral event where a few influential kids from the art scene began wearing Hush Puppies shoes, leading to waves of other teenagers who wanted to join this fashion and a 400%

increase in shoe sales. Gladwell attributes this viral behavioral change to the interaction of three small, but critical roles being filled: (1) Mavens, who start trends because they are highly knowledgeable about certain topics and they like to share that knowledge; (2) Salesmen, who are highly persuasive and therefore can motivate others to assimilate what Mavens have discovered; and (3) Connectors, who have a much larger than average network of friends and acquaintances across different "circles" of people, allowing them to spread what they have assimilated to vastly different social groups. The combination of these roles allows a small set of individuals to influence a much larger group of people, as new behavior moves from one social network to the next.

In a workplace environment such social networks are both formal (for example, the second shift machine operators at the Antwerp plant) and informal (for example, the smokers who gather outside the loading dock at 10:30). Based on their social interactions, members of these groups develop shared meanings of organizational events (Schneider & Reichers, 1983) and similar perceptions of the organization (Rentsch, 1990). The influence that members of each social network have over each other forms the basis of subcultures within the organization. Martin & Siehl (1983) proposed that organizations actually need multiple subcultures as they help maintain a balance between sustaining current behavior and introducing new behaviors. Some subcultures have been found to enhance the dominant culture fervently, as members guard traditions and established behaviors. However, other types of subcultures act as the breeding ground for new behavior. Martin and Siehl describe Orthogonal subcultures, whose members develop new values that are tangential to the dominant culture, and Countercultures, whose members oppose the old norms of behavior and spur innovation.

The key to creating a global planned-change intervention is to seed the right breeding grounds with the right self-replicating behaviors, thus "infecting" the whole organization with coordinated changes deemed necessary for success. The elements of this infectious, self-replicating behavioral change are grounded in existing evidence-based theories that designate (a) who is most likely to initiate new behaviors that will become infectious, (b) how perceived social norms lead individuals to conform, (c) how subtle shifts in the social environment encourage individuals to change their own behavior, and (d) what predictable stages exist when individuals change their own behavior.

## Evidence-Based Psychological Theories of Behavioral Change

Psychological research shows that individuals change their own behavior in predictable ways, suggesting that social environments can be designed to promote behavioral change. The most basic "learning" and "motivational" theories are well known and follow the same basic pattern. First, individuals attain feedback that alerts them to wants and needs. They may look inwardly to realize that they are dissatisfied with their current state, but often this evaluation has a social context. Next, individuals decide to act on one or more of these wants and needs. There is a general tendency to satisfy basic needs (physiological, safety) before addressing more complex needs (social, esteem, or actualization) (Maslow, 1987). Finally, individuals take action and behave in a manner that is intended to satisfy their wants and needs. The actual action is selected because it has worked before (classical conditioning, operant conditioning), it has worked for someone else before (vicarious learning, modeling), or it seems like it should work (expectancy, VIE). However, evidence-based psychological theories of behavioral change go beyond this foundation, and there are four well-supported theories that can be used to change organizations. Each is described below, and the last section of this chapter combines elements from these theories to suggest practical techniques for creating infectious organizational change.

## Individuals Are Predisposed to Play Different Roles During Organizational Change

In any given population there will be some individuals who are relatively more adaptive to change, some who are more anxious about change, some who are more influential in changing others, and some who are more likely to be influenced to change. Although more complex than Gladwell's *Maven-Salesman-Connector* description, personality theory also suggests that employees have different roles to play in an organizational change initiative.

Decades of empirical research have led to the Five Factor Model (FFM) of personality, which uses five broad domains to describe a person's behavioral tendencies that distinguish the individual's identity (see Table 11.1). Though each of these five domains can be broken down into subparts, generally personality boils down to a person's degree of Extroversion, Agreeableness, Conscientiousness, Emotional Stability, and Openness to Experience. The FFM has not only been rigorously validated (see, for example, McCrae & Costa, 1987; Goldberg, 1990; Barrick & Mount, 1991), but it also has been found applicable across multiple societal cultures (Howard & Howard, 2001; Rolland, 2002). As a result the FFM provides an empirically supported set of profiles or roles that can be used to cast an infectious change.

Some individuals are prone to search for novel, unfamiliar experiences and would be classified as scoring high on the Openness to Experience domain. Because these individuals are biological recipients of more dopamine and dopamine receptors in their brains (Howard & Howard, 2001), they display more curiosity and exploration in their thoughts and behaviors. They are willing to change for the sake of change, and they tend to be bored in the absence of change. Thus, employees who are very open to experience are more likely to adopt newly prescribed behaviors. If these new behaviors are likely to create uncertain consequences for the employees, then the most perseverant individuals will likely be those who are relatively high on Emotional Stability, meaning that they tend to be calmer in stressful conditions. A recent study suggests that individuals who have low Emotional Stability have such a high need for certainty that they actually prefer definitive bad news rather than uncertain but possibly good news (Hirsh & Inzlicht, 2008). So, it would seem that only certain employees are prone to be the first to change their behavior to match a new standard, especially with uncertain consequences for making the change.

Making these few early adopters' changes infectious, however, calls for two further circumstances to hold true. The first condition involves Extroversion. Some portion of these early adopters need to be extroverted enough to be perceived as influential (Gladwell's salesman role), and some portion of the individuals being influenced need to be extroverted enough to pass on the

**Table 11.1. The Five-Factor Model of Personality.**

| Personality Domain | Description |
|---|---|
| Openness to Experience | People with high scores seek what is new, think ideally about the future, and are perceived as imaginative, curious, and original. |
| | People with low scores seek familiarity, think practically about the current situation, and are perceived as traditional, consistent, and straightforward. |
| Extroversion | People with high scores prefer being with people, lead or get involved with activities, and are perceived as talkative, assertive, and sociable. |
| | People with low scores prefer being alone, remain private, choose to write more than talk, and are perceived as quiet, aloof, and serious. |
| Agreeableness | People with high scores promote social harmony, tend to compromise, and are described as compassionate, tolerant, and cooperative. |
| | People with low scores promote their interests, persist in an opinion, and are described as tough, independent, and adamant. |
| Emotional Stability | People with high scores handle stress well, tend to be rational, focus on solving problems, and are described as calm and steady. |
| | People with low scores react to stress with excitement, tend to be emotional, focus on seeing problems, and are described as anxious. |
| Conscientiousness | People with high scores work in a linear fashion, rely on preparation and organization, and are described as reliable, rule oriented, and thorough. |
| | People with low scores work in a nonlinear fashion, rely on spontaneity and impulse, and are described as relaxed, flexible, and free-spirited. |

new behavior to others as being worthwhile (Gladwell's Connector role). Extroversion marks a person's need for sensory stimulation, it is mostly expressed by the need to be with other people, and it is positively related to a drive to lead other people (Howard & Howard, 2001). It follows that the more extroverted the early adopters are, the more likely that they will be seen as charismatic leaders whose behavioral changes will be imitated. The same holds true for the "early imitators" who first follow the leader and replicate the behavioral change.

It is this distinction between the leader and the follower that highlights the second condition for infectious change. Those early adopters who are subsequently imitated are *challenging* the established behavioral norm and any social pressure that exists to maintain that norm. Likewise, many of those early imitators must also challenge the status quo. Yet, at some point in a successful intervention, change becomes the norm, meaning that subsequent imitators are not so much challenging others as they are *accommodating* others. Again, the FFM indicates that individuals have different predispositions for challenging or accommodating others. Individuals who score lower on Agreeableness scales tend to be more comfortable with conflict, more willing to express their own opinions, and more apt to stand out from the crowd. So, extroverted early adopters with below average agreeableness have the right profile to start a small counterculture. Conversely, individuals who score high on Agreeableness scales tend to avoid conflict, let others "win," and go with what the crowd wants. Combine these tendencies with high extroversion and high openness to experience, and you have the profile of those who can make that counterculture more mainstream.

To create the psychological equivalent of a domino effect, one needs some assertive individuals to push on others, but one also needs compliant individuals who will fall into place. Although individuals are not always consistent with their personality in all situations, personality does represent individuals' default tendencies. As illustrated in Figure 11.1, I posit that an employee's role in an organizational change initiative can be predicted through the eight possible combinations of dichotomous scores on Openness to Experience, Extroversion, and Agreeableness. By first harnessing the power of Instigators to publicly change their behavior to

**Figure 11.1.  Individual Predispositions to Organizational Change Roles.**

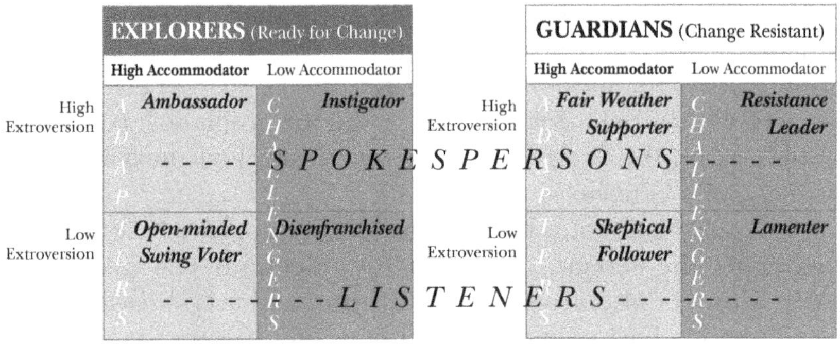

| EXPLORERS (Ready for Change) | | | GUARDIANS (Change Resistant) | | |
|---|---|---|---|---|---|
| High Accommodator | Low Accommodator | | High Accommodator | Low Accommodator | |
| High Extroversion | *Ambassador* | *Instigator* | High Extroversion | *Fair Weather Supporter* | *Resistance Leader* |
| | - - - - - *S P O K E S P E R S O N S* - - - - - | | | | |
| Low Extroversion | *Open-minded Swing Voter* | *Disenfranchised* | Low Extroversion | *Skeptical Follower* | *Lamenter* |
| | - - - - - *L I S T E N E R S* - - - - - | | | | |

(vertical text between Explorer columns: *C H A P L A I N S*; vertical text between Guardian columns: *C H A L L E N G E R S*)

influence their social networks and then relying on Ambassadors to make this behavioral change widely acceptable, an infectious change movement can spread from the Open-Minded Swing Voters and the Disenfranchised to the more accommodating Guardian groups. Though popular personality assessments (e.g., NEO-PI-R, Myers-Briggs Type Indicator) could be used to identify Instigators and Ambassadors, I will discuss in the last section of this chapter how a peer-nominated team will allow these influential early adopters to rise to their necessary position for a successful intervention. Given the cross-cultural validity of the FFM (Howard & Howard, 2001; Rolland, 2002), there is no reason to believe that these profiles would be any less useful outside the United States.

## Perceived Social Norms Lead Individuals to Conform

When in Rome, you do as the Romans do. A large body of research has demonstrated how influential a group can be on an individual's behavior; whether one recycles (Schultz, 1999), laughs at a joke (Smyth & Fuller, 1972), or helps a stranger having a seizure (Darley & Latane, 1968) depends upon the perceived consensus of the people that surround the individual. Robert Cialdini refers to this phenomenon as social proof—if a group of three or more is behaving in a particular manner, other individuals are inclined to join in, especially in an ambiguous situation (Cialdini, 2001).

There are three empirically supported explanations for why individuals change their behavior to conform to others: accuracy, affiliation, and positive self-concept (Cialdini & Goldstein, 2004). Individuals rely on a group consensus to (a) accurately interpret the situation in order to behave correctly, (b) obtain social approval from others, and (c) enhance, protect, or repair their self-esteem (Cialdini & Goldstein, 2004; Deutsch & Gerard, 1955). These motivations are often interrelated. Not surprisingly, individuals are more motivated to conform when they are highly self-conscious and their behavior is being observed by others. Conformity also depends on aspects of the normative information. Knowledge of the social norm needs to be salient when the compliant behavior is to take place—any feedback about what others are doing must either be timely or memorable in order to affect an individual's behavior. Furthermore, normative information comes in two forms: descriptive norms that communicate what *is* being done, and injunctive norms that communicate what *should* be done (Cialdini, 2003; Schultz, Nolan, Cialdini, Goldstein, & Griskevicius, 2007). Conformity is more likely when both of these norms indicate that the same behavior is socially approved.

Different rates of abidance with two traffic laws clearly illustrate these principles. In all likelihood, you rarely drive on the wrong side of the road, no matter how slow traffic is or how late for work you are. In this case the descriptive and injunctive norms are aligned: driving on the correct side is overwhelmingly prevalent and in accordance with traffic law. When you do see a car on the wrong side of the road, something about the situation (there is an animal in the road) or about the person (the driver appears intoxicated) communicates that this is an exception to the social norm. Anyone driving on the wrong side of the road without just cause would be given quick feedback via angry drivers' horns or an officer's traffic citation, and the perpetrator would be perceived as a reckless deviant. For all these reasons, there is strong social power that keeps you driving on the correct side. On the other hand, you are probably not as vigilant about abiding by the posted speed limits. Given similar dangers and potential costs, why would this be? The most obvious reason is that unlike driving on the wrong side of the road, you can easily observe many drivers exceeding the speed limit despite posted fines and warnings—the descriptive norm is incongruent with the injunctive norm. Furthermore, though both the descriptive and the injunctive feedback are provided precisely when you can choose to adjust your speed, the descriptive norm is typically more salient than the injunctive norm. You see many drivers exceeding the speed limit, but you see few being caught in the act. Obeying the speed limit may actually anger some fellow drivers who cannot quickly pass, and "slow" drivers are stereotypically older, more prudish citizens—not a classification that you aspire to join. So, you drive faster than you should, but never on the wrong side of the road—the former is typical, the latter is just wrong.

By analyzing individuals' motivations to conform to descriptive and injunctive norms, it is possible to devise a "Social Norms Marketing Campaign" (Schultz et al., 2007) that projects a social environment that promotes desired behaviors. Schultz and his associates describe a field experiment designed to reduce household energy consumption in a Californian community by correcting individuals' misperceptions regarding energy use. Based on the assumption that people overestimate the prevalence of undesirable behavior, they correctly hypothesized that providing written descriptive norms for energy use would reduce consumption among above-average households. Interestingly, they also correctly hypothesized that providing descriptive norms would *increase* energy consumption among below-average households. However, they eliminated this undesirable boomerang effect by also providing injunctive feedback. By adding nothing more than a handwritten happy face (☺) or sad face (☹) to the feedback, they kept below-average consumption households at their desirable level while improving above-average consumption households' energy use by an average of 1.5 kilowatt hours per day. These are impressive results given how simple the intervention was: targets received two messages, one week apart, that provided feedback on their energy use, the average use in their neighborhood and (in half of the cases) an emoticon to express injunctive norms. One can imagine creating a nearly identical intervention to alter employee behaviors in an organizational setting.

For global organizations, the question is whether a Social-Norms Marketing campaign would be effective across all societal cultures. Because part of the motivation to conform is dependent upon individuals' desires to maintain their self-esteem levels, it is logical to assume that conformity techniques would be less effective on "individuals whose cultures place less of an emphasis on self-concept positivity and related maintenance and enhancement goals (such as Japan) . . ." (Cialdini & Goldstein, 2004, p. 605). On the other hand, Kim & Markus (1999) noted that conformity and nonconformity are evaluated quite differently across cultures. Though nonconformity represents uniqueness in Western cultures, it represents deviance in East Asian cultures, suggesting that conformity tactics may be more effective in that part of the world. Likewise, Cialdini and his associates found that when considering whether to comply with a request, participants were more likely to base their decisions on their peers' actions when from a "collectivistic country" such as Poland than an "individualistic country" such as the United States (Cialdini, Wosinska, Barrett, Butner, & Gornik-Durose, 1999). In summary, while conformity tactics are likely affected by cross-cultural effects, the processes researched in the United States do appear to operate in Europe and Asia as well. Clearly, portraying descriptive and injunctive norms to elicit a specific behavior is best done in consultation with those from the local societal culture.

## Subtle Shifts in the Social Environment Encourage Individuals to Change Their Own Behavior

In 1953 Edgar Schein began working at the Walter Reed Army Institute of Research to help prisoners of war (POWs) repatriate to the United States following the Korean conflict. There was clear evidence that the Chinese had been able to "brainwash" American soldiers such that POWs were sympathetic to communist causes and had collaborated with the enemy in various ways. Schein began to study the socio-psychological process that the Chinese had used to realize these cases of attitudinal and behavioral transformation. The results of his research, documented in his 1961 book *Coercive Persuasion*, were that the Chinese techniques were actually *identical* to the persuasive techniques used to indoctrinate individuals into religious groups, schools, fraternities, and workplaces. The change model is not coercion, which implies being forced to change, but rather coercive persuasion, which manipulates individuals' social interactions, uproots their previous routines, and leads to a change in their self-images that subsequently changes their behaviors.

Schein's change process (2007) has three principles. First, the change agent must create disequilibrium or find where individuals are already dissatisfied, anxious, or feeling guilty. These emotions form "Survival Anxiety" and are forces for change that become a starting point for the process. Second, the change agent must create opportunities where individuals can reestablish equilibrium by learning the desired new behaviors. Because new learning requires unlearning previous behavioral patterns, there will be resistance to change or "Learning Anxiety." Third, change will only occur if Survival Anxiety is greater than Learning Anxiety, which is similar to the DVF Change Equation discussed earlier. However, a key distinction in Schein's model (compared to most other change models) is that escalating Survival Anxiety (for example, dissatisfaction) is NOT seen as a successful method for overcoming Learning Anxiety. Rather it is Learning Anxiety that must be reduced by altering (mostly social) sources of resistance to create "Psychological Safety" that allows behavioral change to occur. Resistance is seen primarily as fear of losing power or position, identity, group membership, and sense of competence—all of which come from an evaluation of individuals' social support system.

Based on these principles, change agents in an organizational setting can target a "captured audience" that is unlikely to leave. They can introduce the new behavior in small, graduated steps while isolating individuals from their previous social group. As a result individuals lose social support for old behaviors, and become immersed in the new manner of thinking—old words and terms become associated with new meanings, old standards are altered to create a new normal state, and the criteria for judging good and bad are redefined. In the midst of this ambiguity, individuals should be placed into a new social group that will reinforce the new behavior and provide support for individuals engaging in the behavior change.

However, shifts in the use of terms, standards, evaluations and other environmental cues need not be drastic. In fact individuals are far less likely to resist behavioral change when they are *unaware* of any change efforts (Tice, 1994). Behavior can be influenced by very subtle alterations to the environment, such as the uneven placement of stripes on Lake Shore Drive in Chicago to promote braking before a dangerous curve, or the placement of fruits and vegetables at eye level in cafeteria lines to improve nutritional intake (Thaler & Sunstein, 2008). The more individuals can find their own way in the process of change (rather than being told), the more likely they are to "internalize" the behavior so that it becomes a part of their self-concept (Schein, 2007). Thus, enticing individuals to behave in a new way (without making the individual feel coerced) leads them to review their own behavior and to adjust their self-concept accordingly. According to Diane Tice (1992; 1994), individuals are more likely to internalize new behaviors when:

- They are outside of their normal environment
- They are in transition points in their lives
- They are induced to behave *publicly* according to the desired regime
- They are likely to interact with others who have seen them behave according to the desired regime
- They frequently recall their own previous behavior that was consistent with the desired regime
- They observe *dissimilar* others behaving in a manner *inconsistent* with the desired regime
- They freely choose to behave according to the desired regime
- They are high self-monitors, who typically regulate their own behavior to fit social cues

Although the workplace environment is not meant to be portrayed as a prisoner-of-war camp, nor organizational leaders as brainwashers, these internalization techniques do have workplace applications, particularly for newly merged organizations or those emerging from crisis. Under these circumstances even the employees most reluctant to change are likely more amenable to new roles, standards, and terminologies. With near-subliminal facilitation from leaders and supervisors, a targeted set of individuals can be guided through steps to maximize behavioral internalization. "Converts" then become effective recruiters because they are so similar to the group from which they came. This self-replicating change process was a highly effective technique for the Chinese (Schein, 1961), and given the international underpinnings of the model, there is every reason to believe that this approach would work across societal cultures.

### Predictable Stages Exist When Individuals Change Their Own Behavior

Perhaps the most researched model in health psychology is the Trans Theoretical Model (TTM) of behavior change, which has been the basis for effective programs for modifying smoking, substance abuse, gambling, physical exercise, sunscreen use, condom use, and other health promotion behaviors (Prochaska, DiClemente, Norcross, 1992; Velicer, Prochaska, Fava, Norman, & Redding, 1998; DiClemente & Prochaska, 1998). TTM conceptualizes change as a process that unfolds over time and involves progress through six stages of change: precontemplation (I won't), contemplation (I might), preparation (I will), action (I am), maintenance (I have), and termination (I do). At each stage, different processes need to occur to help individuals progress to the next stage (Mastrangelo, Prochaska, & Prochaska, 2008). To progress from *I won't* to *I might*, individuals must recognize an increased number of perceived advantages of changing (that is, the pros). However, to progress from *I might* to *I will*, individuals then must recognize a decreased number of perceived disadvantages of changing (that is, the cons). In these first three stages, the processes at work within individuals are likely to be more cognitive (listening to information and education), affective (feeling inspired or afraid), and evaluative (weighing the pros and cons involved in decision making). As individuals progress into the *I am*, *I have*, and *I do* stages, the processes are more behavioral, such as seeking reinforcement from self and others, changing social networks to receive support, reengineering environments, and replacing dysfunctional behaviors with more effective alternatives (Mastrangelo, Prochaska, & Prochaska, 2008).

There are several implications of TTM for large-scale organizational change interventions. First, resistance to change is not the result of employees' failure to be ready for change leaders, but rather change leaders' failure to be ready for employees. Even though fingers may point to "the frozen middle management," the wrong organizational culture, or a disengaged workforce, resistance is actually a logical reaction to people seeking to impose behavior changes on individuals who are not cognitively, socially, or physically prepared. Resistance doesn't stop a successful intervention; resistance is a failed intervention.

A second implication of TTM is that progression through initial stages of change is not overt. Thus, what seems like early failure may be a silent victory, especially if individuals who are now contemplating change can soon feel less anxious about the consequences of changing. However, if the change effort is limited to a communication effort to express the need for change, the vision of the future, and next steps, then the effort attempts only to increase perceived pros, but not to reduce perceived cons. Using Schein's nomenclature (2007), TTM calls for initially increasing survival anxiety (pros), and then decreasing learning anxiety (cons) — a subtly that is completely aligned with Schein's Coercive Persuasion model, but one that is not found in traditional OD change models.

A third implication of TTM is that individuals need continuous, but evolving, support from leaders and change agents. Yes, careful attention to communication is an important element in a large-scale intervention, but it is rarely designed in stages with different focal messages to elicit progression through stages of change. Supervisors are another important element in a large-scale intervention, but they are rarely trained to recognize their direct reports' stages of change and the appropriate feedback they should provide to encourage further progression. Pulse surveys are often used to gauge the progress of the intervention, but they are rarely designed to measure employees' progression through stages of change. Likewise, employees are usually asked to participate in the change intervention only through surveys and feedback groups, but they are rarely asked to commit to their own behavior change (or to help others change their behaviors).

For these and other traditional processes that support large-scale interventions, TTM provides an evidence-based framework that can provide a more comprehensive and aligned organization change effort. The stages of change and the hypothesized changes in pros and cons have been replicated in organizational change efforts to participate in collaborative service delivery, prepare for a company merger, organize high-performance teams, support a managed care model, purchase software, and engage in a continuous quality improvement program (Prochaska, Prochaska, & Levesque, 2001). What is less clear is how applicable TTM is across societal cultures; although some cross-cultural validity has been shown (see Cardinal, Tuominen, & Rintala, 2004), as of yet there appears to be no documentation for the application of TTM to a global organizational setting.

## Putting Theory into Practice

Barring a dramatic crisis within an organization, there is no better impetus for a large-scale change intervention than a global employee survey. To realize this potential, however, the well-known need for "global thinking" in the design, translation, administration, and interpretation of the global survey (Scott & Mastrangelo, 2006) must be matched by global thinking in the action phase of the project. Employees' dissatisfaction with aspects of their work environment differs across societal cultures (House et al., 2004), as do their reactions to post-survey actions (Gomez-Mejia, 1994). Yet, evidence-based psychological theories suggest that change initiatives can be more effective if they involve more than communicating what is being done *to* employees. Instead, an intervention must be designed around how people change (Prochaska, Prochaska, & Levesque, 2001), where the focus is on what is being done *by* employees. The more that employees are participating in a change effort, the more likely they are to embrace change (Wanberg & Banas, 2000). The premise of this chapter is that participation can be garnered through the application of personality differences, social norms, behavior internalization, and stages of change. Indeed, what is missing from post-survey actions is the coordination of activity that involves employees and showcases the changes they have made to entice more employees to commit to their own behavioral change (Mastrangelo & Joseph, 2009).

The most successful post-survey, large-scale interventions that I have facilitated were launched with a peer-nominated survey response team. Instead of inviting volunteers or handpicking members, leaders publicly invited employees to nominate one person who would be knowledgeable, outspoken, and respected as a representative for their workgroup, location, or function. Immediately, all employees had the opportunity to participate in the change process, and their nominations were likely to be the emergent leaders of both formal and informal social groups, making it easy for all employees to get updates and provide feedback. In all cases the head of the unit or division and the HR director were also members. As the external consultant I facilitated the selection of team members, the announcement of the team, and the initial team meeting. Their mission was to review the improvement goals that leaders established, fine-tune measurable criteria for success, conduct root cause analyses, and form initial and long-term action plans. Clearly, a team of 10 individuals cannot cover all actionable areas in a large, global organization. Yet, this team can be used to address a particularly important issue within a subunit where success would benefit the entire organization, and the effort can be showcased continually to the entire organization as a method that others can use to take action.

Each post-survey goal should be associated with iterative action plans, starting with changes that could be implemented in three minutes without budgets or committees, and progressing to plans that would be implemented over the course of three months, and on to three years. This "three minutes, three months, three years" approach allowed for quick wins that gained support for a sustained effort. The general manager of a multimillion-dollar biotech division actually solicited ideas for "three-minute actions" from her entire organization at an all-employee conference and committed to implementing at least three ideas on the spot. This facilitated two-hour event yielded noticeable shifts in body language and many elevator conversations—an excellent start considering how alarming the survey results had been. Their survey response team became an organizational fixture for over two years, and their work not only boosted morale but also led to successful attainment of revenue goals despite dramatic competitive pressure.

The potential applications of the psychological theories described here are boundless. The real challenge to those of us who endeavor to improve global organizations is to focus leaders on behavioral change rather than policy and procedural change. Organizational change is the sum of individuals' behavioral change. Yet, rather than attempting to force change upon employees, the physical and social environment can be designed to guide employees to change their own behavior. Let the employees most open to experience change their behavior and publicly share their experiences to influence their peers. Showcase those employees who have changed their behavior so that others believe that many people are on board with the new standards. Decrease the anxiety associated with leaving the old ways behind, and provide support as employees progress from cognitive preparation to behavioral preparation and ultimately the desired behavior. When individual behavioral change is infectious, global organizational change is no longer elusive.

## References

Barrick, M. R., & Mount, M. K. (1991). The big five personality dimensions and job performance: A meta-analysis. *Personnel Psychology, 44*, 1–26.

Burke, W. W. (2002). *Organization change: Theory and practice*. Thousand Oaks, CA: Sage.

Cardinal, B. J., Tuominen, K. J., Rintala, P. (2004). Cross-cultural comparison of American and Finnish college students' exercise behavior using transtheoretical model constructs. *Research Quarterly for Exercise and Sport, 75* (1), 92–101.

Cialdini, R. B. (2003). Crafting normative messages to protect the environment. *Current Directions in Psychological Science, 12*, 105–109.

Cialdini, R. B. (2001). *Influence: Science and practice* (4th ed.). Boston: Allyn & Bacon.

Cialdini, R. B., & Goldstein, N. J. (2004). Social influence: Compliance and conformity. *Annual Review of Psychology, 55*, 591–621.

Cialdini, R. B., Wosinska, W., Barrett, D. W., Butner, J., & Gornik-Durose, M. (1999). Compliance with a request in two cultures: The differential influence of social proof and commitment/consistency on collectivists and individualists. *Personality & Social Psychology Bulletin, 25,* 1242–1253.

Corporate Leadership Council (2004). *Driving employee performance and retention through engagement: A quantitative analysis of the effectiveness of employee engagement strategies.* Washington: Corporate Executive Board.

Darley, J. M., & Latane, B. (1968). Bystander intervention in emergencies: Diffusion of responsibility. *Journal of Personality and Social Psychology, 8,* 377–383.

Deutsch, M., & Gerard, H. B. (1955). A study of normative and informative social influences upon individual judgment. *Journal of Abnormal Social Psychology, 51,* 629–636.

DiClemente, C. C., & Prochaska, J. O. (1998). Toward a comprehensive transtheoretical model of change. In W. R. Miller & N. Heather (Eds.), *Treating addictive behaviors* (2nd ed.). New York: Springer.

Falletta, S. V., & Combs, W. (2002). Surveys as a tool for organization development and change. In A. H. Church & J. Waclawski (Eds.), *Organization development: A data-driven approach to organizational change.* San Francisco: Jossey-Bass.

Gladwell, M. (2000). *The tipping point: How little things can make a big difference.* New York: Back Bay Books.

Goldberg, L. R. (1990). An alternative "description of personality": The big-five factor structure. *Journal of Personality and Social Psychology, 59,* 1216–1229.

Gomez-Mejia, L. (1994). *Compensation practices in the Maquiladora industry.* Paper presented at the Universidad Autonoma de Mexico, Mexico City.

Hirsh, J. B., & Inzlicht, M. (2008). The devil you know: Neuroticism predicts neural response to uncertainty. *Psychological Science, 19,* 962–967.

Hofstede, G. (2001). *Culture's consequences: International differences in work related values* (2nd ed.). Thousand Oaks, CA: Sage.

Hofstede, G. (1980). *Cultural consequences: International differences in work-related values.* Thousand Oaks, CA: Sage.

Holman, F., & Devane, T. (1999). *The change handbook.* San Francisco: Berrett-Koehler.

House, R. J., Hanges, P. J., Javidan, M., Dorfman, P. W., & Gupta, V. (2004). *Culture, leadership, and organizations: The GLOBE study of 62 societies.* Thousand Oaks, CA: Sage.

Howard, P. J., & Howard, J. M. (2001). *The owner's manual for personality at work: How the big five personality traits affect performance, communication, teamwork, leadership, sales.* Marietta, GA: Bard Press.

Johnson, S. R. (1996). The multinational opinion survey. In A. I. Kraut (Ed.), *Organizational surveys: Tools for assessment and change*. San Francisco: Jossey-Bass.

Kim, H. S., & Markus, H. R. (1999). Deviance or uniqueness, harmony or conformity? A cultural analysis. *Journal of Personality and Social Psychology, 77,* 785–800.

Kotter, J. P. (1996). *Leading change*. Boston: Harvard Business School Press.

Kotter, J. P. (1995). Why transformation efforts fail. *Harvard Business Review, 61* (March-April), 59–67.

Kraut, A. I. (2006). *Getting action from organizational surveys: New concepts, technologies, and applications*. San Francisco: Jossey-Bass.

Kraut, A. I. (1996). *Organizational surveys: Tools for assessment and change*. San Francisco: Jossey-Bass.

Lewin, K. (1951). *Field theory in social science*. New York: Harper.

Martin, J., & Siehl, C. (1983). Organizational culture and counterculture: An uneasy symbiosis. *Organizational Dynamics, 12* (2), 39–64.

Maslow, A. H. (1987). *Motivation and personality* (3rd ed.). New York: Addison Wesley Longman.

Mastrangelo, P. M. (2008). Designing a global employee survey process to realize engagement and alignment. In M. Finney (Ed.), *Building high-performance people and organizations*. Westport, CT: Praeger.

Mastrangelo, P. M., & Corace, C. (2006, May). Comparing survey responses from the GLOBE survey to one global organization's survey. In P. Mastrangelo (Chair), *Patterns across global organizational surveys: Timeliness, norms, structural equation models*. Presentation at the 21st Annual Conference of the Society for Industrial and Organizational Psychology, Dallas, TX.

Mastrangelo, P. M., Johnson, S. R., & Jolton, J. A. (2005, July). *Global differences in employee survey items: How applicable is the 2004 GLOBE study?* Presentation at the International Conference on Advancements in Management, Washington, DC.

Mastrangelo, P. M., & Joseph, C. (2009). Action planning as planned change: The third tier. In A. J. Duffy (Chair), *Innovative approaches to "taking action" on survey results*. Presentation at the 24th Annual Conference of the Society for Industrial and Organizational Psychology, New Orleans, LA.

Mastrangelo, P. M., Prochaska, J. O., & Prochaska, J. M. (2008, April). *How people change: The transtheoretical model of behavior change*. Master's Tutorial at the 23rd Annual Conference of the Society for Industrial and Organizational Psychology, San Francisco, CA.

McCrae, R. R., & Costa, P. T. (1987). Validation of the five-factor model of personality across instruments and observers. *Journal of Personality and Social Psychology, 52,* 81–90.

Prochaska, J. O., DiClemente, C. C., & Norcross, J. C. (1998). Stages of change: Prescriptive guidelines for behavioral medicine and psychotherapy. In G. P. Koocher, J. C. Norcross, & S. S. Hill, III (Eds.), *Psychologists' desk reference.* New York, Oxford: Oxford University Press.

Prochaska, J. M., Prochaska, J. O., & Levesque, D. A. (2001). A transtheoretical approach to changing organizations. *Administration and Policy in Mental Health, 28,* 247–261.

Rentsch, J. R. (1990). Climate and culture: Interaction and qualitative differences in organizational meanings. *Journal of Applied Psychology, 75,* 668–681.

Rolland, J. P. (2002). The cross-cultural generalizability of the five-factor model of personality. In R. R. McCrae & J. Allik (Eds.), *The five-factor model of personality across cultures.* New York: Springer.

Rothwell, W. J., & Sullivan, R. L. (2005). Models for change. In W. J. Rothwell & R. L. Sullivan (Eds.), *Practicing organization development: A guide for consultants* (2nd ed.). San Francisco: Pfeiffer.

Schein, E. H. (1961). *Coercive persuasion: A socio-psychological analysis of the "brainwashing" of American civilian prisoners by the Chinese communists.* Cambridge, MA: Norton.

Schein, E. H. (2007). *The essence of change: Brainwashing, culture evolution and organizational therapy.* Hyannis, MA: Cape Cod Institute.

Schneider, B., & Reichers, A. E. (1983). On the etiology of climates. *Personnel Psychology, 36,* 19–39.

Schultz, P. W. (1999). Changing behavior with normative feedback interventions: A field experiment on curbside recycling. *Basic and Applied Social Psychology, 21,* 25–36.

Schultz, P. W., Nolan, J. M., Cialdini, R. B., Goldstein, N. J., Griskevicius, V. (2007). The constructive, destructive, and reconstructive power of social norms. *Psychological Science, 18,* 429–434.

Scott, J., & Mastrangelo, P. M. (2006). Driving change around the world: Employee surveys in global organizations. In A. Kraut (Ed.), *Getting action from organizational surveys: New concepts, methods, and applications.* Thousand Oaks, CA: Sage.

Smyth, M. M., & Fuller, R. G. C. (1972). Effects of group laughter on responses to humourous materials. *Psychological Reports, 30,* 132–134.

Thaler, R. H., & Sunstein, C. R. (2008). *Nudge: Improving decisions about health, wealth, and happiness.* New Haven, CT: Yale University Press.

Tice, D. M. (1994). Pathways to internalization: When does overt behavior change the self-concept? In T. M. Brinthaupt & R. P. Lipka (Eds.), *Changing the self: Philosophies, techniques, and experiences*. Albany: State University of New York Press.

Tice, D. M. (1992). Self-concept change and self-presentation: The looking glass self is also a magnifying glass. *Journal of Personality and Social Psychology*, *63*, 435–451.

Torgeson-Anderson, K., Gantner, S. M., & Hanson, T. F. (2006). A change model for healthcare organizations. *OD Practitioner*, *38* (3), 42–48.

Velicer, W. F., Prochaska, J. O., Fava, J. L., Norman, G. J., & Redding, C. A. (1998). Detailed overview of the transtheoretical model. *Homeostasis*, *38*, 216–233.

Wanberg, C. R., & Banas, J. T. (2000). Predictors and outcomes of openness to changes in a reorganizing workplace. *Journal of Applied Psychology*, *85*, 132–142.

# CHAPTER 12

# Maximizing the Success and Retention of International Assignees

Paula Caligiuri and Thomas Hippler

International assignees are all employees working outside of their own national borders (for example, parent country nationals, third country nationals, host country nationals). For a variety of strategic reasons, successful international assignments are indispensable for firms operating across borders. To facilitate the success of international employees' assignments, firms use a variety of human resources practices to manage their international assignees including selection, preparation, or training for the assignment, assignee performance management, and the like.

From the perspective of human resources and industrial and organizational psychology, global mobility (or international relocation), and global talent management, this chapter will discuss the need for expatriation and the benefits and challenges of expatriation—both for individuals and their organizations. The second half of this chapter discusses the practice areas of international assignee management, including international assignee selection, cross-cultural training, global organizational management, international assignee performance management, compensation, and work-life balance issues for international assignees and their families.

## The Benefits and Challenges of International Assignments for Individuals and Organizations

International assignments lead to both organizational and personal developments that need to be considered in the context of the associated concerns or challenges. This next section will discuss the positive benefits as well as the challenges of international assignments for individuals and the organizations that employee them.

### Benefits of International Assignments

Edström and Galbraith (1977) identified three principal motives for the global transfer of managers: (1) to *fill positions* that cannot be staffed locally because of a lack of technical or managerial skills; (2) to support *organizational development,* which refers to the coordination and control of international operations through socialization and informal networks; and (3) to support *management development* by enabling high-potential individuals to acquire international experience. If managed well, international assignees may also be more engaged and positive about their organizations (Lundby, Partha, & Kowske, 2008). These assignment motives are not mutually exclusive. More than 30 years after they were originally written, they still remain the dominant strategic benefits of international assignments.

Although the benefits of international assignees are clear, the tasks that international assignees are expected to accomplish while on assignment are as varied as incumbents in those roles. This is important for HR professionals generally (and I/O psychologists specifically) to consider, given that many of our practices are rooted in the knowledge, skills, abilities, personality characteristics, and competencies for a given job or job family. International assignments, as a group of highly diverse jobs accomplished on foreign soil, describe a job context (the foreign country) rather than a job description. Thus, to apply the tools in the I/O psychologists' toolkit with any reasonable efficiency, we need to consider the ways in which assignments can be similar (beyond the mere context of the host-country location).

Based on Caligiuri's taxonomy (1999), all international assignments vary along two dimensions: (1) the extent to which the assignment will require intercultural competence, and (2) the extent to which the assignment is intended to be developmental, enhancing skills for the employee and, in turn, the organization. Using these continua, international assignments fall into four major categories (Caligiuri, 1999):

*Technical Assignments*: There is no intended developmental component for technical international assignments. These assignments require few, if any, intercultural skills in order to be successfully completed. Technical assignees work in the host country solely to complete the job and return home. These individuals are often called in when a given skill set is unavailable in a host country.

*Functional (Tactical) Assignments*: Much like technical assignees, companies send functional assignees to complete a job and return home, usually when a skill set is not present in the host country or when company knowledge (usually headquarter specific) is critical. Also like the technical assignees, employee development is not a stated goal. To be successful, however, functional assignees tend to have significant and important interactions with host national colleagues, clients, and the like and they must be interculturally competent in order to be effective of the assignment.

*Developmental (High-Potential) Assignments*: Despite the need for employees to perform a specific task, the real purpose for such a transfer is developmental. Related to the individual's long-term career growth within the organization, the developmental assignees require the acquisition of intercultural skills. High-potential developmental assignees are often sent to perform various jobs on a rotational basis in order to gain global leadership competence. In general, many international assignees (whether intentionally a developmental assignment or not) find their assignments to be developmental experiences and report having gained tangible skills which are value-added for their organizations (Oddou & Mendenhall, 1991). With these assignments, the developmental goal is stated.

*Strategic (Executive) Assignments*: As a means of fostering the parent corporate culture, international assignees familiar with the organization are placed in key leadership positions in international subsidiaries (Kobrin, 1988; Mayrhofer & Brewster, 1996; Ondrack, 1985; Tung, 1982). In these leadership roles, international assignees are able to enact the parent company "way of doing things." Strategic international assignees in this group hold senior leadership roles within their respective firms. The firm is also sending strategic assignees for organizational development, as these international assignees fill critical leadership positions and also gain new skills, such as managing a larger or more diverse regional market. Global experience, including the use of intercultural skills, is critical for the long-term success and growth within many organizations.

Regardless of the type of assignment, many of the benefits for the international assignees and their family members become visible only upon return to the home country. Though strategically beneficial for the firm for the reasons discussed, international assignments are also beneficial for individuals, both personally and professionally. Personally, former international assignees (or repatriates) report that they are more open-minded and flexible after their assignment. They report that they have developed an appreciation for new things, become more culturally sensitive, and have learned to respect values and customs different from their own (Adler, 1997; Osland, 1995).

International assignments also have professional benefits. Those who have been on international assignments describe their assignments as having a more positive influence on their careers as a whole (Tung, 1998). From a professional standpoint, assignees report that they have developed valuable skills through their international experiences (Tung, 1998), and that these newly developed skills greatly enhance their expertise in both the domestic and the international context (Adler, 1981, 1997; Baughn, 1995; Black, Gregersen, & Mendenhall, 1992a; Napier & Peterson, 1991) either within their current organization or with their subsequent employer (Stahl, Chua, Caligiuri, Cerdin, & Taniguchi, 2009).

## Challenges of International Assignments

Research shows that an international assignment can be a double-edged sword for the individual and the organization. Problems reported in the literature include cross-cultural adjustment problems, underperformance, career derailment, and high costs to the company due to an unsuccessful assignee or mismanaged repatriation (see Black et al., 1992a; Black, Gregersen, & Mendenhall, 1992b; Caligiuri, 1997; Kraimer & Wayne, 2004; Tung, 1998).

One problem that is particularly acute from a talent development perspective is the high turnover rate among repatriated international assignees (see, Lazarova & Cerdin, 2007; Yan, Zhu, & Hall, 2002). Although top managers often claim that international experience is a highly valued asset and a prerequisite for promotion into senior management, the career implications for employees returning from an international assignment may be disappointing. Many companies lack effective expatriate management and repatriation practices and usually fail to integrate international assignments with long-term career development and succession planning (Black et al., 1992b; Caligiuri & Lazarova, 2001a; 2001b; Riusala & Suutari, 2000; Stahl & Cerdin, 2004). Repatriates often perceive that their international assignment had a negative career impact because it may be the case that their reentry positions have less authority and are less satisfying than the positions they held abroad, and that their home organizations do not value their international experience (Adler, 2002; Bolino, 2007; Hammer, Hart, & Rogan, 1998; Stroh, Gregersen, & Black, 1998).

If companies consistently mismanage international assignees and fail to integrate international assignments into long-term career paths, as the above evidence suggests, then why do employees continue to pursue international careers? To explain this paradox, researchers have suggested that employees may accept an international assignment because they see it as a chance to gain the additional skills and experience needed to increase their marketability to other prospective employers (Hippler, 2009; Stahl, Miller, & Tung, 2002; Tung, 1998). This is in line with new career perspectives, such as Schein's (1996) concept of the "internal" or "protean" (Hall, 1996), "aspatial" (Roberts, Kossek, & Ozeki, 1998), "multidirectional" (Baruch, 2004), or "boundaryless" (Arthur & Rousseau, 1996) careers. According to Schein (1996), the internal career involves a subjective sense of where one is going in one's work life, whereas the external career refers to advancement within the organizational hierarchy. Individuals pursuing internal careers may no longer perceive their work life as a progression of jobs within a single organization. Rather, they will move from one company to another (or one country to another) to pursue the best career opportunities (Parker & Inkson, 1999). The "boundaryless" careerist is the highly qualified mobile professional who builds his or her career competencies and market value through continuous learning and transfer across boundaries (Thomas, Lazarova, & Inkson, 2005).

Boundaryless careers are driven by a desire to maintain a permanent state of employability in an environment of increasing economic insecurity and diminished trust between employers and employees (DePhilippi & Arthur, 1996; Lazarova & Tarique, 2005). Collectively, the preceding evidence implies that managers and professionals increasingly seek international assignments to gain new skills and experiences that will make them more marketable—and thus more likely to leave (Stahl et al., 2009). Guenter Stahl and his colleagues surveyed 1,779 expatriates from many countries (and in many countries) and found that expatriates ranked professional development and personal challenge as the most important motivators for accepting the assignments, whereas location was ranked as the least important (many results from this study are reported in Stahl et al., 2009). In this sample, almost 50% were relatively young (between 30 and 39 years old). As this is an age when many are actively building their careers, their expectations for the benefit of the assignment on their careers may, in fact, be higher compared to those closer to retirement age. This age group may be more anxious to leverage their newly acquired cross-cultural skills, whether in their current organization or elsewhere.

## International Assignee Practices

This section focuses on the practice areas of international assignee management in which industrial and organizational psychologists are most likely involved, including international assignee selection, cross-cultural training, global organizational management development, international assignee performance management, and work-life balance issues for international assignees and their families. These are the practice areas in which the field of I/O psychology can make the greatest contribution and also will contribute directly to the success during and retention following international assignments.

## Self-Selection, Assessment, and Selection

International assignee assessment and selection are critical as most firms acknowledge that the wrong international assignee can mean a failed assignment, poor job performance, early repatriation, and emotional problems—not to mention the extreme personal and professional upheaval for the accompanying spouse and children (Caligiuri, 1999). Within the practice of selecting international assignees, there are two areas that have emerged in managing international assignees. The first includes the *individual-level antecedents* of international assignee success, such as personality characteristics, language skills, prior experience of living in a different country, and the family situation. The second includes the *practices* for effectively selecting international assignees, such as realistic previews, self-selection, and assessment (Caligiuri & Tarique, 2006).

## Individual-Level Antecedents of International Assignee Success

Considering that international assignments are job contexts, not job descriptions, the predictors of international assignee success relate more to the idea of living and working in a foreign country as opposed to successfully completing any specific job-related tasks. There are a variety of individual-level antecedents of international assignee success discussed in this section including personality characteristics, language skills, prior experience of living in a different country, and the family situation.

**Personality Characteristics.** Researchers have found that successful and well-adjusted international assignees tend to share certain personality traits (see Black, 1990; Caligiuri, 2000a; 2000b; Church, 1982; Mendenhall & Oddou, 1985; Shaffer, Harrison, Gregersen, Black & Ferzandi, 2006; Stening, 1979) that enable them to be open and receptive to learning the norms of new cultures, to initiate contact with host nationals, to gather cultural information, and to handle the higher amounts of stress associated with the ambiguity of their new environments (Black, 1990; Church, 1982; Mendenhall & Oddou, 1985)—all of which are important for international assignee success. Though many personality characteristics exist, research has found that five factors provide a useful taxonomy for classifying them (Digman, 1990; Goldberg, 1992, 1993; McCrae & Costa, 1987, 1989; McCrae & John, 1992). These five factors have been found repeatedly through factor analyses and confirmatory factor analyses across, time, contexts, and cultures (Buss, 1991; Digman, 1990; Goldberg, 1992, 1993; McCrae & Costa, 1987; McCrae & John, 1992) and are labeled "the Big Five." The Big Five personality factors are:

1. *Extroversion:* It is important to help international assignees learn the work and nonwork social culture in the host country related to international assignee success.
2. *Agreeableness:* The ability to form reciprocal social alliances is achieved through this personality characteristic (Buss, 1991).
3. *Conscientiousness:* Trusted and *conscientious* employees are more likely to become leaders, gain status, get promoted, earn higher salaries, etc.
4. *Emotional Stability:* Given that stress is often associated with living and working in an ambiguous and unfamiliar environment (Richards, 1996), emotional stability is an important personality characteristic for international assignees' adjustment to the host country (Abe & Wiseman, 1983; Black, 1988; Gudykunst, 1988; Gudykunst & Hammer, 1984; Mendenhall & Oddou, 1985) and completion of an international assignment (Ones & Viswesvaran, 1997).
5. *Openness or Intellect:* Openness is related to international assignee success because individuals higher in this personality characteristic will have fewer rigid views of right and wrong, appropriate and inappropriate, and so forth, and are more likely to be accepting of the new culture (see Abe & Wiseman, 1983; Black, 1990; Cui & van den Berg, 1991; Hammer, Gudykunst, & Wiseman, 1978).

Collectively, these personality characteristics could be included in a valid selection system for prospective international assignees. However, the absolute level of each personality characteristic would be contingent upon the type of international assignment under consideration.

**Language Skills.** There is a positive relationship between language skills and international assignee adjustment (see Abe & Wiseman, 1983; Church, 1982; Cui & van den Berg, 1991; Kim & Slocum, 2008). There is some disagreement, however, as to the relative importance of language compared to other factors, such as personality characteristics (see Benson, 1978; Cui & van den Berg, 1991; Dinges, 1983). The disagreement in the importance of language skills has its roots in whether interpersonal contact between people from different cultures leads to increased cultural understanding. At a minimum, in most circumstances an attempt should be made to find a qualified candidate with language skills—but for some positions the language skills may be more critical than with others (Caligiuri & Tarique, 2006).

**Prior International Experience.** From a social learning perspective, the more contact that international assignees have with host nationals and the host culture, the greater their cross-cultural adjustment (Bochner, Hutnik, & Furnham, 1986; Bochner, Mcleod, & Lin, 1977; Brein & David, 1971; Brislin, 1981; Guthrie, 1975). On the other hand, the social cognitive theorists contend that prior foreign experience with the host culture is positively related to adjustment, provided that the experience does not serve to reinforce previously held stereotypical beliefs or foster negative, unrealistic expectations of the foreign culture. There is some evidence that previous experience abroad does not always facilitate adjustment to a new expatriate environment (see Black & Gregersen, 1991; Cui & Awa, 1992; Dunbar, 1992; Nicholson & Imaizumi, 1993; Selmer, 2002). A recent study by Takeuchi, Tesluk, Yun, and Lepak (2005), however, found support for unique moderating effects of past international experiences on the relationship between current assignment tenure and general and work adjustment. Moreover, other recent work by Takeuchi, Wang, and Marinova (2005) suggests that prior international experience may exert its influence on adjustment indirectly via other variables such as psychological workplace strain. They could also demonstrate the importance of whether or not prior international experience was gathered in a culturally similar or dissimilar context (Takeuchi, Wang, &

Marinova, 2005). Kim and Slocum (2008) argue that the type (work, study, travel) and quality (favorable or unfavorable) of previous international experience may also deserve attention. It is possible that significant intercultural experiences that help prepare people to be effective international managers may not necessarily need to happen in the workplace—they may also occur in childhood or young adulthood, as a result of being a member of a multicultural household, studying abroad as a young adult, and the like. Family diversity (that is, being raised in a multicultural household) predicted global leadership effectiveness (Caligiuri & Tarique, 2009).

**Family Situation**. A number of studies have identified a positive influence of the adjustment of an accompanying spouse on the expatriate (Caligiuri, Hyland, Joshi, & Bross, 1998; Takeuchi, Yun, & Tesluk, 2002). Takeuchi, Wang, and Marinova (2005) could also show that the mere physical presence of the spouse while on assignment has a beneficial effect. Expatriates who were not accompanied by their spouse experienced more psychological workplace strain. Takeuchi, Wang, and Marinova (2005) explain this in terms of the logistical, psychological, and physical support an accompanying spouse can provide. Moreover, separation from the spouse while on assignment may lead to worries about the spouse's well-being. Conversely, accompanying children increased psychological workplace strain. Psychological workplace strain was highest when the spouse did not accompany the expatriate but at least one child did (Takeuchi, Wang, & Marinova, 2005). Due to their impact on expatriate adjustment and ultimately performance, spouses and children need to be included in the selection process (Caligiuri, Hyland, Joshi, & Bross, 1998; Takeuchi, Wang, & Marinova, 2005). In addition, Takeuchi, Wang, and Marinova (2005) highlight the responsibility of the human resource professionals to educate themselves of the additional difficulties that single-parent expatriates face on an international assignment in order to provide the expatriates with a realistic job preview and offer additional support for this group.

## Practices for Selecting International Assignees

There are various practices in the research literature regarding international assignee selection. The first is the application of realistic previews to international assignments to help create realistic expectations during (or prior to) selection. The second is the concept of a formal self-selection process which enables international assignee candidates to determine whether the assignment is right for his or her personal situation, family situation, career stage, and so on. The third is traditional candidate assessment that would include many of the dimensions identified in the previous section (personality, language skills, and past experience) in a structured organizational selection program (Caligiuri & Tarique, 2006).

**Realistic Previews for International Assignments.** Preconceived and accurate expectations prior to an international assignment have been shown to influence the international assignment in many important ways (Caligiuri & Phillips, 2003; Searle & Ward, 1990; Weissman & Furnham, 1987). Caligiuri and Phillips (2003) found that providing realistic previews prior to international assignments did not change candidates' interest in possible assignments, but did increase candidates' self-efficacy for an international assignment. This self-efficacy, in turn, could influence the outcome of the international assignment (Caligiuri & Tarique, 2006).

Related to the realistic preview is the look-and-see trip during the decision-making phase. Granting the short-listed candidates and their families the opportunity to visit the host country, city or town, and company unit for a few days before finally committing themselves facilitates forming realistic expectations regarding the cultural and work environment. It also allows them to identify first immediate training needs and to make an informed choice.

**Self-Selection.** Finding people who are willing to accept global assignments is one of the greatest HR challenges (Borstorff, Harris, Field, & Giles, 1997; Collings, Scullion, & Morley, 2007; Selmer, 2001). Given that the demographic profiles and personal situations of the international assignee candidates will vary, self-assessment (or self-selection) has been found to be an effective method for encouraging realistic previews in a tailored and self-directed way (Caligiuri & Phillips, 2003). For example, an unmarried person who is a candidate for an international assignment might have a different set of concerns, compared to a married candidate with a family (Caligiuri, Hyland, Joshi, & Bross,

1998). Likewise, given the many personality characteristics related to cross-cultural adjustment, people who possess different personality characteristics may be differentially suited for certain types of international assignments (Caligiuri 2000a; 2000b; Dalton & Wilson, 2000; Ones & Viswesvaran, 1997, 1999). Firms using self-assessment tools have found that this step fosters the creation of a candidate pool of potential international assignees because individuals have a more realistic sense of the challenges they may experience (Caligiuri & Tarique, 2006).

Long before assignments are available, key employees should consider the viability of a future international assignment—such assignments are not right for every person or every family. Full involvement throughout the process by the employee and all accompanying family members is critical. To further aid in the decision-making process, self-selection or self-assessment tools (such as the SAGE, or the Self-Assessment for Global Endeavors) are useful when employees are contemplating whether to pursue an international assignment. At this early stage, employees and their families are able to critically evaluate themselves on key issues before deciding to accept an international assignment.

Many human resource management professionals note that the desire to accept international assignments has been remaining flat while the need for international assignees has been steadily increasing (GMAC, 2008). The presence of a self-selection tool helps build efficacy among those who may have, without the aid of such a tool, refused an assignment (Caligiuri & Phillips, 2003). Research has shown that self-selection tools help employees make a thoroughly informed and realistic decision before putting their names forward as candidates for international assignments. A common best practice is to offer self-selection tools by casting a net wide enough to generate a candidate pool among those who occupy job titles that are considered logical feeders to the positions most often required internationally.

**Candidate Assessment.** Once the requirements of a given international assignment have been determined, many possibilities exist to assess the candidates on job-related dimensions. Given that international assignments are job contexts, rather than job descriptions, they require different levels of relevant attributes (such as need for language fluency, openness, technical skills). For example, greater emphasis would be placed on personality characteristics (such as sociability and openness) when assessing a candidate for a developmental or strategic assignment—requiring much more host national contact, compared to a more technical international assignment (Caligiuri 2000a; 2000b; 2006a). In a best case, a thorough assessment can be conducted through a variety of valid formal selection methods: paper-and-pencil tests, assessment centers, interviews, behavioral observations, and the like (Caligiuri & Tarique, 2006).

## Cross-Cultural Training

In addition to comprehensive self-selection and selection programs, success in international assignments may be facilitated through the training and development of cross-national competencies (such as cross-cultural knowledge, skills, and abilities) (Caligiuri & Tarique, 2006). The consequent awareness may lower anxiety, reduce culture shock, and encourage appropriate behaviors when living and working in a host culture—thereby improving cross-national competencies among international assignees (Briscoe & Schuler, 2004; Dowling & Welch, 2004; Evans, Pucik, & Barsoux, 2001; Gupta & Govindarajan, 2002).

The goal of cross-cultural predeparture training is to help an international assignee learn the basics of how to function in the country (for example, regarding currency, public transportation, working hours) and some behavioral and social norms to more comfortably live and work in the host country. More recently, research has found that training delivered in-country and sequentially is more likely to produce positive results because international assignees have the opportunity to experience the culture firsthand (Tarique & Caligiuri, 2009).

Cross-national coaches and mentors help international assignees build cultural awareness, work on cultural "blind spots," and help develop competencies for becoming effective in an international environment. Occasionally, cross-national coaches are assigned for a specific task (for example, delivering an important speech in another country, negotiating an international joint venture). Support programs, such as culture coaches, destination services, and online support networks are becoming more popular. In some cases, companies are sponsoring these programs in-house, whereas others are seeking outside vendors (Caligiuri & Lazarova, 2005).

At a more macro level, the international assignments are critical for leadership development and organizational development. International assignees, having successfully completed their assignments, can help establish and expand a firm's international business because they possess firsthand knowledge of particular cultural contexts, including information about specific markets and customers. They understand how the company is perceived in another country and are part of a global social network that can advance the company's business around the world (Downes & Thomas, 1999). They may have an irreplaceable role in organizational learning, given that they can accelerate the transfer of knowledge from host countries to headquarters, and vice versa. For these reasons, many companies view their repatriates as an important human capital investment (Caligiuri & Lazarova, 2001a; 2001b; Downes & Thomas, 1999; Tung, 1998).

## Performance Management

International assignee performance management is another vexing area for practitioners in international human resources given the range of jobs and the number of cross-cultural challenges associated with international assignments. Within the heading of performance management, there are four areas of particular interest. The first includes the dimensions of international assignee performance. The second includes the challenges associated with the way companies evaluate international assignee performance. The third is how international assignee performance is rewarded: international assignment compensation. (It is fair to say that this third category could fill volumes on its own given the extensive tax challenges associated with international assignee compensation. We will focus only on the issues of rewards as they relate to the expertise of talent management and industrial and organizational psychologists.) The fourth, which could also fill volumes, is the career progression of international assignees upon repatriation.

## Dimensions of International Assignee Performance

In the organizational context, there are many challenges when considering the performance evaluation of international assignees living and working outside of their own national borders. Across the various types of international assignments, the technical performance dimensions represent the aspect of work performance in job analytic terms and are represented by the tasks or duties that incumbents perform (Borman & Motowidlo, 1993; Campbell, McCloy, Oppler, & Sager, 1993). These performance dimensions tend to be the same, regardless of location. The way in which these jobs are conducted, however, may be different in practice depending on the country context (Caligiuri, 2006b). In addition to technical performance dimensions, international assignments tend also to include *contextual* performance dimensions (Borman & Motowidlo, 1993), which are aspects of work performance that are not directly related to the technical tasks or duties of the job (Borman & Motowidlo, 1993). In many organizations, these are derived from the core values that the company desires in all employees and, as such, are found on the performance evaluations of employees from the lowest level in the organization to the executive suite (Caligiuri, 2006b).

As mentioned in the previous discussion about the various types of international assignees, some assignees have performance dimensions (or aspects of their assignments) that require intercultural effectiveness; specifically, these assignees have an extensive need for communication with host nationals in order for their assignments to be deemed successful. Job analyses have found that tasks requiring intercultural effectiveness vary, depending on the position. For example, some tasks requiring intercultural effectiveness may include: (a) negotiating an international joint venture, (b) conducting training seminars in another country (in the host national language), (c) working on a multicultural research and development team, (d) presenting to internal or external clients in the host national language, (e) adapting a marketing plan to a local culture, and (f) replacement planning (in cases when an international assignee is training a host national to be his or her replacement). It is also the case that in some highly technical assignments, there is little (if any) need for intercultural effectiveness (Caligiuri, 2006b).

In addition to variation on intercultural dimensions, job analyses have also found a variation across assignments on developmental dimensions. It is worth repeating that the extent to which developmental dimensions are formally recognized as an *expected outcome* of a global assignment will vary greatly depending on the type of assignment. Some assignments are highly functional, with no developmental component. Other assignments are highly developmental—and may even be a part of a global leadership development program (Black et al., 1992a; Caligiuri & Di Santo, 2001). According to Stahl and colleagues (2009) approximately 50% of assignees have some developmental component of their assignment. Sample tasks with developmental components include learning how to conduct business in a host country, building a network of professional relationships in the host country, learning the host country language, and increasing understanding of the company's worldwide structure.

## Assessing International Assignee Performance

There are challenges when developing performance measurement systems to assess the performance of international assignees. Based on Caligiuri (2006b), the first challenge is *determining criteria* that would be applicable for incumbents within the same positions across subsidiaries, regardless of country (Davis, 1998; Ployhart, Wiechmann, Schmitt, Sacco, & Rogg, 2002). This step ensures that the criteria domain among comparable assignees is, in fact, comparable across cultures. Once this is determined, *creating conceptual equivalence* is the next challenge. This may include everything from *language comparability* to developing the *behavioral indices* of various performance dimensions so that raters of their international assignees' performance (who themselves may vary in their cultural backgrounds) can make cross-culturally relevant and comparable ratings. If this level of comparability is desired across similarly placed international assignees, the challenge embedded within conceptual equivalence is that two raters from different countries, observing the same international assignee, would need to observe the same level of performance on a given dimension. This is especially problematic for international assignments with more contextual and less technical performance dimensions within the performance domain (Caligiuri & Day, 2000).

The third challenge, seemingly less onerous than the second, is determining the *performance measurement method* that can be successfully implemented across the cultures where the international assignees are located. Schneider and Barsoux (1997) have suggested that many cultural factors may influence the appropriateness of various methods of performance assessment. *How* performance is assessed will depend on culture difference. For example, the extent to which management by objectives is used may differ depending on the hierarchical culture of the employees—and how comfortable employees are discussing their goals with their managers (Schneider & Barsoux, 1997). Whether performance appraisal involves a dialogue (or a feedback session) with a manager will also vary depending on the cultural context. Performance evaluation will also vary culturally based on *who* is conducting the appraisal. In a sample of Hong Kong Chinese and American managers, Entrekin and Chung (2001) found that supervisor appraisals were more consistent with Chinese values—and more accepted by Hong Kong Chinese managers. Peer and subordinate evaluations (typically found with 360-degree assessment) were considered more acceptable to American managers, consistent with America's egalitarian culture. Thus, in the context of cross-cultural acceptability, it is important to consider both *how* the evaluation is being made and *who* is conducting the evaluation.

Supervisor ratings are especially challenging when international assignees from one culture are rating subordinates from another culture. In these cross-cultural rater-ratee dyads, performance ratings could be biased by the degree of rater-ratee similarity measured in terms of demographic similarity (see Judge & Ferris, 1993; Tsui & O'Reilly, 1989). The degree of similarity between members of a dyad—also referred to as relational demography—has been shown to be positively related to perceived similarity and supervisors' reported liking of a ratee (Wayne & Liden, 1995). Both of these effects have the potential to favorably bias ratings of performance. In the context of performance evaluation of international assignees, national similarity is a type of relational demography that could affect ratings. Similarity of international assignees and their supervisors in terms of national background has been shown to influence performance ratings (Caligiuri & Day, 2000).

Caligiuri and Day (2000) found that the bias of nationality may affect the performance dimensions differently—depending on the type of dimension. They tested both task and contextual performance dimensions and found that rater nationality influenced the ratings of the more subjective contextual performance dimensions, but not the objective task-based performance dimensions. This finding is consistent with research indicating that less ambiguous performance standards increase rater-ratee agreement regarding performance ratings (Schrader & Steiner, 1996). Given that the raters' cultural lens is a potential for bias, supervisors of international assignees should be trained on behavioral indicators for assessing employees' performance. A training intervention, such as frame-of-reference rater training (Bernardin & Buckley, 1981), could be highly effective at reducing the idiosyncratic standards of performance raters (Day & Sulsky, 1995). Frame-of-reference rater training would clarify performance standards across dimensions and across cultures—especially for the more ambiguous subjective dimensions.

Supervisor ratings are also challenging when international assignees are located in a different country from their supervisor. In some cases, the supervisor has no direct observation of the expatriate's performance and must rely on communications or tangible outcomes which may belie the success of the assignments. In other cases, the nonlocal supervisor may not understand the cultural or contextual challenges of the international assignment and rate the expatriates without taking these issues into consideration. Given the myriad challenges it is not surprising that international assignees' performance management will often fall through the cracks of talent management systems.

## Compensating International Assignees

Closely related to performance management is the issue of rewards or compensation of international assignees. The emphasis in the debate of expatriate compensation has shifted over the years. Traditionally, compensation was primarily seen as "a mechanism to calculate differentials and bonuses aimed at promoting international mobility and guaranteeing equity" (Bonache & Fernández, 1997, p. 470). Bonache and Fernández (1997) have then argued to extend the strategic importance compensation policies enjoy in the domestic HR discourse and practice to the international arena and to view compensation as "an instrument that must guide behaviour in order to achieve corporate objectives" (p. 470). More recently, the focus has shifted once more to the influence of expatriate compensation on host-country nationals' perception of fairness (Bonache, Sanchez, & Zárraga-Oberty, 2009; Leung, Zhu, & Ge, 2009; Toh & DeNisi, 2003, 2005).

When expatriate compensation first became a topic of practical and academic interest, the objective it was meant to achieve was straightforward—to make them go. Compensation packages aimed at incentivizing expatriates to accept an international assignment by shielding the expatriates from any adverse monetary effects as well as by offering "a little extra" in recognition of the uprooting that international relocation inevitably involved. Given that multinational companies face an increasing immobility (domestic as well as international) of managerial employees (Borstorff et al., 1997; Collings et al., 2007; Gelb & Hyman, 1987; Horsch, 1995; Magnus & Dodd, 1981; Scullion, 1994; Selmer, 2001) against the background of a fast-increasing demand for expatriates (Collings et al. 2007; GMAC, 2008), this objective is as topical as ever. However, this narrow concern has led to the emergence of a one-size-fits-all approach to expatriate compensation, as Edström and Galbraith (1977) concluded from their interviews with practitioners: "Compensation packages ... do not differ with reasons for transfers; that is, all companies use compensation to maintain the expatriate's standard of living or slightly better it" (p. 253). An exclusive focus on the expatriates has given rise to compensation systems in which pay decisions are primarily based on nationality, country of origin, or cultural identity (Bonache et al., 2009; Leung et al., 2009). The practical manifestation of this orientation is the so-called balance sheet or home country–based approach, aimed at maintaining an expatriate's home-country standard of living while being on assignment. Hardship, housing, cost-of-living, and education allowances as well as income tax equalization regularly feature.

A 2005 survey by PricewaterhouseCoopers found that still more than 60% of the companies surveyed used this approach. Yet even this generous—and generally very expensive—approach to expatriate compensation does not guarantee pay satisfaction. Pay satisfaction is a function of social comparison processes (Williams, McDaniel, & Nguyen, 2006). A plethora of referents is available to expatriates to compare themselves to. Expatriates "can compare themselves not only to other expatriates within the same company and host country, but also to expatriates within the same company and other host countries, expatriates from other companies within their host country, local employees and so on" (Bonache, 2006, p. 166). There is plenty of scope for the expatriates to feel disadvantaged and dissatisfied.

Bonache and Fernández (1997) have argued for a systematic link of expatriate compensation systems to corporate or subsidiary strategy. Expatriates are sent abroad for very different strategic reasons and, depending on their role, the company expects and values very different behaviors. As has long been recognized in domestic compensation schemes, an expatriate compensation scheme must be capable of directing behavior, that is, eliciting the behaviors the different strategic roles require. It is self-evident that a one-size-fits-all approach such as the balance sheet cannot achieve this. The incentive system needs to be tailored to the desired behavior necessary to implement subsidiary strategy. Bonache and Fernández (1997) thus argue for internal and external fit. Internal fit to all other expatriate policies such as those related to selection, training, and career development, and external fit to the type of subsidiary and the role behaviors required. Yet overcoming the balance-sheet approach with a more differentiated compensation system will be an uphill battle. On the surface, the one-size-fits-all approach provides a sense of equity and is comparatively easy to administer (Bonache & Fernández, 1997). It also facilitates reintegration upon repatriation to the home country (Dowling, Festing, & Engle, 2008).

The current debate on expatriate compensation focuses on moving beyond the perspective of the expatriate. It advocates a more holistic view of facilitating the expatriate's adjustment by taking the host nationals' response to the expatriate's compensation scheme into account. Toh and DeNisi (2003) have argued that much of the existing work in the area of expatriate compensation has neglected the HCNs' role in the expatriate's success and put the responsibility largely, but unfairly, on the expatriate's shoulders. Yet a failed assignment is not necessarily or not exclusively the fault of the expatriate, but may have been advanced, albeit unintentionally, by existing expatriate HR practices such as compensation packages (Toh & DeNisi, 2003). Toh and DeNisi (2003) posit that practices aimed at ensuring the expatriates' success may contribute to their failure by alienating the local workforce. No foreign subsidiary can succeed through the efforts of the firms' expatriates alone; they rely on the commitment and cooperation of the local employees.

Host-country nationals frequently receive lower levels of compensation than expatriates working alongside them, even if they are similarly qualified and working in similar or identical jobs (Bonache et al., 2009). This seeming inequity is so entrenched because part of the expatriates' compensation is not based on their actual inputs and performance, but on the very fact that they are on assignment (for example, mobility premiums), for which local employees, by definition, do not qualify (Bonache et al., 2009; Toh & DeNisi, 2003). This situation is exacerbated if expatriates move from economically relatively developed countries to developing countries (Leung et al., 2009; Toh & DeNisi, 2003). If the balance sheet approach is applied, expatriates are remunerated according to the market conditions in their (developed) home country, whereas compensation for the HCNs is determined by the conditions of the local labor market in the developing country. The result is a massive pay differential between expatriates and local employees (Leung et al., 2009). Leung, Smith, Wang, and Sun (1996) refer to Western expatriates in mainland China receiving 20 times the salary of local Chinese managers in similar positions. These large pay gaps lead to the perception of injustice and frustration among local employees (Leung et al., 2009). The effect of this perceived injustice and frustration can result in a number of attitudinal and behavioral outcomes that are detrimental to the local unit, such as low morale, absenteeism, low commitment, poor work performance, and turnover (Bonache et al., 2009; Chen, Choi, & Chi, 2002; Leung et al., 2009; Toh & DeNisi, 2005). Possibly just as detrimental can be the effect on the expatriates. Toh and DeNisi (2003) contend that HCNs may try to restore perceived equity by being unwilling to cooperate with the expatriate, by acting contentiously, discriminating against the expatriate and withholding citizenship behaviors. Yet "local staff could be the expatriate's best on-site trainers" (Toh & DeNisi, 2005, p. 133) when trying to make sense of the new and unfamiliar environment (Louis, 1980). Host-country nationals can act as "a valuable socializing agent and facilitator" (Toh & DeNisi, 2005, p. 134) and thus speed up the expatriate's adjustment to the job, the organization, and the new host country environment (Toh & DeNisi, 2003). Withdrawal behaviors due to perceived injustice may thus have an adverse effect on the amount of time before the expatriates become fully effective and impede their ability to perform effectively on an ongoing basis (Toh & DeNisi, 2003). Perceived pay injustice may thus harm the effectiveness of the local unit as a whole as well as the prospects of the expatriates to complete their assignments successfully (Toh & DeNisi, 2005).

Before addressing managerial implications, a word of warning seems in order. Toh and DeNisi (2003) pointed out that although justice is a "universal human concern" (Leung & Morris, 2000, in Toh & DeNisi, 2003), the idea of what constitutes justice as well as reactions to injustice are culture specific. They point out that certain cultures might value rewards such as recognition, status, and social support much more than pay. Consequently, perceived inequities with regard to these factors might have a much more detrimental effect than those flowing from pay differentials. So attention to the valence of outcomes is of utmost importance. In many Asian cultures, for example, "face" is important. Understanding the concept of "face"—and how this might be affected by perceptions of pay inequity—may also be critical to working in that culture.

The inputs considered when establishing input-outcome ratios (Adams, 1963, 1965) may also vary by culture. As Toh and DeNisi (2003) point out, collectivist societies may give particular importance to seniority and ascription societies may regard social class or race as legitimate inputs. As a consequence, Toh and DeNisi (2003) expect that greater contributions of expatriates may not always merit more generous rewards in the eyes of the HCN, as they may place greater value on organizational tenure, loyalty, or social status. The relationship between pay differential and perceived unfairness may thus also be moderated by national culture (Toh & DeNisi, 2003).

Expatriate compensation is clearly a very sensitive issue for HCNs (Bonache et al., 2009). Therefore, particular attention needs to be paid to how the potentially harmful effects of pay differentials can be avoided or mitigated. The issue of pay differentials can be addressed in two ways: avoiding or reducing them or, where that is not feasible, to make them as acceptable as possible (Bonache et al., 2009). In order to avoid or minimize large pay differentials, companies might give preference to candidates who are intrinsically motivated to accept an international assignment (Bonache et al., 2009). This approach, however, risks dissatisfaction on the part of the expatriate due to perceived inequity if he or she meets other expatriates when on assignment who had to be "bribed" to go. Meeting and interacting with other expatriates (and comparing company compensation practices) is inevitable unless the assignee is the only expatriate in a particular location. Another option might be to make international assignments a valued career development intervention (Bonache et al., 2009). This, however, can only work as an incentive if the company has a proven track record of recognizing international experience in their promotion policy (Hippler, 2009).

If a company can make a credible claim that foreign experience is career enhancing, rewards in terms of pay increases might be reduced. This would be all the more desirable as it would reduce one of the most galling forms of pay discrepancy for the HCNs. An expatriate on a developmental assignment is there to learn from local staff. Not only do the expatriates have no superior expertise or skills, they are abroad to benefit from the skills and experience of the local employees. If this imbalance in knowledge and skills coincides with an inverse imbalance in pay, it will be perceived as particularly indefensible by local employees (Toh & DeNisi, 2005).

Where large pay differentials are unavoidable, recent research suggests a particular emphasis on selection, training, and transparency. Bonache et al. (2009) show that if HCNs perceive the expatriates as making unique contributions (such as providing expert knowledge that is not available locally), they perceive any pay differential as less unfair. Consequently, unless the assignment is primarily developmental, only expatriates with genuinely superior ability should be chosen so that local employees will perceive them as deserving of any more generous compensation (Toh & DeNisi, 2005). The sensitive treatment of locals has also been shown to diminish the perception of pay unfairness (Bonache et al., 2009; Chen et al., 2002). Honesty and integrity promote trustworthiness, which was found to buffer the negative effect of perceived pay injustice on the overall evaluation of the expatriates (Leung et al., 2009). Therefore, personality characteristics and interpersonal skills should play a prominent role in selection decisions and subsequent training. Transparency will facilitate a careful management of HCNs' perceptions of justice (Toh & DeNisi, 2005). Expatriates' unique contributions as well as their special financial needs (such as those related to the loss of the spousal income, fees for international schools, or travel expenses to look after elderly relatives left behind) were demonstrated to make pay differentials more acceptable to HCNs (Bonache et al., 2009). As a result, companies need to raise the HCNs' awareness of these contributions and needs by communicating them very clearly and making the mechanisms by which pay packages are arrived at transparent. Finally, firms should communicate and emphasize the pay advantages that the HCNs might have over other local employees in similar organizations and positions, that is, over another group of relevant referents or "comparison-others" (Adams, 1963, 1965), thus once more mitigating against any negative perception of pay differentials (Bonache et al., 2009; Leung et al., 2009; Toh & DeNisi, 2003, 2005). The design of expatriate compensation packages must take into account their larger effect on all groups of employees, including HCNs (Toh & DeNisi, 2005) to the benefit of both the organization and the individual expatriate.

## Career Progression upon Repatriation

Considering the large investment to develop, maintain, and transfer international assignees, losing an employee with valuable international experience is costly and can affect the firm's bottom line. Moreover, the loss of an internationally proficient employee often indirectly translates into providing an advantage to direct competitors, as repatriates are likely to find jobs with competitors, thus providing them with valuable human assets. In addition, high turnover among repatriates compromises the company's ability to recruit future expatriates because it signals to other employees in the company that, despite the stated message to the contrary, international assignments may have a negative impact on one's career (Downes & Thomas, 1999). Given this strategic human capital issue, ways to predict repatriate retention and lower their turnover is an important challenge facing organizations today (Black, Gregersen, & Mendenhall, 1992a, 1992b; Gregersen & Black, 1995; Stroh, 1995).

Various factors affect whether international assignees remain with their company upon repatriation, which include being placed in unchallenging jobs, lack of promotion opportunities, loss of status and autonomy, lack of career planning and counseling, lack of support on behalf of managers and colleagues, and sluggish career advancement (Adler, 1981; Abueva, 2000; Black et al., 1992b). Of these many factors, it is not surprising that the most important one is the repatriates' perception of how well the firms managed their repatriation process (Feldman & Thompson, 1993). This suggests that if the potential repatriation problems are considered, and appropriately addressed by the firm in advance, repatriate turnover will occur less often (Harvey, 1989). Thus, the repatriates who perceive that they have more support from their organization will be more committed to that organization—and will be more likely to stay with it after repatriation.

Repatriates want their companies to value their international experience. As such, repatriates will mentally calculate an equity equation: comparing their perceptions of the rewards and recognition that the company has given them for taking the assignment, relative to the sacrifices and contributions they have made for their company during the assignment; and the greater the perceived equity, the greater the likelihood that they will remain with the company upon repatriation. This suggests a type of mental exchange, or psychological contract, between expatriates and their employers. The psychological contract is based on the employee's overall perceptions of the long-term exchange of fairness with the company, rather than on any specific (and quantifiable) obligation (Rousseau, 1990).

Given the perceived sacrifice involved in relocating one's family to another country for the sake of the company, it makes intuitive sense that the psychological contract would apply to international assignees upon repatriation (Guzzo, Noonan, & Elron, 1994; Haslberger & Brewster, 2009). Caligiuri and Lazarova (2001b) offer some proactive recommendations for firms wishing to manage the career progression of their international assignees and increase retention upon repatriation:

1. Organizations should make an effort to manage expectations upon repatriation. This will be helpful in reducing the expatriate's ambiguity while on assignment (Black, 1992; Conference Board, 1996; Hammer, Hart, & Rogan, 1998). Organizations should give detailed briefings before the international assignee leaves for his or her global assignment, detailing for the expatriate what to expect while on the assignment and what to expect upon return (Conference Board, 1996).

2. Career planning is another critical function for retaining expatriates upon repatriation. Between 6 and 12 months before the end of the global assignment, firms should offer multiple reentry sessions or career-planning sessions to discuss the expatriate's concerns regarding repatriations; for example, career objectives and performance (Adler, 1981, 1997; Black, 1992; Black et al., 1992b; Conference Board, 1996). The intention of these career-planning reentry sessions is to give the expatriate a sense of security regarding his or her future with the company (Black et al., 1992b).

3. To reduce ambiguity about the expatriates' future, offer a written guarantee or repatriation agreement. This repatriation agreement outlines the type of position the international assignee will be placed in upon return from global assignment (Gomez-Mejia & Balkin, 1987).

4. One popular practice used in proactive repatriation systems is mentoring. Mentors keep the expatriate abreast of important occurrences while he or she is on global assignment and help the expatriate stay connected with the organization (Black et al., 1992b; Conference Board, 1996; Gomez-Mejia & Balkin, 1987; Napier & Peterson, 1991). A mentor also guides the expatriate's future career with the organization by being his or her internal champion.

5. Organizations should offer a reorientation program to brief returning expatriates on the changes in the company, such as in policies, personnel, and strategy (Gomez-Mejia & Balkin, 1987; Harvey, 1982). This should be provided immediately upon return from the assignment, when the repatriate returns to work.

6. Repatriation training seminars should be offered to employees and their families. These repatriation training seminars will address expatriates' emotional concerns upon returning home (Black, 1992, 1994; Black et al., 1992a, 1992b; Conference Board, 1996; Hammer et al., 1998). This repatriation training should improve reentry adjustment.

7. Another recommendation is financial counseling and financial or tax assistance. This counseling helps repatriates adjust back to their lifestyles without the additional allowances of the international position (Gomez-Mejia & Balkin, 1987; Harvey, 1982; Kendall, 1981).

8. Lifestyle counseling is also beneficial to employees and their families, as their lifestyles are likely to change dramatically when they return to their home countries (Black, 1994; Harvey, 1989; Kendall, 1981).

9. Firms can also offer a repatriation adjustment period for the employees to reintegrate without added pressure from the organization (Harvey, 1989; Kendall, 1981). Given the stresses of repatriation both at home and at work, some organizations will reduce the repatriates' travel time, give more vacation time, and so forth.

10. While the individuals are still on assignment, firms should offer opportunities for communication with their home office. For example, the assignee could be offered extended home visits during which he or she is expected to be visible at the office (Black, 1994; Gomez-Mejia & Balkin, 1987; Gregersen & Stroh, 1997). Another possibility is to encourage communication between an assignee and colleagues back home to maintain his or her network, and so on (Adler, 1997).

11. Organizations should show visible signs that they value the international experience (for example, promoting the repatriate upon return, maintaining position prestige and status, or providing additional compensation for completing the

assignment). This will create the perception within the organization that global experience is beneficial for one's career (Adler, 1981, 1997; Black et al., 1992b; Black, 1994; Gomez-Mejia & Balkin, 1987; Gregersen & Black, 1995). This will also help produce a culture in which global experience should not be disregarded as "different, and not relevant here" (Adler 1981, 1997; Hammer et al., 1998).

## Work-Life Balance and International Assignee Support Practices

The last practice area of interest to industrial psychologists involved in the management of international assignees is the assistance that firms offer regarding work-life balance practices for their international assignees, or more often, for their families. Work-life balance initiatives in the international assignment context can be especially challenging because they often involve far more than the employees of the organization; a spouse or partner and a child or children, who often accompany an international assignee to the host country, have their lives disrupted for the sake of the assignees' job. Their experiences can often have a profound influence on the assignees' sense of work-life balance and, subsequently, on the outcome of international assignments (Caligiuri & Lazarova, 2005). For example, many accompanying partners' careers are put on hold due to visa regulations. In today's dynamic environment of professional careers, such loss of career continuity may be quite damaging (Caligiuri & Lazarova, 2005). Moreover, for many of those employed prior to the assignment, inability to get engaged in productive activities outside the home can contribute to increased stress (Punnett, 1997).

Spouses who have been out of work for the duration of the assignment may find resuming their careers upon return equally challenging. A period of unemployment after returning home does not only prolong and exacerbate the spouse's stress with possible additional effects for the relationship and subsequent spill-over effects into the repatriate's work domain. Losing not only an often very generous compensation package but all the expatriate perks frequently available (such as a company car, a maid, excellent accommodations, memberships in exclusive clubs) in itself requires some readjustment. Losing the spouse's income as well when compared to the preassignment situation presents a burden on the family finances that can exert an additional strain on the relationship.

As Riusala and Suutari (2000) found, there are many discrepancies between the career needs of the accompanying partner and the extent to which they are met in organizations. The 2008 Global Relocation Trends Survey found that 33% of the companies offered education or training assistance for accompanying partners, 19% offered career enhancement reimbursement, 20% offered career planning assistance, and 21% offered assistance in finding employment (GMAC, 2008). There are other tangible services that companies offer accompanying partners on global assignments. These include monetary policies such as paying fees required by employment agencies in the host countries, offering seed money to start a new business, paying fees to join professional associations, compensation of the accompanying partner's lost wages and benefits, or offering financial support to engage in volunteer service (Pellico & Stroh, 1997; Punnett, 1997). Other tangible services companies offer are nonmonetary but are also considered extremely useful for accompanying partners. These include organization-sponsored support groups for partners (Punnett, 1997), employment networks coordinated with other global firms (Punnett, 1997), and office space in the host location for the purpose of job hunting (Elron & Kark, 2000).

Between 2002 and 2008, the percentage of spouses not employed prior to relocation in the Global Relocation Trend Surveys has averaged 45% (GMAC, 2008). The support needs of accompanying spouses who do not work abroad are somewhat different from that of the expatriates and their employed counterparts. The stay-at-home spouses' environment differs considerably from that of the expatriate or working spouses. The work environment (and, for the children, the school environment) offers sources of an emerging social support network, whereas the stay-at-home spouse may have little natural social contact. Social support for these spouses thus has to aim at combating the spouse's potential isolation and establishing his or her own social support network. Beyond addressing the immediate social needs, the company should assist the spouse in creating a meaningful life abroad (Adler, 1997).

In addition to accompanying partners, children of international assignees will also influence an assignee's sense of work-life balance. Uprooting a child from a place that is an important identity source can be a stressful experience (Harvey, 1985). In addition to concerns over availability of high-quality education, one also needs to consider the emotional stress that children undergo during periods of transition. Children can face obstacles such as saying good-bye to friends, making new friends, starting a new school, communicating through language barriers, having inadequate peer relations, lacking in peer acceptance (especially problematic for teenagers), and overall disruption to personal life. If not adequately supported by the parents, children may feel lonely and isolated, uncertain about their identity, and experience diminished self-esteem. The transition poses extraordinary demands on children of all ages, and it is critical that parents acknowledge this and that organizations provide the resources for parents to do their best to help children through this adjustment phase (Borstorff et al., 1997; Brett, 1980; DeLeon & McPartlin, 1995; Harvey, 1985).

In general, for organizations to help their international assignees achieve a greater sense of work-life balance, increasing opportunities for social support and social interaction (such as club memberships, housing in an expatriate community, trips home) are helpful. These practices can create a sense of belonging, enhance psychological security and self-esteem, and reduce anxiety (Caligiuri & Lazarova, 2002). Given the profound impact that social networks and social support can have on an international assignee's success, organizations should encourage opportunities to support such interactions.

## The Future: Strategic Alignment and Expatriate Management Practices

An area where I/O psychologists could greatly influence the professional practice of international assignee management in the future is in the strategic alignment of the practices with the way in which firms compete globally. According to Adler and Ghadar (1990), international assignee management practices, namely who the firm considers as possible international assignees, how the firm selects and trains them, what criteria the firm uses to assess their performance, and what impact the international experience has on the careers of international assignees, should all fit the external environment in which the firm operates, as well as its strategic intent. Adler and Ghadar have stated that "the central issue for MNCs is not to identify the best international policy per se, but rather to find the best fit between the MNC's external environment, its overall strategy, and its HRM policy and implementation" (p.190). Currently, however, there is little strategic differentiation among the firms in their international assignee management practices, such as selection and performance management (Caligiuri & Colakoglu, 2007). This is not surprising given that international assignees historically have been managed mostly administratively (from the compensation and relocation functions)—and without involvement of the more strategic HR and I/O psychology areas.

Today, more I/O psychologists are being called in to work with international assignee management programs as these assignments are being integrated and managed as a part of broader leadership development and talent management programs. These next-generation international assignee management practices include the activities related to managing the performance and development of employees on international assignee assignments to ensure, at an organizational level, that the right people are in the right place at the right time—doing what they were sent to do and developing the competencies needed at a firm level. This approach is newer and has a more strategic orientation given that the activities are aimed at firm-level development and improved outcomes through human talent. The field of international assignee management is changing rapidly and more industrial/organizational psychologists are becoming involved with the selection, training, development, and succession of international assignees.

## Practical Reality for Industrial/Organizational Psychologists and the Management of International Assignees

Although often located down the same corridor in the Human Resources wing of most corporate headquarters, the directors of global or international mobility and talent development (where I/O psychologists often work) lead their respective complementary, but not often strategically integrated, functions. As *complementary HR functions*, talent development professionals identify the firm's talent deemed ready for international assignments, when (and sometimes where) they should be assigned, and what they will be expected to do. Once talent has been identified, global mobility professionals manage the many complexities (and vendors)—everything from their tax and visas to the movement of their household goods and international schools. In these complementary roles, the collaboration is generally minimal once a prospective international assignee is handed off from the talent management professionals to the global mobility professionals. As a matter of practicality, there is some efficiency-based value in global mobility and talent management operating as *complementary HR functions* (especially in firms with international assignee populations predominantly placed in less developmental—and more technical and functional—assignments).

Though efficient, global mobility and talent management operating in *complementary HR functions*, however, is *rarely effective* from the perspective of global HR strategy. In brief, there is a growing strategic need in most firms to produce more culturally agile leaders through systematic global leadership development programs. This strategic HR need has led to a paradigm shift, as the global mobility and talent management functions are being reconfigured to be more *strategically integrated HR partners*.

As *strategically integrated HR partners*, both talent management and global mobility professionals work together under one set of strategic business goals guiding where international assignees should be placed *and why*. For example, as *strategically integrated HR partners*, the talent management professionals have a deeper knowledge of the specific global competencies needing to be developed for any given high potential; they are able to readily identify who is predisposed to achieve the desired developmental gains from a given international assignment. Global mobility professionals, also operating as *strategically integrated HR partners*, possess the same knowledge of the desired developmental global competencies, and, in turn, are able to design international assignments with associated support practices to increase the probability that the desired developmental competencies will be gained.

In firms where the global mobility and talent management functions operate as *strategically integrated HR partners*, three elements are recognized by both functions: (1) not all international assignments are intentionally developmental, (2) not all individuals have the ability to develop from the experience of international assignments, and (3) the completion of an assignment is not the same as gaining desired developmental competencies. These three elements represent a significant paradigm shift within the HR function. This change seems to be affecting talent management and global mobility professionals equally, as they both need to gain new knowledge about the repertoire of possible developmental competencies potentially inherent in international assignments, how to craft the experiences to elicit those developmental competencies, and how to identify talent most likely to experience the developmental gain. Given the speed of globalization and the need for effective expatriates, the time is right for the involvement of the science and practice of I/O psychologists and their integration with strategic international mobility.

## References

Abe, H., & Wiseman, R. (1983). A cross-cultural confirmation of the dimensions of intercultural effectiveness. *International Journal of Intercultural Relations, 7*, 53–67.

Abueva, J. E. (2000, May 17). Management: Return of the native executive; many repatriations fail, at huge cost to companies. *The New York Times*, p. C8.

Adams, J. S. (1965). Inequity in social exchange. In L. Berkowitz (Ed.), *Advances in experimental social psychology, 2*, 267–299, New York: Academic Press.

Adams, J. S. (1963). Wage inequities, productivity and work quality. *Industrial Relations, 3*, 3–16.

Adler, N. J. (2002). *International dimensions of organizational behaviour* (4th ed.). Cincinnati, OH: South-Western.

Adler, N. J. (1997). *International dimensions of organizational behaviour* (3rd ed.). Cincinnati, OH: South-Western.

Adler, N. J. (1981). Re-entry: Managing cross-cultural transitions. *Group and Organization Studies, 6*, 341–356.

Adler, N. J., & Ghadar F. (1990). Strategic human resource management: A global perspective. In R. Pieper (Ed.), *Human resource management: An international comparison.* New York: de Gruyter.

Arthur, M. B., & Rousseau, D. M. (1996). *The boundaryless career: A new employment principle for a new organisational era*. New York: Oxford University Press.

Baruch, Y. (2004). Transforming careers: From linear to multidirectional career paths. *Career Development International, 9*(1), 58–73.

Baughn, C. (1995). Personal and organizational factors associated with effective repatriation. In J. Selmer (Ed.), *Expatriate management: New ideas for international business*. Westport, CT: Quorum Books.

Benson, P. (1978). Measuring cross-cultural adjustment: The problem of criteria. *International Journal of Intercultural Relations, 2*, 21–37.

Bernardin, H. J., & Buckley, M. R. (1981). Strategies in rater training. *Academy of Management Review, 6*, 205–212.

Black, J. S. (1994). O Kaerinasai: Factors related to Japanese repatriation adjustment. *Human Relations, 47*(12), 1489–1508.

Black, J. S. (1992). Coming home: The relationship of expatriate expectations with repatriation adjustment and job performance. *Human Relations, 45*, 177–192.

Black, J. S. (1990). Factors related to the adjustment of Japanese expatriate managers in America. In K. M. Rowland & G. R. Ferris (Eds.), *Research in personnel and human resources management, Supp. 2*. Greenwich, CT: JAI Press.

Black, J. S. (1988). Workrole transitions: A study of American expatriate managers in Japan. *Journal of International Business Studies, 19*, 274–291.

Black, J. S., & Gregersen, H. B. (1991). When Yankee comes home: Factors related to expatriate and spouse repatriation adjustment. *Journal of International Business Studies, 22*(4), 671–695.

Black, J. S., Gregersen, H. B., & Mendenhall, M. E. (1992a). *Global assignments*. San Francisco: Jossey-Bass.

Black, J. S., Gregersen, H . B., & Mendenhall, M. E. (1992b). Toward a theoretical framework of repatriation adjustment. *Journal of International Business, 24*, 737–760.

Bochner, S., Hutnik, N., & Furnham, A. (1986). The friendship patterns of overseas students and host students in an Oxford student resident hall. *Journal of Social Psychology, 125*, 689–694.

Bochner, S., McLeod, B. M., & Lin, A. (1977). Friendship patterns of overseas students: A functional model. *International Journal of Psychology, 12*, 277–294.

Bolino, M. C. (2007). Expatriate assignments and intra-organizational career success: Implications for individuals and organizations. *Journal of International Business Studies, 38*, 819–835.

Bonache, J. (2006). The compensation of expatriates: a review and a future research agenda. In G. K. Stahl & I. Björkman (Eds.), *Handbook of Research in International Human Resource Management.* Cheltenham, UK: Edward Elgar.

Bonache, J., & Fernández, Z. (1997). Expatriate compensation and its link to the subsidiary strategic role: a theoretical analysis. *International Journal of Human Resource Management, 8,* 457–475.

Bonache, J., Sanchez, J., & Zárraga-Oberty, C. (2009) The interaction of expatriate pay differential and expatriate inputs on host country nationals' pay unfairness. *International Journal of Human Resource Management, 20*(10), 2135–2149.

Borman, W. C., & Motowidlo, S. J. (1993). Expanding the criteria domain to include elements of contextual performance. In N. Schmitt, W. C. Borman, & Associates (Eds.), *Personnel selection in organizations.* San Francisco: Jossey-Bass.

Borstorff, P. C., Harris, S. G., Field, H. S., & Giles, W. F. (1997). Who'll go? A review of factors associated with employee willingness to work overseas. *Human Resource Planning, 20,* 29–40.

Brein, M., & David, K. (1971). Intercultural communication and the adjustment of the sojourner. *Psychological Bulletin, 76,* 215–230.

Brett, J. M. (1980). The effect of job transfer on employees and their families. In C. L. Cooper & R. Payne (Eds.), *Current concerns in occupational stress.* Chichester, UK: Wiley.

Briscoe, D., & Schuler, R. (2004). *International human resource management: Policies and practices for the global enterprise* (2nd ed). New York: Routledge.

Brislin, R. (1981). *Cross-cultural encounters: Face-to-face encounters.* New York: Pergamon.

Buss, D. (1991). Evolutionary personality psychology. In M. R. Rosenzweig & L. W. Porter (Eds.), *Annual Review of Psychology, 42,* 459–492. Palo Alto, CA: Annual Reviews Inc.

Caligiuri, P. (2006a). Developing global leaders. *Human Resource Management Review, 16,* 219–228.

Caligiuri, P. (2006b). Performance measurement in a cross-national context. In W. Bennett, D. Woehr, & C. Lance (Eds.), *Performance measurement: Current perspectives and future challenges.* Mahwah, NJ: Erlbaum.

Caligiuri, P. (2000a). Selecting expatriates for personality characteristics: A moderating effect of personality on the relationship between host national contact and cross-cultural adjustment. *Management International Review, 40,* 61–80.

Caligiuri, P. (2000b). The big five personality characteristics as predictors of expatriate desire to terminate the assignment and supervisor-rated performance. *Personnel Psychology, 53*(1), 67–88.

Caligiuri, P. (1999). Strategic expatriate selection systems: Getting the right people, in the right assignment, at the right time. *Innovations in International HR, 25*(4), 1–5.

Caligiuri, P. (1997). Assessing expatriate success: Beyond just "being there." In D. M. Saunders (Series Ed.) & Z. Aycan (Volume Ed.), *New approaches to employee management* (Vol. 4) *Expatriate management: Theory and practice.* Greenwich, CT: JAI Press.

Caligiuri, P., & Colakoglu, S. (2007). A strategic contingency approach to expatriate assignment management. *Human Resource Management Journal, 17*(4), 393–410.

Caligiuri, P., & Day, D. (2000). Effects of self-monitoring on technical, contextual, and assignment-specific performance: A study of cross-national work performance ratings. *Group & Organization Management, 25*(2), 154–175.

Caligiuri, P., & Di Santo, V. (2001). Global competence: What is it, and can it be developed through global assignments? *Human Resource Planning Journal, 24*(3), 27–38.

Caligiuri, P., Hyland, M., Joshi, A., & Bross, A. (1998). A theoretical framework for examining the relationship between family adjustment and expatriate adjustment to working in the host country. *Journal of Applied Psychology, 83*, 598–614.

Caligiuri, P., & Lazarova, M. (2005). Work-life balance and the effective management of global assignees. In S. Poelmans (Ed.), *Work and family: An international research perspective.* Mahwah, NJ: Erlbaum.

Caligiuri, P., & Lazarova, M. (2002). The influence of social interaction and social support on female expatriates' cross-cultural adjustment. *International Journal of Human Resource Management, 13*(5), 1–12.

Caligiuri, P., & Lazarova, M. (2001a). Retaining repatriates: The role of organizational support practices. *Journal of World Business, 36*(4), 389–401.

Caligiuri, P., & Lazarova, M. (2001b). Strategic repatriation policies to enhance global leadership development. In M. Mendenhall, T. Kuehlmann, & G. Stahl (Eds.), *Developing global business leaders: Policies, processes, and innovations.* Westport, CT: Quorum Books.

Caligiuri, P., & Phillips, J. (2003). An application of self-assessment realistic job previews to expatriate assignments. *International Journal of Human Resource Management, 14*, 1102–1116.

Caligiuri, P. & Tarique, I. (2009). Predicting Effectiveness in Global Leadership Activities. *Journal of World Business, 44*, 336–346.

Caligiuri, P., & Tarique, I. (2006). International assignee selection and cross-cultural training and development. In I. Björkman & G. Stahl (Eds.), *Handbook of Research in International Human Resource Management*. Cheltenham, UK: Edward Elgar.

Campbell, J. P., McCloy, R. A., Oppler, S. H., & Sager, C. E. (1993). A theory of performance. In N. Schmitt, W. C. Borman, & Associates (Eds.), *Personnel selection in organizations*. San Francisco: Jossey-Bass.

Chen, C. C., Choi J., & Chi, S.-C. (2002). Making justice sense of local-expatriate compensation disparity: mitigation by local referents, ideological explanations, and interpersonal sensitivity in China-foreign joint ventures. *Academy of Management Journal, 45*, 807–817.

Church, A. (1982). Sojourner adjustment. *Psychological Bulletin, 9*, 540–572.

Collings, D. G., Scullion, H., & Morley, M. J. (2007). Changing patterns of global staffing in the multinational enterprise: challenges to the conventional expatriate assignment and emerging alternatives. *Journal of World Business, 42*, 198–213.

Conference Board (1996). *Managing expatriates return: A research report* (Report Number 1148–96-RR). New York: The Conference Board, Inc.

Cui, G., & Awa, N. E. (1992). Measuring intercultural effectiveness: An integrative approach. *International Journal of Intercultural Relations, 16*, 311–328.

Cui, G., & van den Berg, S. (1991). Testing the construct validity of intercultural effectiveness. *International Journal of Intercultural Relations, 15*, 227–241.

Dalton, M., & Wilson, M. (2000). The relationship of the five-factor model of personality to job performance for a group of middle eastern international assignee managers. *Journal of Cross-Cultural Psychology, 18*, 250–258.

Davis, D. D. (1998). International performance measurement and management. In J. W. Smither (Ed.), *Performance appraisal: State of the art in practice*. San Francisco: Jossey-Bass.

Day, D. V., & Sulsky, L. M. (1995). Effects of frame-of-reference training and information configuration on memory organization and rating accuracy. *Journal of Applied Psychology, 80*, 158–167.

DeLeon, C. T., & McPartlin, D. (1995). Adjustment of expatriate children. In J. Selmer (Ed.), *Expatriate management: New ideas for international business*. Westport, CT: Quorum Books.

DePhilippi, R. J., & Arthur, M. B. (1996). Boundaryless contexts and careers: A competency-based perspective. In M. B. Arthur & D. M. Rousseau (Eds.), *The boundaryless career: A new employment principle for a new organizational era*. New York: Oxford University Press.

Digman, J. (1990). Personality structure: The emergence of the five-factor model. *Annual Review of Psychology, 41*, 417–440.

Dinges, N. (1983). Intercultural competence. In D. Landis, & R. W. Brislin (Eds.), *Handbook of intercultural training: Issues in theory and design, 1*, 176–202. New York: Pergamon Press.

Dowling, P., Festing, M., & Engle, A. D. (2008). *International human resource management* (5th ed.). London: Thomson Learning.

Dowling, P. J., & Welch, D. E. (2004). *International human resource management: Managing people in a global context* (4th ed.). London: Thomson Business Press.

Downes, M., & Thomas, A. S. (1999). Managing overseas assignments to build organizational knowledge. *Human Resource Planning, 22*(4), 33–48.

Dunbar, E. (1992). Adjustment and satisfaction of expatriate U.S. personnel. *International Journal of Intercultural Relations, 16*, 1–16.

Edström, A., & Galbraith J.R. (1977). Transfer of managers as a coordination and control strategy in multinational organizations. *Administrative Science Quarterly, 22*(2), 248–263.

Elron, E., & Kark, R. (2000). Women managers and international assignments: Some recommendations for bridging the gap. In M. Mendenhall & G. Oddou (Eds.), *Readings in international human resource management*. Cincinnati, OH: South-Western.

Entrekin, L., & Chung, Y. (2001). Attitudes toward different sources of executive appraisal. *International Journal of Human Resource Management, 12*, 965–987.

Evans, P., Pucik, V., & Barsoux, J. L. (2001). *The global challenge: Frameworks for international human resource management*. New York: McGraw-Hill/Irwin.

Feldman, D. C., & Thompson, H. B. (1993). Expatriation, repatriation, and domestic geographical relocation: An empirical investigation of adjustment to new job assignments. *Journal of International Business Studies, 24*, 507–529.

Gelb, B. D., & Hyman, M. R. (1987). Reducing reluctance to transfer. *Business Horizons*, (Mar.-Apr.), 39–43.

GMAC Global Relocation Services (2008). *Global relocation trends 2008 survey report*. Woodridge, IL: GMAC Global Relocation Services.

Goldberg, L. (1993). The structure of phenotypic personality traits. *American Psychologist, 48*, 26–34.

Goldberg, L. (1992). The development of markets for the big-five factor structure. *Psychological Assessment, 4,* 26–42.

Gomez-Mejia, L., & Balkin, D. B. (1987). The determinants of managerial satisfaction with the expatriate and repatriate process. *Journal of Management Development, 6,* 7–17.

Gregersen, H. B., & Black, J. S. (1995). Keeping high performers after international assignments: A key to global executive development. *Journal of International Management, 1*(1), 3–21.

Gregersen, H. B., & Stroh, L. K. (1997). Coming home to the Arctic cold: Antecedents to Finnish expatriate and spouse repatriation adjustment. *Personnel Psychology, 50,* 635–654.

Gudykunst, W. (1988). Uncertainty and anxiety. In Y. Kim & W. Gudykunst (Eds.), *Theories in intercultural communication.* Newbury Park, CA: Sage.

Gudykunst, W., & Hammer, M. (1984). Dimensions of intercultural effectiveness: Culture specific or cultural general? *International Journal of Intercultural Relations, 8,* 1–10.

Gupta, A., & Govindarajan, V. (2002). Cultivating a global mindset. *The Academy of Management Executive, 16,* 116–126.

Guthrie, G. (1975). A behavioral analysis of cultural learning. In R. W. Brislin, S. Bochner, & W. J. Lonner (Eds.), *Cross-cultural perspectives on learning.* New York: Wiley.

Guzzo, R . A., Noonan, K . A., & Elron, E. (1994). Expatriate managers and the psychological contract. *Journal of Applied Psychology, 79,* 617–626.

Hall, D. T. (Ed.). (1996). *The career is dead—Long live the career: A relational approach to careers.* San Francisco: Jossey-Bass.

Hammer, M., Gudykunst, W., & Wiseman, R. (1978). Dimensions of inter-cultural effectiveness: An exploratory study. *International Journal of Intercultural Relations, 2,* 382–392.

Hammer, M. R., Hart, W., & Rogan, R. (1998). Can you go home again? An analysis of the repatriation of corporate managers and spouses. *Management International Review, 38*(1), 67–86.

Harvey, M. G. (1989). Repatriation of corporate executives: An empirical study. *Journal of International Business Studies, 19,* 131–144.

Harvey, M. G. (1985). The executive family: An overlooked variable in international assignments. *Columbia Journal of World Business, 20,* 84–92.

Harvey, M. G. (1982). The other side of foreign assignments: Dealing with the repatriation dilemma. *Columbia Journal of World Business, 17*(1), 53–59.

Haslberger, A., & Brewster, C. (2009). Capital gains: Expatriate adjustment and the psychological contract in international careers. *Human Resource Management, 48*, 379–397.

Hippler, T. (2009). Why do they go? Empirical evidence of employees' motives for seeking or accepting relocation. *International Journal of Human Resource Management, 20*, 1381–1401.

Horsch, J. (1995). *Auslandseinsatz von Stammhaus-Mitarbeitern: eine Analyse ausgewählter personalwirtschaftlicher Problemfelder multinationaler Unternehmen mit Stammsitz in der Bundesrepublik Deutschland.* Frankfurt am Main: Peter Lang.

Judge, T. A., & Ferris, G. R. (1993). Social context of performance evaluation decisions. *Academy of Management Journal, 36*, 80–105.

Kendall, D. (1981). Repatriation: An ending and a beginning. *Business Horizons, (Nov.-Dec.)*, 21–25.

Kim, K., & Slocum, J. W. (2008). Individual differences and expatriate assignment effectiveness: The case of U.S.-based Korean expatriates. *Journal of World Business, 43*, 109–126.

Kobrin, S. J. (1988). Expatriate reduction and strategic control in American multinational corporations. *Human Resource Management, 27*, 63–75.

Kraimer, M. L., & Wayne, S. J. (2004). An examination of perceived organizational support as a multidimensional construct in the context of expatriate assignment. *Journal of Management, 30*, 209–237.

Lazarova, M. B., & Cerdin, J.-L. (2007). Re-visiting repatriation concerns: Organizational support vs. career and contextual influences. *Journal of International Business Studies, 38*, 404–429.

Lazarova, M. B., & Tarique, I. (2005). Knowledge transfer upon repatriation. *Journal of World Business, 40*, 361–373.

Leung, K., Smith, P. B., Wang, Z., & Sun, H. (1996). Job satisfaction in joint venture hotels in China: An organizational justice analysis. *Journal of International Business Studies, 27*, 947–962.

Leung, K., Zhu, Y., & Ge, C. (2009). Compensation disparity between locals and expatriates: moderating the effects of perceived injustice in foreign multinationals in China. *Journal of World Business, 44*, 85–93.

Louis, M. R. (1980). Surprise and sense making: What newcomers experience in entering unfamiliar organizational settings. *Administrative Science Quarterly, 25*, 226–251.

Lundby, K., Partha, S., & Kowske, B. (2008). What's driving your globetrotters and how do you keep them? Employee engagement among expatriates in Asia. *EvolveHR Magazine, 2*(5), 26–30.

Magnus, M., & Dodd, J. (1981). Relocation: changing attitudes and company policies. *Personnel Journal, 60*, 538–548.

Mayrhofer, W., & Brewster, C. (1996). In praise of ethnocentricity: expatriate policies in European multinationals. *The International Executive, 38*, 749–778.

McCrae, R., & Costa, P. (1989). More reasons to adopt the five-factor model. *American Psychologist, 44*, 451–452.

McCrae, R., & Costa, P. (1987). Validation of the five-factor model of personality across instruments and observers. *Journal of Personality and Social Psychology, 52*, 81–90.

McCrae, R., & John, O. (1992). An introduction to the five factor model and its applications. *Journal of Personality, 60*, 175–216.

Mendenhall, M., & Oddou, G. (1985). The dimensions of expatriate acculturation. *Academy of Management Review, 10*, 39–47.

Napier, N., & Peterson, R. (1991). Expatriate re-entry: What do expatriates have to say? *Human Resource Planning, 14*, 19–28.

Nicholson, N., & Imaizumi, A. (1993). The adjustment of Japanese expatriates to living and working in Britain. *British Journal of Management, 4*, 119–134.

Oddou, G., & Mendenhall, M. (1991). Succession planning for the 21st century: How well are we grooming our future business leaders? *Business Horizons, (September-October)*, 26–34.

Ondrack, D. A. (1985). International human resource management in European and North American firms. *International Studies of Management and Organizations, 15*, 26–32.

Ones, D., & Viswesvaran, C. (1999). Relative importance of personality dimensions for international assignee selection: A policy capturing study. *Human Performance, 12*, 275–294.

Ones, D., & Viswesvaran, C. (1997). Personality determinants in the prediction of aspects of expatriate job success. In D. M. Saunders (Series Ed.) & Z. Aycan (Volume Ed.), *New approaches to employee management* (Vol. 4) *Expatriate management: Theory and practice.* Greenwich, CT: JAI Press.

Osland, J. (1995). *The adventure of living abroad: Hero tales from the global frontier.* San Francisco: Jossey-Bass.

Parker, P., & Inkson, K. (1999). New forms of career: The challenge to human resource management. *Asia Pacific Journal of Human Resources, 37*(1), 76–85.

Pellico, M . T., & Stroh, L . K. (1997). Spousal assistance programs: An integral component of the international assignment. In D. M. Saunders (Series Ed.) & Z. Aycan (Volume Ed.), *New approaches to employee management* (Vol. 4) *Expatriate management: Theory and practice*. Greenwich, CT: JAI Press.

Ployhart, R., Wiechmann, D., Schmitt, N., Sacco, J., & Rogg, K. (2002). The cross-cultural equivalence of job performance ratings. *Human Performance, 16,* 49–79.

PricewaterhouseCoopers (2005). *International assignments: Global policy and practice: Key trends 2005*. PricewaterhouseCoopers.

Punnett, B. J. (1997). Towards effective management of expatriate spouses. *Journal of World Business, 32,* 243–257.

Richards, D. (1996). Strangers in a strange land: Expatriate paranoia and the dynamics of exclusion. *International Journal of Human Resource Management, 7,* 553–571.

Riusala, K., & Suutari, V. (2000). Expatriation and careers: Perspectives of expatriates and spouses. *Career Development International, 5*(2), 81–90.

Roberts, K., Kossek, E. E., & Ozeki, C. (1998). Managing the global workforce: Challenges and strategies. *Academy of Management Executive, 12*(4), 93–106.

Rousseau, D. M. (1990). New hire perceptions of their own and their employer's obligations: A study of psychological contracts. *Journal of Organizational Behavior, 11,* 389–400.

Schein, E. H. (1996) Career anchors revisited: Implications for career development in the 21st century. *Academy of Management Executive, 10*(4), 80–88.

Schneider, S. C., & Barsoux, J. L. (1997). *Managing across cultures*. London: Prentice Hall.

Schrader, B. W., & Steiner, D. D. (1996). Common comparison standards: An approach to improving agreement between self and supervisory performance ratings. *Journal of Applied Psychology, 81,* 813–820.

Scullion, H. (1994). Creating international managers: recruitment and development issues. In P. S. Kirkbride (Ed.), *Human resource management in Europe: Perspectives for the 1990s*. London: Routledge.

Searle, W., & Ward, C. (1990). The prediction of psychological and sociocultural adjustment during cross-cultural transitions. *International Journal of Intercultural Relations, 14,* 449–464.

Selmer, J. (2002). Practice makes perfect? International experience and expatriate adjustment. *Management International Review, 42,* 71–87.

Selmer, J. (2001), *(S)he'll do! Expatriate selection when people are not exactly queuing-up for the job*. Paper presented at the Human Resources Global Management Conference, Barcelona, Spain.

Shaffer, M. A., Harrison, D. A., Gregersen, H., Black, J. S., & Ferzandi, L. A. (2006). You can take it with you: Individual differences and expatriate effectiveness. *Journal of Applied Psychology, 91*, 109–125.

Stahl, G. K., & Cerdin, J. L. (2004). Global careers in French and German multinational corporations. *Journal of Management Development, 23*, 885–902.

Stahl, G. K., Chua, C. H., Caligiuri, P., Cerdin, J. L., & Taniguchi, M. (2009). Predictors of turnover intentions in learning-driven and demand-driven international assignments: The role of repatriation concerns, satisfaction with company support, and perceived career advancement opportunities. *Human Resource Management, 48*(1), 89–109.

Stahl, G. K., Miller, E., & Tung. R. (2002). Toward the boundaryless career: A closer look at the expatriate career concept and the perceived implications of an international assignment. *Journal of World Business, 37*, 216–227.

Stening, B. W. (1979). Problems of cross-cultural contact: A literature review. *International Journal of Intercultural Relations, 3*, 269–313.

Stroh, L. K. (1995). Predicting turnover among repatriates: Can organizations affect retention rates? *International Journal of Human Resource Management, 6*, 443–456.

Stroh, L. K., Gregersen, H. B., & Black, J. S. (1998). Closing the gap: Expectations versus reality among repatriates. *Journal of World Business, 33*(2), 111–124.

Takeuchi, R., Tesluk, P., Yun, S., & Lepak, D. (2005). An integrative view of international experiences: An empirical examination. *Academy of Management Journal, 48*, 85–100.

Takeuchi, R., Wang, M., & Marinova, S. V. (2005). Antecedents and consequences of psychological workplace strain during expatriation: A cross-sectional and longitudinal investigation. *Personnel Psychology, 58*, 925–948.

Takeuchi, R., Yun, S., & Tesluk, P. E. (2002). An examination of crossover and spillover effects of spousal and expatriate cross-cultural adjustment on expatriate outcomes. *Journal of Applied Psychology, 87*, 655–666.

Tarique, I. & Caligiuri, P. (2009). Effectiveness of in-country cross cultural training: Role of cross-cultural absorptive capacity. *International Journal of Training and Development. 13*, 148–164.

Thomas, D. C., Lazarova, M. B., & Inkson, K. (2005). Global careers: New phenomenon or new perspectives? *Journal of World Business, 40*, 340–347.

Toh, S. M., & DeNisi, A. S. (2005). A local perspective to expatriate success. *Academy of Management Executive*, *19*, 132–146.

Toh, S. M., & DeNisi, A. S. (2003). Host country national reactions to expatriate pay policies: a model and implications. *Academy of Management Review*, *28*, 606–621.

Tsui, A. S., & O'Reilly, C. A., III. (1989). Beyond simple demographic effects: The importance of relational demography in superior-subordinate dyads. *Academy of Management Journal*, *32*, 402–423.

Tung, R. L. (1998). American expatriates abroad: From neophytes to cosmopolitans. *Journal of World Business*, *33*, 125–144.

Tung, R. L. (1982). Selection and training procedures of U.S., European, and Japanese multinationals. *California Management Review*, *25*, 57–71.

Wayne, S. J., & Liden, R. C. (1995). Effects of impression management on performance ratings: A longitudinal study. *Academy of Management Journal*, *38*, 232–260.

Weissman, D., & Furnham, A. (1987). The expectations and experience of a sojourning temporary resident abroad: A preliminary study. *Human Relations*, *40*, 313–326.

Williams, M. L., McDaniel, M. A., & Nguyen, N. T. (2006). A meta-analysis of the antecedents and consequences of pay level satisfaction. *Journal of Applied Psychology*, *91*, 392–413.

Yan, A., Zhu, G., & Hall, D. T. (2002). International assignment for career building: A model of agency relationships and psychological contracts. *Academy of Management Review*, *27*, 373–391.

# CHAPTER 13

# Work and Family in a Global Context

Tammy D. Allen, Kristen M. Shockley, and Andrew Biga

## Introduction

Work and family issues have captured the attention of both researchers and practitioners during the last several decades. It has been suggested that balancing personal demands and career aspirations may be one of the greatest challenges individuals face in contemporary society (Halpern, 2004). Organizations too are grappling with the task of trying to identify ways to help individuals successfully meet both their work and nonwork responsibilities. The work-family dilemma is evident not only in the United States but also in countries across the globe. Currently there is little information available to help guide multinational companies in terms of relationships between cultural context, work-life effectiveness, and use of flexible work arrangement(s) (FWA).

The objective of this chapter is threefold. First, we provide an overview of flexible work arrangements within organizations, followed by a brief review of what is known regarding work-family issues in a global context. Although most of the research regarding work and family issues has been conducted in the United States and other Western countries, cross-country comparative studies have recently emerged that suggest Western models may not generalize. Second, based on data from a global company, Procter

& Gamble, we compare reports of individual work-family effectiveness across cultural dimensions. We also examine two major forms of flexibility, schedule flexibility (that is, flextime) and location flexibility (that is, telecommuting) in relation to individual work-life effectiveness. We close the chapter with a discussion of the results of our data analyses, the challenges that multinational organizations face in developing strategies for helping individuals manage work and family, and recommendations for best practices.

Although a complete discussion of various work-family constructs and terms is outside the scope of this chapter, a few issues are important for clarity at this juncture. Most of the research literature has focused on work-family conflict, which is defined as the extent that demands from work and family roles are mutually incompatible (Greenhaus & Buetell, 1985). Although this is the term most often used in the academic literature, many organizations refrain from using such language. Instead, they employ terminology with a more positive and inclusive connotation, such as work-life effectiveness. For the purpose of this chapter, we use the term work-family conflict when referring to findings from the research literature and the term work-life effectiveness when referring to data originating from our current organizational analysis.

## Organizational Flexibility Practices

Within the work-family literature, considerable attention has been focused on ways that organizations can facilitate the ability of employees to manage their work and nonwork responsibilities. Of the various family-friendly benefits available, flexibility has received the most attention from both the research and the practice communities (Galinsky & Backon, 2008).

Flexible work arrangements facilitate the management of competing demands from work and nonwork through increases in temporal flexibility (when work is done) and in spatial flexibility (where work is done) (Rau, 2003). Although a variety of different initiatives exist that fall under the FWA umbrella, the two most common are flextime and flexplace. Flextime refers to flexibility in the timing of work. For example, employees may be offered a range of starting and ending times for the workday. Flexplace involves flexibility in the location where work is completed, often referring to work conducted at home (also known as telework or telecommuting). Based on data from the 2008 National Study of Employers, 79% of the organizations surveyed offered some degree of time flexibility, and 31% offered flextime on a daily basis (Galinsky, Bond, Sakai, Kim, & Giuntoli, 2008). Moreover, in 2006, an estimated 45 million American employees practiced some degree of telecommuting (WorldatWork, 2006).

Flextime was first introduced within a West German aerospace firm in 1967 (Avery & Zabel, 2001) and was rapidly adopted by firms in Switzerland, France, and Scandinavia. The first British experiment with flextime occurred in 1972. Hewlett-Packard is thought to have been the first U.S. company to implement flextime in 1972 (Giglio, 2005). It is noteworthy that Hewlett-Packard only introduced the policy within the United States after trying it in its German division.

Interest in telecommuting grew in the 1970s due to the oil crisis in the United States. Over one-third of IBM's global employee population works outside of the office at least some of the time (Frauenheim, 2004). Flexplace options may be particularly useful to global companies in which employees are required to travel. As an example, Cisco Systems has a global workforce with employees in 97 countries, many of whom travel. Cisco has had a formalized teleworking program since 1993 (Giglio, 2005) that allows employees to work any time, any place.

One of the most radical examples of flexibility is the "results-only work environment" (ROWE) at Best Buy (Conlon, 2006). Corporate employees are free to work where and whenever they want as long as they complete their assignments. Work is viewed as something that gets done, not a place. Clearly this type of arrangement is not possible for all types of jobs (for example, nursing), but the ROWE program helps demonstrate how far the concept of flexibility has developed.

Positive work-related outcomes have been associated with the use of FWA. In a meta-analytic review of intervention studies, Baltes et al. (1999) reported the effects of flexible and compressed work schedules on a variety of work outcomes and found that they related positively to productivity, job satisfaction, and work schedule satisfaction, and related negatively to absenteeism. Based on a qualitative review of the research on FWA and work-family conflict (WFC), Allen and Shockley (2009) found mixed support for a relationship between work-family conflict and FWA. Although there is a robust relationship between FWA and organizational variables such as productivity and absenteeism, the evidence regarding WFC is considerably more equivocal. The type of flexibility also makes a difference; specifically, there is some evidence that flextime availability is more effective in terms of minimizing WFC than is flexplace availability (Shockley & Allen, 2007).

## Work-Family Literature from a Global Perspective

Comparative studies of work-family issues across countries are relatively rare. There are two issues of interest. One is the prevalence with which conflicts between work and family occur. The other is the generalizability of relationships between work-family conflict and other variables across countries. With regard to prevalence, we are aware of only one study that has looked at this directly. Spector, Allen, Poelmans, Cooper, et al. (2005) compared work-family pressures of managers in 18 countries and found significant mean differences. Specifically, individuals from Taiwan and Hong Kong reported the greatest work-family pressure whereas individuals from the United Kingdom and Australia reported the least.

A greater number of studies have examined the generalizability of relationships. Most of this research has inferred that differences in relationships between work-family conflict and other variables are based on differences in collectivism (see Spector, Cooper, Poelmans, Allen et al, 2004; Spector, Allen, Poelmans, & Lapierre et al., 2007; Yang, 2005; Yang, Chen, Choi, & Zhou, 2000). These studies find that relations between work-family conflict and predictors (such as work demands) and between work-family conflict and outcomes (such as job satisfaction) are weaker in more collectivistic societies than in less collectivistic (aka individualist) societies (see Spector et al., 2004; Spector et al., 2007). This is thought to occur because in collectivist cultures work is viewed as something that is done for the family, but in individualistic cultures work is thought to be something that is done for the self. However, not all comparative studies show differences. In a 48-country study, Hill, Yang, Hawkins, and Ferris (2004) demonstrated that a model that linked work demands to WIF held universally across four country clusters. What is notable about this study is that although the participants came from different countries, they were all employees of IBM. Thus, it is possible that organizational culture or organizational policies and practices played a role in the findings.

Raghuram, London, and Larsen (2001) examined the amount of variance accounted for in FWA use by culture versus country. Culture was measured based on Hofstede's (1991) value indices. They asked personnel heads of 14 European countries with 200 or more employees to estimate the percentage of employees who used telework. Country culture was based on the location of the company's corporate headquarters versus the country in which the employee was living. They concluded that national differences between flexible employment practices were explained by cultural differences. However, no relationship between telework and collectivism was detected. They did find that high femininity cultures use a greater proportion of telework. In the next section we elaborate on the cultural dimensions thought important to understanding the effectiveness of flexibility in a global context.

## Relevant Cultural Dimensions

The effectiveness of human resource practices such as FWA intended to help employees manage work and nonwork may be impacted by the norms and values of the home country (Raghuram et al., 2001). Culture can be defined as "shared motives, values, beliefs, identities, and interpretations or meanings of significant events that results from common experiences of members of collectives that are transmitted over generations" (House & Javidan, 2004, p. 15).

Building on existing work, we believe there are four cross-cultural value dimensions that are particularly relevant for understanding the relationship between FWA use and work-family effectiveness. Those dimensions are gender egalitarianism, humane orientation, collectivism, and performance orientation.

Gender egalitarianism refers to the extent that a society minimizes gender role differences while promoting equality between the genders (House & Javidan, 2004). Societies that espouse stronger gender egalitarian values eschew rigid social norms that dictate gender roles and behaviors based on biological sex (Emrich, Denmark, & Den Hartog, 2004). In other words, men and women are viewed as equal in ability. Countries high on gender egalitarianism include Russia, Denmark, and Sweden. Countries low on gender egalitarianism include South Korea, Mexico, and Middle Eastern countries such as Kuwait. The United States is moderate in terms of gender egalitarianism.

Humane orientation is the extent to which members of a society are fair, altruistic, friendly, caring, and kind (House & Javidan, 2004). Characteristics of high humane orientation societies include the consideration of the interests of others as important, the encouragement of members to promote the well-being of others, and the motivation of members by the need to belong and affiliate with others as opposed to the need for power and material possessions. Examples of high humane orientation countries include Zambia, the Philippines, and Ireland. Examples of low–humane orientation countries include several Western European countries (including Greece, Spain, and Germany). The United States falls in the low-to-middle part of the spectrum.

Collectivism refers to how people see themselves in reference to others. In more collectivistic societies, people tend to view themselves in terms of a network of social connections that include extended family and groups. In less collectivistic societies (that is, individualistic societies), people focus on personal achievement and independence (Markus & Kitayama, 1991). Project GLOBE includes two forms of collectivism. Institutional collectivism pertains to the degree to which organizational and societal institutional practices encourage and reward the collective distribution of resources. In-group collectivism refers to the extent that societies express pride, loyalty, and interdependence in their families. As mentioned previously, Raghuram et al. (2001) found no relationship between collectivism and telework use. However, their sample was limited to European countries and was based on Hofstede's value indices (1991). The Philippines, Georgia, and India are highly in-group collectivistic cultures, whereas Scandinavian and Western European countries are generally very low. The United States also ranks as one of the countries lowest in in-group collectivism.

Performance orientation is the extent to which society encourages and rewards group members for performance improvement and excellence (House et al., 1999). Societies high in performance orientation value training and development, expect direct and explicit communication, and value what one does more than who one is. Countries high in performance orientation include Switzerland, Singapore, and Hong Kong, and countries that score low on this dimension include Venezuela, Greece, and Russia. The United States scores relatively high on this dimension.

In the following section we report the results of analyses that examine work-life effectiveness across cultural dimensions and by use of flexplace and flextime. Our analyses were designed to answer two questions: (1) do reports of work-life effectiveness vary across cultural contexts, and (2) is the use of flextime and flexplace associated with greater work-life effectiveness within specific cultural contexts (for example, high versus low collectivism).

## Investigation of Flexibility Use at Procter & Gamble

Participants were 24,327 managers employed by Procter & Gamble in 50 countries throughout the globe. The majority were male (57.7%) and were low- to mid-level managers (63.2%). The average tenure with the organization was in the range of six to ten years. Data were collected via Procter & Gamble's annual employee opinion survey. The majority of surveys were administered online. Participation was voluntary.

*Work-life effectiveness* was measured with three items ("When I leave work, I continue to have energy for the things I enjoy," "My workload keeps me from my personal/family activities more than is reasonable" (reverse scored), "My work environment prevents me from living a fit and healthy lifestyle" (reverse scored). Response options were based on a five-point scale that ranged from strongly disagree to strongly agree. Higher scores represent greater work-life effectiveness. Coefficient alpha was .62.

*Cultural values* were not measured explicitly; rather, the values obtained for each country by Project GLOBE (House et al., 2004) were imputed based on participants' reported country of employment. Project GLOBE sampled middle managers from 951 organizations in 62 countries to create country-level assessments of several cultural dimensions. Cultural values were based on Project GLOBE's societal practices ("as is") ratings rather than on societal ideal values ("should be").

*Gender egalitarianism* mean country scores ranged from 2.50 to 4.08 (M=3.36, SD=.34). Higher scores indicate greater gender equality. Project GLOBE created the gender egalitarianism index from a multi-item scale. Emrich et al. (2004) provide detailed information regarding scale development and scoring.

*Humane orientation* mean country scores ranged from 3.29 to 5.12 (M=4.05, SD=.38), with higher scores representing stronger humane orientation. The initial scale used to obtain mean scores in Project GLOBE included five questions that assessed the degree to which individuals in a society are concerned, sensitive toward others, friendly, tolerant of mistakes, and generous. Kabasakal and Bodur (2004) provide a detailed description of scale development.

*Collectivism* was imputed from Project GLOBE's in-group collectivism measure. Scores ranged from 3.53 to 5.92 (M=4.67, SD=.66), and higher scores indicated greater collectivism. The initial scale used to obtain mean scores in Project GLOBE included four questions that assessed the degree to which individuals express pride, loyalty, and interdependence in their families. Detailed information regarding the Project GLOBE scale development can be found in Gelfand, Bkawuk, Nishii, and Bechtold (2004).

*Performance orientation* mean country scores ranged from 3.20 to 4.90 (M=4.27, SD=.34). The original measure was based on three items relating to current societal practices regarding innovation, improvement, and reward systems. Further scale information can be found in Javidan (2004).

High, medium, and low bands were based on the bands created by Project GLOBE for each cultural dimension. In order to categorize societies into meaningful groups, Project GLOBE researchers used test-banding techniques, which assume that all scores within a particular band are not meaningfully different. The number of scores within each band is driven by statistics (standard error of the difference); thus, the number of countries within each band of a given cultural value varies. For more information, see Hanges, Dickson, and Sipe (2004).

For countries that include within-country sectors with vast cultural differences (Switzerland, South Africa, and Germany), Project GLOBE reported multiple mean scores. In the present study, we were not able to determine which part of the country participants were from, and thus could not code cultural values according to these factors. Instead, when the multiple mean scores from one country were in the same band, we used the average of the two scores. If the mean scores were in different bands, we excluded the country from that particular analysis.

## Findings

*Gender egalitarianism (GE).* As shown in Table 13.1, means for work-life effectiveness WLE ranged from a low of 2.72 to a high of 3.23 across the different GE bands. Individuals in moderate GE countries reported the greatest WLE. Those in low GE countries (represented solely by South Korea in our sample) reported the least WLE.

As shown in Table 13.2, when taking FWA use into account, the means ranged from a low of 2.63 to a high of 3.29. Flextime use versus nonuse was associated with greater WLE only for those in high GE countries. Flexplace use versus nonuse was associated with greater WLE for those in high and medium GE countries. However, it is important to note that there are differences in statistical power across the various bands. For example, the mean difference for use versus nonuse of flexplace in the low GE band is .32, but not statistically significant. The mean difference for use versus nonuse of flexplace in the medium GE band is only .06 but statistically significant due to greater statistical power within that band.

*Humane orientation (HO).* See Tables 13.3 and 13.4. As shown in Table 13.3, means for WLE ranged from a low of 3.05 to a high of 3.27 across the different HO bands. Individuals in medium-low HO countries reported the highest level of WLE. There were no significant differences between the other clusters.

As shown in Table 13.4, when taking FWA into account, means ranged from a low of 2.96 to a high of 3.35. Flextime use versus nonuse was associated with greater WLE by individuals in high and in low HO countries. No significant differences emerged

**Table 13.1. Mean WLE by Gender Egalitarianism.**

| | Bands | | |
|---|---|---|---|
| | High | Medium | Low |
| | **Asia** | **Asia** | **Asia** |
| | Philippines | Australia | South Korea |
| | Malaysia | Thailand | |
| | Hong Kong | Indonesia | |
| | **CEEMEA** | New Zealand | |
| | Hungary | Japan | |
| | Russia | Taiwan | |
| | Poland | China | |
| | Slovenia | India | |
| | Kazakhstan | **CEEMEA** | |
| | Albania | Israel | |
| | **Latin America** | Nigeria | |
| | Mexico | Turkey | |
| | Venezuela | Morocco | |
| | Costa Rica | Egypt | |
| | Argentina | **Latin America** | |
| | **North America** | Brazil | |
| | Canada | Ecuador | |
| | **Western Europe** | Guatemala | |
| | Denmark | **North America** | |
| | Sweden | United States | |
| | England | **Western Europe** | |
| | Portugal | Switzerland | |
| | France | Finland | |
| | Netherlands | Italy | |
| | Greece | Ireland | |
| | | Germany | |
| | | Austria | |
| | | Spain | |
| N | 6057 | 16753 | 210 |
| Mean WLE | 3.07[a] | 3.23[b] | 2.72[c] |
| SD | .96 | .95 | .94 |

Note: South Africa removed from analyses. CEEMEA = Central and Eastern Europe, Middle East, and Africa. Means with different subscripts significantly differ from each other.

## Table 13.2. Mean WLE by Gender Egalitarianism and FWA Use.

| | High | | | | Medium | | | | Low | | | |
|---|---|---|---|---|---|---|---|---|---|---|---|---|
| | Flextime | | Flexplace | | Flextime | | Flexplace | | Flextime | | Flexplace | |
| | No Use | Use | No Use | Use | No Use | Use | No Use | Use | No Use | Use | No Use | Use |
| N | 4586 | 1125 | 4077 | 1634 | 12356 | 3516 | 11848 | 4024 | 97 | 92 | 151 | 38 |
| MeanWLE | 3.06[a] | 3.14[b] | 3.03[a] | 3.19[b] | 3.24[a] | 3.25[a] | 3.23[a] | 3.29[b] | 2.66[a] | 2.74[a] | 2.63[a] | 2.95[a] |
| SD | .96 | 1.00 | .97 | .94 | .94 | .97 | .96 | .92 | .92 | .97 | .95 | .89 |

Note: Countries in each band are the same as in Table 13.1. Means with different subscripts significantly differ from each other.

### Table 13.3. Mean WLE by Humane Orientation.

| | Bands | | |
|---|---|---|---|
| **High** | **Medium High** | **Medium Low** | **Low** |
| **Asia** | **Asia** | **Asia** | **Asia** |
| Philippines | Indonesia | Taiwan | Singapore |
| Malaysia | India | Hong Kong | **CEEMEA** |
| Thailand | China | South Korea | Poland |
| **CEEMEA** | New Zealand | **CEEMEA** | Hungary |
| Egypt | Japan | Nigeria | **Western Europe** |
| **Western Europe** | Australia | Israel | Italy |
| Ireland | **CEEMEA** | Kazakhstan | Germany |
| | Albania | Turkey | France |
| | Morocco | Russia | Greece |
| | **Latin America** | Slovenia | Spain |
| | Ecuador | **Latin America** | |
| | Costa Rica | Argentina | |
| | Venezuela | Mexico | |
| | **North America** | Guatemala | |
| | Canada | Colombia | |
| | **Western Europe** | Brazil | |
| | Denmark | **North America** | |
| | | U.S. | |
| | | **Western Europe** | |
| | | Sweden | |
| | | Finland | |
| | | Switzerland | |
| | | Portugal | |
| | | Netherlands | |
| | | Austria | |
| | | England | |
| N | 1163 | 4410 | 13157 | 3684 |
| Mean WLE | 3.05[a] | 3.11[a] | 3.27[b] | 3.07[a] |
| SD | .97 | .95 | .95 | .97 |

Note: South Africa and Switzerland removed from analyses. CEEMEA = Central and Eastern Europe, Middle East, and Africa. Means with different subscripts significantly differ from each other.

**Table 13.4. Mean WLE by Humane Orientation and FWA Use.**

| | High Bands | | | | | | | |
|---|---|---|---|---|---|---|---|---|
| | High | | | | Medium High | | | |
| | Flextime | | Flexplace | | Flextime | | Flexplace | |
| | No Use | Use | No Use | Use | No Use | Use | No Use | Use |
| N | 523 | 522 | 663 | 382 | 2594 | 1523 | 3032 | 1085 |
| MeanWLE | 2.96[a] | 3.18[b] | 3.04[a] | 3.12[a] | 3.10[a] | 3.13[a] | 3.09[a] | 3.19[b] |
| SD | .96 | .95 | .98 | .93 | .95 | .97 | .96 | .93 |

| | Low Bands | | | | | | | |
|---|---|---|---|---|---|---|---|---|
| | Medium Low | | | | Low | | | |
| | Flextime | | Flexplace | | Flextime | | Flexplace | |
| | No Use | Use | No Use | Use | No Use | Use | No Use | Use |
| N | 10521 | 2028 | 9270 | 3279 | 2527 | 911 | 2587 | 851 |
| MeanWLE | 3.28[a] | 3.29[a] | 3.25[a] | 3.35[b] | 3.01[a] | 3.24[b] | 3.06[a] | 3.11[a] |
| SD | .94 | .96 | .95 | .91 | .96 | .99 | .98 | .94 |

Note: Countries in each band are the same as in Table 13.3. Means with different subscripts significantly differ from each other.

between use and nonuse within medium-high and medium-low HO countries. The reverse was found with regard to flexplace. Flexplace use versus nonuse was associated with greater WLE by individuals in medium-high and in medium-low HO countries. No significant differences emerged between use and nonuse within high and low HO countries.

*Collectivism.* As shown in Table 13.5, means for WLE ranged from a low of 2.97 to a high of 3.33 across the collectivism bands. Individuals in low collectivism countries reported the greatest WLE whereas individuals in low collectivism countries reported the least WLE.

As shown in Table 13.6, when taking FWA into account, means ranged from a low of 2.94 to a high of 3.39. Flextime use versus nonuse was associated with greater WLE at all levels

**Table 13.5.  Mean WLE by Collectivism.**

| | Bands | | |
|---|---|---|---|
| | High | Medium | Low |
| | **Asia** | **Asia** | **Asia** |
| | Philippines | Hong Kong | Australia |
| | India | Japan | New Zealand |
| | China | **CEEMEA** | **North America** |
| | Thailand | Kazakhstan | Canada |
| | Indonesia | Hungary | U.S. |
| | Singapore | South Africa | **Western Europe** |
| | Taiwan | Israel | England |
| | South Korea | **Latin America** | Finland |
| | Malaysia | Brazil | Switzerland |
| | **CEEMEA** | Costa Rica | Netherlands |
| | Turkey | **Western Europe** | Sweden |
| | Morocco | Greece | Denmark |
| | Albania | Ireland | |
| | Egypt | Italy | |
| | Russia | Austria | |
| | Nigeria | France | |
| | Poland | | |
| | Slovenia | | |
| | **Latin America** | | |
| | Ecuador | | |
| | Colombia | | |
| | Mexico | | |
| | Guatemala | | |
| | Venezuela | | |
| | Argentina | | |
| | **Western Europe** | | |
| | Portugal | | |
| | Spain | | |
| N | 5926 | 3751 | 12241 |
| Mean WLE | 2.97[a] | 3.03[b] | 3.33[c] |
| SD | .96 | .98 | .92 |

Note: Germany removed from analyses. CEEMEA = Central and Eastern Europe, Middle East, and Africa. Means with different subscripts significantly differ from each other.

**Table 13.6. Mean WLE by Collectivism and FWA Use.**

| | Bands | | | | | | | | | | | |
|---|---|---|---|---|---|---|---|---|---|---|---|---|
| | High | | | | Medium | | | | Low | | | |
| | Flextime | | Flexplace | | Flextime | | Flexplace | | Flextime | | Flexplace | |
| | No Use | Use | No Use | Use | No Use | Use | No Use | Use | No Use | Use | No Use | Use |
| N | 3904 | 1493 | 4115 | 1282 | 2288 | 1238 | 2962 | 600 | 10192 | 1593 | 8191 | 3594 |
| MeanWLE | 2.94[a] | 3.05[b] | 2.94[a] | 3.07[b] | 3.00[a] | 3.11[b] | 3.04[a] | 3.01[a] | 3.32[a] | 3.39[b] | 3.32[a] | 3.37[b] |
| SD | .96 | .95 | .96 | .94 | .97 | 1.00 | .98 | .97 | .92 | .92 | .93 | .90 |

Note: Countries in each band are the same as in Table 13.5. Means with different subscripts significantly differ from each other.

of collectivism. Flexplace use versus nonuse was associated with greater WLE in high and in collectivism countries only. There were no significant differences between flexplace use and nonuse in medium collectivism countries.

*Performance orientation (PO).* As shown in Table 13.7, means for WLE ranged from a low of 2.96 to a high of 3.29 across the PO bands. Individuals in high PO countries reported the greatest WLE. Individuals in low PO countries reported the least WLE.

As shown in Table 13.8, when taking FWA into account, means ranged from a low of 2.90 to a high of 3.34. Flextime use versus nonuse was associated with greater WLE in medium and in low PO countries. There were no significant differences in high PO countries. Flexplace use versus nonuse was associated with greater WLE in high and medium PO countries. There were no significant differences in low PO countries.

## Practical Implications and Recommendations

Our data, based on a large sample of managers working across the globe, indicate that reports of work-life effectiveness vary across cultural contexts. Gender egalitarianism was associated with the greatest variation in work-life effectiveness. Work-life effectiveness appears to suffer the most in cultural contexts marked by low levels of gender egalitarianism. However, this finding should be considered with caution given that our data were represented by only one country within this band. Perhaps what is somewhat surprising is that work-life effectiveness was greater in medium gender egalitarian countries than in high gender egalitarian countries. That is, a moderate level of GE rather than a low or a high level appears to be most highly associated with work-life effectiveness. Although highly prescribed gender roles may make it difficult to effectively manage work and nonwork, the findings also suggest that highly fluid gender roles might provide the opportunity for confusion or misunderstandings with regard to appropriate ways to manage work and nonwork.

Humane orientation was associated with the least variation in work-life effectiveness. Although it might be expected that members of cultures high in humane orientation would provide greater support for managing work-life challenges (Francesco, &

## Table 13.7. Mean WLE by Performance Orientation.

| | Bands | | |
|---|---|---|---|
| | High | Medium | Low |
| | Asia | Asia | CEEMEA |
| | Singapore | India | Slovenia |
| | Hong Kong | Japan | Kazakhstan |
| | New Zealand | Thailand | Hungary |
| | Taiwan | CEEMEA | Russia |
| | South Korea | Egypt | Latin America |
| | Philippines | Israel | Argentina |
| | China | Morocco | Venezuela |
| | Indonesia | Nigeria | Western Europe |
| | Australia | Poland | Portugal |
| | Malaysia | Turkey | Italy |
| | CEEMEA | Latin America | Greece |
| | Albania | Ecuador | |
| | North America | Costa Rica | |
| | Canada | Mexico | |
| | U.S. | Brazil | |
| | Western Europe | Colombia | |
| | Austria | Guatemala | |
| | Ireland | Western Europe | |
| | Netherlands | Germany | |
| | | Denmark | |
| | | France | |
| | | England | |
| | | Spain | |
| | | Finland | |
| | | Sweden | |
| N | 12073 | 7688 | 2083 |
| Mean WLE | 3.29[a] | 3.10[b] | 2.96[c] |
| SD | .93 | .99 | .97 |

Note: Switzerland and South Africa removed from analyses. CEEMEA = Central and Eastern Europe, Middle East, and Africa. Means with different subscripts significantly differ from each other.

# Table 13.8. Mean WLE by Performance Orientation and FWA Use.

| | Bands | | | | | | | | | | | |
| --- | --- | --- | --- | --- | --- | --- | --- | --- | --- | --- | --- | --- |
| | High | | | | Medium | | | | Low | | | |
| | Flextime | | Flexplace | | Flextime | | Flexplace | | Flextime | | Flexplace | |
| | No Use | Use | No Use | Use | No Use | Use | No Use | Use | No Use | Use | No Use | Use |
| N | 9392 | 2070 | 7982 | 3480 | 5125 | 2126 | 5608 | 1643 | 1496 | 418 | 1649 | 265 |
| MeanWLE | 3.31[a] | 3.28[a] | 3.28[a] | 3.34[b] | 3.08[a] | 3.17[b] | 3.09[a] | 3.16[b] | 2.90[a] | 3.16[b] | 2.94[a] | 3.02[a] |
| SD | .92 | .93 | .93 | .90 | .97 | 1.01 | .99 | .96 | .96 | .98 | .97 | .93 |

Note: Countries in each band are the same as in Table 13.7. Means with different subscripts significantly differ from each other.

Ying, 2009), our results showed no difference between the high and low bands and that the medium-low band was associated with the greatest work-life effectiveness. The results regarding gender egalitarianism and humane orientation demonstrate that the relationship between cultural values and work-life effectiveness cannot be assumed to be linear.

We did find linear patterns for collectivism and for performance orientation. Greater WLE effectiveness was associated with less collectivism and with greater performance orientation. Powell et al. (2009) speculated that members of collectivist cultures were more likely to receive greater social support and therefore would experience less work-family conflict. In contrast, our data suggests that greater work-life effectiveness is reported in less collectivistic contexts. These findings are consistent with Spector et al. (2005) who found that two countries considered more collectivistic (Taiwan and Hong Kong) reported the greatest work-family pressure whereas two countries considered more individualistic (United Kingdom and Australia) reported the least. This may be explained by the fact that individuals within highly collectivistic cultures typically have the burden of providing a great deal of social support to others because of tight-knit kinship systems and therefore may experience greater family demands.

Greater WLE effectiveness was associated with greater performance orientation. Perhaps societies with greater performance orientation emphasize performance in all domains of life. Accordingly, individuals within high performance orientation contexts may learn efficiencies that help them manage both work and nonwork effectively.

Multinational companies face unique challenges in developing solutions to help individuals manage work and family. Policies that are effective within the home country of the organization may not translate to units based in countries outside the home country. Our results show that the use of flextime and flexplace were generally associated with greater work-life effectiveness. Although not all comparisons were significant, in no cultural context did we find that flexible work arrangement use was associated with significantly less work-life effectiveness.

The effectiveness of any benefit intended to be family-supportive may be influenced by culture-specific procedures, local regulations, and norms. We did find some variability in the effectiveness of FWA as a function of cultural values. For example, flextime appears to be especially helpful in low performance orientation countries. In high performance orientation countries, where work-life effectiveness is already at a greater level, flextime is not associated with greater work-life effectiveness. Similar results were found for humane orientation. Flextime is especially helpful under low and high levels of human orientation, but does not raise the level of work-life effectiveness when it is already generally at a higher rate. Thus, the overall pattern of results suggest that flextime policies can help compensate for cultural contexts that may make the achievement of work-life effectiveness more difficult. In terms of practical significance, flexplace appears to have the most potential for impact within contexts where work-life effectiveness is lower as associated with gender egalitarianism. Working from home, and thus more isolated from society, may temper the negative effects associated with very fluid or very rigid gender roles.

It is also interesting to note that the pattern of results did not suggest that one form of flexibility was uniformly more effective than the other. This is in contrast to some research that has suggested that flextime is more effective in terms of mitigating work-family conflict than is flexplace (Shockley & Allen, 2007). One difference may be that the current analysis is based exclusively on a sample of managers. Perhaps individuals in managerial positions cultivate the skills needed to be effective across work and family roles while working in various locations.

In crafting human resource policies designed to help working families from a global perspective, local regulations and norms may also need to be taken into consideration. Family-related supports provided by the government vary greatly across countries. For example, the United States is frequently criticized as lagging behind other industrialized nations in terms of social policies (such as paid parental leave) that help individuals balance work and family (Waldfogel, 2001). However, it is interesting to note that across every cultural value, work-life effectiveness was the highest in the band that contained the United States. In addition, the United States was the only country that consistently appeared in the highest work-life effectiveness band across all four cultural values. It seems possible that this finding may be due to the fact that the data come from a multinational company headquartered in the United States. That is, there may be work-life advantages for employees working in the country within which a large multinational organization is headquartered. Yet, the findings are again consistent with those of Spector et al. (2005); in this study, participants were employed in different organizations. Of the 18 diverse countries included in Spector et al. (2005), managers in the United States reported the fourth lowest level of work-family pressure. This suggests that there is more to work-life effectiveness than country-level social policy, leaving the door open for individual organizations to have a major impact on the work-life effectiveness of employees.

There are a variety of factors for organizations to consider in terms of the implementation of FWA across the globe. For example, in some locations in Latin America and Africa where the number of family members living at home tends to be large, the houses small, and the technology less advanced, it may be especially difficult to implement telecommuting. However, in these countries, where the roads and infrastructure tend to be poor and employees spend long hours commuting from home to work, the use of flexible working hours could significantly reduce time-based forms of work-family conflict (Masuda, Poelmans, & Allen, 2008). When implementing FWA policies, a consideration of commute times, traffic congestion patterns, and access to public transportation can be useful.

The challenge of effectively implementing FWA programs and policies is akin to other organizational change efforts. To have a truly agile organization, flexibility is a base organizational requirement. It is not enough to develop and set FWA policy; at some level, organizational culture change must occur to facilitate use and acceptance of these programs as vital to the company's success (Allen, 2001). Understanding the local culture at the country or region level is one way that companies can better enable this change effort. However, a tradeoff exists between standardization and customization based on the local culture. Standardization of FWA polices across regions and cultural context offers the benefits of efficiency. The development of differentiated HR systems in an effort to fit diverse cultural contexts may have its benefits, but often involves costs and a loss of efficiency (Palich & Gomez-Mejia, 1999; Raghuram et al., 2001). Depending on the size and complexity of the organization, a balance needs to be found between standardization and customization.

Another area of practical importance in dealing with FWA change efforts is performance management. Implementing FWA policies and programs offers organizations the opportunity to reevaluate their performance management practices. Without the reliance on face-time as a possible driver for performance evaluations, companies must become more skilled at quantifying performance across different roles, levels, and local cultures in a global context. Traditional performance management systems may be more susceptible to face-time bias, local cultural preferences, and other potentially non-work-related biases. The shift to a more agile work environment requires new and different ways of managing performance. Having clear guidelines and uniform training for managers about FWA implementation may create less room for cultural biases and immediate manager preferences that may impact the efficacy of FWA policies. Ensuring that it is not a matter of immediate manager preference and that an agile workforce is a business strategy will enable broader and more robust adoption of these programs.

Timothy Flynn, chairman and CEO of KPMG, has stated that, "Providing employees with flexibility and family-friendly programs is more than a 'nice to have' fringe benefit; it's critical to our success" (Forte, 2008). With appropriate caution regarding causal inferences, our data support this line of thought and suggest that the use of FWA can make a positive difference in the work-life effectiveness of employees and can do so within a variety of cultural contexts. Understanding the relationship between HR practices and country culture can assist multinational organizations with the development and adaptation of culturally appropriate practices.

## References

Allen, T. D. (2001). Family-supportive work environments: The role of organizational perceptions. *Journal of Vocational Behavior*, *58*, 414–435.

Allen, T. D., & Shockley, K. M. (2009). Flexible work arrangements: Help or hype? In D. R. Crane, & E. J. Hill (Eds.), *Handbook of families and work: Interdisciplinary perspectives.* Lanham, MD: University Press of America.

Avery, C., & Zabel, D. (2001). *The flexible workplace: A sourcebook of information and research.* Westport, CT: Quorum Books.

Baltes, B. B., Briggs, T. E., Huff, J. W., Wright, J. A., & Neuman, G. A. (1999). Flexible and compressed workweek schedules: A meta-analysis of their effects on work-related criteria. *Journal of Applied Psychology, 84* (4), 496–513.

Conlon, M. (2006). Smashing the clock. *BusinessWeek,* December 11. Retrieved from www.businessweek.com/magazine/content/06_50/b4013001.htm.

Emrich, C. G., Denmark, F. L., & Den Hartog, D. N. (2004). Cross-cultural differences in gender egalitarianism: Implications for societies, organizations, and leaders. In R. J. House, P. J. Hanges, M. Javidan, P. W. Dorfman, & V. Gupta (Eds.), *Culture, leadership, and organizations: The GLOBE study of 62 societies* (pp. 343–394). Thousand Oaks, CA: Sage.

Forte, T. (2008). Focus on the 100 Best—Top 10 2008. *Working Mother.* Retrieved April 17, 2009, from www.workingmother.com/web?service=direct/1/ViewArticlePage/dlinkFullArticle&sp=1658&sp=94.

Frauenheim, E. (2004). At tech firms, time again for flextime? *TechRepublic.* November 15, 2004. Retrieved April 17, 2009, from http://articles.techrepublic.com.com/5100–22_11–5452865.html.

Galinksy, E., & Backon, L. (2008). *2008 guide to bold new ideas for making work work.* New York: Families and Work Institute.

Galinsky, E., Bond, J. T., Sakai, K, Kim, S. S., & Giuntoli, N. (2008). *The 2008 national study of employees.* New York: Families and Work Institute.

Gelfand, M. J., Bhuwak, D. P. S., Nishii, L. H., Bechtold, D. J. (2004). Individualism and collectivism. In R. J. House, P. J. Hanges, M. Javidan, P. W. Dorfman, & V. Gupta (Eds.), *Culture, leadership and organizations: The GLOBE study of 62 societies* (pp. 437–512). Thousand Oaks, CA: Sage.

Giglio, K. (2005). *Workplace flexibility case study.* Sloan Work and Family Network.

Greenhaus, J. H., & Beutell, N. J. (1985). Sources and conflict between work and family roles. *Academy of Management Review, 10,* 76–88.

Halpern, D. F. (2004). *Public policy, work, and families: The report of the APA presidential initiative on work and families.* Washington, DC: The American Psychological Association. Available online from www.apa.org/work-family/.

Hanges, P. J., Dickson, M. W., & Sipe, M. T. (2004). Rationale for GLOBE statistical analyses: Societal ratings and tests of hypotheses. In R. J. House, P. J. Hanges, M. Javidan, P. W. Dorfman, & V. Gupta (Eds.), *Culture, leadership and organizations: The GLOBE study of 62 societies* (pp. 437–512). Thousand Oaks, CA: Sage.

Hill, E. J., Yang, C., Hawkins, A. J., & Ferris, M. (2004). A cross-cultural test of the work-family interface in 48 countries. *Journal of Marriage and Family, 66,* 1300–1316.

Hofstede, G. (1991). *Cultures and organizations.* London: HarperCollins.

House, R. J., Hanges, P. J., Javidan, M., Dorfman, P. W., & Gupta, V. (Eds.), *Culture, leadership and organizations: The GLOBE study of 62 societies* (pp. 437–512). Thousand Oaks, CA: Sage.

House, R. J., & Javidan, M. (2004). Overview of GLOBE. In R. J. House, P. J. Hanges, M. Javidan, P. W. Dorfman, & V. Gupta (Eds.), *Culture, leadership, and organizations: The GLOBE study of 62 societies* (pp. 9–28). Thousand Oaks, CA: Sage.

Javidan, M. (2004). Performance orientation. In R. J. House, P. J. Hanges, M. Javidan, P. W. Dorfman, & V. Gupta (Eds.), *Culture, leadership and organizations: The GLOBE study of 62 societies* (pp. 437–512). Thousand Oaks, CA: Sage.

Kabasakal, H., & Bodur, M. (2004). Humane orientation in societies, organizations, and leader attributes. In R. J. House, P. J. Hanges, M. Javidan, P. W. Dorfman, & V. Gupta (Eds.), *Culture, leadership and organizations: The GLOBE study of 62 societies* (pp. 437–512). Thousand Oaks, CA: Sage.

Lyness, K. S., & Kropf, M. B. (2005). The relationships of national gender equality and organizational support with work-family balance: A study of European managers. *Human Relations, 58,* 33–60.

Markus, H. R., & Kitayama, S. (1991). Culture and the self: Implications for cognition, emotion, and motivation. *Psychological Review, 98,* 224–253.

Masuda, A. D., Poelmans, S. A. Y., & Allen, T. D. (2008, August). *National culture and the use of flexible work arrangements: An analysis of two country clusters.* Paper presented at the annual meeting of the Academy of Management, Anaheim, CA.

Palich, L. E., & Gomez-Mejia, L. R. (1999). A theory of global strategy and firm efficiencies: Considering the effects of cultural diversity. *Journal of Management, 25,* 587–606.

Powell, G. N., Francesco, A. M., & Ying, Y. (2009). Towards culture-sensitive theories of the work-family interface. *Journal of Organizational Behavior, 30,* 597–616.

Raghuram, S., London, M., & Larsen, H. H. (2001), Flexible employment practices in Europe: Country versus culture. *International Journal of Human Resource Management, 12,* 738–53.

Rau, B. L. (2003). Flexible work arrangements. *Sloan online work and family encyclopedia.* Available from http://wfnetwork.bc.edu/encyclopedia _entry.php?id=240&area=All.

Shockley, K. M., & Allen, T. D. (2007). When flexibility helps: Another look at the availability of flexible work arrangements and work-family conflict. *Journal of Vocational Behavior, 71* (3), 479–493.

Spector, P. E., Allen, T. D., Poelmans, S., Cooper, C. L., et al. (2005). An international comparative study of work-family stress and occupational strain (pp. 71–86). In Poelmans, S. A. Y. (Ed.), *Work and family: An international research perspective.* Mahwah, NJ: Erlbaum.

Spector, P. E., Allen, T. D., Poelmans, S., Lapierre, L. M., Cooper, C. L., O'Driscoll, et al. (2007). Cross-national differences in relationships of work demands, job satisfaction and turnover intentions with work-family conflict. *Personnel Psychology, 60,* 805–835.

Spector, P. E., Cooper, C. L., Poelmans, S., O'Driscoll, M., Sanchez, J. I., Siu, O. L., Dewe, P., Hart, P., & Lu, L. (2004). A cross-national comparative study of work-family stressors, working hours, and well-being: China and Latin America versus the Anglo world. *Personnel Psychology, 57,* 119–142.

Waldfogel, J. (2001). International policies toward parental leave and child care. *The Future of Children, 11,* 99–111.

WorldatWork. (2006). *Telework trendlines for 2006.* Retrieved August 22, 2007, from www.workingfromanywhere.org/news/Trendlines _2006.pdf.

Yang, N. (2005). Individualism-collectivism and work-family interfaces: A Sino-U.S. comparison. In S. A. Y. Poelmans (Ed.), *Work and family: An international research perspective* (pp. 287–318). Mahwah, NJ: Erlbaum.

Yang, N., Chen, C. C., Choi, J., & Zhou, Y. (2000). Sources of work-family conflict: A Sino-U.S. comparison of the effects of work and family demands. *Academy of Management Journal, 41,* 113–123.

# The Editor

**Kyle Lundby** is a consultant with nearly 15 years experience working with global organizations. Having just completed a multiyear assignment in Asia, he has a unique perspective on the current opportunities and challenges faced by organizational leaders in that part of the world. Over the course of his career, Kyle has consulted and facilitated large-scale change efforts, working with leaders from the C-suite down to the line level. His clients have included such global organizations as HSBC, ANZ, Medtronic, General Motors, Subaru, and Foster's, to name a few. Kyle has held executive consultant and director positions with a variety of leading consulting firms. He holds a Ph.D. in industrial/organizational psychology and is the author of numerous publications and presentations in North America and Asia. Kyle is a longtime and active member of the Society for Industrial and Organizational Psychology (SIOP) and currently sits on the editorial board for SIOP's Professional Practice Series.

# Subject Index

Page references following *fig* indicate an illustrated figure; following *t* indicate a table.

# Name Index